N.Y. Yankees Collectibles

A Price Guide to Memorabilia for America's Favorite Team

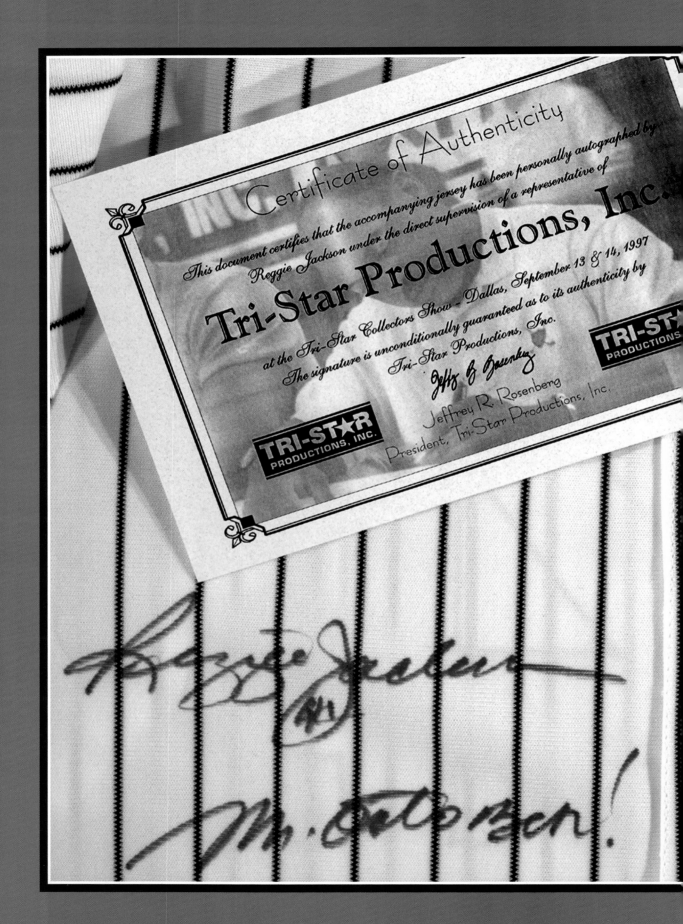

N.Y. Yankees Collectibles

A Price Guide To Memorabilia For America's Favorite Team

PRESENTED BY BECKETT PUBLICATIONS

Frontispiece: Reggie Jackson Autographed Jersey

N.Y. Yankees Collectibles: A Price Guide to Memorabilia for America's Favorite Team
Copyright ©1999 by Dr. James Beckett
All rights reserved under International and Pan-American Copyright Conventions.
Published by: Beckett Publications
15850 Dallas Parkway
Dallas, TX 75248
ISBN: 1-887432-65-5
Beckett® is a registered trademark of Beckett Publications.

First Edition: May 1999
Beckett Corporate Sales and Information (972) 991-6657

Printed in Canada

Your Value Guide

When it comes to reporting on values for secondary market collectibles, Beckett Publications is recognized and respected worldwide as the most trusted authority. Founded in 1984 by Dr. James Beckett, the company has sold millions of price guide books and magazines to collectors of sports cards, sports memorabilia, toys and other licensed collectible products.

Presently, Beckett Publications publishes eight popular monthly magazines on collectibles. They are *Beckett Baseball Card Monthly*, *Beckett Basketball Card Monthly*, *Beckett Football Card Monthly*, *Beckett Hockey Collector*, *Beckett Sports Collectibles and Autographs*, *Beckett Racing & Motorsports Marketplace*, *Beckett Hot Toys* and *Beckett Sci-Fi Collector*.

This reference book is intended to provide an objective and unbiased representation of values for the subject collectibles on the secondary market. The independent pricing contained in this guide reflects current retail rates determined just prior to printing. They do not reflect for-sale prices by the author, distributors or any retailers of collectibles or memorabilia who've contributed their skills and knowledge to the production of this guide. All values are in U.S. dollars and are for informational purposes only.

The values published in this guide were compiled in a joint effort by a staff of full-time expert Beckett Publications analysts and independent contributors knowledgeable in this field of collecting. The information was gathered from actual buy/sell transactions at collectibles conventions, hobby shops and on-line sites, and, to a lesser extent, from buy/sell advertisements in hobby publications, for-sale prices from collectibles dealers' catalogs and price lists, as well as discussions with leading hobbyists in the U.S. and Canada.

Great care and diligence were taken in determining the prices reported within this book. Our desire to supply independent pricing that is more accurate and reliable than what may be supplied by any other source is paramount to our efforts. It is also a prime reason why the Beckett name is synonymous with collecting and memorabilia. Collectors have come to know Beckett as the hobby's most reliable and relied upon source.

Contents

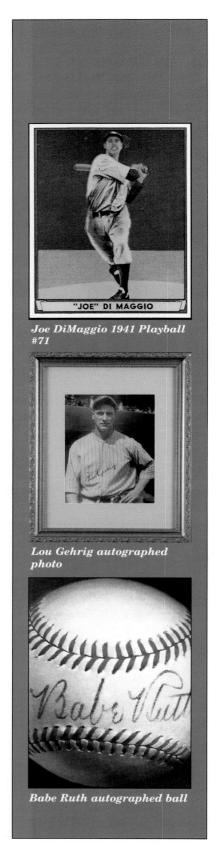

Joe DiMaggio 1941 Playball #71

Lou Gehrig autographed photo

Babe Ruth autographed ball

Introduction
By Marty Appel

1973 Yankees Old Timers Day

It begins, of course, with the 'Voice of God,' the voice of Bob Sheppard, who has handled the public address assignment at Yankee Stadium since bleacher seats were 50 cents, since Mickey Mantle wore his rookie No. 6, and since Casey Stengel wore a long-sleeve manager's uniform as Joe McCarthy had. The Yankee top hat logo was four years old; the Yankees Yearbook, two, and the No. 4 elevated train was passing behind the bleachers, over Joe DiMaggio's shoulders.

And when Bob Sheppard says

'Good after-NOON, ladies and gentlemen, and WEL-come to YANK-ee STAD-ium', you know that the House that Ruth Built is in order, that everything is properly arranged, and that you are in the sacred cutout in south Bronx that is unlike any sports arena ever known in America.

And that is how it all begins. The No. 4 train out there, Bob Sheppard up here, pinstripes down there, and the world's most celebrated franchise, bringing forth love or hate but always passion, grabbing our attention. These are the New York Yankees.

If you are a fan of the Beatles, and are asked to list your top 50 songs of all time, you know that there is your top 50 list, and your top 50 Beatles list. The two do not blend. 'Johnny B Goode' may be the national anthem of rock and roll, but nothing can give you the special feeling that 'She Loves You' invokes. It's apples and oranges.

So to is it with the New York Yankees, that most storied and celebrated sports franchise, which, for all the occasional hoopla about the Atlanta Braves or the Dallas Cowboys, is truly America's team. It is the team they have heard of in Berlin and Beijing, and the team that, love 'em or hate 'em, stands apart from the crowd.

There are nearly 120 pro teams today in the four major sports, and it even tests the best fan's knowledge when the nicknames flash by on the bottom of the screen reeling off the scores. But there is only one Yankees, and there is no problem identifying them to your 87-year-old Ukrainian-born grandmother in her

Babe Ruth game-worn cap

retirement home in California.

Why is this? Why does the collectible bearing the pinstripes or the top hat or the interlocking NY or the vision of Yankee Stadium set hearts racing? Why do we have our sports collectibles here, and our Yankees collectibles there?

The answer is three-fold.

It is first, the cult of personality the team has honed since 1920. It is second the consistency of style anchored by solvent ownership and a dedication to a 'look.'

And third, it is the ballpark itself, the majestic Yankee Stadium.

Humble beginnings

It wasn't always like this. The team itself was forced onto the American League by Ban Johnson, the founder and first league president, two years after the other teams had made their debut in the 'junior circuit.'

The franchise was originally in Baltimore when the league began play in 1901. Johnson knew that he

Reggie Jackson autographed photo

wasn't truly 'big league,' on a par with the National League, until he planted a franchise in New York, the nation's largest city at just less than 3.5 million people. But New York was a problem; the Giants 'owned it.' The Giants were politically well connected, and able to block just about any attempt to let competition in. When at last Johnson was successful, he could only manage to put the team in a rickety wooden field called Hilltop Park, well beyond where the subway line ended in upper Manhattan.

This was a sorry franchise, although Johnson, manipulating its creation, got Clark Griffith, the great 19th century pitcher, to become player/manager — and added Wee Willie Keeler, a Brooklyn native of 'hit 'em where they ain't fame' and Jack Chesbro, a star pitcher from Pittsburgh.

Hilltop Park (best represented today in a 1989 lithograph by William Feldman through the catalogue of Bill Goff Inc.), was no tourist attraction. The so-called 'Highlanders' (the park was at Manhattan's highest elevation), almost won the 1904 pennant (Chesbro, a record-setting 41 wins under his belt, tossed a wild pitch that cost them the flag), but made little impact for the rest of their existence. It wasn't America's Team; it was barely on the minds of New Yorkers. It was the Giants of John McGraw and Christy Mathewson who were the darlings of the sporting set in New York, the toast of the Broadway crowd, and the favorites of the political gang from Tammany Hall.

Little of the Highlanders era is favored by collectors, although its antiquity makes it a curiosity at this stage. Its value is in its age, far more than its link to the Yankees. The tobacco cards of Highlanders are no more popular than those of other teams, particularly because there were so few stars during the Highlanders era of 1903-1913.

The era limped to a close with the changing of the team's name to Yankees (although it had been used in newspaper headlines for years), the move of the team to share the Polo Grounds with the Giants as tenants, and a year later, the purchase of the club by Col. Jacob Ruppert and Captain Tillinghast L'Hommedieu Huston.

Ruppert and Huston were New York society, not gambling house operators and corrupt police chiefs like the previous ownership. Ruppert had even been a three-term U.S. Congressman from Manhattan and operated one of the city's major breweries. Huston was an engineer. It would only be a matter of a few years before they were able to find themselves on equal footing with the lordly Giants, and would, in fact, outdraw them. That insult would lead to the Giants telling Ruppert, 'find your own place.'

The key to this shift in popularity occurred on Jan. 5, 1920, when the Boston Red Sox sold Babe Ruth to the Yankees. It changed baseball. From that moment on, the Yankees would become the most successful sports franchise in all the land, the most star-studded, glamorous team yet conceived, far beyond what the Colonel or the Captain could have ever dreamed. And it is no coincidence that baseball has thrived when the Yankees have been strong.

During a period in the early '70s, for example, baseball was said to be out of favor. Attendance was flat. An exciting 1975 World Series was said to have 'revived' the game. But it is also hard to overlook that in 1976, the Yankees ended a 12-year drought in the pennant department, returned to a refurbished Yankee Stadium, and all of baseball enjoyed the beginning of a period of

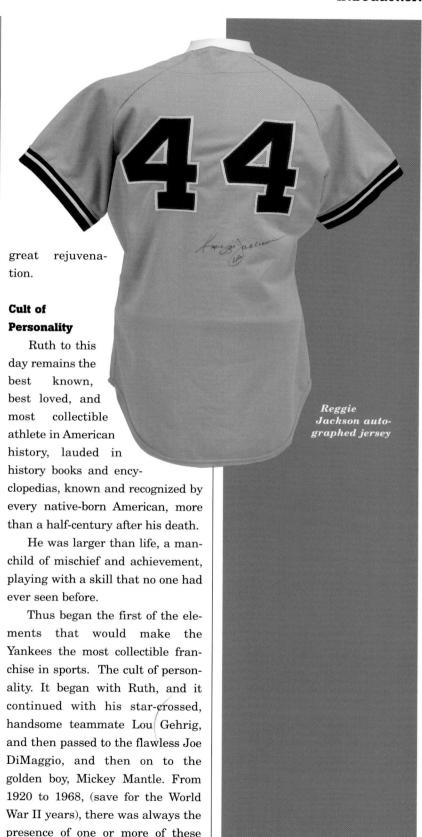

Reggie Jackson autographed jersey

great rejuvenation.

Cult of Personality

Ruth to this day remains the best known, best loved, and most collectible athlete in American history, lauded in history books and encyclopedias, known and recognized by every native-born American, more than a half-century after his death.

He was larger than life, a man-child of mischief and achievement, playing with a skill that no one had ever seen before.

Thus began the first of the elements that would make the Yankees the most collectible franchise in sports. The cult of personality. It began with Ruth, and it continued with his star-crossed, handsome teammate Lou Gehrig, and then passed to the flawless Joe DiMaggio, and then on to the golden boy, Mickey Mantle. From 1920 to 1968, (save for the World War II years), there was always the presence of one or more of these

Above: Mickey Mantle autographed ball. Below: 1932 World Series ticket

heroes, each in turn the most popular player of his day. That there were 29 pennants in a span of 44 seasons during those years added to the mystique.

It is often asked why Mantle collectibles so out-value Willie Mays collectibles. Both began in the same year, in the same town, both were remarkably skilled, and in the end, even Mantle conceded that Mays was the better player and had the better career.

Some are quick to suggest that it could be a racial element, the white player vs. the black player. But when one views the collectible value of a Michael Jordan, a Ken Griffey, Jr. or a Muhammad Ali, that argument fades.

It was the Yankees. It was that Mantle was in 12 World Series in his first 14 years, to Mays' two. Mantle enjoyed the national spotlight each fall, the network coverage, the Life magazine covers. Mays' Giants, by then, had become the No. 3 team in town, before leaving for San Francisco. It was the Yankees.

Bobby Richardson was a heckuva second baseman, as was Junior Gilliam of the Dodgers. Bobby hit a career .266 with 34 homers and topped out at 99 runs scored in his best year. Gilliam hit .265, had 65 homers and surpassed 100 runs four times, playing for a well-known and collectible team. According to *Beckett's Almanac of Baseball Cards and Collectibles,* a 1960 Topps Richardson, near-mint, is worth $14. Gilliam's, same year, $6. It's the Yankees.

The supporting cast — be they Tony Lazzeri, Earle Combs, Bill Dickey, Lefty Gomez, Red Ruffing, Phil Rizzuto, Tommy Henrich, Yogi Berra, Roger Maris, Whitey Ford, Bobby Murcer, Thurman Munson, Catfish Hunter, Graig Nettles, Reggie Jackson, Ron Guidry, Don Mattingly, Dave Winfield, Bernie Williams, Derek Jeter, Tino Martinez, and Paul O'Neill — were all made larger by the wearing of the uniform. Being a Yankee didn't earn you a free pass to Cooperstown; but it certainly enhanced your national recognition.

The consistency of style

This is the second element of the Yankee lore. The uniform, essentially unchanged over all these years, and the first to bear numbers on its back (1929), was rumored to employ pinstripes to camouflage Ruth's ample girth. It's probably not true. Babe's waistline was not vast, nor problematic when the pinstripes first appeared. But the pinstripes developed into a classic look, one that works for the Yankees, but has never worked quite as well for the imitators, whether they be Mets, Padres, Brewers or Braves. The interlocking NY, seen as early as the Highlander years, is itself a standard. Then you have the top hat logo, designed for its first appearance in the 1947 World Series, commissioned by the promotion-minded owner Larry MacPhail. It's the style and it's the standards. It's a team that knows that its great tradition is best preserved by consistency of look. It's why the clubhouse man, (Pete Sheehy), and the broadcaster, (Mel Allen), and the general managers (Ed Barrow, George Weiss) and the publicist (Bob Fishel) and the groundskeeper (Jimmy Esposito), and the aforementioned P.A. announcer all became household names to Yankee fans. They maintained a standard of excellence, each in their own field. There was a comfort level for dads, passing on the game to sons, saying 'this is how it has always been.'

The Stadium

Finally, there is the Stadium, periodically rumored to be a burden to the team, holding back attendance. In the end, it is the place to go. Few tourists arriving in New York are told that they are 'not to miss Shea Stadium.' Yankee Stadium, on the other hand, commands attention, even a subway ride up to the Bronx when the team is off. Visiting National League players have been known to make the excursion when in town to play the Mets, just for a look.

Yankee Stadium was the nation's first triple-decked ballpark, and was in fact, the first to be called a stadium. Hastily constructed with Ruppert-Huston money, it has become the world's most celebrated sports facility, more than 75 years later. (The Coliseum in Rome is sometimes mentioned in the same

breath, but it is a stretch to call lions devouring Christians a sport). The graceful facade, which first encircled the grandstand and now rests proudly on the bleacher walls, is 'the look,' but there is also a haunting majesty found in its odd shape, left field so much deeper than right. And then there is monument park, way out there, home to monuments and plaques for those who exceeded even the honor of the Hall of Fame or of the retired number. (For those who want retired numbers, no team has more — 13 at last count).

For Yankee Stadium, it is about character and majesty and grace

Babe Ruth

*Lou Gehrig /
Babe Ruth*

and style and beauty. It can be intimidating for the visiting player — it can be intimidating for the home players — but as many have said when first playing on its well-manicured lawn, 'NOW, I'm in the big leagues.'

You see that ticket stub from the day Lou Gehrig said he was 'the luckiest man on the face of the earth?'

It is, at once, both a sports col-lectible and a slice of American his-tory.

There has never been a team like it. Anything that somehow touches the rich history of this fran-chise is, to someone, a very special collectible.

Whether it's a yearbook, a button, a trading card, a photo, a scorecard, a matchbook, a poster, an ashtray, an autograph, a figurine, a book, a seat, a cap, a ticket or Babe Ruth's camelhair coat — it needs to be displayed over here; apart from all those other things, over there.

1955 World Series pennant

The Five Most Collectible Yankees Price Guide

Joe DiMaggio Trading Cards

Year	Set Name	Card No.	Price
1933-36	Zeenuts (B and W)	108	2500.00
1933-36	Zeenuts (B and W)	109	3000.00
1935	Pebble Beach	2	1500.00
1936	Goudey Wide Pen Premiums R314	A117	175.00
1936	Goudey Wide Pen Premiums R314	C6	600.00
1936	National Chicle Fine Pen Premiums R313	105	250.00
1936	R311 Premiums	L12	350.00
1936	R312 Pastel Photos	9	500.00
1936	World Wide Gum V355	51	3500.00
1936-38	Overland Candy R301	13	*
1937	Exhibits Four-in-One W463-7	13	800.00
1937	Goudey Flip Movies R326	4A	200.00
1937	Goudey Flip Movies R326	4B	200.00
1937	Goudey Thum Movies R342	4	350.00
1937	O-Pee-Chee Batter Ups V300	118	4500.00
1937	Wheaties BB14	5	500.00
1937	Wheaties BB6	11	350.00
1937	Wheaties BB7	29I	400.00
1937	Wheaties BB8	3	400.00
1937	Wheaties BB9	5	400.00
1938	Baseball Tabs	7	300.00
1938	Exhibits Four-in-One	13	1000.00
1938	Goudey Heads Up R323	250	4500.00
1938	Goudey Heads Up R323	274	4500.00
1938	Our National Game Tabs	7	175.00
1938	Wheaties BB10	11	400.00
1938	Wheaties BB15	2	400.00
1939	Goudey Premiums R303A	13	250.00
1939	Goudey Premiums R303B	6	200.00
1939	Orcajo Photo Art PC786	7	750.00
1939	Play Ball R334	26	2400.00
1939	World Wide Gum Trimmed Premiums V351B	13	250.00
1939	World Wide Gum V351A	11	600.00
1939-46	Exhibits Salutation	13	125.00
1940	Play Ball R335	1	2700.00
1940	Wheaties M4	2A	200.00
1940	Wheaties M4	2B	200.00
1941	Double Play R330	63	750.00
1941	Play Ball R336	71	2600.00
1941	Wheaties M5	17	200.00

1938 Goudey Heads Up #274

Year	Set Name	Card No.	Price
1943	MP and Co. R302-1	9	75.00
1946-49	Sports Exchange W603	4-7	150.00
1947	Homogenized Bond	10	250.00
1947	Yankees Team Issue	8	50.00
1947-66	PM10 Stadium Pins 1 3/4"	45	200.00
1947-66	PM10 Stadium Pins 1 3/4"	46	200.00
1947-66	PM10 Stadium Pins 1 3/4"	47	75.00
1947-66	PM10 Stadium Pins 1 3/4"	48	200.00
1947-66	PM10 Stadium Pins 1 3/4"	49	200.00
1947-66	PM10 Stadium Pins 1 3/4"	50	275.00
1948	Swell Sport Thrills	15	100.00
1948	Yankees Team Issue	6	75.00
1948-49	Blue Tint R346	16	200.00
1949	Leaf	1	2200.00
1949	MP and Co. R302-2	105	60.00
1949	Yankees Team Issue	8	50.00
1950	Yankees Team Issue	9	35.00
1950-56	Callahan HOF W576	27	200.00
1951	Berk Ross	B5	175.00
1951	R423 Small Strip	25	15.00
1952	Berk Ross	13	1250.00
1953	Exhibits Canadian	28	200.00
1953-63	Artvue Hall of Fame Postcards	29	*
1958	Jay Publishing All-Time Greats	2	15.00
1960	Nu-Card Hi-Lites	7	40.00
1960	Nu-Card Hi-Lites	38	40.00
1960	Rawling's Glove Tags	5	*
1961	Golden Press	9	35.00
1961	Nu-Card Scoops	438	15.00
1961	Nu-Card Scoops	467	15.00
1963	Baseball Magazine M118	20	*
1963	Gad Fun Cards	33	5.00
1963	Hall of Fame Busts	5	100.00
1967	Topps Venezuelan	145	400.00
1968	Laughlin World Series	36	5.00
1969	A's Jack in the Box	5	40.00
1970	House of Jazz	5	40.00
1970	Sports Cards for Collectors Old-Timer Postcards	10	4.00
1970	Yankee Clinic Day Postcards	13	10.00
1972	Laughlin Great Feats	1	5.00
1972	TCMA's the 30's	20	8.00
1972-87	Bowery Bank DiMaggio	1	12.50
1973	Hall of Fame Picture Pack	6	3.00
1973	Syracuse Chiefs Team Issue	7	*
1974	Laughlin All-Star Games	39	4.00
1974	Syracuse Chiefs Team Issue	5	*
1975	McCallum Cobb	15	4.00
1975	Shakey's Pizza	1	15.00
1975	Sports Hobbyist Baseball Greats	2	*
1975	TCMA House of Jazz	5	5.00
1975	Yankee Dynasty 1936-39 TCMA	11	6.00
1975	Yankee Dynasty 1936-39 TCMA	51	4.00
1975	Yankee Dynasty 1936-39 TCMA	53	4.00
1975	Yankees All-Time Team TCMA	2	5.00
1976	Galasso Baseball's Great Hall of Fame	7	3.00
1976	Laughlin Diamond Jubilee	25	6.00
1976	Rowe Exhibits	4	1.50
1976	Shakey's Pizza	74	5.00
1976	SSPC Yankees Old-Timers Day	2	3.00
1976	Taylor/Schmierer Bowman 47	4	15.00
1976	Taylor/Schmierer Bowman 47	49	15.00
1977	Shakey's Pizza	24	5.00
1977-79	Sportscaster	208	10.00
1977-84	Galasso Glossy Greats	1	3.00
1977-84	Galasso Glossy Greats	235	3.00
1978	Dexter Hall of Fame Postcards	9	7.50
1979	Diamond Greats	1	5.00
1979	TCMA 50'S	1	5.00
1980	Marchant Exhibits HOF	10	1.00
1980	Yankees Greats TCMA	7	2.50

Year	Set Name	Card No.	Price
1980-83	Pacific Legends	5	2.50
1980-87	SSPC HOF	75	1.50
1980-96	Perez-Steele Hall of Fame Postcards	75	60.00
1981	San Diego Sports Collectors	14	2.00
1981	San Diego Sports Collectors	19	.75
1981	Sportrait Hall of Fame	14	3.00
1982	Baseball Card News	8	1.50
1982	Baseball Card News	18	3.00
1982	Davco Hall of Fame Boxes	5	4.00
1982	Diamond Classics	1	2.00
1982	GS Gallery All-Time Greats	6	3.00
1982	TCMA Greatest Hitters	3	3.00
1982	TCMA Greatest Sluggers	44	3.00
1982	TCMA Stars of the 50's	16	5.00
1983	ASA Joe DiMaggio	1	200.00
1983	ASA Joe DiMaggio	2	2.00
1983	ASA Joe DiMaggio	3	2.00
1983	ASA Joe DiMaggio	4	4.00
1983	ASA Joe DiMaggio	5	2.00
1983	ASA Joe DiMaggio	6	4.00
1983	ASA Joe DiMaggio	7	2.00
1983	ASA Joe DiMaggio	8	2.00
1983	ASA Joe DiMaggio	9	4.00
1983	ASA Joe DiMaggio	10	2.00
1983	ASA Joe DiMaggio	11	2.00
1983	ASA Joe DiMaggio	12	2.00
1983	MLBPA Pins	4	4.00
1983	TCMA Playball 1942	2	3.00
1983	Yankee A-S Fifty Years	10	1.50
1983	Yankee Yearbook Insert TCMA	1	2.50
1984	ASA Willie Mays 90	44	.75
1984	TCMA Bruce Stark Postcards	BS1	5.00
1984-85	Sports Design Products West	5	1.00
1984-89	O'Connell and Son Ink	50	2.00
1985	Big League Collectibles 30s	17	3.00
1985	TCMA Home Run Champs	3	3.00
1985	TCMA Playball 1948	30	3.00
1985	Ultimate Baseball Card	9	7.50
1985-86	Sportflics Prototypes	1	75.00
1986	Sportflics Decade Greats	20	3.00
1986	Sports Design J.D. McCarthy	11	1.50
1986	TCMA	8	2.00
1986	TCMA Superstars Simon	9	1.50
1986	TCMA Superstars Simon	18	2.00
1986	TCMA Superstars Simon	25	2.00
1987	Hygrade All-Time Greats	15	1.00
1988	Pacific Legends I	100	2.50
1988	Willard Mullin Postcards	4	2.00
1989	CMC Mantle	15	1.50
1989	HOF Sticker Book	39	2.00
1990	Baseball Wit	49	1.50
1990	HOF Sticker Book	39	2.00
1990	Yankees Monument Park Rini Postcards	12	2.00
1992	Score DiMaggio	1	30.00
1992	Score DiMaggio	2	30.00
1992	Score DiMaggio	3	30.00
1992	Score DiMaggio	4	30.00
1992	Score DiMaggio	5	30.00
1992	Score DiMaggio	AU0	550.00
1992	Score Factory Inserts	B12	1.50
1992	Score Factory Inserts	B13	1.50
1992	Score Factory Inserts	B14	1.50
1992	Yankees WIZ All-Stars	18	5.00
1992	Yankees WIZ HOF	9	5.00
1993	Diamond Stars Extension Set	126	2.00
1993	Pinnacle DiMaggio	1	.75
1993	Pinnacle DiMaggio	2	.75
1993	Pinnacle DiMaggio	3	.75
1993	Pinnacle DiMaggio	4	.75

Continued on page 24

Joe DiMaggio

He's No Average Joe

1941 Play Ball #71

Befitting his stature as one of baseball's icons, Joe DiMaggio boasts memorabilia that's among the most treasured in the hobby

By Mike Pagel

His image became larger than life for people of all ages. He made a name for himself in baseball during a time when television broadcasts from America's ballparks were a dream of the future. Just a select few personally witnessed him building an image of greatness.

So why does Joe DiMaggio remain so popular among so many Americans, reflected in the still-voracious appetite for his memorabilia, more than 45 years after his retirement?

From the sandlots of San Francisco to the hallowed Yankee Stadium, Joe DiMaggio lived the American dream. Many baseball fans lived out their own similar dreams through DiMaggio's actions, not only on the field, but off it as well. Joe was the consummate player and gentleman.

In leading the New York Yankees to nine World Series championships in his 13 seasons with the team, Joe DiMaggio became a hero to many and a living legend to others.

As he's come to occupy a special place in American lore, it seems as if everyone wants a part of him. And because Americans do not have access to the man himself, they accept the next best thing: Joe DiMaggio memorabilia. A renewal of interest in DiMaggio's collectibles coincided with headlines of the baseball legend's declining health.

From his early days as a minor league outfielder with the San Francisco Seals, to his days as a spokesman for Bowery Savings Bank and Mr. Coffee, DiMaggio always has been in high demand. From bats, balls and jerseys to menus, glasses and match covers from his restaurant in San Francisco, interest remains high in any item associated with Joe.

Because DiMaggio's time with the San Francisco Seals coincided with the depths of the Great Depression, memorabilia from this period is difficult to locate. Of course, Pacific Coast League programs featuring the Seals include his name in the lineup. Most Depression programs were four-page scorecards, but they do turn up with some regularity and remain in heavy demand.

DiMaggio's first baseball card is a Zeenut issue, produced in 1934. Zeenuts are black-and-white cards that were inserted into confectionery products sold on the West Coast. Names on the Zeenut cards of the three DiMaggio brothers all are spelled "DeMaggio," and because kids used to play card games similar to pitching pennies, Mint Zeenuts are scarce. A Joe "DeMaggio" card in Near-Mint or better condition commands a four-figure premium.

A second "DeMaggio" Zeenut was issued in 1935, and is in equal demand as the first. But there is another DiMaggio card from 1935, and it is scarce beyond belief. San Francisco radio station KYA unveiled a promotion in which fans could send in a penny postcard each week and in return receive a postcard featuring a member of either the Seals, the Oakland Oaks or the San Francisco Missions baseball clubs. There are seven known versions of baseball player cards that were mailed out.

Each card had a notation next to the player's name, "Compliments of Pebble Beach," a local clothing producer. Each card was personally signed by the player. Joe's autograph read "J. DiMaggio," noting the correct spelling of his last name along with only his first initial. The

Joe DiMaggio autographed bats have been among the Yankee Clipper's most popular memorabilia items.

Most collectors view DiMaggio's locker as a treasure chest of memorabilia items.

Collectors can expect to pay a hefty price for a DiMaggio-worn jersey.

GAIL DOCEKAL

JOE DI MAGGIO, Yankees

abbreviated autograph seemed to be the norm for Joe during his Seals years. Scarce as they are, Pebble Beach cards in Mint or Near-Mint condition change hands for as much as $5,000.

Photos of Joe as a Seal have proven to be relatively common. Because he was so popular in the PCL, an abundance of photos were

Supply and DiMand

The demand for Joe DiMaggio cards far exceeds the limited supply the market has to offer

Looking for Joe DiMaggio cards? Haven't had much luck finding any? There's a simple explanation for that. The number of cards Joe DiMaggio appears on is quite limited.

DiMaggio played baseball in an era when cards were not mass-produced as they are today. In fact, during World War II and through 1947, hardly any cards were produced at all. When Bowman and Topps, the two card manufacturers at the time, resumed production of cards, DiMaggio didn't sign a contract with either one and therefore wasn't included in their major sets. In 1951, Joe retired from the game, and soon thereafter card companies discontinued their pursuit of him.

However, DiMaggio appears on several pre-war vintage issues such as 1939 Play Ball #92, 1940 Play Ball #1, 1941 Play Ball #71 and 1941 Double Play #63. These popular issues range in value from $750 for the '41 Double Play card to $2,700 for the '40 Play Ball card. DiMaggio's 1938 Goudey Heads Up #274 issue, which is valued at $4,500, has become one of his most prominent Yankees cards.

In the '50s, Joe was featured on several oddball issues such as 1952 Berk Ross #13, which sells for $1,250 in Mint condition.

Nearly a decade later, the Nu-Card Company produced two newspaper style card sets that feature cards of the Yankee Clipper. Those most notable include his 1960 Nu-Card Hi-Lites #38 and his 1961 Nu-Card Scoops #438. Both cards carry the theme of

DiMaggio's 56-game hitting streak and sell in the more affordable range of $15-$40.

In 1992, Score honored DiMaggio with a five-card insert set. Joe autographed 2,500 of these cards, 2,495 of which were randomly inserted into Series I packs. The other five were given away through a mail-in sweepstakes. The autographed issue sells for as much as $500, while the regular inserts sell for about $30 each.

Three additional DiMaggio cards were included in the 1992 Score Factory Inserts set. Although their value is between 60 cents and $1.50, these cards generally are not as available as singles since few dealers are willing to break the set.

One year later, Pinnacle capitalized on Joe's renewed popularity by producing a 30-card set commemorating his life and career. DiMaggio signed 9,000 cards that were randomly inserted into the 209,000 sets produced.

And in 1995, Signature Rookies included Joe DiMaggio in its 36-card set (#JD1). DiMaggio signed 250 issues for insertion into the Old Judge Signatures set. The autographed cards list for as much as $400.

So you see, there are DiMaggio cards in circulation. Sure, locating and obtaining the cards may not be an easy task, but for the devoted DiMaggio collector, it certainly is a rewarding one.

1993
Pinnacle
DiMaggio
Set #25

PINNACLE

JOE DIMAGGIO

taken. Many have been reproduced for signing sessions. Most of these reproduced photos were signed with a Sharpie pen. Autographed photos of Joe during his San Francisco Seals days sell for about $150.

While equipment from that era is hard to find, a few DiMaggio bats from his Seals days reportedly have survived. These are in heavy demand and generally require a substantial premium of as much as $20,000 each, depending on their condition.

DiMaggio's family-operated restaurant, which closed in 1986 after nearly 50 years of business, brought to the market some interesting memorabilia

Items such as match covers, napkins, menus and water glasses from the San Francisco restaurant exist but are not easily found.

As many as 15 different versions of the match covers exist and sell for as much as $40 each. DiMaggio's napkins, perhaps the most avail-

NATIONAL BASEBALL LIBRARY AND ARCHIVE/COOPERSTOWN, N.Y.

able restaurant item, can be obtained for about $25 each. And a vintage DiMaggio's menu, which is one of the most difficult of these items to locate, sells in the $350 range with Joe's signature and $150 without.

DiMaggio's restaurant stopped using the famed water glasses in the mid-1970s because many customers continually stole the glasses as they left the premises. The small glass features a rendition of Joe swinging a bat, etched in blue. The script on the glass also is blue and simply reads: "DiMaggio's." Today, the glasses are valued at about $100 each.

Swizzle sticks, sugar packets and postcards also remain as souvenirs from the restaurant. These are considered less significant items and can be obtained for a much smaller fee. Most postcards sell for $25-$35. But the most popular postcard, which is made of linen and features the three DiMaggio baseball brothers, sells for up to $75. Pennants and ashtrays also are available as souvenirs from the DiMaggio restaurant. They have been known to sell in the $500 price range.

DiMaggio's most popular memorabilia continues to be items from his glorious Yankees days.

DiMaggio's game-worn Yankees jerseys have ranged in price from $50,000 to $200,000 each, while a game-used, autographed bat commanded a $22,000 premium not long ago. Also, DiMaggio's game-used Yankees caps have been known to sell for as much as $18,000 in the last several years, although only a few are known to exist.

Hundreds of magazine covers also exist for DiMaggio memorabilia collectors. The most popular DiMaggio magazine cover is the first issue of *Sport*, which hit newsstands in September 1946. The magazine, which features Joe holding his young son on his lap, sells for about $700 in Near-Mint condition. Joe also appeared on *Sport* magazine covers in each of the next three years. DiMaggio also graces the cover of a number of non-sports magazines such as *Life*, *Time* and *Look*. The magazine covers will run between $150-$550 for Near-Mint copies.

In October 1991, Scoreboard signed Joe to an exclusive two-year contract to sign balls and photos. During that time, DiMaggio honored his relationship with Scoreboard by not signing any other baseballs. The demand and the price for a DiMaggio-signed baseball skyrocketed. Scoreboard retailed the autographed balls at $390 but reduced the price to as low as $249 because of a low number of sales at the original price. Obtaining DiMaggio's autograph in person always rates as a difficult task because of Joe's low profile. Joe rarely made public appearances primarily because of health concerns. DiMaggio occasionally signed at shows, but his high appearance fee discouraged many promoters from seeking him. It has been reported that DiMaggio commanded $100,000 for an appearance, which led promoters to charge no less than $150 for his autograph.

DiMaggio's exceptional demands in the hobby industry were justified in part due to his direct contributions to the Joe DiMaggio Children's Hospital in Hollywood, Fla. Much of the hospital's expenses have been funded by DiMaggio himself. The hospital accepts all children in need of medical treatment, whether or not their families can afford it.

At one of DiMaggio's last card show appearances — The 16th Long Island Classic in New York three years ago — DiMaggio signed 1,300 autographs and graciously allowed all customers the opportunity to have their picture taken with him. The price range for Joe's autograph at the show was $150 for baseballs, $175 for flat items, and $350 for caps and helmets.

There are some items that DiMaggio generally wouldn't sign. Like other big-name sports celebrities, Joe refused to sign bats, jerseys, original art, statues and photo balls. Nor would he autograph any Mr. Coffee memorabilia or Marilyn Monroe memorabilia.

DiMaggio's restaurant in San Francisco remained a popular attraction for nearly 50 years before closing in 1986.

23

Joe DiMaggio Trading Cards continued

Year	Set Name	Card No.	Price
1993	Pinnacle DiMaggio	5	.75
1993	Pinnacle DiMaggio	6	.75
1993	Pinnacle DiMaggio	7	.75
1993	Pinnacle DiMaggio	8	.75
1993	Pinnacle DiMaggio	9	.75
1993	Pinnacle DiMaggio	10	.75
1993	Pinnacle DiMaggio	11	1.50
1993	Pinnacle DiMaggio	12	.75
1993	Pinnacle DiMaggio	13	.75
1993	Pinnacle DiMaggio	14	.75
1993	Pinnacle DiMaggio	15	.75
1993	Pinnacle DiMaggio	16	.75
1993	Pinnacle DiMaggio	17	.75
1993	Pinnacle DiMaggio	18	.75
1993	Pinnacle DiMaggio	19	.75
1993	Pinnacle DiMaggio	20	.75
1993	Pinnacle DiMaggio	21	1.00
1993	Pinnacle DiMaggio	22	.75
1993	Pinnacle DiMaggio	23	.75
1993	Pinnacle DiMaggio	24	.75
1993	Pinnacle DiMaggio	25	.75
1993	Pinnacle DiMaggio	26	.75
1993	Pinnacle DiMaggio	27	.75
1993	Pinnacle DiMaggio	28	.75
1993	Pinnacle DiMaggio	29	.75
1993	Pinnacle DiMaggio	30	.75
1993	Pinnacle DiMaggio Autographs	1	300.00
1993	Pinnacle DiMaggio Autographs	2	300.00
1993	Pinnacle DiMaggio Autographs	3	300.00
1993	Pinnacle DiMaggio Autographs	4	300.00
1993	Pinnacle DiMaggio Autographs	5	300.00
1995	Signature Rookies Old Judge	JD1	10.00
1995	Signature Rookies Old Judge Joe DiMaggio	1	10.00
1995	Signature Rookies Old Judge Joe DiMaggio	2	400.00
1995	Signature Rookies Old Judge Signatures	JD1	400.00

Lou Gehrig Trading Cards

Year	Set Name	Card No.	Price
1925	Exhibits	97	800.00
1926	Exhibits	99	750.00
1927	Exhibits	49	400.00
1928	Exhibits	50	400.00
1928	Portraits and Action R315	A10	400.00
1928	Portraits and Action R315	B10	400.00
1928	Star Player Candy E-Unc.	24	1500.00
1928	W502	26	125.00
1928	W560 Playing Cards	C3	*
1928	Yuenglings	26	450.00
1929	Portraits and Action R316	28	400.00
1929-30	Exhibits Four-in-One	26	750.00
1930	Schutter-Johnson R332	20	350.00
1930	W554	4	250.00
1931	W517	35	900.00
1931-32	Exhibits Four-in-One	26	1250.00
1932	U.S. Caramel R328	26	1000.00
1933	Butterfinger Canadian V94	18	300.00
1933	Cracker Jack Pins	7	100.00
1933	Delong R333	7	3500.00
1933	Goudey Canadian V353	55	3500.00
1933	Goudey R319	92	2500.00
1933	Goudey R319	160	2500.00
1934	Baby Ruth Gum	25	*
1934	Butterfinger Premiums R310	24	300.00
1934	Exhibits Four-in-One W463-4	13	750.00
1934	Goudey Canadian V354	92	3500.00
1934	Goudey R320	37	2700.00
1934	Goudey R320	61	2700.00
1935	Al Demaree Die Cuts R304	9	1500.00
1935	Exhibits Four-in-One W463-5	13	600.00
1935	Wheaties BB1	13	450.00
1936	Exhibits Four-in-One W463-6	13	600.00
1936	Wheaties BB3	4	400.00
1936	Wheaties BB4	2	350.00

1934 Goudey R320

Year	Set Name	Card No.	Price
1936	World Wide Gum V355	96	2500.00
1936-38	Overland Candy R301	15	*
1936-39	Hall of Fame Postcards	11	*
1937	Exhibits Four-in-One W463-7	13	800.00
1938	Baseball Tabs	11	300.00
1938	Exhibits Four-in-One	13	1000.00
1938	Our National Game Tabs	11	175.00
1939-46	Exhibits Salutation	18	2000.00
1939-52	Albertype Hall of Fame PC754-2	22	60.00
1946-49	Sports Exchange W603	3-4	200.00
1947-66	PM10 Stadium Pins 1 3/4"	68	350.00
1947-66	PM10 Stadium Pins 1 3/4"	69	300.00
1948	Exhibit Hall of Fame	12	75.00
1948	Swell Sport Thrills	14	125.00
1948-49	Blue Tint R346	29	200.00
1949	Leaf Premiums	3	500.00
1950-56	Callahan HOF W576	33	100.00
1951	R423 Small Strip	35	15.00
1951	Topps Connie Mack All-Stars	5	2000.00
1953-63	Artvue Hall of Fame Postcards	37	*
1958	Jay Publishing All-Time Greats	3	15.00
1960	Fleer	28	80.00
1960	Key Chain Inserts	18	30.00
1960	Nu-Card Hi-Lites	24	50.00
1960	Rawling's Glove Tags	8	*
1960-61	Exhibits Wrigley HOF	11	40.00
1961	Fleer	31	75.00
1961	Golden Press	16	35.00
1961	Nu-Card Scoops	424	15.00
1961	Topps	405	80.00
1962	Topps	140	50.00
1962	Topps Venezuelan	140	50.00
1963	Baseball Magazine M118	29	*
1963	Bazooka ATG	15	50.00
1963	Gad Fun Cards	5	5.00
1963	Gad Fun Cards	43	5.00
1963	Hall of Fame Busts	8	100.00
1967	Topps Venezuelan	141	400.00
1968	Laughlin World Series	25	7.50
1968	Sports Memorabilia All-Time Greats	12	3.00
1969-70	Bazooka	4	50.00
1969-70	Bazooka	5	100.00
1969-70	Bazooka	7	60.00
1969-73	Equitable Sports Hall of Fame	BB5	12.50
1970	Fleer World Series	25	6.00
1970	Fleer World Series	29	6.00
1970	Fleer World Series	35	4.00
1970	House of Jazz	8	40.00
1970	Metropolitan Museum of Art Burdick	2	25.00
1970	Sports Cards for Collectors Old-Timer Postcards	1	4.00
1970	Sports Cards for Collectors Old-Timer Postcards	9	4.00

Year	Set Name	Card No.	Price
1971	Fleer World Series	26	5.00
1972	Fleer Famous Feats	5	3.00
1972	Kellogg's ATG	13	6.00
1972	Laughlin Great Feats	8	5.00
1973	Hall of Fame Picture Pack	8	3.00
1973	O-Pee-Chee	472	18.00
1973	Seven-Eleven Trading Cups	23	20.00
1973	Syracuse Chiefs Team Issue	8	*
1973	Topps	472	15.00
1974	Capital Publishing	2	4.00
1974	Fleer Baseball Firsts	5	1.50
1974	New York News This Day in Sports	20	5.00
1974	Syracuse Chiefs Team Issue	8	*
1975	Sports Hobbyist Baseball Greats	5	*
1975	TCMA House of Jazz	8	5.00
1975	Yankee Dynasty 1936-39 TCMA	16	6.00
1975	Yankee Dynasty 1936-39 TCMA	51	4.00
1975	Yankee Dynasty 1936-39 TCMA	52	1.50
1975	Yankee Dynasty 1936-39 TCMA	53	4.00
1975	Yankee Dynasty 1936-39 TCMA	54	4.00
1975	Yankees 1927 TCMA	8	5.00
1975	Yankees All-Time Team TCMA	4	5.00
1976	Galasso Baseball's Great Hall of Fame	11	3.00
1976	Laughlin Diamond Jubilee	28	6.00
1976	O-Pee-Chee	341	15.00
1976	Rowe Exhibits	4	1.50
1976	Shakey's Pizza	18	5.00
1976	Topps	341	12.00
1977	Sertoma Stars	10	3.00
1977	Shakey's Pizza	10	6.00
1977-84	Galasso Glossy Greats	46	3.00
1977-84	Galasso Glossy Greats	181	3.00
1977-84	Galasso Glossy Greats	236	3.00
1978	Dexter Hall of Fame Postcards	17	7.50
1979	Sports Legends	3	25.00
1979	Yankees 1927 TCMA	11	5.00
1980	Laughlin 300/400/500	29	2.50
1980	Laughlin Famous Feats	10	1.50
1980	Marchant Exhibits	9	1.00
1980	Yankees Greats TCMA	1	2.50
1980-83	Pacific Legends	13	2.50
1980-87	SSPC HOF	22	1.50
1980-96	Perez-Steele Hall of Fame Postcards	22	35.00
1981	Conlon TSN	5	7.50
1981	San Diego Sports Collectors	17	2.00
1981	San Diego Sports Collectors	18	1.00
1981	San Diego Sports Collectors	19	.75
1981	Sportrait Hall of Fame	6	3.00
1981	Tigers Detroit News	50	.75
1982	BHCR Sports Legends	3	*
1982	Davco Hall of Fame Boxes	9	3.00
1982	Diamond Classics	35	2.00
1982	TCMA Greatest Hitters	23	3.00
1982	TCMA Greatest Sluggers	19	3.00
1983	Big League Collectibles Original All-Stars	9	3.00
1983	Conlon Marketcom	3	2.00
1983	TCMA Ruth	2	4.00
1983	Yankee A-S Fifty Years	15	1.50
1984	Galasso Hall of Famers Ron Lewis	18	2.00
1984	Yankees 1927 Galasso	1	2.00
1984-89	O'Connell and Son Ink	98	2.00
1984-89	O'Connell and Son Ink	174	2.00
1985	Big League Collectibles 30s	49	3.00
1985	Circle K	14	.75
1985	Donruss	635	1.50
1985	Donruss HOF Sluggers	3	1.50
1985	Donruss Wax Box Cards	PUZ	.75
1985	Feg Murray's Cartoon Greats	7	1.00
1985	George Steinbrenner Menu	2	5.00
1985	Leaf/Donruss	635	.50
1985	TCMA Photo Classics	5	2.50
1985	TCMA Photo Classics	16	1.00
1985	Ultimate Baseball Card	4	7.50
1985	Woolworth's	14	.75
1986	Conlon Series 1	1	1.50
1986	Conlon Series 1	17	1.50
1986	Conlon Series 1	52	1.50
1986	Conlon Series 1	57	1.50
1986	Sportflics Decade Greats	10	3.00

Year	Set Name	Card No.	Price
1986	TCMA	17	2.00
1986	TCMA Superstars Simon	9	1.50
1986	TCMA Superstars Simon	28	2.00
1987	Conlon Series 2	1	1.50
1987	Hygrade All-Time Greats	20	1.00
1987	Nestle Dream Team	1	1.50
1987	Sports Cube Game	2	10.00
1987	Sports Reading	28	12.50
1987	Yankees 1927 TCMA	8	2.00
1988	Conlon American All-Stars	10	1.50
1988	Conlon Hardee's/Coke	3	2.00
1988	Conlon Series 5	12	1.50
1988	Grenada Baseball Stamps	30	2.00
1989	CMC Baseball's Greatest	3	.75
1989	HOF Sticker Book	1	2.00
1989	Pacific Legends II	174	1.50
1989	Rini Postcards Gehrig	1	.50
1989	Rini Postcards Gehrig	2	.50
1989	Rini Postcards Gehrig	3	.50
1989	Rini Postcards Gehrig	4	1.00
1989	Rini Postcards Gehrig	5	.50
1989	Rini Postcards Gehrig	6	.50
1989	Rini Postcards Gehrig	7	.50
1989	Rini Postcards Gehrig	8	.50
1989	Rini Postcards Gehrig	9	.50
1989	Rini Postcards Gehrig	10	.50
1989	Swell Baseball Greats	25	2.00
1989	Topps Baseball Talk/LJN	21	6.00
1989	USPS Legends Stamp Cards	2	6.00
1989	Yankee Citgo All-Time Greats	2	5.00
1990	Baseball Wit	73	1.25
1990	Collect-A-Books	34	1.25
1990	HOF Sticker Book	38	2.00
1990	Swell Baseball Greats	25	2.00
1990	Yankees Monument Pk. Rini Postcards	1	2.00
1990-97	Perez-Steele Great Moments	4	15.00
1991	Cadaco Ellis Discs	23	8.00
1991	Conlon TSN	111	.75
1991	Conlon TSN	310	.75
1991	Denver BallPark	4	*
1991	Homers Cookies Classics	9	2.50
1991	Swell Baseball Greats	125	2.00
1991	U.S. Game Systems Baseball Legends	3C	.50
1991	U.S. Game Systems Baseball Legends	3D	.50
1991	U.S. Game Systems Baseball Legends	3H	.50
1991	U.S. Game Systems Baseball Legends	3S	.50
1991-92	Conlon TSN Prototypes	111	10.00
1992	Conlon TSN	529	.75
1992	Megacards Ruth	81	.75
1992	Megacards Ruth	122	.40
1992	Megacards Ruth Prototypes	154	3.00
1992	O-Pee-Chee	40	4.00
1992	Pinnacle	286	.50
1992	Score	881	.25
1992	St. Vincent HOF Heroes Stamps	5	3.00
1992	Topps	40	2.00
1992	Topps Gold	40	15.00
1992	Topps Gold Pre-Production Sheet	40	10.00
1992	Topps Gold Winners	40	4.00
1992	Topps Micro	40	*
1992	Whitehall Legends to Life	2	4.00
1992	Whitehall Prototypes	2	4.00
1992	Yankees WIZ All-Stars	22	5.00
1992	Yankees WIZ HOF	11	4.00
1992-93	Conlon TSN Color Inserts	3	4.00
1992-93	Conlon TSN Color Inserts	8	4.00
1992-97	Sports Illustrated For Kids II	108	3.00
1993	Action Packed ASG	97	1.50
1993	Action Packed ASG 24K	31G	50.00
1993	Cadaco Discs	24	6.00
1993	Conlon Masters BW	3	3.00
1993	Conlon TSN	673	.75
1993	Diamond Stars Extension Set	130	2.00
1993	Hoyle	3	2.00
1993	Spectrum HOF II	1	2.00
1993	Ted Williams	63	1.50
1993	Ted Williams	122	1.50
1993	Ted Williams POG Cards	23	2.00
1993	Ted Williams POG Cards	24	1.50
1993	Upper Deck All-Time Heroes	58	2.00

Year	Set Name	Card No.	Price
1993	Upper Deck All-Time Heroes	131	1.50
1993	Upper Deck All-Time Heroes	133	1.50
1993-94	Legendary Foils	3	6.00
1993-97	Bleachers	32	35.00
1993-97	Bleachers	33	18.00
1994	Conlon TSN	1082	.75
1994	Conlon TSN	1249	.75
1994	Conlon TSN Burgundy	1082	5.00
1994	Conlon TSN Burgundy	1249	5.00
1994	Conlon TSN Color Inserts	31	6.00
1994	Megacards Ruthian Shots	3	4.00
1994	Ted Williams	147	1.00
1994	Ted Williams Locklear Collection	LC13	8.00
1994	Ted Williams Trade for Babe	T5	5.00
1994	Upper Deck All-Time Heroes	4	1.50
1994	Upper Deck All-Time Heroes	40	1.50
1994	Upper Deck All-Time Heroes	112	1.00
1994	Upper Deck All-Time Heroes	160	.75
1994	Upper Deck All-Time Heroes 125th	4	4.00
1994	Upper Deck All-Time Heroes 125th	40	4.00
1994	Upper Deck All-Time Heroes 125th	112	2.00
1994	Upper Deck All-Time Heroes 125th	160	2.00
1994	Upper Deck: The American Epic	37	2.00
1995	Conlon TSN	1421	1.50
1995	Conlon TSN Griffey Jr.	2	2.50
1995	Conlon TSN Prototypes	1421	4.00
1995	Megacards Ruth	3	.75
1995	Megacards Ruth	6	1.00
1995	Megacards Ruth	12	1.50
1995	Megacards Ruth	13	1.00
1995	Upper Deck Sonic Heroes of Baseball	4	.75
1996-98	Highland Mint Mini Mint-Cards	19	400.00
1996-98	Highland Mint Mini Mint-Cards	21	225.00
1996-98	Highland Mint Mini Mint-Cards	23	100.00

Mickey Mantle Trading Cards

Year	Set Name	Card No.	Price
1947-65	PM10 Stadium Pins 2 1/8"	21	250.00
1947-66	Exhibits	146A	150.00
1947-66	Exhibits	146B	250.00
1947-66	Exhibits	146C	150.00
1947-66	Exhibits	146D	600.00
1947-66	PM10 Stadium Pins 1 3/4"	119	175.00
1947-66	PM10 Stadium Pins 1 3/4"	120	160.00
1947-66	PM10 Stadium Pins 1 3/4"	121	160.00
1947-66	PM10 Stadium Pins 1 3/4"	122	100.00
1947-66	PM10 Stadium Pins 1 3/4"	123	50.00
1947-66	PM10 Stadium Pins 1 3/4"	124	275.00

1996 Topps #7

1953 Bowman #59

Year	Set Name	Card No.	Price
1947-66	PM10 Stadium Pins 1 3/4"	125	60.00
1951	Bowman	253	8000.00
1952	Berk Ross	37	1800.00
1952	Bowman	101	2500.00
1952	Star Cal Large	70G	1000.00
1952	Tip Top	24	1750.00
1952	Topps	311	20000.00
1953	Bowman Color	44	675.00
1953	Bowman Color	59	3000.00
1953	Stahl Meyer	6	2500.00
1953	Topps	82	3000.00
1953-54	Briggs	34	2500.00
1953-55	Dormand	111	125.00
1953-55	Dormand	111A	200.00
1953-55	Dormand	111B	300.00
1953-55	Dormand	111C	300.00
1954	Bowman	65	1400.00
1954	Dan Dee	17	1800.00
1954	New York Journal American	51	500.00
1954	Red Heart	18	500.00
1954	Stahl Meyer	6	3000.00
1955	Armour Coins	13A	125.00
1955	Armour Coins	13B	250.00
1955	Big League Inc. Statues	11	300.00
1955	Bowman	202	900.00
1955	Dairy Queen Statues	11	300.00
1955	Stahl Meyer	6	3000.00
1955-62	Don Wingfield	31	50.00
1956	Mantle Holiday Inn Postcard	1	35.00
1956	Topps	135	1400.00
1956	Yankees Jay Publishing	8	40.00
1956	Yankees Team Issue	14	50.00
1956	Yellow Basepath Pins	20	900.00
1957	Topps	95	1000.00
1957	Topps	407	500.00
1957	Yankees Jay Publishing	10	60.00
1958	Jay Publishing All-Stars	11	35.00
1958	Jay Publishing Sluggers	5	25.00
1958	Topps	150	800.00
1958	Topps	418	275.00
1958	Topps	487	175.00
1958	Yankees Jay Publishing	9	25.00
1958-63	Hartland Statues	1	*
1959	Bazooka	14	1750.00
1959	Home Run Derby	12	1350.00
1959	Oklahoma Today Major Leaguers	12	75.00
1959	Topps	10	600.00
1959	Topps	461	130.00
1959	Topps	564	300.00

Continued on page 28

The Mick's Magic

Mickey Mantle may have worn No. 7, but he's still No. 1 in the hearts of many collectors

by Marty Appel

After Mickey Mantle's retirement, he became a spring training batting instructor for the Yankees. The job offered him six weeks in Fort Lauderdale, Fla., and gave the Yankees a touch of glamour and a thread to their glory days.

His primary job? Posing for photos, not only with fans, but also with rookies. Yes, even in the pre-memorabilia age of the early 1970s, young players knew they could not pass on a chance to have a picture taken with their "teammate," The Mick.

Ten years later, everything had taken on a price, and Mickey was at the head of the class. He can still inspire awe. When he uncoiled and hit those rockets and set off with blazing speed for first base, his No. 7 seemed to signify the lashing out of the power and speed at once, not unlike a lightning bolt illustrating a comic book panel.

True, when he arrived as a 19-year-old rookie in 1951, they gave him No. 6, and it was clearly meant that he follow in the footsteps of No. 3 (Babe Ruth), No. 4 (Lou Gehrig) and No. 5 (Joe DiMaggio), not to put too much pressure on the teen-age product of the dust bowl off Route 66 in Oklahoma. But No. 6 didn't fit, even if the jersey did. The 6 looked, somehow, unmajestic. It worked fine for Stan Musial in St. Louis and Al Kaline in Detroit, but it didn't quite capture Mick. So when Casey Stengel shipped him back to the minors in the summer of 1951, the holder of No. 7, Cliff Mapes, was traded. When Mantle returned in August,

Mickey Mantle

he donned No. 7 and kept it thereafter. Lucky 7 has been worn hundreds of times on the backs of players since, but none wore it quite as Mantle did. He defined it. Flat against his broad back, it was part of the art that defined Mickey Mantle on a baseball field.

Today, flannel jerseys that actually brushed against his T-shirts and muscular arms are among the most valued collectibles in all of sports. And they are only a small part of the empire of collectibles that has risen in the wake of this legendary superstar.

As Marilyn Monroe transcended the film industry and Elvis Presley the music industry, Mickey has grown larger than sports. The emotion he stirs among baby boomers has taken him to a level reached by few Americans.

In a sense, it began with trading cards, when, long before anyone knew the term "chase card," a Mantle card tucked in a nickel pack of Topps was a jewel. Many still can cite the street corner on which they stood when they opened that wax pack and saw that handsome face and alliterative name, seemingly cast in Hollywood.

A decade after his retirement, there he was again, giving rise to the birth of the so-called secondary market, and with it, the weekend card show. When his early cards began to sell for big bucks, when the stories of those sales crept into the nation's newspapers, everyone began running to their attics in search of their cards. Yes, the moms of America had thrown out most of them. But for those who held on to their

Mickey Mantle monogram

stash, happiness reigned.

And so the memorabilia market grew, and Mantle, predecessor Joe DiMaggio and Boston rival Ted Williams became the champions of the autograph market.

Then, with a declining market and a nasty baseball strike, the trading card business began to falter, and yes, one more time, even in death, Mantle rode to the rescue. Topps reprinted his original cards, inserted them in its 1996 products, and people started buying cards again, visiting hobby stores and buying everything possible to touch Mantle's legend.

Was that a Styrofoam coffee cup Mickey had sipped from during a radio interview? You can bet it was preserved by a sharp radio producer. Was that the golf ball Mickey discarded after the ninth hole at Preston Trails in Dallas? You can bet some caddie has that sitting at home as a souvenir.

The fascination with items relating to Mantle never seems to wane. He touched America in a

way few ever had, and because he played in an era that preceded our hunger for memorabilia; everything sought in his wake involved the charm of the hunt. No one stood outside the Yankees clubhouse to gather his historic baseballs and rush them off to auction. No one encouraged him to sell his uniform shirts or donate his bats. (One eager hotel bellhop however, did offer Mantle's toenail clippings in a letter to Topps two years ago).

As a young employee in the Yankees public relations department in the summer of 1968, I was standing by Mantle's locker when he broke open a box of spikes and said, to no one in particular, "Well, this'll be my last pair of these." Not knowing the life span of shoes, I could not assume he was announcing that 1968 would be his last season. For all I knew, a pair of spikes could go into 1969.

But we were so naive that it never occurred to me to see what became of his discarded pair. Today, every bandage he removed would be hermetically sealed in a mayonnaise jar. After his liver transplant, even Mantle joked (on national television) by asking whether noted collector Barry Halper, who was in the room, "got my old liver."

Michael Jordan, Wayne Gretzky, Tiger Woods, Joe Montana — all arrived after a collectibles industry was in place. As important as those men always will be to their sports and to collectors, Mantle's career predated the industry, leaving a combination of scarcity and adulation that will forever have him at the top of the roll call in auction houses.

Mickey Mantle

Mickey Mantle Trading Cards continued

Year	Set Name	Card No.	Price
1959	Topps Venezuelan	10	1500.00
1959	Yoo-Hoo	4	1750.00
1960	Armour Coins	14	100.00
1960	Bazooka	31	275.00
1960	Key Chain Inserts	31	40.00
1960	Nu-Card Hi-Lites	22	50.00
1960	Nu-Card Hi-Lites	50	50.00
1960	Post	7	2500.00
1960	Rawling's Glove Tags	17	*
1960	Topps	160	140.00
1960	Topps	350	475.00
1960	Topps	563	325.00
1960	Topps Tattoos	31	400.00
1960	Topps Tattoos	92	175.00
1960	Topps Venezuelan	160	350.00
1960	Yankees Jay Publishing	7	25.00
1961	Bazooka	2	275.00
1961	Nu-Card Scoops	422	30.00
1961	Nu-Card Scoops	450	30.00
1961	Post	4A	150.00
1961	Post	4B	150.00
1961	Rawlings	5	75.00
1961	Topps	44	100.00
1961	Topps	300	500.00
1961	Topps	307	100.00
1961	Topps	406	100.00
1961	Topps	475	200.00
1961	Topps	578	425.00
1961	Topps Dice Game	8	3000.00
1961	Topps Stamps Inserts	196	60.00
1961	Yankees Jay Publishing	8	35.00
1962	Baseball Pens	3	*
1962	Bazooka	23	275.00
1962	Exhibit Stat Back	23	150.00
1962	Jello	5	1000.00
1962	Post	5A	150.00
1962	Post	5B	150.00

Year	Set Name	Card No.	Price
1962	Post Canadian	5	350.00
1962	Salada Plastic Coins	41	150.00
1962	Shirriff Plastic Coins	41	175.00
1962	Topps	18	200.00
1962	Topps	53	110.00
1962	Topps	200	450.00
1962	Topps	318	150.00
1962	Topps	471	200.00
1962	Topps Bucks	54	200.00
1962	Topps Stamps Inserts	88	60.00
1962	Topps Venezuelan	18	500.00
1962	Topps Venezuelan	53	250.00
1962	Yankees Jay Publishing	9	35.00
1963	Baseball Magazine M118	54	*
1963	Bazooka	1	225.00
1963	Exhibit Stat Back	41	150.00
1963	Jello	15	275.00
1963	Post	15	350.00
1963	Salada Metal Coins	56	125.00
1963	Topps	2	50.00
1963	Topps	173	175.00
1963	Topps	200	500.00
1963	Topps Stick-Ons Inserts	26	80.00
1963	Yankees Jay Publishing	7	35.00
1964	Auravision Records	10	75.00
1964	Bazooka	1	200.00
1964	Challenge The Yankees	16	150.00
1964	Topps	50	300.00
1964	Topps	331	150.00
1964	Topps Coins Inserts	120	80.00
1964	Topps Coins Inserts	131A	60.00
1964	Topps Coins Inserts	131B	60.00
1964	Topps Giants	25	30.00
1964	Topps Stamps	53	75.00
1964	Topps Stand Ups	45	550.00
1964	Topps Tattoos Inserts	51	300.00
1964	Topps Venezuelan	50	750.00

Year	Set Name	Card No.	Price
1964	Topps Venezuelan	331	450.00
1964	Yankees Jay Publishing	7	35.00
1964-5	Rawlings	5	50.00
1965	Bazooka	1	175.00
1965	Challenge The Yankees	13	150.00
1965	O-Pee-Chee	3	50.00
1965	O-Pee-Chee	5	50.00
1965	O-Pee-Chee	134	100.00
1965	Old London Coins	30	125.00
1965	Topps	3	40.00
1965	Topps	5	40.00
1965	Topps	134	75.00
1965	Topps	350	550.00
1965	Topps Embossed Inserts	11	60.00
1965	Topps Transfers Inserts	57	100.00
1966	Bazooka	7	175.00
1966	O-Pee-Chee	50	300.00
1966	Topps	50	200.00
1966	Topps Rub-Offs Inserts	57	75.00
1966	Topps Venezuelan	50	500.00
1966	Yankees Team Issue	7	25.00
1967	Bazooka	7	200.00
1967	Coke Caps Yankees and Mets	V8	20.00
1967	Dexter Press	132	50.00
1967	O-Pee-Chee	103	25.00
1967	O-Pee-Chee	150	350.00
1967	O-Pee-Chee Paper Inserts	6	100.00
1967	Topps	103	20.00
1967	Topps	150	300.00
1967	Topps Giant Stand Ups	8	1500.00
1967	Topps Posters Inserts	6	20.00
1967	Topps Test Foil	11	400.00
1967	Topps Venezuelan	192	750.00
1968	Atlantic Oil	7	50.00
1968	Bazooka	11	250.00
1968	Laughlin World Series	61	7.50
1968	Topps	280	250.00
1968	Topps	490	175.00
1968	Topps Action Stickers	7B	350.00
1968	Topps Action Stickers	10A	100.00
1968	Topps Game Card Inserts	2	40.00
1968	Topps Plaks	9	1500.00
1968	Topps Posters	18	75.00
1968	Topps Venezuelan	280	600.00
1969	Topps	412	15.00
1969	Topps	500A	350.00
1969	Topps	500B	1000.00
1969	Topps Decals Inserts	23	125.00
1969	Topps Stamps	205	35.00
1969	Topps Super	24	1000.00
1969	Topps Team Posters	19	175.00
1969	Transogram Statues	30	275.00
1969	Yankees Malanga	5	10.00
1969-73	Equitable Sports Hall of Fame	BB11	*
1970	Yankee Clinic Day Postcards	13	10.00
1970	Yankees Photos SCFC	23	10.00
1971	Yankee Clinic Day Postcards	10	25.00
1972	Laughlin Great Feats	33	6.00
1973	Seven-Eleven Trading Cups	41	25.00
1973	Syracuse Chiefs Team Issue	15	*
1973-97	Book Promotional Cards	16	10.00
1974	New York News This Day in Sports	18	10.00
1974	Syracuse Chiefs Team Issue	14	*
1975	O-Pee-Chee	194	18.00
1975	O-Pee-Chee	195	30.00
1975	O-Pee-Chee	200	18.00
1975	SSPC 42	37	20.00
1975	SSPC Samples	4	15.00
1975	Syracuse Chiefs Team Issue	9	*
1975	TCMA All-Time Greats	21	5.00
1975	TCMA House of Jazz	17	8.00
1975	Topps	194	20.00
1975	Topps	195	25.00
1975	Topps	200	20.00
1975	Topps Mini	194	20.00
1975	Topps Mini	195	25.00
1975	Topps Mini	200	20.00
1975	Yankees All-Time Team TCMA	6	5.00
1976	Galasso Baseball's Great Hall of Fame	17	4.00

Year	Set Name	Card No.	Price
1976	Great Plains Greats	41	3.00
1976	Shakey's Pizza	145	7.50
1976	Sportstix	D	75.00
1976	SSPC Yankees Old-Timers Day	7	3.00
1976	UPI Superstars	7	40.00
1977-79	Sportscaster	716	12.00
1977-84	Galasso Glossy Greats	7	3.00
1977-84	Galasso Glossy Greats	232	3.00
1978	Dexter Hall of Fame Postcards	34	7.50
1978	TCMA 60'S I	262	7.50
1979	Baseball Greats	72	7.50
1979	TCMA 50'S	7	7.50
1980	Laughlin 300/400/500	18	4.00
1980	Mickey Mantle Reserve Life	1	10.00
1980	Yankees Greats TCMA	6	3.00
1980-83	Pacific Legends	6	3.00
1980-87	SSPC HOF	145	1.50
1980-96	Perez-Steele Hall of Fame Postcards	145	60.00
1981	San Diego Sports Collectors	10	2.50
1981	San Diego Sports Collectors	11	2.50
1981	San Diego Sports Collectors	12	1.50
1981	San Diego Sports Collectors	13	1.00
1981	Sportrait Hall of Fame	15	4.00
1981	TCMA 60's II	303	5.00
1981	TCMA 60's II	474	2.50
1982	Baseball Card News	1	4.00
1982	Cracker Jack	6	5.00
1982	Davco Hall of Fame Boxes	15	5.00
1982	Diamond Classics	55	3.00
1982	K-Mart	1	.75
1982	TCMA Greatest Sluggers	3	5.00
1982	TCMA Stars of the '50s	19	6.00
1983	Donruss HOF Heroes	7	2.50
1983	Donruss HOF Heroes	43	2.50
1983	MLBPA Pins	12	4.00
1983	O'Connell and Son Baseball Greats	10	5.00
1983	Tigers Al Kaline Story	14	2.50
1983	Tigers Al Kaline Story	16	1.50
1983	Tigers Al Kaline Story	35	2.50
1983	Topps Reprint 52	311	50.00
1983	Yankee A-S Fifty Years	1	1.00
1983	Yankee A-S Fifty Years	26	2.00
1983	Yankee Yearbook Insert TCMA	15	3.00
1983	Yankees 1961	7	3.00
1983-91	Topps Traded Bronze Premiums	4	50.00
1984	ASA Willie Mays 90	29	.75
1984	Donruss Champions	50	3.00
1984	Fifth National Convention Tickets	11	7.50
1984-85	Sports Design Products West	4	1.50
1984-89	O'Connell and Son Ink	25	2.50
1984-89	O'Connell and Son Ink	100	2.50
1984-89	O'Connell and Son Ink	140	2.50
1984-89	O'Connell and Son Ink	150	2.50
1984-89	O'Connell and Son Ink	207	2.50
1985	Circle K	6	1.50
1985	Donruss HOF Sluggers	6	2.50
1985	George Steinbrenner Menu	5	7.50
1985	Woolworth's	23	1.00
1986	Big League Chew	6	2.00
1986	Donruss Highlights	10	1.00
1986	Sportflics Decade Greats	26	4.00
1986	Sports Design J.D. McCarthy	4	2.00
1986	TCMA	20	2.50
1986	TCMA Superstars Simon	4	2.50
1986	TCMA Superstars Simon	7	2.50
1986	TCMA Superstars Simon	9	1.50
1986	TCMA Superstars Simon	11	2.50
1986	TCMA Superstars Simon	18	2.00
1986	TCMA Superstars Simon	23	2.50
1986	TCMA Superstars Simon	24	2.50
1987	Astros Shooting Stars-Series One	26	3.00
1987	Hygrade All-Time Greats	31	1.50
1987	K-Mart	5	2.00
1987	Leaf Special Olympics	H1	4.00
1987	Nestle Dream Team	17	3.00
1987	Yankees 1961 TCMA	2	2.50
1988	Grenada Baseball Stamps	46	2.00
1988	Houston Show	9	15.00
1988	Pacific Legends I	7	3.00

Year	Set Name	Card No.	Price
1988	Willard Mullin Postcards	23	3.00
1989	Bowman Reprint Inserts	5	.75
1989	Bowman Reprint Inserts	6	.50
1989	Bowman Reprint Inserts Tiffany	5	.75
1989	Bowman Reprint Inserts Tiffany	6	.50
1989	Bowman Tiffany	R5	2.00
1989	Bowman Tiffany	R6	2.00
1989	CMC Mantle	1	.50
1989	CMC Mantle	2	.50
1989	CMC Mantle	3	.50
1989	CMC Mantle	4	.50
1989	CMC Mantle	5	.50
1989	CMC Mantle	6	1.00
1989	CMC Mantle	7	.50
1989	CMC Mantle	8	.75
1989	CMC Mantle	9	.50
1989	CMC Mantle	10	.75
1989	CMC Mantle	11	.50
1989	CMC Mantle	12	.50
1989	CMC Mantle	13	.50
1989	CMC Mantle	14	.75
1989	CMC Mantle	15	1.50
1989	CMC Mantle	16	.50
1989	CMC Mantle	17	.50
1989	CMC Mantle	18	.50
1989	CMC Mantle	19	.50
1989	CMC Mantle	20	.50
1989	HOF Sticker Book	40	2.00
1989	Perez-Steele Celebration Postcards	28	10.00
1990	Baseball Wit	3	2.00
1990	HOF Sticker Book	49	2.00
1990	Yankees 61 Ron Lewis	7	5.00
1990	Yankees Monument Pk. Rini Postcards	6	2.50
1990-92	Perez-Steele Master Works	6	15.00
1990-92	Perez-Steele Master Works	7	15.00
1990-92	Perez-Steele Master Works	8	15.00
1990-92	Perez-Steele Master Works	9	15.00
1990-92	Perez-Steele Master Works	10	15.00
1990-97	Perez-Steele Great Moments	19	20.00

Year	Set Name	Card No.	Price
1990-97	Perez-Steele Great Moments	87	10.00
1991	Mantle Video	1	3.00
1991	Score Mantle	1	30.00
1991	Score Mantle	2	30.00
1991	Score Mantle	3	30.00
1991	Score Mantle	4	30.00
1991	Score Mantle	5	30.00
1991	Score Mantle	6	30.00
1991	Score Mantle	7	30.00
1991	Score Mantle	AU0	500.00
1991	Topps Archives 1953	82	20.00
1991	Topps East Coast National	2	8.00
1991	Yankees Rini Postcards 1961 3	1	2.00
1992	Pinnacle Mantle	1	1.00
1992	Pinnacle Mantle	2	.75
1992	Pinnacle Mantle	3	.75
1992	Pinnacle Mantle	4	.75
1992	Pinnacle Mantle	5	.75
1992	Pinnacle Mantle	6	.75
1992	Pinnacle Mantle	7	.75
1992	Pinnacle Mantle	8	.75
1992	Pinnacle Mantle	9	.75
1992	Pinnacle Mantle	10	.75
1992	Pinnacle Mantle	11	.75
1992	Pinnacle Mantle	12	.75
1992	Pinnacle Mantle	13	.75
1992	Pinnacle Mantle	14	.75
1992	Pinnacle Mantle	15	.75
1992	Pinnacle Mantle	16	.75
1992	Pinnacle Mantle	17	.75
1992	Pinnacle Mantle	18	.75
1992	Pinnacle Mantle	19	.75
1992	Pinnacle Mantle	20	.75
1992	Pinnacle Mantle	21	.75
1992	Pinnacle Mantle	22	.75
1992	Pinnacle Mantle	23	.75
1992	Pinnacle Mantle	24	1.50
1992	Pinnacle Mantle	25	1.00
1992	Pinnacle Mantle	26	1.00

Joe DiMaggio/
Mickey Mantle

Year	Set Name	Card No.	Price
1992	Pinnacle Mantle	27	1.00
1992	Pinnacle Mantle	28	.75
1992	Pinnacle Mantle	29	.75
1992	Pinnacle Mantle	30	1.00
1992	Score Franchise	2	12.00
1992	Score Franchise	4	10.00
1992	Score Franchise	AU2	500.00
1992	Score Franchise	AU4	1500.00
1992	TV Sports Mailbag/		
	Photo File 500 Home Run Club	6	5.00
1992	Yankees WIZ 60s	78	10.00
1992	Yankees WIZ All-Stars	43	7.50
1992	Yankees WIZ HOF	22	5.00
1992-98	Highland Mint Mint-Coins	69	12.00
1993	Select Triple Crown	1	60.00
1993	Upper Deck All-Time Heroes	87	3.00
1993	Upper Deck All-Time Heroes	134	1.50
1993	Upper Deck All-Time Heroes	135	1.00
1993	Upper Deck All-Time Heroes	137	1.25
1993	Upper Deck All-Time Heroes	140	1.00
1993	Upper Deck All-Time Heroes	141	1.00
1993	Upper Deck All-Time Heroes	165	1.25
1993	Upper Deck All-Time Heroes Preview	1	1.50
1993	Upper Deck All-Time Heroes Preview	2	1.50
1993	Upper Deck All-Time Heroes Preview	4	1.50
1993	Upper Deck Then And Now	TN17	15.00
1993-97	Bleachers	19	12.00
1993-97	Bleachers	20	18.00
1993-97	Bleachers	21	18.00
1993-97	Bleachers	22	18.00
1993-97	Bleachers	23	18.00
1993-97	Bleachers	24	18.00

Year	Set Name	Card No.	Price
1994	Metallic Impressions Mantle	1	3.00
1994	Metallic Impressions Mantle	2	3.00
1994	Metallic Impressions Mantle	3	3.00
1994	Metallic Impressions Mantle	4	3.00
1994	Metallic Impressions Mantle	5	3.00
1994	Metallic Impressions Mantle	6	3.00
1994	Metallic Impressions Mantle	7	3.00
1994	Metallic Impressions Mantle	8	3.00
1994	Metallic Impressions Mantle	9	3.00
1994	Metallic Impressions Mantle	10	3.00
1994	Ted Williams 500 Club	4	8.00
1994	Upper Deck	GM1	1200.00
1994	Upper Deck	MM1	600.00
1994	Upper Deck All-Star Jumbos	46	2.50
1994	Upper Deck All-Star Jumbos Gold	46	25.00
1994	Upper Deck All-Time Heroes	7	.75
1994	Upper Deck All-Time Heroes	10	1.25
1994	Upper Deck All-Time Heroes	100	2.00
1994	Upper Deck All-Time Heroes	116	1.00
1994	Upper Deck All-Time Heroes	135	.25
1994	Upper Deck All-Time Heroes	168	1.00
1994	Upper Deck All-Time Heroes	222	1.00
1994	Upper Deck All-Time Heroes	225	.75
1994	Upper Deck All-Time Heroes 125th	7	2.00
1994	Upper Deck All-Time Heroes 125th	10	4.00
1994	Upper Deck All-Time Heroes 125th	100	4.00
1994	Upper Deck All-Time Heroes 125th	116	2.00
1994	Upper Deck All-Time Heroes 125th	135	1.00
1994	Upper Deck All-Time Heroes 125th	168	2.00
1994	Upper Deck All-Time Heroes 125th	222	2.00
1994	Upper Deck All-Time Heroes 125th	225	2.00
1994	Upper Deck All-Time Heroes		

Year	Set Name	Card No.	Price
	1954 Archives	259	40.00
1994	Upper Deck All-Time Heroes		
	Autographs	3	350.00
1994	Upper Deck Mantle Heroes	64	12.00
1994	Upper Deck Mantle Heroes	65	12.00
1994	Upper Deck Mantle Heroes	66	12.00
1994	Upper Deck Mantle Heroes	67	12.00
1994	Upper Deck Mantle Heroes	68	12.00
1994	Upper Deck Mantle Heroes	69	12.00
1994	Upper Deck Mantle Heroes	70	12.00
1994	Upper Deck Mantle Heroes	71	12.00
1994	Upper Deck Mantle Heroes	72	12.00
1994	Upper Deck Mantle Heroes	NNO0	12.00
1994	Upper Deck Mantle Phone Cards	1	8.00
1994	Upper Deck Mantle Phone Cards	2	8.00
1994	Upper Deck Mantle Phone Cards	3	8.00
1994	Upper Deck Mantle Phone Cards	4	8.00
1994	Upper Deck Mantle Phone Cards	5	8.00
1994	Upper Deck Mantle Phone Cards	6	8.00
1994	Upper Deck Mantle Phone Cards	7	8.00
1994	Upper Deck Mantle Phone Cards	8	8.00
1994	Upper Deck Mantle Phone Cards	9	8.00
1994	Upper Deck Mantle Phone Cards	10	8.00
1994	Upper Deck Mantle's Long Shots	MM21	15.00
1994	Upper Deck Mantle's Long Shots	NNO	12.00
1994	Upper Deck Mantle's Long Shots	NNO	6.00
1994	Upper Deck Mantle's Long Shots		
	Electric Diamond	MM21	18.00
1994	Upper Deck Sheets	10	2.00
1994	Upper Deck: The American Epic	63	2.50
1994	Upper Deck: The American Epic	BC3	5.00
1994	Upper Deck: The American Epic GM	5	1.25
1994	Upper Deck: The American Epic		
	Little Debbies	LD12	1.50
1994-98	Highland Mint		
	Magnum Series Medallions	5	250.00
1994-98	Highland Mint		
	Magnum Series Medallions	6	150.00
1994-98	Highland Mint		
	Magnum Series Medallions	7	50.00
1994-98	Highland Mint Mint-Cards Pinnacle/UD	8	750.00
1994-98	Highland Mint Mint-Cards Pinnacle/UD	9	300.00
1994-98	Highland Mint Mint-Cards Pinnacle/UD	10	75.00
1995	Mantle Donor Card	1	1.00
1995	Upper Deck Mantle Metallic Impressions	1	*
1995	Upper Deck Mantle Metallic Impressions	2	*
1995	Upper Deck Mantle Metallic Impressions	3	*
1995	Upper Deck Mantle Metallic Impressions	4	*
1995	Upper Deck Mantle Metallic Impressions	5	*
1995	Upper Deck Mantle Metallic Impressions	6	*
1995	Upper Deck Mantle Metallic Impressions	7	*
1995	Upper Deck Mantle Metallic Impressions	8	*
1996	Bazooka	NNO	4.00
1996	Bowman	M20	10.00
1996	Bowman's Best	NNO	8.00
1996	Bowman's Best	NNO	20.00
1996	Bowman's Best	NNO	40.00
1996	Bowman's Best Atomic Refractors	NNO	*
1996	Bowman's Best Refractors	NNO	*
1996	Stadium Club Mantle	MM1	15.00
1996	Stadium Club Mantle	MM2	15.00
1996	Stadium Club Mantle	MM3	15.00
1996	Stadium Club Mantle	MM4	15.00
1996	Stadium Club Mantle	MM5	15.00
1996	Stadium Club Mantle	MM6	15.00
1996	Stadium Club Mantle	MM7	15.00
1996	Stadium Club Mantle	MM8	15.00
1996	Stadium Club Mantle	MM9	15.00
1996	Stadium Club Mantle	MM10	8.00
1996	Stadium Club Mantle	MM11	8.00
1996	Stadium Club Mantle	MM12	8.00
1996	Stadium Club Mantle	MM13	8.00
1996	Stadium Club Mantle	MM14	8.00
1996	Stadium Club Mantle	MM15	8.00
1996	Stadium Club Mantle	MM16	8.00
1996	Stadium Club Mantle	MM17	8.00
1996	Stadium Club Mantle	MM18	8.00
1996	Stadium Club Mantle	MM19	8.00
1996	Topps	7	4.00

Mickey Mantle

Year	Set Name	Card No.	Price
1996	Topps	F7	15.00
1996	Topps Chrome	7	15.00
1996	Topps Chrome Refractors	7	120.00
1996	Topps Gallery	NNO	20.00
1996	Topps Mantle	1	15.00
1996	Topps Mantle	2	20.00
1996	Topps Mantle	3	10.00
1996	Topps Mantle	4	8.00
1996	Topps Mantle	5	8.00
1996	Topps Mantle	6	8.00
1996	Topps Mantle	7	8.00
1996	Topps Mantle	8	8.00
1996	Topps Mantle	9	8.00
1996	Topps Mantle	10	8.00
1996	Topps Mantle	11	8.00
1996	Topps Mantle	12	8.00
1996	Topps Mantle	13	8.00
1996	Topps Mantle	14	8.00
1996	Topps Mantle	15	12.00
1996	Topps Mantle	16	12.00
1996	Topps Mantle	17	12.00
1996	Topps Mantle	18	12.00
1996	Topps Mantle	19	12.00
1996	Topps Mantle Case	1	100.00
1996	Topps Mantle Case	2	120.00
1996	Topps Mantle Case	3	60.00
1996	Topps Mantle Case	4	50.00
1996	Topps Mantle Case	5	50.00
1996	Topps Mantle Case	6	50.00
1996	Topps Mantle Case	7	50.00
1996	Topps Mantle Case	8	50.00
1996	Topps Mantle Case	9	50.00
1996	Topps Mantle Case	10	50.00
1996	Topps Mantle Case	11	50.00
1996	Topps Mantle Case	12	50.00
1996	Topps Mantle Case	13	50.00
1996	Topps Mantle Case	14	50.00
1996	Topps Mantle Case	15	60.00
1996	Topps Mantle Case	16	60.00
1996	Topps Mantle Case	17	60.00
1996	Topps Mantle Case	18	60.00
1996	Topps Mantle Case	19	60.00
1996	Topps Mantle Finest	1	15.00
1996	Topps Mantle Finest	2	20.00
1996	Topps Mantle Finest	3	10.00
1996	Topps Mantle Finest	4	8.00
1996	Topps Mantle Finest	5	8.00
1996	Topps Mantle Finest	6	8.00
1996	Topps Mantle Finest	7	8.00
1996	Topps Mantle Finest	8	8.00
1996	Topps Mantle Finest	9	8.00
1996	Topps Mantle Finest	10	8.00
1996	Topps Mantle Finest	11	8.00
1996	Topps Mantle Finest	12	8.00
1996	Topps Mantle Finest	13	8.00
1996	Topps Mantle Finest	14	8.00
1996	Topps Mantle Finest	15	12.00
1996	Topps Mantle Finest	16	12.00
1996	Topps Mantle Finest	17	12.00
1996	Topps Mantle Finest	18	12.00
1996	Topps Mantle Finest	19	12.00
1996	Topps Mantle Finest Refractors	1	60.00
1996	Topps Mantle Finest Refractors	2	80.00
1996	Topps Mantle Finest Refractors	3	40.00
1996	Topps Mantle Finest Refractors	4	30.00
1996	Topps Mantle Finest Refractors	5	30.00
1996	Topps Mantle Finest Refractors	6	30.00
1996	Topps Mantle Finest Refractors	7	30.00
1996	Topps Mantle Finest Refractors	8	30.00
1996	Topps Mantle Finest Refractors	9	30.00
1996	Topps Mantle Finest Refractors	10	30.00
1996	Topps Mantle Finest Refractors	11	30.00
1996	Topps Mantle Finest Refractors	12	30.00
1996	Topps Mantle Finest Refractors	13	30.00
1996	Topps Mantle Finest Refractors	14	30.00
1996	Topps Mantle Finest Refractors	15	40.00
1996	Topps Mantle Finest Refractors	16	40.00
1996	Topps Mantle Finest Refractors	17	40.00
1996	Topps Mantle Finest Refractors	18	40.00
1996	Topps Mantle Finest Refractors	19	40.00
1996	Topps Mantle Redemption	1	30.00
1996	Topps Mantle Redemption	2	40.00
1996	Topps Mantle Redemption	3	20.00
1996	Topps Mantle Redemption	4	15.00
1996	Topps Mantle Redemption	5	15.00
1996	Topps Mantle Redemption	6	15.00
1996	Topps Mantle Redemption	7	15.00
1996	Topps Mantle Redemption	8	15.00
1996	Topps Mantle Redemption	9	15.00
1996	Topps Mantle Redemption	10	15.00
1996	Topps Mantle Redemption	11	15.00
1996	Topps Mantle Redemption	12	15.00
1996	Topps Mantle Redemption	13	15.00
1996	Topps Mantle Redemption	14	15.00
1996	Topps Mantle Redemption	15	15.00
1996	Topps Mantle Redemption	16	15.00
1996	Topps Mantle Redemption	17	15.00
1996	Topps Mantle Redemption	18	15.00
1996	Topps Mantle Redemption	19	15.00
1997	Scoreboard Mantle	1	4.00
1997	Scoreboard Mantle	2	.50
1997	Scoreboard Mantle	3	.50
1997	Scoreboard Mantle	4	.50
1997	Scoreboard Mantle	5	.50
1997	Scoreboard Mantle	6	4.00
1997	Scoreboard Mantle	7	4.00
1997	Scoreboard Mantle	8	.50
1997	Scoreboard Mantle	9	.50
1997	Scoreboard Mantle	10	.50
1997	Scoreboard Mantle	11	.50
1997	Scoreboard Mantle	12	.50
1997	Scoreboard Mantle	13	.50
1997	Scoreboard Mantle	14	.50
1997	Scoreboard Mantle	15	.50
1997	Scoreboard Mantle	16	.50
1997	Scoreboard Mantle	17	.50
1997	Scoreboard Mantle	18	.50
1997	Scoreboard Mantle	19	.50
1997	Scoreboard Mantle	20	.50
1997	Scoreboard Mantle	21	.50
1997	Scoreboard Mantle	22	.50
1997	Scoreboard Mantle	23	.50
1997	Scoreboard Mantle	24	.50
1997	Scoreboard Mantle	25	.50
1997	Scoreboard Mantle	26	.50
1997	Scoreboard Mantle	27	.50
1997	Scoreboard Mantle	28	1.50
1997	Scoreboard Mantle	29	.50
1997	Scoreboard Mantle	30	.50
1997	Scoreboard Mantle	31	.50
1997	Scoreboard Mantle	32	.50
1997	Scoreboard Mantle	33	.50
1997	Scoreboard Mantle	34	.50
1997	Scoreboard Mantle	35	.50
1997	Scoreboard Mantle	36	.50
1997	Scoreboard Mantle	37	.50
1997	Scoreboard Mantle	38	.50
1997	Scoreboard Mantle	39	.50
1997	Scoreboard Mantle	40	.50
1997	Scoreboard Mantle	41	.50
1997	Scoreboard Mantle	42	.50
1997	Scoreboard Mantle	43	.50
1997	Scoreboard Mantle	44	.50
1997	Scoreboard Mantle	45	.50
1997	Scoreboard Mantle	46	.50
1997	Scoreboard Mantle	47	.50
1997	Scoreboard Mantle	48	.50
1997	Scoreboard Mantle	49	.50
1997	Scoreboard Mantle	50	.50
1997	Scoreboard Mantle	51	.75
1997	Scoreboard Mantle	52	.75
1997	Scoreboard Mantle	53	.75
1997	Scoreboard Mantle	54	.75
1997	Scoreboard Mantle	55	.75
1997	Scoreboard Mantle	56A	.75
1997	Scoreboard Mantle	56B	.75
1997	Scoreboard Mantle	57	.75
1997	Scoreboard Mantle	58	.75
1997	Scoreboard Mantle	59	.75
1997	Scoreboard Mantle	60	.75
1997	Scoreboard Mantle	61	.75
1997	Scoreboard Mantle	62	.75
1997	Scoreboard Mantle	63	.75
1997	Scoreboard Mantle	64	.75
1997	Scoreboard Mantle	65	.75
1997	Scoreboard Mantle	66	.75
1997	Scoreboard Mantle	67	.75
1997	Scoreboard Mantle	68	.75
1997	Scoreboard Mantle	69	.75
1997	Scoreboard Mantle	70	5.00
1997	Scoreboard Mantle	71	1.50
1997	Scoreboard Mantle	72	.50
1997	Scoreboard Mantle	73	.50
1997	Scoreboard Mantle	74	5.00
1997	Scoreboard Mantle	P1	1.50
1997	Scoreboard Mantle	P7	1.50
1997	Scoreboard Mantle 7	1	8.00
1997	Scoreboard Mantle 7	2	8.00
1997	Scoreboard Mantle 7	3	8.00
1997	Scoreboard Mantle 7	4	8.00
1997	Scoreboard Mantle 7	5	10.00
1997	Scoreboard Mantle 7	6	8.00
1997	Scoreboard Mantle 7	7	50.00
1997	Topps Mantle	21	8.00
1997	Topps Mantle	22	8.00
1997	Topps Mantle	23	8.00
1997	Topps Mantle	24	8.00
1997	Topps Mantle	25	8.00
1997	Topps Mantle	26	8.00
1997	Topps Mantle	27	8.00
1997	Topps Mantle	28	8.00
1997	Topps Mantle	29	8.00
1997	Topps Mantle	30	8.00
1997	Topps Mantle	31	8.00
1997	Topps Mantle	32	8.00
1997	Topps Mantle	33	8.00
1997	Topps Mantle	34	8.00
1997	Topps Mantle	35	8.00
1997	Topps Mantle	36	8.00
1997	Topps Mantle Finest	21	8.00
1997	Topps Mantle Finest	22	8.00
1997	Topps Mantle Finest	23	8.00
1997	Topps Mantle Finest	24	8.00
1997	Topps Mantle Finest	25	8.00
1997	Topps Mantle Finest	26	8.00
1997	Topps Mantle Finest	27	8.00
1997	Topps Mantle Finest	28	8.00
1997	Topps Mantle Finest	29	8.00
1997	Topps Mantle Finest	30	8.00
1997	Topps Mantle Finest	31	8.00
1997	Topps Mantle Finest	32	8.00
1997	Topps Mantle Finest	33	8.00
1997	Topps Mantle Finest	34	8.00
1997	Topps Mantle Finest	35	8.00
1997	Topps Mantle Finest	36	8.00
1997	Topps Mantle Finest Refractors	21	40.00
1997	Topps Mantle Finest Refractors	22	40.00
1997	Topps Mantle Finest Refractors	23	40.00
1997	Topps Mantle Finest Refractors	24	40.00
1997	Topps Mantle Finest Refractors	25	40.00
1997	Topps Mantle Finest Refractors	26	40.00
1997	Topps Mantle Finest Refractors	27	40.00
1997	Topps Mantle Finest Refractors	28	40.00
1997	Topps Mantle Finest Refractors	29	40.00
1997	Topps Mantle Finest Refractors	30	40.00
1997	Topps Mantle Finest Refractors	31	40.00
1997	Topps Mantle Finest Refractors	32	40.00
1997	Topps Mantle Finest Refractors	33	40.00
1997	Topps Mantle Finest Refractors	34	40.00
1997	Topps Mantle Finest Refractors	35	40.00
1997	Topps Mantle Finest Refractors	36	40.00
1997-98	Highland Mint Elite Series Coins	20	80.00
1997-98	Highland Mint Elite Series Coins	21	40.00
1997-98	Highland Mint Elite Series Coins	22	20.00
1998	Fleer	536	5.00
1998	Fleer Mantle and Sons	NNO	10.00
1998	Fleer Mantle and Sons	NNO	3.00
1998	Fleer Mickey Mantle		

Year	Set Name	Card No.	Price	Year	Set Name	Card No.	Price	Year	Set Name	Card No.	Price
	Monumental Moments	1	25.00	1998	Fleer Mickey Mantle Monumental Moments	10	25.00	1998	Fleer Mickey Mantle Monumental Moments Gold	8	300.00
1998	Fleer Mickey Mantle Monumental Moments	2	25.00	1998	Fleer Mickey Mantle Monumental Moments Gold	1	300.00	1998	Fleer Mickey Mantle Monumental Moments Gold	9	300.00
1998	Fleer Mickey Mantle Monumental Moments	3	25.00	1998	Fleer Mickey Mantle Monumental Moments Gold	2	300.00	1998	Fleer Mickey Mantle Monumental Moments Gold	10	300.00
1998	Fleer Mickey Mantle Monumental Moments	4	25.00	1998	Fleer Mickey Mantle Monumental Moments Gold	3	300.00	1998	Fleer Vintage '63	67	5.00
1998	Fleer Mickey Mantle Monumental Moments	5	25.00	1998	Fleer Mickey Mantle Monumental Moments Gold	4	300.00	1998	Fleer Vintage '63 Classic	67	500.00
1998	Fleer Mickey Mantle Monumental Moments	6	25.00	1998	Fleer Mickey Mantle Monumental Moments Gold	5	300.00	1998	Sports Illustrated World Series Fever	1	3.00
1998	Fleer Mickey Mantle Monumental Moments	7	25.00	1998	Fleer Mickey Mantle Monumental Moments Gold	6	300.00	1998	Sports Illustrated World Series Fever Autumn Excellence	7	25.00
1998	Fleer Mickey Mantle Monumental Moments	8	25.00	1998	Fleer Mickey Mantle Monumental Moments Gold	7	300.00	1998	Sports Illustrated World Series Fever Autumn Excellence Gold	7	100.00
1998	Fleer Mickey Mantle Monumental Moments	9	25.00					1998	Sports Illustrated World Series Fever Extra Edition	1	300.00
								1998	Sports Illustrated World Series Fever First Edition	1	*

* These cards are not priced due to lack of market information.

Bonus Mickey Mantle

1953	N.Y Sunday News Poster (20" X 14")*	150
1954	PF Flyers Canvas Shoe Cardboard Sign	500
1957	Rawlings Glove Silk Banner	750
1961	Cooper Tires Poster	750
1961	Mantle/Maris Home Run Derby TV Show Poster	400
1961	Rawlings Advisory Photo (8" X 10" B/W)	75
1962	Big Yank Pants Poster (18" X 24")	450

1962	Jello Card Promotion Poster (34" X 28")	2500
1962	Lifeboy "How I Hit" Poster (11" X 14")	250

1960's	Mantle/Maris Kids Cap (Blue)	250
1960's	Mantle/Maris Kids Cap (Red)	250
1960's	Mantle/Maris Sneakers in the Box	500
1960's	Mantle/Maris Official Kid's Uniform	600

Coins-Buttons-Pins

1953	N.Y. Yankee Team Photo Button 3 1/2" dia."*	500
1955	Armour Coin (Corrected Version)	250
1955	Armour Coin (Error)	125
1956	Yellow Basepath Pin	1000
1960	Armour Coin	100
1961	Mantle/Ruth/Maris "61 in 61" Button (6")	3000
1962	Salada Coin	125
1962	Shirriff Coin	200
1963	Salada Coin	125
1965	Old London Coin	125
1967	Coca Cola Soda Cap	25
1967	Fresca Soda Cap	50
1967	Tab Soda Cap	50

1969	"A Day to Remember" Photo Button (3 1/2")	75
1947-66	PM10 Pin "I Love Mickey" (1 3/4")	75
1947-66	PM10 Pin Batting Right Handed (1 3/4")	200
1947-66	PM10 Pin Both Hands Showing (1 3/4")	60
1947-66	PM10 Pin Eyes Almost Closed (1 3/4")	325
1947-66	PM10 Pin Head & Shoulder shot (1 3/4")	200
1947-66	PM10 Pin Left Hand Missing (1 3/4")	125
1947-66	PM10 Pin Light Gray Background (2 1/8")	300
1947-66	PM10 Pin Right Ear Missing (1 3/4")	200

The annual Manny's Baseball Land souvenir catalog (1964 edition pictured above) was a great collectibles source for America's favorite ballplayer of the 1950s and 1960s, Mickey Mantle. "Mick's" many fans not privy to the Bronx retail landmark were able to purchase their favorite "Commerce Comet" memorabilia through this catalog. It's been said that Manny's, located adjacent to Yankee Stadium, sold more Mickey Mantle memorabilia than any other single source in America between 1954 and 1969, including major retail stores. The following Mickey Mantle price guide is composed of various types of collectibles, all of which were available during, or shortly after the Mick's playing days. Values were determined from actual sales information, sales offers and auction results.

* Denotes multi-player cover art.

Advertising

1962	Yoo-Hoo Counter Display (11" X 14")	1100
1962	Yoo-Hoo Window Poster (28" X 36")	2500
1963	Kodak Film Poster (16" X 32")	750
1964	Rawlings Glove Promo Photo (8" X 10" Color)	100
1965	Dell Publications All-Star Poster (18" X 53")*	350
1965	Louisville Slugger Poster (11" X 17")	400
1950's	Mantle/Musial Wonder Bread Sign (16" X 44")	1500
1950's	Rawlings Glove Cardboard Sign (24" X 21")	5000
1960's	Louisville Slugger Silk Banner	1000
1960's	YMCA Poster (10" X 18")	900

Clothing

1962	Mantle/Maris Kids T-Shirt	350
1950s	Mickey Mantle "Champion Slugger" Kids T-Shirt	250

Ephemera

1949	First Baseball contract	20,000
1950	Signed Joplin, Mo. Minor League	
	Team Photo (8 X 10)	6500
1954	Red Heart Dog Food Label	150
1956	"I Love Mickey" Sheet Music	100
1960	Yoo-Hoo One-Page Endorsement Contract	2300
1961	Mantle/Maris Radio Brochure	200

1962	Batting Tips By Mickey Mantle Brochure	40
1962	Post Cereal Box Front	100
1964	Phillies Cigar Premium Photo (8" x 10")	150
1965	Quality of Courage Book Club Brochure	35
1968	Sports Illustrated Poster	250

Game Used Equipment

1961	N.Y. Yankee Home Jersey	50,000
1962	Game-Used Bat	5,000
1967	N.Y Yankee Road Jersey	7000
1968	Complete Home Uniform	85,000
1951-59	Game-Used Bat K-55	6,800

Hardcover Books

1953	The Mickey Mantle Story	150
1956	My Greatest Thrills in Baseball Comic Book	250
1957	Mickey Mantle Baseball's King	75
1958	Mickey Mantle of the Yankees	100
1961	Mickey Mantle	75
1962	Mickey Mantle-Yankee Slugger	100
1963	Mickey Mantle, Mr. Yankee	75
1964	The Quality of Courage	75
1966	The Mickey Mantle Album	100
1967	The Education of a Baseball Player	40
1967	The Education of a Baseball Player (signed)	150
1972	Mickey Mantle Slugs it Out	35

Hollywood

1961	Safe at Home Lobby Card Set (8)	750
1962	Mantle/Maris Safe at Home	
	8mm Movie in the Box	400

1962	Safe at Home 1-Sheet Movie Poster	
	('27 X 41')	600
1962	Safe at Home 3-Sheet Movie Poster	3000

1962	Safe at Home Press Book	300
1962	That Touch of Mink lobby card	200

Publications

1947	High School Yearbook	1000
1948	High School Yearbook	1000
1951	Baseball Magazine (Aug.)	250
1951	The Sporting News (4/25)	275
1952	Look Magazine*	100
1953	Baseball All-Stars Magazine*	75
1953	Baseball Digest (April)*	40
1953	Baseball Magazine (July)*	40
1953	Dell Baseball Annual	75
1953	Guideposts Magazine (Sept.)	75
1953	Inside Baseball Magazine	75
1953	Quick Magazine (April)	75

1953	Sport Magazine (April)	150
1953	Street & Smith Yearbook	200
1953	The Sporting News (6/17)*	60
1953	The Sporting News (7/1)*	60
1953	Time Magazine (7/1)	200

1953	True Baseball Yearbook*	40
1954	How to Play Championship Baseball*	50
1956	Baseball Digest (July)	60
1956	Baseball Magazine (July)	50
1956	Dell Baseball Stars Magazine	75
1956	"How I Hit" Booklet	75
1956	Life Magazine (6/25)	75
1956	My Greatest Thrills in Baseball Comic Book	125

1956	N.Y Yankee Yearbook (Jay)	75
1956	Newsweek Magazine (6/25)	85
1956	Sport Magazine (April)	50
1956	Sport Magazine (Oct)	100
1956	Sports Illustrated (10/1)	75
1956	Sports Illustrated (6/18)	150
1956	Sports Illustrated (7/9)*	50
1956	Street & Smith Yearbook*	175
1956	The Sporting News (10/10)*	100
1956	The Sporting News (11/28)*	50
1956	The Sporting News (6/13)*	50
1956	True Baseball Yearbook*	50
1957	Baseball All-Stars Magazine*	50

1957	Baseball Stars Magazine*	50
1957	Baseball's Best Hitters Magazine*	35
1957	Confidential Magazine (Sept)*	25
1957	Dell Baseball Annual	75

Year	Item	Price
1957	Famous Slugger Yearbook*	30
1957	Mickey Mantle Magazine	100
1957	Sport Magazine (March)	75
1957	Sporting News Baseball Guide	100
1957	Sporting News Dope Book	50
1957	Sports Illustrated (3/4)	100
1957	Street & Smith Yearbook*	150
1957	The Sporting News (1/2)*	100
1957	The Sporting News (1/23)*	35
1957	True Baseball Yearbook*	50
1957	Who's Who in Baseball	60
1957	Who's Who in Sports Magazine	25
1958	Baseball's All-Stars Magazine*	35
1958	How to Play and Enjoy Baseball*	40
1958	Sports Illustrated (7/7)	50
1958	Sports Review Baseball Magazine	75
1958	True Baseball Yearbook*	40

Year	Item	Price
1959	Sport Magazine (Aug.)*	50
1959	Sport Magazine (June)*	50
1959	Street & Smith Yearbook*	125
1959	True Baseball Yearbook*	50
1959	Who's Best In Sports Magazine*	40
1959	Who's Who in the Big Leagues Magazine	75
1960	Baseball Photo Album Magazine*	50
1960	Sport Magazine (Aug.)	60

Year	Item	Price
1960	True Baseball Yearbook*	40
1960	Who's Best In Sports Magazine*	25
1961	Baseball Digest (Oct)	25
1961	Baseball Photo Album*	50
1961	Baseball Thrills Magazine*	40
1961	Inside Baseball Magazine*	35
1961	Life Magazine (8/18)*	60
1961	Sport Magazine (May)*	50
1961	Sport Magazine (Sept.)*	75
1961	The Sporting News (3/29)	30
1961	The Sporting News (6/28)	100
1961	The Sporting News (7/12)	30
1961	Who's Best In Sports Magazine*	25
1962	All Sports Magazine (July)	45
1962	American League Red Book*	40
1962	Baseball Digest (June)	35
1962	Baseball Photo Album*	50
1962	Baseball's All-Stars Magazine*	40
1962	Complete Baseball Magazine (Oct.)	35
1962	Complete Sports Magazine (June)*	35
1962	Great Moments in Sports Magazine (July)	45
1962	Great Moments in Sports Magazine (Nov.)*	35
1962	Great Moments in Sports Magazine (Sept.)*	35
1962	Home Run Hitters Magazine*	60
1962	Major League Baseball Magazine	35

Year	Item	Price
1962	Mantle/Maris Pictorial Magazine	75
1962	Mickey Mantle & Willie Mays Magazine*	45
1962	N.B.C. Baseball Magazine	75
1962	N.Y. Yankees Yearbook (Jay)*	75
1962	Popular Sports Quiz Magazine*	45
1962	Sport Magazine (July)	50
1962	Sport World Magazine (July)*	35

Year	Item	Price
1962	Sports All-Stars Baseball Magazine	45
1962	Sports Illustrated (7/2)	100
1962	Sports Review Baseball Magazine (June)*	50
1962	Sports Stars Baseball Magazine	45
1962	True Baseball Yearbook*	35
1963	Baseball Photo Album*	45
1963	Complete Sports World Series Magazine	75
1963	Major League Baseball Magazine*	25
1963	Sport Heroes Magazine (Oct.)*	35
1963	Sport Magazine (May)*	40
1963	Sport Magazine (Oct.)	30
1963	Sport World Magazine (July)*	35
1963	True Baseball Yearbook*	40
1963	Who's Best In Sports Magazine*	25
1964	All-American Athlete Magazine (April)	35
1964	Baseball 1964	45
1964	Baseball Review Magazine*	35
1964	Big Time Baseball	45
1964	Complete Sports World Series Magazine	45
1964	Dell Baseball Stars Magazine*	30
1964	Dell Sports Magazine (May)*	25
1964	Mickey Mantle Scrapbook Magazine	50
1964	N.Y. Mirror Sunday Magazine	75
1964	Sport Annual Magazine*	25
1964	Sport Magazine (Sept.)	40
1964	Sports Special Baseball Magazine (Spring)*	35
1964	Street & Smith Yearbook	75
1964	True Baseball Yearbook*	35
1964	Who's Best In Sports Magazine*	25
1965	Baseball 1965*	35
1965	Baseball Illustrated*	35
1965	Complete Sports Baseball Issue* (Spring)	35
1965	Complete Sports World Series Magazine	50
1965	Life Magazine (7/30)	50
1965	N.Y. News Sunday Magazine	60
1965	Press Box Baseball Magazine	45
1965	Pro Sports Magazine (Sept.)*	25
1965	Sport Annual Magazine*	25
1965	Sport Magazine (Aug.)	40
1965	Sport World Magazine (Aug.)*	35
1965	Sport World Magazine*	35
1965	Sports All-Stars Baseball Magazine	50
1965	Sports Illustrated (6/21)	75
1965	Sporting News World Series Record Book	30
1965	Sports Review Magazine (July)	40
1965	Sports Special Baseball (Spring)	35
1965	True Baseball Yearbook*	35
1965	Who's Best In Sports Magazine*	25
1966	Sport Magazine (July)	35
1967	Baseball Illustrated*	30
1967	Pro Sports Magazine (July)*	25
1967	Sport Magazine (May)	40
1967	Sport World Magazine (Oct.)*	25
1967	True Baseball Yearbook*	35
1968	Sport Heroes Magazine* (Summer)	25
1968	Sports Illustrated (5/8)*	25
1969	Baseball Digest (Feb.)	20

Year	Item	Price
1969	Boys Life Magazine (June)	60
1969	Mickey Mantle Day Program	75
1969	Pro Sports Magazine (May)*	25
1969	Super Sports Magazine (May)*	25
1969	The Sporting News (4/6)	45

Records

Year	Item	Price
1956	I Love Mickey (45 rpm)	90
1958	My Favorite Hits--Mickey Mantle (33 rpm)	150
1959	Mickey Mantle of the Yankees — 2 record set of Gene Schoor's book	175
1964	That Hollar Guy*	200
1969	A Day to Remember (33 rpm)	75
1964	Auravision Record	75

Restaurant-Hotel

Year	Item	Price
1950s	Country Cookin Restaurant Menu	150
1950s	Country Cookin Restaurant 5-pc. Dinner Setting	300
1950s-60s	Holiday Inn Brochure	100
1950s-60s	Holiday Inn Key Fob	400
1950s-60s	Holiday Inn Magazine (March)*	50
1950s-60s	Holiday Inn Matchbooks (2-Diff.)	75
1950s-60s	Holiday Inn Postcards (3 different) (each)	40

Year	Item	Price
1950s-60s	Holiday Inn Restaurant Menu	200
1960s	Holiday Inn Soap Bar	400
1960s	Holiday Inn Pennant	300
1960s	Holiday Inn 2-pc Stationary Set	350

Sporting Goods

Year	Item	Price
1964	32" H&B Kids Decal Bat	450
1964	Phillies Cigar Kids Glove in the Box (Premium)	700
1950s	All-Pro kids glove	150
1950s	Rawlings Big-8 Glove Box	450
1950s	Rawlings MM4 Autograph Series Glove	200

1950s	Rawlings MM5 Pro Model Glove	300
1950s	Rawlings MM8 Pro Model Glove	125
1950s	Rawlings MM8 Pro Model Glove in the Box	500

1960s	H&B 125 Store Model Bat	200
1960s	Rawlings MM3 Autograph Series Glove	250
1960s	Rawlings MM9 Youth Triple Crown Glove	125
1961-63	Adirondack White Leather Model Bat	350
1970s	Rawlings MM6 kids glove	450

Stadium Souvenirs

1950s 16" Dk. Brown Mini Bat	250
1950s Picture Pack Photos (Jay)	60-75(Ea.)
1960s 16" Lt. Brown Mini Bat	125
1960s Picture Pack Photo (Jay)	30-45(Ea.)

Toys-Games

1950s	Pitch to Mickey Mantle	250
1956	Big League Statue	250
1956	Dairy Queen Statue	300
1956	Mickey Mantle Game by Gardner	250
1957	"Year of the Slugger" Mobile	300
1957	Mickey Mantle's Grand Slam Baseball	1500
1957	Mickey Mantle's Home Run Game	250
1958	All-Star Mr. Baseball Battery Operated Toy	300
1960	Mickey Mantle's Big League Baseball	325
1960s	Mantle and Mays Spring Training Camp in the Box*	350
1960s	Transogram Pitch-O-Matic Mantle/ Mays Batting Trainer*	200

1960s	Official Autograph Baseball and Baseball Manual	150
1961	Bobbin Head Doll	500

1961	Bobbin Head Doll in Box	800
1961	Mantle/Maris Table Radio	1200
1961	Mickey Mantle's Backyard Baseball	300
1961	Mini Bobbin Head Doll	1200
1962	Mantle/Maris "Pitch-N-Hit"	250

1962	Mantle/Maris Jig-Saw Photo Puzzle (8" X 10")	400
1962	Mickey Mantle On Deck Toy	250
1962	Mickey Mantle's Big League Baseball	200
1962	Mini Bobbin Head Doll in the Box	1800

1963	Mickey Mantle's Zoom Ball in Package	200
1964	Mantle/Mays Transogram Bat-Ball-Helmet Set	350
1965	Mantle/Mays Pitch Up Device	200
1965	Mickey Mantle's Bat Master	150
1969	Zippe Baseball (Mantle/Mays)	125
1950s	Mantle/Mays Transogram Bat-N-Ball Set	150
1950s	Mantle/Mays Transogram Wiffle Ball Pack (3)	150
1950s	Mickey Mantle Official Rawlings League Ball and Box	300
1950s	Transogram Statue w/o Box	125
1958-63	Hartland Lamp	1200
1958-63	Hartland Statue	400
1958-63	Hartland Statue Box	250
1958-63	Hartland Statue ID Tag	225
1958-63	Mickey Mantle's Switch Hitter	250
1960s	Famous Sluggers Plastic Bat Rack Bank	200
1960s	All-Stars Mr. Baseball Jr. Game in the Box	1200
1960s	Big-6 Sports Game	150
1960s	Mickey Mantle's All-American Baseball	200
1960s	Mickey Mantle's Baseball Action in the Box	600
1960s	Mickey Mantle's Four-Bagger Bean Bag Game	300
1960s	Mickey Mantle's On-Deck Bat in the Package	150
1960s	Mickey Mantle's Sky-Hi in the Package	150
1960s	Mickey Mantle's Swing-T in the Box	250
1960s	Minute-A-Day Gym in the Box	125
1960s	Paint by Numbers Kit	150

1960s	Pitch to Mickey Mantle Toy	200
1960s	Stretch-O-Matic Gym in the Box	75
1960s	Yankee Stadium Model Kit (Mantle Photo on Box)	300
1970s	Paint-A-Player Paint Kit*	150

Miscellaneous

1950s	Rawlings Baseball Shoe Tag	250
1951	Dairylea Decal Transfer	500
1953	Louisville Slugger Bat Decal	125
1953	Rawlings Facamile Signed Baseball in the Box	500
1955	Mickey Mantle's Pencil Set (2)	75
1956	All-Star Stationary in the Box*	200
1960	Key Chain Insert	100
1962	Yoo-Hoo 6-oz Beverage Can*	75
1962	Yoo-Hoo Bottle Cap	35
1964	Mantle/Mays/Maris All-Star Watch In the Box	1000
1969	Mickey Mantle Day Pennant	150
1972	7-Eleven Plastic Slurpee Cup	40
1973	HOF 7-Eleven Plastic Slurpee Cup	20
1960s	Big Yank Denim Jeans Tag*	200

1960s	Louisville Slugger Mini Wood Pen-Pencil Set	250
1960s	Photo Linen Emblem	75
1962	"Me For Yoo-Hoo" Complete Matchbook	200

Certain Bonus Price Guide photos are courtesy of Mastro & Steinbach, Lelands, Hunt Auctions, Inc., Oregon Trail Sports Auctions and Robert Edward Auctions. All material graded in NR-MT condition or better.

* Denotes multi-player cover art.

Roger Maris Trading Cards

Year	Set Name	Card No.	Price
1947-65	PM10 Stadium Pins 2 1/8"	22	150.00
1947-65	PM10 Stadium Pins 2 1/8"	23	125.00
1947-66	Exhibits	148	50.00
1947-66	PM10 Stadium Pins 1 3/4"	128	60.00
1947-66	PM10 Stadium Pins 1 3/4"	129	40.00
1947-66	PM10 Stadium Pins 1 3/4"	130	125.00
1955-62	Don Wingfield	32	25.00
1957	Indians Sohio	8	225.00
1957	Indians Team Issue	13	25.00
1958	Indians Team Issue	12	20.00
1958	Topps	47	450.00
1958-63	Hartland Statues	18	*
1959	Topps	202	125.00
1960	Key Chain Inserts	32	20.00
1960	Topps	377	90.00
1960	Topps	565	90.00
1960	Topps Tattoos	32	50.00
1960	Yankees Jay Publishing	8	10.00
1961	Bazooka	5	75.00
1961	Nu-Card Scoops	416	7.50
1961	Post	7A	30.00
1961	Post	7B	30.00
1961	Seven-Eleven	25	50.00
1961	Topps	2	175.00
1961	Topps	44	100.00
1961	Topps	478	60.00
1961	Topps	576	175.00
1961	Topps Stamps Inserts	197	15.00

Year	Set Name	Card No.	Price
1961	Yankees Jay Publishing	9	20.00
1962	Baseball Pens	4	*
1962	Bazooka	14	75.00
1962	Exhibit Stat Back	24	30.00
1962	Gold-Mine	1	*
1962	Jello	6	175.00
1962	Post	6A	25.00
1962	Post	6B	25.00
1962	Post Canadian	6	150.00
1962	Salada Plastic Coins	23	35.00
1962	Shirriff Plastic Coins	23	35.00
1962	Topps	1	250.00
1962	Topps	53	110.00
1962	Topps	234	25.00
1962	Topps	313	40.00
1962	Topps	401	60.00
1962	Topps Bucks	55	50.00
1962	Topps Stamps Inserts	89	20.00
1962	Topps Venezuelan	1	500.00
1962	Topps Venezuelan	53	250.00
1962	Yankees Jay Publishing	10	15.00
1963	Baseball Magazine M118	55	*
1963	Exhibit Stat Back	42	35.00
1963	Jello	16	100.00
1963	Post	16	175.00
1963	Salada Metal Coins	57	40.00
1963	Topps	4	20.00
1963	Topps	120	50.00
1963	Topps	144	12.00
1963	Yankees Jay Publishing	8	15.00
1964	Auravision Records	11	10.00
1964	Challenge The Yankees	17	50.00

Year	Set Name	Card No.	Price
1964	Topps	225	60.00
1964	Topps	331	150.00
1964	Topps Venezuelan	225	125.00
1964	Topps Venezuelan	331	450.00
1964	Yankees Jay Publishing	8	15.00
1965	Challenge The Yankees	14	50.00
1965	O-Pee-Chee	155	50.00
1965	Old London Coins	31	35.00
1965	Topps	155	60.00
1966	Topps	365	40.00
1966	Topps Venezuelan	365	80.00
1966	Yankees Team Issue	8	15.00
1967	O-Pee-Chee	45	45.00
1967	Topps	45	35.00
1967	Topps Venezuelan	328	75.00
1968	Atlantic Oil Play Ball Contest Cards	26	15.00
1968	Topps	330	35.00
1968	Topps Venezuelan	330	75.00
1969	O-Pee-Chee	164	10.00
1969	Topps	164	12.00
1972	Laughlin Great Feats	50	1.50
1975	O-Pee-Chee	198	1.00
1975	O-Pee-Chee	199	3.00
1975	Topps	198	2.00
1975	Topps	199	3.00
1975	Topps Mini	198	2.00
1975	Topps Mini	199	3.00
1976	Great Plains Greats	18	1.00
1976	Laughlin Diamond Jubilee	30	1.50
1976	UPI Superstars	8	15.00
1977-79	Sportscaster	716	12.00
1977-84	Galasso Glossy Greats	226	.75
1978	Reading Remembers	14	5.00
1978	TCMA 60s I	11	1.00
1979	Diamond Greats	25	1.50
1979	TCMA 50'S	161	2.50
1979	Topps	413	2.00
1980	Marchant Exhibits	18	.50
1980-83	Pacific Legends	101	.35
1981	San Diego Sports Collectors	15	1.50
1981	San Diego Sports Collectors	16	1.50
1981	TCMA 60s II	303	5.00
1981	TCMA 60s II	382	2.50
1981	TCMA 60s II	474	2.50
1982	Baseball Card News	5	1.00
1982	GS Gallery All-Time Greats	16	1.00
1982	TCMA Greatest Sluggers	2	1.00
1983	Yankee A-S Fifty Years	27	1.25
1983	Yankees 1961	1	1.50
1984-89	O'Connell and Son Ink	28	1.00
1985	George Steinbrenner Menu	6	4.00
1985	TCMA Photo Classics	22	4.00
1985	Woolworth's	24	.50
1986	Sports Design J.D. McCarthy	5	1.00
1986	TCMA Superstars Simon	9	1.50
1986	TCMA Superstars Simon	32	1.00
1986	Topps	405	.10
1986	Topps Tiffany	405	.10
1987	K-Mart	7	.25
1987	Yankees 1961 TCMA	8	1.00
1988	Pacific Legends I	89	.50
1989	CMC Mantle	6	1.00
1989	CMC Mantle	10	.75
1990	AGFA	10	.75
1990	HOF Sticker Book	63	.20
1990	Yankees 61 Ron Lewis	3	2.50
1990	Yankees Monument Park Rini Postcards	11	1.00
1991	Yankees Rini Postcards 1961 2	1	1.00
1992	Yankees WIZ 60s	79	4.00
1992	Yankees WIZ All-Stars	44	2.00
1994	Ted Williams	139	.15
1994	Ted Williams Memories	M27	6.00
1994	Ted Williams Roger Maris	ES1	1.50
1994	Ted Williams Roger Maris	ES2	1.50
1994	Ted Williams Roger Maris	ES3	1.50
1994	Ted Williams Roger Maris	ES4	1.50
1994	Ted Williams Roger Maris	ES5	1.50
1994	Ted Williams Roger Maris	ES6	1.50

Roger Maris autographed photo

ROGER MARIS

Year	Set Name	Card No.	Price
1994	Ted Williams Roger Maris	ES7	1.50
1994	Ted Williams Roger Maris	ES8	1.50
1994	Ted Williams Roger Maris	ES9	1.00
1994	Upper Deck: The American Epic	67	.25
1994	Yoo-Hoo	9	5.00
1996	Stadium Club Mantle	MM12	8.00
1997	Topps Mantle	36	8.00
1997	Topps Mantle Finest	36	8.00
1997	Topps Mantle Finest Refractors	36	40.00
1998	Topps Gold Label Home Run Race	HR1	12.00
1998	Topps Gold Label Home Run Race Black	HR1	36.00
1998	Topps Gold Label Home Run Race Red	HR1	240.00

Babe Ruth Trading Cards

Year	Set Name	Card Number	Price
1914	Baltimore Orioles Ruth	1	15000.00
1915	Sporting News M101-5	151	6000.00
1916	Sporting News M101-4	151	6000.00
1917	Collins-McCarthy E135	147	1200.00
1917	Holsum Bread D327	87	*
1919	W514	2	200.00
1920	W516-1	1	175.00
1921	Koester's Bread World Series Issue D383	49	500.00
1921	Neilson's V61	37	1800.00
1921	Oxford Confectionery E253	15	1800.00
1921	Pathe Ruth	1	*
1921-22	E121 Series of 120	86A	750.00
1921-22	E121 Series of 120	86B	1000.00
1921-22	E121 Series of 120	86C	750.00
1921-22	E121 Series of 120	86D	1000.00
1921-22	E121 Series of 120	86E	750.00
1921-23	National Caramel E220	86	1200.00
1921-24	Exhibits	148	400.00
1921-24	Exhibits	149	800.00
1922	American Caramel E122	57	1000.00
1922	E120	71	800.00
1922	W572	88	1000.00
1922	W575	112	250.00
1922	William Paterson V89	25	1250.00
1923	Maple Crispette V117	8	2000.00
1923	W501	49	500.00
1923	W503	32	500.00
1923	W515	3	150.00
1923	W515	47	150.00
1923	W551	7	200.00
1923	Willards Chocolates V100	139	1200.00
1924	Mrs. Sherlock's Bread Pins	7	900.00
1925	Exhibits	100	1000.00
1926	Exhibits	102	1000.00
1926	Sport Company of America	36	500.00
1926	Sporting News Supplements M101-7	2	450.00
1927	American Caramel E126	38	1500.00
1927	Exhibits	52	600.00
1927	York Caramel E210	6	1300.00
1928	Babe Ruth Candy Company E-Unc.	1	250.00
1928	Babe Ruth Candy Company E-Unc.	2	250.00
1928	Babe Ruth Candy Company E-Unc.	3	250.00
1928	Babe Ruth Candy Company E-Unc.	4	250.00
1928	Babe Ruth Candy Company E-Unc.	5	250.00
1928	Babe Ruth Candy Company E-Unc.	6	1000.00
1928	Exhibits	51	600.00
1928	Fro Joy	1	150.00
1928	Fro Joy	2	100.00
1928	Fro Joy	3	100.00
1928	Fro Joy	4	100.00
1928	Fro Joy	5	100.00
1928	Fro Joy	6	100.00
1928	Portraits and Action R315	A31	500.00
1928	Portraits and Action R315	B31	500.00
1928	Star Player Candy E-Unc.	57	2000.00
1928	W502	6	200.00
1928	W512	6	125.00
1928	W560 Playing Cards	JOK	*
1928	Yuenglings	6	800.00
1929	Portraits and Action R316	79	350.00

Year	Set Name	Card No.	Price
1929-30	Exhibits Four-in-One	26	750.00
1930	Schutter-Johnson R332	26	700.00
1930	Schutter-Johnson R332	42	700.00
1930	Uncle Jack	24	*
1930	W554	15	350.00
1931	W517	4	1500.00
1931	W517	20	1800.00
1931-32	Exhibits Four-in-One	26	1250.00
1932	R337 Series Of 24	402	1000.00
1932	U.S. Caramel R328	32	1200.00
1933	Butter Cream R306	23	15000.00
1933	Butterfinger Canadian V94	41	400.00
1933	Exhibits Four-in-One	13	1250.00
1933	Goudey Canadian V353	80	5000.00
1933	Goudey Canadian V353	93	5000.00
1933	Goudey R319	53	4000.00
1933	Goudey R319	144	3000.00
1933	Goudey R319	149	4000.00
1933	Goudey R319	181	4000.00
1933	Rittenhouse Candy E285	1S	400.00
1933	Rittenhouse Candy E285	13C	400.00
1933	Sport Kings R338	2	3500.00
1934	Baby Ruth Gum	54	*
1934	Butterfinger Premiums R310	53	350.00
1934	Exhibits Four-in-One W463-4	13	750.00
1934	Goudey Canadian V354	28	5000.00
1934	Goudey Premiums R309-1	4	600.00
1935	Al Demaree Die Cuts R304	4	2000.00
1935	Clark's Bread D-381-2	4	*
1935	Exhibits Four-in-One W463-5	1	750.00
1935	Goudey Puzzle R321	1J	1000.00
1935	Goudey Puzzle R321	3A	1000.00
1935	Goudey Puzzle R321	14A	1500.00
1935	Goudey Puzzle R321	15A	1500.00
1935	Quaker Babe Ruth Pin	1	200.00
1936	National Chicle Fine Pen Premiums R313	84	15.00
1936-39	Hall of Fame Postcards	21	*
1938	Quaker Oats Ruth	1	200.00
1939-52	Albertype Hall of Fame PC754-2	4	75.00
1946-49	Sports Exchange W603	8-4	250.00
1947-66	PM10 Stadium Pins 1 3/4'	192	375.00
1948	Babe Ruth Story	1	150.00
1948	Babe Ruth Story	25	150.00
1948	Babe Ruth Story	26	150.00
1948	Babe Ruth Story	27	150.00
1948	Babe Ruth Story	28	150.00
1948	Babe Ruth Story Premium	1	5000.00
1948	Exhibit Hall of Fame	25A	50.00
1948	Exhibit Hall of Fame	25B	300.00
1948	Swell Sport Thrills	12	200.00
1949	Leaf	3	2500.00
1949	Leaf Premiums	7	750.00
1950	Four Mighty Heroes H801-6	3	750.00
1950-56	Callahan HOF W576	63	150.00
1951	R423 Small Strip	92	20.00
1951	Topps Connie Mack All-Stars	9	2500.00
1953-63	Artvue Hall of Fame Postcards	74	*
1956	Topps Hocus Focus	B1	400.00
1958	Jay Publishing All-Time Greats	9	20.00
1958-63	Hartland Statues	2	*
1959	Fleer Ted Williams	2	100.00
1959	Fleer Ted Williams	75	50.00
1960	Fleer	3	125.00
1960	Key Chain Inserts	41	40.00
1960	Nu-Card Hi-Lites	1	40.00
1960	Nu-Card Hi-Lites	16	40.00
1960	Nu-Card Hi-Lites	47	40.00
1960	Rawling's Glove Tags	28	*
1960-61	Exhibits Wrigley HOF	20	75.00
1961	Fleer	75	125.00
1961	Golden Press	3	40.00
1961	Nu-Card Scoops	447	30.00
1961	Nu-Card Scoops	455	25.00
1962	Topps	401	50.00
1962	Topps	135	20.00
1962	Topps	136	20.00
1962	Topps	137	20.00
1962	Topps	138	20.00
1962	Topps	139A	30.00

Year	Set Name	Card No.	Price
1962	Topps	140	50.00
1962	Topps	141	20.00
1962	Topps	142	20.00
1962	Topps	143	20.00
1962	Topps	144	20.00
1962	Topps Venezuelan	135	50.00
1962	Topps Venezuelan	136	50.00
1962	Topps Venezuelan	137	50.00
1962	Topps Venezuelan	138	50.00
1962	Topps Venezuelan	139	60.00
1962	Topps Venezuelan	140	50.00
1962	Topps Venezuelan	141	50.00
1962	Topps Venezuelan	142	50.00
1962	Topps Venezuelan	143	50.00
1962	Topps Venezuelan	144	50.00
1963	Baseball Magazine M118	73	*
1963	Bazooka ATG	17	75.00
1963	Gad Fun Cards	1	7.50
1963	Gad Fun Cards	34	7.50
1963	Hall of Fame Busts	16	125.00
1966	Aurora Sports Model Kits	4	*
1967	Topps Venezuelan	147	500.00
1968	Atlantic Oil	10	50.00
1968	Laughlin World Series	12	7.50
1968	Laughlin World Series	13	7.50
1968	Laughlin World Series	20	7.50
1968	Laughlin World Series	25	7.50
1968	Laughlin World Series	29	7.50
1968	SCFS Old Timers	1	5.00
1968	Sports Memorabilia All-Time Greats	11	5.00
1969-70	Bazooka	5	100.00
1969-70	Bazooka	9	60.00
1969-70	Bazooka	10	60.00
1969-70	Bazooka	11	60.00
1969-73	Equitable Sports Hall of Fame	BB20	15.00
1970	Fleer World Series	12	6.00
1970	Fleer World Series	13	6.00
1970	Fleer World Series	20	6.00
1970	Fleer World Series	25	6.00
1970	Fleer World Series	29	6.00
1970	House of Jazz	25	50.00
1970	Metropolitan Museum of Art Burdick	6	30.00
1970	Sports Cards for Collectors Old-Timer Postcards	1	4.00
1970	Sports Cards for Collectors Old-Timer Postcards	8	5.00
1970	Sports Cards for Collectors Old-Timer Postcards	31	5.00
1970	Sports Cards for Collectors Old-Timer Postcards	32	5.00
1971	Fleer World Series	16	7.50
1971	Fleer World Series	30	7.50
1972	Fleer Famous Feats	20	4.00
1972	Kellogg's ATG	6	8.00
1972	Kellogg's ATG	14	8.00
1972	Laughlin Great Feats	32	5.00
1973	Hall of Fame Picture Pack	15	3.00
1973	O-Pee-Chee	1	50.00
1973	O-Pee-Chee	474	20.00
1973	Seven-Eleven Trading Cups	65	30.00
1973	Syracuse Chiefs Team Issue	24	*
1973	Topps	1	40.00
1973	Topps	474	20.00
1973-97	Book Promotional Cards	11	25.00
1973-97	Book Promotional Cards	17	3.00
1974	Capital Publishing	1	5.00
1974	Laughlin All-Star Games	33	6.00
1974	Syracuse Chiefs Team Issue	23	*
1974	TCMA Nicknames	2	10.00
1975	Syracuse Chiefs Team Issue	17	*
1975	TCMA All-Time Greats	30	7.50
1975	TCMA All-Time Greats	31	7.50
1975	TCMA House of Jazz	27	8.00
1975	Yankees 1927 TCMA	3	8.00
1975	Yankees All-Time Team TCMA	11	8.00
1976	Galasso Baseball's Great Hall of Fame	25	4.00
1976	Laughlin Diamond Jubilee	32	7.50
1976	Motorola Old Timers	9	10.00
1976	O-Pee-Chee	345	18.00
1976	Rowe Exhibits	16	1.00

Year	Set Name	Card No.	Price
1976	Shakey's Pizza	2	7.50
1976	Taylor/Schmierer Bowman 47	3	20.00
1976	Taylor/Schmierer Bowman 47	49	15.00
1976	Taylor/Schmierer Bowman 47	113	7.50
1976	Topps	345	15.00
1977	Sertoma Stars	21	5.00
1977	Shakey's Pizza	20	7.50
1977-79	Sportscaster	511	8.00
1977-79	Sportscaster	6818	4.00
1977-84	Galasso Glossy Greats	69	4.00
1977-84	Galasso Glossy Greats	91	4.00
1977-84	Galasso Glossy Greats	165	4.00
1977-84	Galasso Glossy Greats	193	4.00
1977-84	Galasso Glossy Greats	227	4.00
1978	Dexter Hall of Fame Postcards	43	10.00
1979	Sports Legends	14	30.00
1979	Yankees 1927 TCMA	28	8.00
1980	Franchise Babe Ruth	1	1.50
1980	Franchise Babe Ruth	2	1.50
1980	Franchise Babe Ruth	3	1.50
1980	Franchise Babe Ruth	4	1.50
1980	Franchise Babe Ruth	5	1.50
1980	Franchise Babe Ruth	6	1.50
1980	Franchise Babe Ruth	7	1.50
1980	Franchise Babe Ruth	8	1.50
1980	Franchise Babe Ruth	9	1.50
1980	Franchise Babe Ruth	10	1.50
1980	Franchise Babe Ruth	11	1.50
1980	Franchise Babe Ruth	12	1.50
1980	Franchise Babe Ruth	13	1.50
1980	Franchise Babe Ruth	14	1.50
1980	Franchise Babe Ruth	15	1.50
1980	Franchise Babe Ruth	16	1.50
1980	Franchise Babe Ruth	17	1.50
1980	Franchise Babe Ruth	18	1.50
1980	Franchise Babe Ruth	19	1.50
1980	Franchise Babe Ruth	20	1.50
1980	Franchise Babe Ruth	21	1.50
1980	Franchise Babe Ruth	22	1.50
1980	Franchise Babe Ruth	23	1.50
1980	Franchise Babe Ruth	24	1.50
1980	Franchise Babe Ruth	25	1.50
1980	Franchise Babe Ruth	26	1.50
1980	Franchise Babe Ruth	27	1.50
1980	Franchise Babe Ruth	28	1.50
1980	Franchise Babe Ruth	29	1.50
1980	Franchise Babe Ruth	30	1.50
1980	Franchise Babe Ruth	31	1.50
1980	Franchise Babe Ruth	32	1.50
1980	Franchise Babe Ruth	33	1.50
1980	Franchise Babe Ruth	34	1.50
1980	Franchise Babe Ruth	35	1.50
1980	Franchise Babe Ruth	36	1.50
1980	Franchise Babe Ruth	37	1.50
1980	Franchise Babe Ruth	38	1.50
1980	Franchise Babe Ruth	39	1.50
1980	Franchise Babe Ruth	40	1.50
1980	Franchise Babe Ruth	41	1.50
1980	Franchise Babe Ruth	42	1.50
1980	Franchise Babe Ruth	43	1.50
1980	Franchise Babe Ruth	44	1.50
1980	Franchise Babe Ruth	45	1.50
1980	Franchise Babe Ruth	46	1.50
1980	Franchise Babe Ruth	47	1.50
1980	Franchise Babe Ruth	48	1.50
1980	Franchise Babe Ruth	49	1.50
1980	Franchise Babe Ruth	50	1.50
1980	Franchise Babe Ruth	51	1.50
1980	Franchise Babe Ruth	52	1.50
1980	Franchise Babe Ruth	53	1.50
1980	Franchise Babe Ruth	54	1.50
1980	Franchise Babe Ruth	55	1.50
1980	Franchise Babe Ruth	56	1.50
1980	Franchise Babe Ruth	57	1.50
1980	Franchise Babe Ruth	58	1.50
1980	Franchise Babe Ruth	59	1.50
1980	Franchise Babe Ruth	60	1.50
1980	Franchise Babe Ruth	61	1.50
1980	Franchise Babe Ruth	62	1.50

1994 Conlon TSN Color Inserts

Year	Set Name	Card No.	Price
1980	Franchise Babe Ruth	63	1.50
1980	Franchise Babe Ruth	64	1.50
1980	Franchise Babe Ruth	65	1.50
1980	Franchise Babe Ruth	66	1.50
1980	Franchise Babe Ruth	67	1.50
1980	Franchise Babe Ruth	68	1.50
1980	Franchise Babe Ruth	69	1.50
1980	Franchise Babe Ruth	70	1.50
1980	Franchise Babe Ruth	71	1.50
1980	Franchise Babe Ruth	72	1.50
1980	Franchise Babe Ruth	73	1.50
1980	Franchise Babe Ruth	74	1.50
1980	Franchise Babe Ruth	75	1.50
1980	Franchise Babe Ruth	76	1.50
1980	Franchise Babe Ruth	77	1.50
1980	Franchise Babe Ruth	78	1.50
1980	Franchise Babe Ruth	79	1.50
1980	Franchise Babe Ruth	80	1.50
1980	Laughlin 300/400/500	2	4.00
1980	Laughlin Famous Feats	16	2.00
1980	Yankees Greats TCMA	5	3.00
1980-83	Pacific Legends	1	3.00
1980-87	SSPC HOF	1	2.00
1980-96	Perez-Steele Hall of Fame Postcards	4	60.00
1981	Conlon TSN	4	10.00
1981	Sportrait Hall of Fame	3	4.00
1982	Baseball Card News	20	4.00
1982	BHCR Sports Legends	2	*
1982	Davco Hall of Fame Boxes	20	5.00
1982	Diamond Classics	13	3.00
1982	TCMA Greatest Hitters	19	5.00
1982	TCMA Greatest Sluggers	18	5.00
1983	Big League Collectibles		
	Original All-Stars	20	5.00
1983	Conlon Marketcom	17	3.00
1983	TCMA Ruth	1	4.00
1983	TCMA Ruth	5	4.00
1983	TCMA Ruth	6	4.00
1983	Topps/O-Pee-Chee Stickers	2	3.00
1984	Cubs Brickhouse Playing Cards	13H	4.00
1984	Donruss Champions	1	2.00
1984	Galasso Hall of Famers Ron Lewis	2	2.50
1984	Yankees 1927 Galasso	2	3.00
1984-89	O'Connell and Son Ink	90	2.50
1985	Big League Collectibles 30s	54	5.00
1985	Circle K	2	1.50
1985	Donruss HOF Sluggers	1	2.00
1985	Feg Murray's Cartoon Greats	15	1.50
1985	Feg Murray's Cartoon Greats	16	1.50
1985	George Steinbrenner Menu	8	7.50

Year	Set Name	Card No.	Price
1985	TCMA Photo Classics	4	8.00
1985	TCMA Photo Classics	8	4.00
1985	TCMA Photo Classics	9	4.00
1985	Ultimate Baseball Card	3	10.00
1985	Woolworth's	31	1.00
1986	Big League Chew	2	2.00
1986	Conlon Series 1	13	2.00
1986	Conlon Series 1	20	2.00
1986	Conlon Series 1	48	2.00
1986	Conlon Series 1	50	2.00
1986	Conlon Series 1	54	2.00
1986	Sportflics Decade Greats	1	3.00
1986	TCMA	12	2.50
1986	TCMA Superstars Simon	2	1.25
1986	TCMA Superstars Simon	9	1.50
1986	TCMA Superstars Simon	14	1.25
1986	TCMA Superstars Simon	42	2.50
1986	TCMA Superstars Simon	43	2.50
1986	Topps Rose	87	.15
1987	Hygrade All-Time Greats	38	1.50
1987	Nestle Dream Team	5	3.00
1987	Sports Cube Game	1	15.00
1987	Sports Reading	2	15.00
1987	Yankees 1927 TCMA	9	2.50
1988	Conlon American All-Stars	21	2.00
1988	Conlon Series 3	25	2.00
1988	Grenada Baseball Stamps	81	2.00
1988	Willard Mullin Postcards	5	2.00
1989	Cadaco Ellis Discs	45	10.00
1989	CMC Baseball's Greatest	4	1.00
1989	CMC Ruth	1	.50
1989	CMC Ruth	2	.50
1989	CMC Ruth	3	.50
1989	CMC Ruth	4	.50
1989	CMC Ruth	5	.50
1989	CMC Ruth	6	.50
1989	CMC Ruth	7	.50
1989	CMC Ruth	8	.50
1989	CMC Ruth	9	.50
1989	CMC Ruth	10	.50
1989	CMC Ruth	11	.50
1989	CMC Ruth	12	.50
1989	CMC Ruth	13	.50
1989	CMC Ruth	14	.50
1989	CMC Ruth	15	.75
1989	CMC Ruth	16	.50
1989	CMC Ruth	17	.75
1989	CMC Ruth	18	.50
1989	CMC Ruth	19	.50
1989	CMC Ruth	20	.50
1989	CMC Ruth	P1	1.00
1989	Dodgers Smokey Greats	26	3.00
1989	HOF Sticker Book	47	2.00
1989	Pacific Legends II	176	2.00
1989	Swell Baseball Greats	1	2.50
1989	Topps Baseball Talk/LJN	20	7.50
1989	USPS Legends Stamp Cards	4	7.50
1989	Yankee Citgo All-Time Greats	5	7.50
1989-91	Sports Illustrated For Kids I	216	4.00
1990	Baseball Wit	86	2.00
1990	Collect-A-Books	10	1.50
1990	HOF Sticker Book	25	2.50
1990	Swell Baseball Greats	10	2.50
1990	Yankees Monument Park Rini		
	Postcards	2	2.50
1990-97	Perez-Steele Great Moments	1	20.00
1991	Cadaco Ellis Discs	44	10.00
1991	Conlon TSN	110	1.00
1991	Conlon TSN	145	1.00
1991	Denver BallPark	3	*
1991	Homers Cookies Classics	1	3.00
1991	Swell Baseball Greats	124	2.50
1991	U.S. Game Systems Baseball Legends	2C	.75
1991	U.S. Game Systems Baseball Legends	2D	.75
1991	U.S. Game Systems Baseball Legends	2H	.75
1991	U.S. Game Systems Baseball Legends	2S	.75
1991-92	Conlon TSN Prototypes	145	15.00
1992	Conlon TSN	426	1.00
1992	Conlon TSN 13th National	663	7.50

Year	Set Name	Card No.	Price
1992	Conlon TSN All-Star Program	663G	10.00
1992	Delphi Ruth	1	2.00
1992	Gold Entertainment Ruth	1	2.00
1992	Gold Entertainment Ruth	2	3.00
1992	Gold Entertainment Ruth	3	2.00
1992	Gold Entertainment Ruth	4	3.00
1992	Gold Entertainment Ruth	5	2.00
1992	Megacards Ruth	1	.40
1992	Megacards Ruth	2	.15
1992	Megacards Ruth	3	.15
1992	Megacards Ruth	4	.15
1992	Megacards Ruth	5	.15
1992	Megacards Ruth	6	.15
1992	Megacards Ruth	7	.15
1992	Megacards Ruth	8	.15
1992	Megacards Ruth	9	.25
1992	Megacards Ruth	10	.15
1992	Megacards Ruth	11	.15
1992	Megacards Ruth	12	.15
1992	Megacards Ruth	13	.15
1992	Megacards Ruth	14	.15
1992	Megacards Ruth	15	.15
1992	Megacards Ruth	16	.15
1992	Megacards Ruth	17	.15
1992	Megacards Ruth	18	.15
1992	Megacards Ruth	19	.15
1992	Megacards Ruth	20	.15
1992	Megacards Ruth	21	.15
1992	Megacards Ruth	22	.15
1992	Megacards Ruth	23	.15
1992	Megacards Ruth	24	.15
1992	Megacards Ruth	25	.15
1992	Megacards Ruth	26	.15
1992	Megacards Ruth	27	.15
1992	Megacards Ruth	28	.15
1992	Megacards Ruth	29	.15
1992	Megacards Ruth	30	.15
1992	Megacards Ruth	31	.15
1992	Megacards Ruth	32	.15
1992	Megacards Ruth	33	.15
1992	Megacards Ruth	34	.15
1992	Megacards Ruth	35	.15
1992	Megacards Ruth	36	.15
1992	Megacards Ruth	37	.15
1992	Megacards Ruth	38	.15
1992	Megacards Ruth	39	.15
1992	Megacards Ruth	40	.15
1992	Megacards Ruth	41	.15
1992	Megacards Ruth	42	.15
1992	Megacards Ruth	43	.15
1992	Megacards Ruth	44	.15
1992	Megacards Ruth	45	.15
1992	Megacards Ruth	46	.15
1992	Megacards Ruth	47	.15
1992	Megacards Ruth	48	.15
1992	Megacards Ruth	49	.15
1992	Megacards Ruth	50	.15
1992	Megacards Ruth	51	.15
1992	Megacards Ruth	52	.15
1992	Megacards Ruth	53	.15
1992	Megacards Ruth	54	.15
1992	Megacards Ruth	55	.15
1992	Megacards Ruth	56	.15
1992	Megacards Ruth	57	.15
1992	Megacards Ruth	58	.15
1992	Megacards Ruth	59	.15
1992	Megacards Ruth	60	.15
1992	Megacards Ruth	61	.15
1992	Megacards Ruth	62	.15
1992	Megacards Ruth	63	.15
1992	Megacards Ruth	64	.15
1992	Megacards Ruth	65	.15
1992	Megacards Ruth	66	.15
1992	Megacards Ruth	67	.15
1992	Megacards Ruth	68	.15
1992	Megacards Ruth	69	.15
1992	Megacards Ruth	70	.15
1992	Megacards Ruth	71	.15
1992	Megacards Ruth	72	.15
1992	Megacards Ruth	73	.15
1992	Megacards Ruth	74	.15
1992	Megacards Ruth	75	.15
1992	Megacards Ruth	76	.15
1992	Megacards Ruth	77	.15
1992	Megacards Ruth	78	.15
1992	Megacards Ruth	79	.15
1992	Megacards Ruth	80	.15
1992	Megacards Ruth	81	.75
1992	Megacards Ruth	82	.25
1992	Megacards Ruth	83	.15
1992	Megacards Ruth	84	.15
1992	Megacards Ruth	85	.15
1992	Megacards Ruth	86	.15
1992	Megacards Ruth	87	.15
1992	Megacards Ruth	88	.15
1992	Megacards Ruth	89	.15
1992	Megacards Ruth	90	.15
1992	Megacards Ruth	91	.15
1992	Megacards Ruth	92	.25
1992	Megacards Ruth	93	.15
1992	Megacards Ruth	94	.15
1992	Megacards Ruth	95	.25
1992	Megacards Ruth	96	.25
1992	Megacards Ruth	97	.25
1992	Megacards Ruth	98	.15
1992	Megacards Ruth	99	.15
1992	Megacards Ruth	100	.15
1992	Megacards Ruth	101	.15
1992	Megacards Ruth	102	.15
1992	Megacards Ruth	103	.15
1992	Megacards Ruth	104	.15
1992	Megacards Ruth	105	.15
1992	Megacards Ruth	106	.15
1992	Megacards Ruth	107	.15
1992	Megacards Ruth	108	.15
1992	Megacards Ruth	109	.15
1992	Megacards Ruth	110	.15
1992	Megacards Ruth	111	.15
1992	Megacards Ruth	112	.15
1992	Megacards Ruth	113	.15
1992	Megacards Ruth	114	.15
1992	Megacards Ruth	115	.15
1992	Megacards Ruth	116	.15
1992	Megacards Ruth	117	.15
1992	Megacards Ruth	118	.15
1992	Megacards Ruth	119	.15
1992	Megacards Ruth	120	.15
1992	Megacards Ruth	121	.15
1992	Megacards Ruth	122	.40
1992	Megacards Ruth	123	.25
1992	Megacards Ruth	124	.25
1992	Megacards Ruth	125	.60
1992	Megacards Ruth	126	.40
1992	Megacards Ruth	127	.15
1992	Megacards Ruth	128	.15
1992	Megacards Ruth	129	.15
1992	Megacards Ruth	130	.15
1992	Megacards Ruth	131	.15
1992	Megacards Ruth	132	.15
1992	Megacards Ruth	133	.15
1992	Megacards Ruth	134	.15
1992	Megacards Ruth	135	.15
1992	Megacards Ruth	136	.15
1992	Megacards Ruth	137	.15
1992	Megacards Ruth	138	.15
1992	Megacards Ruth	139	.15
1992	Megacards Ruth	140	.25
1992	Megacards Ruth	141	.15
1992	Megacards Ruth	142	.15
1992	Megacards Ruth	143	.15
1992	Megacards Ruth	144	.15
1992	Megacards Ruth	145	.15
1992	Megacards Ruth	146	.15
1992	Megacards Ruth	147	.15
1992	Megacards Ruth	148	.15
1992	Megacards Ruth	149	.40
1992	Megacards Ruth	150	.15
1992	Megacards Ruth	151	.15
1992	Megacards Ruth	152	.15
1992	Megacards Ruth	153	.15
1992	Megacards Ruth	154	.15
1992	Megacards Ruth	155	.15
1992	Megacards Ruth	156	.15
1992	Megacards Ruth	157	.15
1992	Megacards Ruth	158	.25
1992	Megacards Ruth	159	.15
1992	Megacards Ruth	160	.15
1992	Megacards Ruth	161	.15
1992	Megacards Ruth	162	.15
1992	Megacards Ruth	163	.15
1992	Megacards Ruth Prototypes	14	3.00
1992	Megacards Ruth Prototypes	31	3.00
1992	Megacards Ruth Prototypes	75	3.00
1992	Megacards Ruth Prototypes	106	3.00
1992	Megacards Ruth Prototypes	124	3.00
1992	Megacards Ruth Prototypes	129	3.00
1992	Megacards Ruth Prototypes	134	3.00
1992	Megacards Ruth Prototypes	138	3.00
1992	Megacards Ruth Prototypes	154	3.00
1992	PM Gold Ruth Prototype	1	3.00
1992	Score	879	.40
1992	St. Vincent HOF Heroes Stamps	9	3.00
1992	TV Sports Mailbag/Photo File 500 Home Run Club	12	5.00
1992	Whitehall Legends to Life	3	6.00
1992	Whitehall Prototypes	3	6.00
1992	Yankees WIZ All-Stars	72	7.50
1992	Yankees WIZ HOF	29	5.00
1992-93	Conlon TSN Color Inserts	4	6.00
1993	Action Packed ASG	94	2.00
1993	Action Packed ASG 24K	28G	75.00
1993	Cadaco Discs	47	10.00
1993	Conlon Masters BW	2	6.00
1993	Conlon Masters Color	5	6.00
1993	Conlon TSN	663	1.00
1993	Conlon TSN	888	1.00
1993	Conlon TSN Prototypes	888	5.00
1993	Hoyle	6	2.50
1993	Spectrum HOF I	1	2.00
1993	Ted Williams	121	2.50
1993	Ted Williams Locklear Collection	6	10.00
1993	Upper Deck All-Time Heroes	110	3.00
1993	Upper Deck All-Time Heroes	131	1.50
1993	Upper Deck All-Time Heroes	133	1.50
1993	Upper Deck All-Time Heroes	134	1.50
1993	Upper Deck All-Time Heroes	146	1.50
1993	Upper Deck All-Time Heroes	149	1.50
1993	Upper Deck All-Time Heroes	151	1.50
1993	Upper Deck All-Time Heroes	152	1.00
1993-94	Legendary Foils	9	7.50
1993-94	Legendary Foils Hawaii IX	1	5.00
1993-97	Bleachers	37	35.00
1994	Conlon TSN	1080	1.00
1994	Conlon TSN Burgundy	1080	7.50
1994	Conlon TSN Color Inserts	33	7.50
1994	Conlon TSN Color Inserts	35	6.00
1994	Megacards Ruthian Shots	1	3.00
1994	Megacards Ruthian Shots	2	2.00
1994	Megacards Ruthian Shots	3	4.00
1994	Megacards Ruthian Shots	4	2.00
1994	Megacards Ruthian Shots	5	2.00
1994	Ted Williams 500 Club	6	6.00
1994	Ted Williams Trade for Babe	T1	5.00
1994	Ted Williams Trade for Babe	T2	5.00
1994	Ted Williams Trade for Babe	T3	5.00
1994	Ted Williams Trade for Babe	T4	5.00
1994	Ted Williams Trade for Babe	T5	5.00
1994	Ted Williams Trade for Babe	T6	5.00
1994	Ted Williams Trade for Babe	T7	5.00
1994	Ted Williams Trade for Babe	T8	5.00
1994	Ted Williams Trade for Babe	T9	4.00
1994	Upper Deck All-Star Jumbos	45	5.00
1994	Upper Deck All-Star Jumbos Gold	45	15.00
1994	Upper Deck All-Time Heroes	60	2.00
1994	Upper Deck All-Time Heroes	110	1.00
1994	Upper Deck All-Time Heroes	165	1.00
1994	Upper Deck All-Time Heroes 125th	60	4.00

Ruth sent thank-you

Babe Ruth was still a pitcher with the Boston Red Sox when he signed a 1917 contract giving Louisville Slugger the right to use his name in exchange for $100. After receiving his check, Ruth wrote a thank-you note to the company — a rare gesture for an athlete of any generation.

Babe Ruth autographed photo

Year	Set Name	Card No.	Price
1994	Upper Deck All-Time Heroes 125th	110	2.00
1994	Upper Deck All-Time Heroes 125th	165	2.00
1994	Upper Deck: The American Epic	30	2.00
1994	Upper Deck: The American Epic	BC1	5.00
1994	Upper Deck: The American Epic GM	8	1.25
1994-98	Highland Mint Magnum Series Medallions	19	250.00
1994-98	Highland Mint Magnum Series Medallions	20	150.00
1994-98	Highland Mint Magnum Series Medallions	21	50.00
1995	Conlon TSN	1405	2.00
1995	Conlon TSN	NNO	2.00
1995	Conlon TSN Griffey Jr.	1	3.00
1995	Conlon TSN Prototypes	3C	5.00
1995	Conlon TSN Prototypes	1535	5.00
1995	Megacards Ruth	1	.40
1995	Megacards Ruth	2	.40
1995	Megacards Ruth	3	.75
1995	Megacards Ruth	4	.40
1995	Megacards Ruth	5	.40
1995	Megacards Ruth	6	1.00
1995	Megacards Ruth	7	.40
1995	Megacards Ruth	8	.40
1995	Megacards Ruth	9	.75
1995	Megacards Ruth	10	.40
1995	Megacards Ruth	11	.40
1995	Megacards Ruth	12	1.50
1995	Megacards Ruth	13	1.00
1995	Megacards Ruth	14	1.50

Year	Set Name	Card No.	Price
1995	Megacards Ruth	15	.40
1995	Megacards Ruth	16	.40
1995	Megacards Ruth	17	.40
1995	Megacards Ruth	18	.60
1995	Megacards Ruth	19	.40
1995	Megacards Ruth	20	.40
1995	Megacards Ruth	21	1.50
1995	Megacards Ruth	22	.40
1995	Megacards Ruth	23	.40
1995	Megacards Ruth	24	.60
1995	Megacards Ruth	25	.40
1995	Topps	3	2.00
1995	Upper Deck Ruth Heroes	73	15.00
1995	Upper Deck Ruth Heroes	74	15.00
1995	Upper Deck Ruth Heroes	75	15.00
1995	Upper Deck Ruth Heroes	76	15.00
1995	Upper Deck Ruth Heroes	77	15.00
1995	Upper Deck Ruth Heroes	78	15.00
1995	Upper Deck Ruth Heroes	79	15.00
1995	Upper Deck Ruth Heroes	80	15.00
1995	Upper Deck Ruth Heroes	81	15.00
1995	Upper Deck Ruth Heroes	NNO	15.00
1995	Upper Deck Sonic Heroes of Baseball	3	1.25
1996	Bally's HOF 1936 Chips	4	20.00
1996	Collector's Choice	500	1.00
1996	Collector's Choice Gold Signature	500	25.00
1996	Collector's Choice Silver Signature	500	3.00
1997-98	Fleer Million Dollar Moments	3	1.50
1997-98	Fleer Million Dollar Moments Redemption	3	*
1998	Sports Illustrated World Series Fever Autumn Excellence	3	20.00
1998	Sports Illustrated World Series Fever Autumn Excellence Gold	3	80.00
1999	Upper Deck A Piece of History	PH	2500.00
1999	Upper Deck A Piece of History	LCPH	*
1999	Upper Deck Black Diamond	90	5.00
1999	Upper Deck Black Diamond Dominance	D30	50.00
1999	Upper Deck Black Diamond Dominance Emerald	D30	*
1999	Upper Deck Black Diamond Double	90	30.00
1999	Upper Deck Black Diamond Mystery Numbers	M1	200.00
1999	Upper Deck Black Diamond Mystery Numbers Emerald	M1	*
1999	Upper Deck Black Diamond Quadruple	90	250.00
1999	Upper Deck Black Diamond Triple	90	60.00

* These cards are not priced due to lack of market information.

Bonus Babe Ruth

The following Babe Ruth Price Guide is composed of various types of collectibles and cards. Values were determined from actual sales information, sales offers, auction results and listed values from the 2nd edition of the annual *Beckett Almanac of Baseball Cards and Collectibles*. Certain photos are courtesy of Lelands, Mastro Fine Sports Auctions, Hunt Auctions Inc. and Oregon Trail Sports Auctions.

All material is graded and valued in Nr-Mt condition or better.

*Denotes multi-player cover art.

Advertising

1927	Ruth/Gehrig Louisville Slugger Bats Poster (18" X 26")	1000
1929	Benrus Watch Cardboard Sign (10" X 13")	1500
1929	Benrus Watch Poster (12" X 8")	800

| 1933 | Goudey Cardboard Counter Sign | 1500 |
| 1935 | Goudey Gum Card Window Poster (6" X 10") | 850 |

1935	Quaker Oats Cereal Cardboard Sign (16" X 20")	
		2000
1935	Quaker Oats Cereal Cardboard Sign (19" X 23")	
		1500

1935	Quaker Oats Cereal Cardboard Sign (26" X 35")	
		800
1939	Louisville Slugger Hall of Fame Poster (22" X 29")	
		2500

1920's	"Celebrities in the World of Sport" Poster*	350
1920's	Spalding Bats Cardboard Sign (16" X 25")	2000
1920's	Turret Tobacco Silk-Screened Sign (22" X 37")	1800
1930's	Kaywoodie Pipes Cardboard Sign (25" X 16")	2000
1940's	Raleigh Cigarettes Cardboard Sign (38" X 48")	3000

Autographs

1916	Player Contract From 1916-17 Season	30,000
1920	Sales Document Between Red Sox & Yankees (6-Pages)	100,000
1923	Yankees Team Baseball (21 Signatures)	3,500
1925	Yankees Team Baseball (13 Signatures)	1,200
1926	"Along Came Ruth" Sheet Music (Signed)	2,800

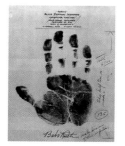

1926	"The All-America Team"Participants Certificate (Signed)	2,500
1927	"Busting Babes Vs Larruping Lou's" Baseball	3,500
1927	Personalized Photo (11" X 17")	3,500

1927	Signed 60th Home Run Print (35" X 24")	20,000
1927	Yankees Team Baseball (27 Signatures) (Nr-Mt-Mt)	27,000
1927	Yankees Team Photo (7" X 9") (48 Signatures)	36,000

1928	Yankees Team Baseball (21 Signatures)	4,000
1928	Yankees Team Baseball (24 Signatures) (Mint)	20,000
1932	Yankees Player Contract	40,000
1932	Yankees Team Baseball (16 Signatures) (Mint)	7,500

1932	Yankees Team Photo (22" X 18")	1,500
1933	All-Star Game Baseball (18 Signatures)	9,000
1933	Goudey Gum Card (#144)	3,000
1933	Goudey Gum Card (#149)	4,000
1933	Yankees Team Baseball (22 Signatures)	2,500
1934	1-Page Typed Letter on Babe's Stationary (6" X 8")	2,000
1934	Babe's Typed & Signed Retirement Letter From Yankees	40,000

1935	Photo in Braves Uniform (5" X 8")	900
1936	Yankees Team Baseball (18 Signatures) (Vg)	1000
1938	Dodgers Team Baseball (20 Signatures)	2800
1938	George Burke Signed Dodgers Photo (4" X 6")	2100
1939	Hall of Fame Inductees Baseball (11 Signatures)	63000

1939	NY Worlds Fair "Academy of Sport" Participants Diploma	2800
1939	NY Worlds Fair "School of Baseball" Laurel Card	900
1944	Dodgers Team Baseball (27 Signatures)	1400
1946	Canceled Bank Check	1600
1947	Ford Luncheon Dinner Program	2500

1947	World Series Ticket Stub (Game #2)	1400
1948	Copy of "The Babe Ruth Story" Hardcover Book	2000
1930s	Gehrig/Ruth Baseball	7500
1930s	Signed Ink Hand Print	13000
1930s	Spring Training Photo (Personalized, (8" X 10")	2800
1930s	Store Model Bat (40BR)	6000
1940s	Spalding Sports Show Program	1800

Ephemera

1914	Baltimore Orioles Schedule/Card	27000
1916	Matted Red Sox Team Cabinet Photo (11" X 9")	3500
1916	Ticket Stub to Ruth's First World Series Game	1200
1919	"Batterin' Babe" Sheet Music	325
1919	"Play Ball" Children's Notebook	400

1920	"Oh! You "Babe" Ruth" Sheet Music	300
1921	Pathe Record Company Premium (7" X 9")	3000
1922	"He's A Home Run Guy" Sheet Music	350

1926	"Along Came Ruth" Sheet Music	250
1926	Kingston, NY Real Photo Postcard	750
1927	60th Home Run Game Ticket Stub (9/30)	1200
1928	Babe Ruth! Babe Ruth! "We Know What He Can Do" Sheet Music	175
1928	Fro-Joy Ice Cream Premium	1600
1928	R315 Uncut Strip Card Strip	500
1929	D & M Athletic Goods Catalog (Spring/Summer)*	250
1932	"Fair Boy's Dept." Advertising Trade Card	450
1932	Complete World Series Proof Ticket (Game #3)	1200

1932	World Series Ticket Stub (Called Shot, Game #3)	2800
1933	The Daily Ghost Dinner Program (12/17)	275
1934	700th Home Run Game Ticket Stub (7/13)	1000
1934	Babe Ruth's Boys Club Newspaper (1/3)	150
1934	Quaker Oats Premium Photo (Facsimile Signature, 8" X 10")	200
1935	Quaker Oats Brochure Promoting Ruth Offer (9" X 8")	175
1936	Hall of Fame Induction Group Photo Postcard.	500
1940	Brown & Bigelow Wall Calendar (16" X 33")	550
1941	Wall Calendar, Springfield Savings & Loan (16" X 25")	275
1947	"Babe" Sheet Music	75
1947	Babe Ruth Day Ticket Stub (4/27)	600
1947	The Sporting News Insert Photo (6" X 9")	100
1948	Exhibit Card Machine Cardboard Paper Insert Front	250
1950	Wall Calendar (11" X 23")	100
1952	Callahan Hall of Fame Booklet (Many Sponsors)	60
1955	Milwaukee Braves Pocket Schedule (Geo. H. Hotton & Son)*	25
1920s	"Batterin Babe" "Look at Him Now" Sheet Music	700
1920s	Ruth's Home Run Candy Bar Wrapper	1500

1930s	"Play Ball" Radio Show Brochure	100
1930s	Reach Gloves Pictorial Tag	700
1950s	Brown & Bigelow Ink Blotter (Waltham Citizens National Bank)	100

Game Used

1929	Yankees Home White Jersey	140000
1935	Braves Road Gray Jersey	56000
1938	Dodgers Cap	25000
1938	Dodgers Home White Jersey	75000
1938	Dodgers Road Gray Jersey and Pants	100000
1920's	Louisville Slugger 125 Bat (36")	15000

Hardcover Books

1920	"The Home Run King" with Pictorial Dustcover	375
1930	Babe Ruth "Idol of the American Boy" (Daniel)	125
1947	Babe Ruth (Meany)	150
1948	The Babe Ruth Story (Considine)	175
1948	The Real Babe Ruth (Daniel)	50
1952	Pictorial History of American Sports (Leather Bound)	75
1954	Babe Ruth-Baseball Boy (Van Riper)	60
1966	Babe Ruth-His Story In Baseball (Allen)	50
1930s	"Babe Ruth's New Tatics of Baseball" (Japan)	500

Hollywood

1920	"Headin Home" Lobby Card (B & W)	750
1920	"Headin Home" Movie Herald	300
1921	"Headin Home" Japaneese 2-Sheet Movie Poster (16" X 43")	5000
1922	"Lion Brand" "Home Run" Movie Flip Book	1200

1927	"Babe Comes Home" Lobby Card	450
1927	"Babe Comes Home" One Sheet Movie Poster	6000
1928	"Speedy" Lobby Card	400

1948	"Spalding Sport Show" Poster Promoting "The Babe Ruth Story" (11" X 17")	175
1948	"The Babe Ruth Story" One-Sheet Movie Poster (27" X 41")	1450
1948	"The Babe Ruth Story" Pressbook (2-Diff)	125
1948	"The Babe Ruth Story" Promotional Slide	50
1949	"The Babe Ruth Story" 1-Sheet	

1949	Movie Poster (22" X 28")	450
1949	"The Babe Ruth Story" Belgian Movie Poster (20" X 14")	300
1949	"The Pride Of The Yankees" Movie Poster (14" X 22") (Reissue)	700
1949	"The Pride Of The Yankees" One-Sheet Movie Poster (27" X 41")	1800
1949	"The Pride Of The Yankees" Presentation Ink Blotter w/Cast-Signed Baseball	2000
1949	"The Pride Of The Yankees" Title Lobby Card (Reissue)	600

Memorabilia

1920s	"Babe and Lou-The Home Run Twins" Record Album (78RPM)	150
1920	"Babe" Ruth's Home Run Story Record Album (Actuelle)	225
1930	Babe Ruth Underwear in the Box (Pictorial)	450

1934	Quaker Oats "Home Run Special" Baseball	500
1934	Quaker Oats "Home Run Special" Baseball in the Box	1500
1934	Quaker Oats Premium "Babe Ruth Champions" Photo Pin (1" Dia.).	200

| 1934 | Quaker Oats Premium "Babe Ruth Champions" Shirt Patch | 125 |
| 1934 | Quaker Oats Premium Brass Ring | 300 |

1934	Quaker Oats Premium Kids Cap	450
1934	Quaker Oats Premium Pen & Pencil Set	350
1935	Quaker Oats Premium Pocket Knife	250

1949	"60th" Home Run Electric Table Clock	2400
1949	"Babe Ruth Story" Promotional Pen Holder	1000
1949	"Sultan of Swat" Pocket Watch	700
1949	Exacta Wristwatch	500
1949	Exacta Wristwatch in Plastic Baseball Container	1200
1920s	"Bambino" Cigerette Papers (Pack)	350

1920s	"Bambino" Vest-Pocket Tobacco Tin	3000
1920s	Celluloid Baseball Scorer (N.Y. American)	300
1930s	"Babe's Musical Bat" Harmonica (3 3/4")	250
1930s	Bambino Candy Box	1000
1930s	Brass Locker Tag (2" Dia.)	2500
1930s	Felt Mini-Pennant	300

1930s	Set of Personal Golf Clubs in the Bag	3000
1930s	Souvenir Brass Belt Buckle	400
1930s	Souvenir H & B Mini-Bat (14")	250
1940s	"George Babe Ruth" H & B Mini-Bat (16")	150
1950s	"The Greatest Moments in Sports Record w/Pictorial Sleeve (33RPM)	100
1950s	"The Greatest Moments in Sports Record w/Pictorial Sleeve (45RPM)	50

Photographs

1916	Red Sox Matted Team Cabinet Photo (11" X 9")	4000
1925	Yankees Team Panorama (20" X 8")	900
1929	Yankees Team Panorama (21" X 8")	600

1948	Babe with Joe DiMaggio (8" X 10" Wirephoto)	400
1916-19	Babe Pitching For The Red Sox (6" X 9")	600
1930's	Ruth Signing a Bushel Basket Full of Baseballs (8" X 10")	300
1930's	Ruth Standing on Dougout Steps (8" X 10")	400
1940's	8" X 10" Wirephoto, "The Babe Lies in State"	450
1940's	8" X 10" Wirephoto, Babe on Set of "The Babe Ruth Story"	250

1930	Babe Signing Bat (8" X 10")	150
1931	Yankees Team Panorama (13" X6")	600
1932	Ruth & Gehrig on Dougout Steps (8" X 10")	600
1933	Babe With Duke Kahanamoka at the Beach (8" X 10" Wirephoto)	450

1924	Mrs. Sherlock's Bread (1" Dia.)	600
1928	Babe Ruth! Babe Ruth! "We Know What He Can Do"	100
1934	Quaker Oats Premium "Babe Ruth Champions" Membership (Celluloid)	150
1934	Quaker Oats Premium "Member" (Celluloid)	125
1934	Quaker Oats Premium Brass Membership Badge.	125

1935	Babe Golfing (8" X 10" Wirephoto)	400
1935	Babe Posed with House of David Ballplayer (8" X 10" Wirephoto)	400
1938	Babes Debut as Dodgers Coach (8" X 10" Wirephoto)	200

1961	"Shootin For 61 in '61" Mantle/Maris/Ruth (6")	3200
1930s	"Babe Ruth Club" (3/4" Dia)	175
1930s	"Babe Ruth's Own Team" (1" Dia.).	175
1930s	"Hello Babe" (3/4" Dia.).	150
1930s	Celluloid Scorer (B on Cap)	225
1930s	Celluloid Scorer (NY on Cap)	250
1930s	Esso Gas "Babe Ruth's Boys Club" Membership	125
1930s	Mrs Sherlock's Bread (7/8" Dia.)	600
1930s	Texaco Gas "Ask Me" (3" Dia.)	1600
1940s	"Never Forgotten" w/Whitehead & Hoag paper back (1 1/2" Dia.)	225
1947-66	PM10 Stadium Pins (1 3/4" Dia.)	200

1939	Group Shot of Hall of Fame's First Inductees (8" X 10")	300
1941	8" X 10" Wirephoto, Babe on Set `of "Pride of Yankees"	250
1941	The Babe at Lou Gehrig's Funeral (8" X 10")	250
1942	Babe with Walter Johnson	200
1946	Babe Poses with Joe Louis and Govenor Dewey (8" X 10" Wirephoto)	400
1947	Babe Ruth Day (8" X 10")	400

Publications

1916	Baseball Magazine (Dec.)*	600
1916	World Series Program (Red Sox Edition)	4000
1920	Baseball Magazine (Apr.)	350
1920	Baseball Magazine (Oct.)*	400
1920	Mid-Week Pictorial (8/5)	400
1920	The Sporting News Record Book	150

1920	Who's Who in Baseball	750
1921	Baseball Magazine (Oct.)*	350
1921	Baseball Magazine, Inside Cover Photo (Sept.)*	150

1921	Mid-Week Pictorial (4/14)	400
1921	The Sporting News Record Book*	100
1921	Who's Who in Baseball	800
1923	Baseball Magazine (Dec.)*	400
1923	Baseball Magazine, Inside Cover Photo (Dec.)*	150
1926	Baseball Magazine (Dec.)*	350
1926	Mid-Week Pictorial (4/22)	300
1927	Baseball Magazine, Inside Cover Photo w/Gehrig (Sept.)	500
1927	Police Gazette	600
1927	Spalding Equiptment Catalog	150
1928	Baseball Magazine, Inside Cover Photo (Aug.)	125

1929	The Sporting News Record Book*	125
1931	The Sporting News Dealer Directory.	150
1932	The Sporting News (10/6)	250
1932	The Sporting News (10/6)*	400
1934	Baseball Magazine (Jan.)*	250
1934	Baseball Magazine, Inside Cover Photo (Oct.)	125
1934	Newsweek Magazine (2/17)*	250
1935	Baseball Magazine (May)*	200
1935	Baseball Magazine (Nov.)*	200

1935	Baseball Magazine, Inside Cover Photo (June)*	125
1935	Program From Final Ballgame (Good Cond.)	500

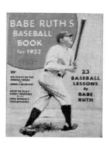

1935	Quaker Oates Premium, "How To" Booklet Set (4)	200
1935	The Sporting News (6/6)	200
1936	Babe Ruth's Baseball Advice Magazine	125
1938	Baseball Magazine, Inside Cover Photo (Aug.)	100
1938	The Sporting News (6/23)	150
1938	The Sporting News (6/23)	150
1938	The Sporting News (7/14)	150
1939	Baseball Magazine, Inside Cover Photo (July)	150
1942	The Sporting News (7/2)*	200
1943	Baseball Magazine, Inside Cover Photo (Oct.)*	75
1947	The Sporting News (4/23)	200
1947	The Sporting News (4/23)	350
1948	Babe Ruth "As I Knew Him" Magazine	125
1948	Baseball Magazine, Inside Cover Photo (Oct.)	100
1948	Hollywood Stars Game Program*	300
1948	Sport Magazine (May)	75
1948	The Sporting News (6/23)	200
1948	The Sporting News (6/23)	300
1948	The Sporting News (8/25)	350
1948	The Sporting News (8/25)	400
1952	Baseball Heroes Comic Book*	200
1952	Baseball Heroes Comic Book*	200

1952	Baseball Magazine, Babe Ruth Anniversary Issue (Sept.)	75
1960	Sport Magazine (Oct.)*	25
1965	Official Babe Ruth League Magazine	20
1920s	Reach Glove Die-Cut Catalog	275
1940s	The Hall of Fame Story Book	75
1949-51	Babe Ruth Sports Comics (Set of 10)	1200
1938	The Sporting News (6/23)	150
1938	The Sporting News (7/14)	150
1939	Baseball Magazine, Inside Cover Photo (July)	150
1942	The Sporting News (7/2)*	200

1943	Baseball Magazine, Inside Cover Photo (Oct.)*	75
1947	The Sporting News (4/23)	200
1947	The Sporting News (4/23)	350
1948	Babe Ruth "As I Knew Him" Magazine	125
1948	Baseball Magazine, Inside Cover Photo (Oct.)	100
1948	Hollywood Stars Game Program*	300
1948	Sport Magazine (May)	75
1948	The Sporting News (6/23)	200
1948	The Sporting News (6/23)	300
1948	The Sporting News (8/25)	350
1948	The Sporting News (8/25)	400
1952	Baseball Heroes Comic Book*	200
1952	Baseball Heroes Comic Book*	200
1952	Baseball Magazine, Babe Ruth Anniversary Issue (Sept.)	75
1960	Sport Magazine (Oct.)*	25
1965	Official Babe Ruth League Magazine	20
1920s	Reach Glove Die-Cut Catalog	275
1940s	The Hall of Fame Story Book	75
1949-51	Babe Ruth Sports Comics (Set of 10)	1200

Softcover Books

1928	Babe Ruth's Own Book of Baseball (Ruth)	100
1930	How To Play Baseball (Cosmopolitan)	75
1932	Babe Ruth's Baseball Book For 1932 (Oversize)	200
1935	Quaker Oats Premium, "Babe Ruth's Big Book of Baseball"	175

1948	Babe Ruth "As I Knew Him"	35
1948	Babe Ruth (Welden)	40
1948	The Babe Ruth Story (Meany)	60
1948	The Real Babe Ruth (Daniel)	50
1953	Baseball's Immortals Series Booklet	25
1954	Babe Ruth Baseball Boy (Bobbs-Merrill)	35
1955	The King of Swat (Father Ted)	35
1956	I Was With Babe Ruth At St. Mary's (Leisman)	75
1959	"The Babe and I" (Avon Books)	20
1959	"The Babe and I" (Slocum)	40
1963	The Babe Ruth Story (Considine)	125
1966	Babe Ruth, His Story in Baseball (Allen)	15
1967	Babe Ruth (Richards)	15

Tours

1927	Busting Babes vs Larruping Lou's Program (Oakland, Ca)	2500
1927	Busting Babe's vs Larruping Lou's Ticket Stub	175
1934	Japan Tour Postcard w/Facsimile Signature	350
1934	Japan Tour Postcard w/Facsimile Signature (Gehrig/Ruth)	350

1934	Tour of Japan Baseball (19 Signatures) (Gem Condition)	16,000

1934	Tour of Japan Newspaper Supplement (Facsimile Signatures on Cover)*	500
1934	Tour of Japan Program (Ruth/Gehrig/Foxx Cover)	3500

1920s	Lake Oscawana Barnstorming Poster (13" X 19")	3500
1930s	Bustin Babe Tour Photo (w/Kid)	250
1930s	Busting Babe's vs Larruping Lou's Signed Photo (8" X 10")	8500
1930s	Signed Black Hills, SD Barnstorming Program	1500

Toys — Games

1933	Feen-A-Mint "Home Run" Halloween Mask	2000
1963	Hall of Fame Bust Statue in the Box	125
1966	Aurora "Great Moments in Sports" Model Kit in the Box	450

1920s	"Babe Ruth National Game of Baseball" Pictorial Game Board	1500
1930s	"Babe Ruth's Baseball Game" (Ex Condition)	750
1930s	"Bambino" Pinball Machine Glass Front (19" X 17")	800
1958-63	Hartland Statue	375
1958-63	Hartland Statue in the Box	750

Trading Cards
By Dan Schlossberg

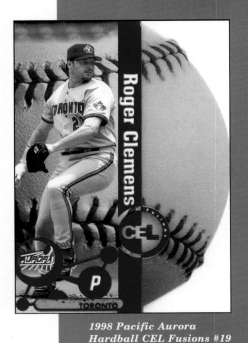

1998 Topps Gold Label Home Run Race #HR1

1998 Pacific Aurora Hardball CEL Fusions #19

The most famous bridge in New York has nothing to do with Brooklyn, Verrazano or George Washington.

It's actually a baseball bridge that spans four generations, from Babe Ruth's arrival with the Yankees in 1920 through the memorabilia boom that mushroomed some 60 years later.

Ruth and Lou Gehrig anchor the bridge on one end, with Joe DiMaggio in the middle and Mickey Mantle at the other pillar.

As players, Ruth (a Yankee from 1920-34) passed the baton to Gehrig (1923-39), DiMaggio (1936-51) and Mantle (1951-68).

All four were not only larger-than-life giants of the game but bastions of what would become the sports hobby industry.

It was Ruth who created the concept of autograph hunting, DiMaggio who discovered its lucrative potential, and Mantle who gave birth to the modern baseball card industry. Gehrig, Ruth's cerebral contemporary, bridged the two-year gap between the Babe and DiMaggio.

"The mentality of collecting was different in Ruth's day," said Greg Schwalenberg, curator of the Babe Ruth Museum. "People got his autograph just because they wanted to say they met the Babe.

It had nothing to do with the value of the autograph. We have tons of pictures of him signing things and many Babe Ruth balls that people donated. Babe really did stay outside the stadium for hours after the game, signing for everybody."

Ruth, more than anyone else, was responsible for creating autograph awareness.

"He never turned down a request," said the curator of the Baltimore museum, located near Ruth's birthplace. "You don't find a lot of signed baseballs from before his era. There was demand for having a connection with the Babe — especially from kids."

One of the signed balls in the museum's collection came from Johnny Sylvester, portrayed in "The Babe Ruth Story" as the hospitalized youth who begs Ruth to hit a home run for him. The truth is a little different.

"Hollywood tends to glamorize a lot of things," said Schwalenberg. "The fact is the Yankees got a letter from Johnny's father saying his son was in the hospital and might feel better if he got something from the team. The Babe heard about it and sent him a ball that said, 'I'll knock a homer for you in Wednesday's game.'"

"He actually hit three home

runs (in Game 3 of the 1926 World Series) but visited Johnny only after the fact. But Johnny received the ball before the game."

Among the museum's benefactors are his adopted daughter, Julia Ruth Stevens, and his wife Claire, who was still alive when it opened in 1974. They not only donated bats, balls, and other equipment, but Ruth's first scorebook and even a kimono he received during a tour of Japan.

The museum's card collection is sparse — only a couple of Goudeys and some strip cards — but local collectors fill the void during special exhibitions.

There are four different Babe Ruth cards in a 240-card set issued by the Goudey Company in 1933. Though book value ranges up to $4,000 for Mint condition, cards rated very good would still command $2,000.

A Mint-condition baseball signed by Ruth could command $8,000, while a 3x5 file card is valued at $750.

Though hobby historians revere Ruth as the father of the autograph craze, they also credit DiMaggio for parlaying it into a moneymaking industry.

Long after his retirement in 1951, the silver-haired Yankee Clipper realized he could make more money in a single year than he did in his entire 13-season playing career. All he had to do was sign his name to selected items of baseball memorabilia.

Joe DiMaggio carefully cultivated the same dignified persona off the field that he had as a player. He had stayed in the public eye by throwing out the first ball at Yankee openers, appearing at Old Timers games, and endorsing various products (Mr. Coffee) and services (Bowery Savings Bank). His short-lived but much-publicized marriage to movie star Marilyn Monroe, plus his habit of sending fresh roses to her grave daily for years after her death, added to his image as a talented athlete to whom privacy was more vital than fame.

The first former player to charge higher prices for signed balls, bats and uniforms than he did for pictures, DiMaggio was also the first to refuse signing certain items. He stopped signing lithographs, paintings, large photos, and eventually bats — raising the value of DiMaggio signatures acquired previously.

He also became the top choice of card show promoters who realized that a marquee autograph guest would increase attendance dramatically. As demand for DiMaggio appearances went up, so did his price — enabling him to command almost as much for a weekend show as he made in his best year as a player ($100,000). In his last appearances, individual tickets for DiMaggio autographs sold for $150-$175 each.

When he eventually agreed to sign a limited run of 1941 bats (celebrating the season of his record 56-game hitting streak), DiMaggio realized a profit estimated at $3 million. In 1993 alone, he doubled that income, and beyond, through an exclusive memorabilia signing contract with Score Board Inc., a Cherry Hill, N.J., firm that has since gone out of business.

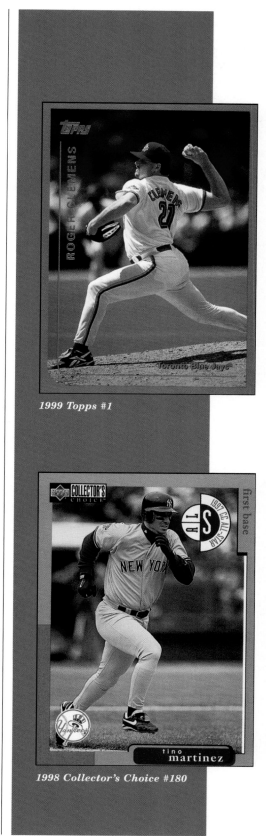

1999 Topps #1

1998 Collector's Choice #180

1998 Pinnacle EPIX Play Orange #E17

1996 Pacific Prisms Flame Throwers #FT3

Thanks to catalog marketing and personal DiMaggio appearances on the QVC home shopping network, the 1941 bats sold for $3,000 each and DiMaggio-signed balls went for $349 apiece. At least those signatures were authentic; before his autograph became so pricey, DiMaggio had his sister sign his name on a mountain of outgoing fan mail.

Mickey Mantle did for the card industry what DiMaggio did for autographing.

According to former Yankee publicist Marty Appel, now spokesman for The Topps Company, "Mantle's importance to the card world can be measured three times over. He was such a popular player in the 1950s that people got a Mantle card in a Topps pack and treated it as an insert card. His was the chase card — the one you wanted to get.

"When his card started to sell in garage sales in the late 1970s and the AP did a story on one of his old cards going for $2,500, that started the weekend card shows big-time.

"Then, after he passed away, Topps reprinted all of his original cards when the trading card world was really down after the (1994-95) baseball strike. It suddenly brought new life to the industry with people running after reprints of Mantle originals."

Topps also announced that it would honor Mantle by permanently retiring No. 7 from its annual series.

Because of its scarcity, the 1952 Mantle rookie — the first card in a late-issued fourth series (#311 overall) — has sold for more than $100,000. So has the original painting that served as the design for the 1953 Topps Mantle. And a Mint-condition set of the 407-card Topps 1952s, including the Mantle rookie, once sold for $145,000.

Those figures don't shock most Mantle collectors. He meant so much to the hobby that Upper Deck once gave him a three-year, $9 million contract to assure the authenticity of his signature on any new memorabilia.

Fellow former Yankee Reggie Jackson, a collector himself, also signed a seven-figure deal with Upper Deck Authenticated — formed specifically to market expensive collectibles — and served on the parent company's board of directors.

The Mantle estate later won a $4.9 judgment against Upper Deck for selling Mantle memorabilia after the star's demise in 1996. Like the game of baseball itself, a one-time sport had become a big business.

"People who want Mantle memorabilia are willing to spend big money," said Bill Jacobowitz, owner of Skybox Baseball Cards in

Livingston, N.J. "I bought a collection a year-and-a-half ago: sixty-four signed 8x10 black-and-whites of Mantle. My first buyer bought thirty-two of them. Out of those original sixty-four, I have seven or eight left. That's because I don't display them."

Getting an autographed card doesn't have to cost a fortune, said Jacobowitz, a dealer, store owner, and card show promoter for 24 years.

"Kids come into my store, look at my Yankee section of signed cards and come across Sparky Lyle," he suggested. "They may not know Sparky Lyle was a Cy Young Award winner but their father, who's probably 35 or 40, might say, 'He was great. He was a real closer for the Yankees.' So they'll buy the card for $6 or $7. They wind up with a signed card of a Cy Young Award winner at a very reasonable price."

Verifying authenticity can be a problem, Jacobowitz admitted.

"Any purchase of autographs involves a certain degree of faith," he said. "You don't want to buy at a show unless the dealer can show you business cards, has a store address, or has a reputation you know about. It's best to buy from somebody you know, so that two or three years down the line, if some question comes up, you can find the guy and return the item. If you get burned for $5, that's one thing. But it's a little different if you're buying something for $400-$500.

"There are some bad people out there: I know a guy who can do a fabulous Mickey Mantle. You just won't know the difference."

Forged Mantle or DiMaggio signatures are more common than forged Ruths or Gehrigs. Color glossies and blue Sharpies, plus perfected counterfeiting techniques, all arrived long after the deaths of Gehrig (1941) and Ruth (1948). A hallmark of a true Ruth or Gehrig autograph is the age of the paper.

According to Bill Jacobowitz, "I bought a collection from a guy whose aunt worked in the Boston Braves' offices from 1929-32. One of the things she had was this little kid's autograph book. The first third of the book is just pages and pages of signatures. On one page alone, there are only two signatures: Lou Gehrig and Babe Ruth. The last two-thirds consists of all these 'roses are red, violets are blue' phrases. There's no way you can even get that kind of autograph book in that kind of condition. And you can tell by the type of pen used that the signatures are genuine."

An autograph collector himself, Jacobowitz has more than 20,000 different signatures, including Ruth, DiMaggio, and Mantle. His next-to-impossible goal is to get one of every man who's ever worn a major league uniform.

The ultimate collection — for both autographs and cards — probably belongs to the Baseball Hall of Fame. It has 130,000 cards and 4,000 baseballs — many of them signed.

Jeff Idelson, the former Yankee publicist who is now communica-

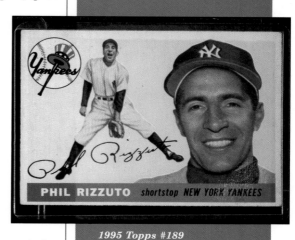

1995 Topps #189

1997 Donruss Elite Passing the Torch Autographs #12

Top 10 Yankee Cards

1. 1952 Topps Mickey Mantle #311. Topps produced four series (the fourth numbered 311-407) with a lower print run on the high-numbered last set. The first Topps Mantle card, listed at $52,000 in mint condition, has sold for more than $100,000.

2. 1951 Bowman Mickey Mantle #253. A true Mantle rookie (1951 was his first year), this horizontal card has commanded as much as $22,753.

3. 1940 Play Ball Joe DiMaggio. This vertical card carried an extra art element that said "1939 Pennant" and has sold for $8,885.

4. 1977 Topps Unissued Proof — Reggie Jackson. An unissued proof version of this card, showing Jackson in an Orioles uniform on a Yankee card, sold in 1994 for $3,500, then a record for a post-1950s card. Only a half-dozen are known to exist. Topps airbrush artists corrected the official version to show Jackson, who spent part of the preceding season in Baltimore after a trade from Oakland, in a Yankee uniform.

5. 1933 Goudey Babe Ruth #144. This card, from the first Goudey set, is valued at $3,000.

6. 1953 Topps Mickey Mantle #82. The only set in which Topps used paintings. The original artwork sold for $100,000 at auction, though the card's value is $4,800.

7. 1949 Leaf Babe Ruth #3. This card is valued at $4,000.

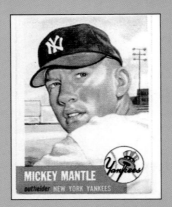

Above: 1953 Topps #82. Below: 1999 Upper Deck — A Piece of History.

8. 1999 Upper Deck Babe Ruth — A Piece of History. This recent card includes an authentic chip from a Babe Ruth game-used bat. It's valued at $2,500.

9. 1956 Topps Mickey Mantle #135. This horizontal Mantle was part of the last oversized, regular-issue cards and the first Topps set after it bought out Bowman. Valued at $2,400.

10. 1950 Bowman Yogi Berra #46. The first high-quality set from the Philadelphia- based company consisted of horizontal cards produced from paintings. Valued at $500.

— Dan Schlossberg

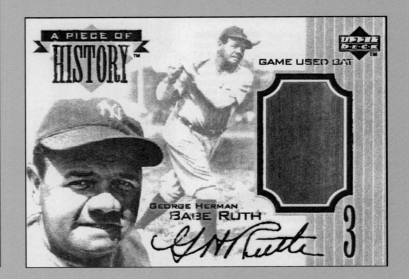

tions director for the Cooperstown museum, said players decide whether to sign the memorabilia they donate.

"We leave it up to the player," he said. "We have signed balls from every no-hitter since 1940. And we have dozens and dozens of balls from every Hall of Famer, as well as many autographed team balls from championship years."

Single-signed balls are sometimes more valuable than team-signed versions, he noted. It depends upon the historical significance.

"A team ball from the 1997 Florida Marlins is very telling," said Idelson, "because so few of those players remained in 1998. But a ball signed by Al Leiter, who had a no-hitter for Florida that year, is also special."

The Hall is the biggest repository of Yankee cards, autographs and other memorabilia. Among them is the only existing ball bearing the autographs of Babe Ruth and the men who broke his single-season and career home run records, Roger Maris and Hank Aaron. The signatures were obtained by long-time collector Bob Woytych between 1927 and 1974.

"We have the Mantle rookie and every other prominent Yankee card you can think of," said Idelson. "We have an autographed ball from David Wells' perfect game last year and Joe Torre's signed lineup card from Sept. 25, 1998, when the Yankees broke the American League record with their 112th victory of the season."

The September opening of the Barry Halper Changing Exhibit Gallery will add much more memorabilia — much of it signed.

"Major League Baseball acquired and donated 200 pieces from Barry's collection," he said. "Some of that is Yankee related, including the contract selling Babe Ruth from Boston to New York. Many are of great historical value.

"We're always looking to add new elements to our exhibitory and this will be an important exhibit for our visitors to see. It also assures a legacy for Barry, which is much-deserved since he spent his whole life collecting these important pieces of baseball history."

Halper's 50-year-old collection, divided between the Hall of Fame and Sotheby's auction house, once consisted of 30,000 cards and 1,053 uniforms — 663 of them signed.

According to Halper, a one-time paper products executive who still owns a piece of the Yankees, Cooperstown got 20 percent of his collection, Sotheby's got 79.5 percent, and he kept the remaining 0.5 percent for personal reasons.

"The items I kept are so personal to me that it might detract from someone else unless he was also named Barry," he said. "I kept anything Joe DiMaggio signed personally. I have so many things that say, 'To my dear friend Barry.' He put little comments on paintings, pictures, and other things. Same thing with Mickey.

"Joe gave me the nicest thing anybody ever gave me at a card show in Kansas City years ago. It might have been the first show he ever did.

"I gave him the No. 1 print of a lithograph that showed him

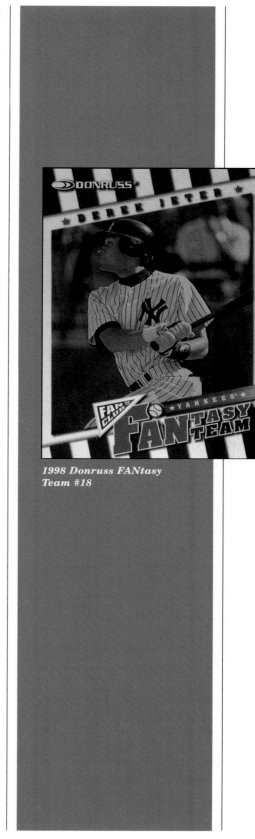

1998 Donruss FANtasy Team #18

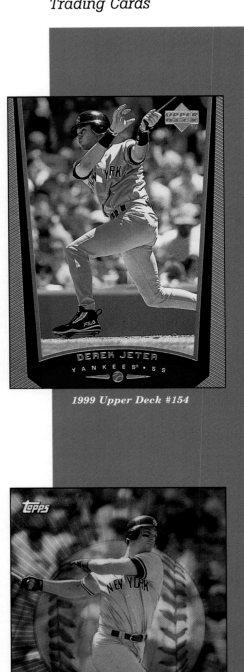

1999 Upper Deck #154

1998 Topps Mystery Finest Borderless #M11

swinging the bat. He gave it back to me and wrote, 'To my friend Barry. The #1 issue from this painting, deserving of the #1 collector. My good wishes, Joe DiMaggio.'"

Before his collection went public, Halper had a world-class stash of Ruth items. One of them was a rare 1914 Ruth rookie card, issued by the Baltimore News, showing him in the uniform of the Boston Red Sox. Another was a three-year Yankee contract for 1923-25 stipulating an annual salary of $52,000.

"I was speaking with (Ruth biographer) Robert Creamer one day and he explained that number to me," Halper said. "According to Creamer, Ruth said he'd know he made it big in life if he ever made a grand a week."

Though Ruth signed tons of autographs, his messages were invariably short and sweet, Halper said, while Lou Gehrig was more effusive.

"Because he went to Columbia, Lou signed more balls with messages than anybody else," said the world-famous collector from his Livingston, N.J. home. "He would write something like, 'Aunt Sue, hope you're feeling better. Cordially yours, Lou Gehrig.' The Babe would write, 'To Dan, Babe Ruth.'"

Halper lamented the fact that today's players don't sign with the same legibility of their predecessors. In addition to overwhelming demand on their time, many players fear the motives of autograph hunters are private profit rather than personal pleasure.

"When you see a team picture signed by the 1937 Yankees, 1947 Yankees, or 1956 Yankees, you can read every name," Halper said. "Today, you know who the player is only if he also signs his number."

Signing for pay poses other problems. A Halper-owned picture showing Yankee teammates hoisting David Wells on their shoulders after his 1998 perfect game bears the signatures of everyone but the pitcher.

"Everybody got different amounts to sign it," Halper said, "and David didn't get along with the person who made the deal to get all the Yankees to sign. He said he'll sign it for me eventually."

Halper, one of the first collectors to realize the significance of group signings (hitters with 500 homers, pitchers with 300 wins, etc.), still has an eye out for items of value.

"I'm not out of the collecting business entirely," he admitted. "If I see something and can purchase it, I know what I can do with it. I know where the bodies are buried and who likes what. If I make up my mind to do something, I do it 100 percent.

"After the 1998 World Series, I bought big pictures autographed by everybody and I have a bat autographed by everybody. Those things I don't want to sell because if that was the best team ever, I should hold onto them. I was an owner when all that happened and I still am an owner."

Halper's influence extends in all directions — north to the Hall of Fame, south to the Babe Ruth

Museum, and east to the Yogi Berra Museum, for example.

"Barry's been a great help to us," said Berra museum director Dave Kaplan. "A lot of our materials came from him."

Every Yogi card, including a 1947 rookie that lists him by his real name of Larry Berra, is on display at the Montclair, N.J. museum. Its gift shop even sells a 1985 Topps father and son card of Yogi and Dale Berra ($10), plus a Yogi-signed 1954 Topps reprint ($13) and a Yogi-signed baseball ($37.95).

Prices of cards and autographs vary widely. The four primary determinants are demand, scarcity, age and condition — plus the status of the signee. If he's in the legends class, collectors can expect a hefty price tag.

Autographed DiMaggio items remain high: usually $175 for Hall of Fame plaque postcards, $125 for 8x10s, $275 for balls, $300 for Perez-Steele postcards (issued from 1981-98), but much more for bats, jerseys or original art. The "Just Joe" painting by Dick Perez is valued at $21,000.

A bat signed by Mantle, Jackson and nine other living members of the 500 Home Run Club (all but Eddie Murray) costs $1,500, but the Hillerich & Bradsby M110 signature model signed only by Mantle is almost the same price ($1,300). Mantle-signed balls usually go for $225, while his autographed Perez-Steele is worth $250.

Yogi Berra's signatures vary from bat ($150) to ball ($40) to Perez-Steele ($25), but predecessor

Bill Dickey's are worth more: $700 on a bat, $300 on a ball and $75 on a Perez-Steele card. Whitey Ford's go for $100, $35 and $25, respectively.

Even a rare signed 1941 spring training photo of Yankee executive Ed Barrow, who never played in the majors, is worth nearly $500, while a signed 1977 Thurman Munson promotional contract, on the letterhead of Frank Scott Associates, costs $750.

Because prices for autographs are rising more quickly than the stock market, many collectors are returning to cards as their primary targets. In addition to the wide variety of regular sets and inserts, there are numerous special series featuring Yankees past and present. In 1995, for example, the Highland Mint issued a double Lou Gehrig/Cal Ripken Jr. mini-set as a tribute to baseball's old and new Iron Men.

There's still a debate about the value of signatures on cards. Some hobbyists insist that any autographed card — no matter how valuable — is no longer in Mint condition. But all agree that cards remain the cornerstone of the collecting hobby.

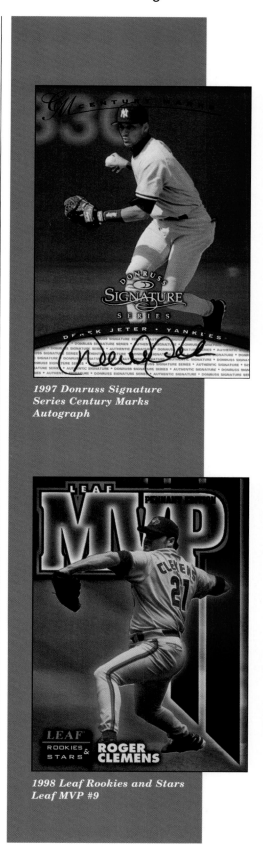

1997 Donruss Signature Series Century Marks Autograph

1998 Leaf Rookies and Stars Leaf MVP #9

Yankees Trading Card Checklist

1959 Topps #180

1948 Bowman #6

Yogi Berra

Year	Set Name	Card No.
1946-49	Sports Exchange W603	5-11
1947	Homogenized Bond	2
1947	Tip Top	46
1947	Yankees Team Issue	1
1947-65	PM10 Stadium Pins 2 1/8'	4
1947-66	Exhibits	20A
1947-66	Exhibits	20B
1947-66	PM10 Stadium Pins 1 3/4'	9
1947-66	PM10 Stadium Pins 1 3/4'	10
1947-66	PM10 Stadium Pins 1 3/4'	11
1948	Bowman	6
1948	Yankees Team Issue	2
1949	Bowman	60
1949	MP and Co. R302-2	117
1949	Yankees Team Issue	2
1950	Bowman	46
1950	Drake's	24
1950	Yankees Team Issue	3
1951	Berk Ross	B4
1951	Bowman	2
1951	R423 Small Strip	5
1951	Topps Current All-Stars	1
1951	Topps Red Backs	1
1952	Berk Ross	3
1952	Bowman	1
1952	National Tea Labels	2
1952	Red Man	AL3
1952	Star Cal Large	70C
1952	Star Cal Small	84B
1952	Tip Top	2
1952	Topps	191
1952	Wheaties	4A
1952	Wheaties	4B
1953	Bowman Color	44
1953	Bowman Color	121
1953	Red Man	AL3
1953	Topps	104
1953-55	Dormand	102
1954	Bowman	161
1954	New York Journal American	41
1954	Red Man	AL20
1954	Topps	50
1955	Armour Coins	2
1955	Big League Inc. Statues	3
1955	Bowman	168
1955	Dairy Queen Statues	3
1955	Red Man	AL16
1955	Topps	198
1956	Topps	110
1956	Topps Pins	27
1956	Yankees Jay Publishing	2
1956	Yankees Team Issue	2
1956	Yellow Basepath Pins	7
1957	Topps	2
1957	Topps	407
1957	Yankees Jay Publishing	2
1958	Jay Publishing Sluggers	2
1958	Topps	370
1958	Yankees Jay Publishing	2
1958	Yoo-Hoo Match Book Cover	1
1958-63	Hartland Statues	8
1959	Topps	180
1959	Topps Venezuelan	180
1959	Yoo-Hoo	1
1960	Bazooka	8
1960	Key Chain Inserts	7
1960	Nu-Card Hi-Lites	28
1960	Topps	480

Year	Set Name	Card No.
1960	Topps Tattoos	6
1960	Yankees Jay Publishing	1
1961	Chemstrand Patches	2
1961	Nu-Card Scoops	453
1961	Post	1A
1961	Post	1B
1961	Seven-Eleven	22
1961	Topps	425
1961	Topps	472
1961	Topps Magic Rub-Offs	23
1961	Topps Stamps Inserts	189
1961	Yankees Jay Publishing	1
1962	Exhibit Stat Back	4
1962	Jello	7
1962	Post	7
1962	Post Canadian	7
1962	Salada Plastic Coins	33
1962	Shirriff Plastic Coins	33
1962	Topps	88
1962	Topps	360
1962	Topps Bucks	9
1962	Topps Stamps Inserts	83
1962	Topps Venezuelan	88
1962	Yankees Jay Publishing	2
1963	Baseball Magazine M118	11
1963	Exhibit Stat Back	7
1963	Jello	17
1963	Post	17
1963	Salada Metal Coins	62
1963	Topps	340
1963	Yankees Jay Publishing	1
1963-67	Yankee Requena K Postcards	2
1964	Challenge The Yankees	1
1964	Topps	21
1964	Topps Venezuelan	21
1964	Yankees Jay Publishing	1
1965	Mets Jay Publishing	2
1965	Mets Postcards	1
1965	Topps	470
1966	Mets Team Issue	1
1966	Mets Volpe Tumblers	2
1967	Mets Team Issue	1
1967	Topps Venezuelan	179
1969	Mets Team Issue	2
1971	Mets Team Issue	2
1973	Hall of Fame Picture Pack	1
1973	Mets All-Time Ed Broder	1
1973	New York Sunday News M138	1
1973	O-Pee-Chee	257
1973	Seven-Eleven Trading Cups	5
1973	Topps	257A
1973	Topps	257B
1974	Mets Dairylea Photo Album	13
1974	Mets Japan Ed Broder	1
1974	New York News This Day in Sports	1
1974	New York News This Day in Sports	11
1974	New York News This Day in Sports	28
1974	O-Pee-Chee	179
1974	Topps	179
1975	Mets SSPC	19
1975	O-Pee-Chee	189
1975	O-Pee-Chee	192
1975	O-Pee-Chee	193
1975	O-Pee-Chee	421
1975	SSPC 18	5
1975	SSPC 42	40
1975	Topps	189
1975	Topps	192
1975	Topps	193
1975	Topps	421
1975	Topps Mini	189

Year	Set Name	Card No.
1975	Topps Mini	192
1975	Topps Mini	193
1975	Topps Mini	421
1976	Galasso Baseball's Great Hall of Fame	3
1976	Great Plains Greats	22
1976	Shakey's Pizza	127
1976	Taylor/Schmierer Bowman 47	10
1978	Yankees Photo Album	2
1979	Baseball Greats	71
1979	TCMA 50'S	2
1979	Yankees Picture Album	3
1980	Yankees Photo Album	1
1980-83	Pacific Legends	67
1980-87	SSPC HOF	127
1980-96	Perez-Steele Hall of Fame Postcards	127
1981	Donruss	351
1981	TCMA 60's II	382
1981	TCMA 60's II	407
1981	TCMA 60's II	474
1982	Baseball Card News	4
1982	Donruss	387
1982	TCMA Greatest Sluggers	15
1982	TCMA Stars of the 50's	18
1983	ASA Johnny Mize	11
1983	ASA Yogi Berra	1
1983	ASA Yogi Berra	2
1983	ASA Yogi Berra	3
1983	ASA Yogi Berra	4
1983	ASA Yogi Berra	5
1983	ASA Yogi Berra	6
1983	ASA Yogi Berra	7
1983	ASA Yogi Berra	8
1983	ASA Yogi Berra	9
1983	ASA Yogi Berra	10
1983	ASA Yogi Berra	11
1983	ASA Yogi Berra	12
1983	Donruss HOF Heroes	24
1983	Franchise Brooks Robinson	9
1983	MLBPA Pins	2
1983	O'Connell and Son Baseball Greats	3
1983	Topps Reprint 52	191
1983	Yankee A-S Fifty Years	4
1983	Yankee Yearbook Insert TCMA	8
1983	Yankees 1961	8
1983	Yankees Photo Album	3
1983-96	Kellogg's Cereal Boxes	8
1984	Fifth National Convention Tickets	2
1984	Topps Traded	13T
1984	Topps Traded Tiffany	13T
1984-89	O'Connell and Son Ink	39
1984-89	O'Connell and Son Ink	136
1985	Circle K	33
1985	George Steinbrenner Menu	1
1985	TCMA Playball 1948	29
1985	Topps	132
1985	Topps	155
1985	Topps Tiffany	132
1985	Topps Tiffany	155
1985	Woolworth's	4
1985	Yankees TCMA Postcards	2
1986	Astros Police	26
1986	Sportflics Decade Greats	31
1986	TCMA	11
1986	TCMA Superstars Simon	9
1986	TCMA Superstars Simon	39
1987	Astros Mother's	27
1987	Astros Police	26
1987	Hygrade All-Time Greats	5
1987	Leaf Special Olympics	H2
1987	Nestle Dream Team	19
1987	Topps	531
1987	Topps Tiffany	531
1987	Yankees 1961 TCMA	6
1988	Astros Mother's	27
1988	Houston Show	11
1988	Pacific Legends I	53
1989	Astros Lennox HSE	14

Year	Set Name	Card No.
1989	Astros Mother's	27
1989	Astros Smokey	5
1989	Bowman Reprint Inserts	2
1989	Bowman Reprint Inserts Tiffany	2
1989	CMC Mantle	10
1989	Mets Rini Postcards 1969	35
1989	Perez-Steele Celebration Postcards	6
1990	AGFA	22
1990	Baseball Wit	24
1990	Pacific Legends	7
1990	Swell Baseball Greats	105
1990	Yankees 61 Ron Lewis	8
1990-92	Perez-Steele Master Works	26
1990-92	Perez-Steele Master Works	27
1990-92	Perez-Steele Master Works	28
1990-92	Perez-Steele Master Works	29
1990-92	Perez-Steele Master Works	30
1990-97	Perez-Steele Great Moments	53
1991	Collect-A-Books	35
1991	Kellogg's 3D	11
1991	Kellogg's Stand Ups	3
1991	Line Drive	7
1991	MDA All-Stars	11
1991	Mets WIZ	36
1991	Swell Baseball Greats	8
1991	Topps Archives 1953	104
1991	Upper Deck Sheets	8
1991	Yankees Rini Postcards 1961 1	1
1992	Action Packed ASG	1
1992	Action Packed ASG 24K	1G
1992	Action Packed ASG Prototypes	1
1992	Bazooka Quadracard '53 Archives	4
1992	Front Row Berra	1
1992	Front Row Berra	2
1992	Front Row Berra	3
1992	Front Row Berra	4
1992	Front Row Berra	5
1992	MDA MVP	1
1992	MVP 2 Highlights	4
1992	MVP Game	2
1992	Pinnacle Mantle	25
1992	Yankees WIZ 60s	8
1992	Yankees WIZ All-Stars	3
1992	Yankees WIZ HOF	3
1992	Ziploc	10
1992-93	Revolutionary Legends 1	10
1992-93	Revolutionary Legends 1	11
1992-93	Revolutionary Legends 1	12
1992-97	Sports Illustrated For Kids II	212
1993	Action Packed ASG Coke/Amoco	1
1993	Metallic Images	3
1993	Ted Williams	58
1993	Ted Williams Locklear Collection	1
1993	Ted Williams POG Cards	21
1993	Upper Deck All-Time Heroes	9
1993	Yoo-Hoo	2
1994	Mets '69 Capital Cards Postcard Promos	4
1994	Mets '69 Commemorative Sheet	3
1994	Mets '69 Tribute	30
1994	Ted Williams Memories	M25
1994	Topps Archives 1954	50
1994	Topps Archives 1954 Gold	50
1994	Upper Deck All-Time Heroes	114
1994	Upper Deck All-Time Heroes	145
1994	Upper Deck All-Time Heroes	158
1994	Upper Deck All-Time Heroes 125th	114
1994	Upper Deck All-Time Heroes 125th	145
1994	Upper Deck All-Time Heroes 125th	158
1994	Upper Deck: The American Epic	62
1995	Ball Park Franks	1
1995	Stouffer Pop-ups	1
1997	Donruss Signature Significant Signatures	3
1997	Jimmy Dean	1
1997	New York Lottery	1
1997	Sports Illustrated Cooperstown Collection	2
1997	Topps Mantle	21
1997	Topps Mantle	23

Year	Set Name	Card No.
1997	Topps Mantle Finest	21
1997	Topps Mantle Finest	23
1997	Topps Mantle Finest Refractors	21
1997	Topps Mantle Finest Refractors	23
1998	Bowman Chrome Reprints	1
1998	Bowman Chrome Reprints Refractors	1
1998	Donruss Signature Significant Signatures	2
1998	Sports Illustrated Then and Now	4
1998	Sports Illustrated Then and Now Extra Edition	4
1998	Sports Illustrated Then and Now Great Shots	23
1998	Sports Illustrated World Series Fever Autumn Excellence	8
1998	Sports Illustrated World Series Fever Autumn Excellence Gold	8
1998	Upper Deck Retro	66
1998	Upper Deck Retro Sign of the Times	YB
1999	Topps Hall of Fame Collection	HOF10

Chris Chambliss

Year	Set Name	Card No.
1970	Wichita Aeros McDonald's	6
1972	O-Pee-Chee	142
1972	Topps	142
1973	Arthur Treacher Cups	3
1973	Indians Team Issue	7
1973	O-Pee-Chee	11
1973	Topps	11
1973-74	Linnett Portraits	61
1974	O-Pee-Chee	384
1974	Topps	384
1974	Topps Deckle Edge	15
1974	Topps Stamps	162
1975	O-Pee-Chee	585
1975	Topps	585
1975	Topps Mini	585
1975	Yankees SSPC	14
1976	Hostess	58
1976	Hostess Twinkie	58
1976	O-Pee-Chee	65
1976	SSPC	434
1976	Topps	65
1977	Burger Chef Discs	173
1977	Hostess	98
1977	Kellogg's	52
1977	O-Pee-Chee	49
1977	RC Cola Cans	18
1977	Topps	220
1977	Topps	276
1977	Yankees Burger King	12
1977	Yankees Nedicks Cups	1
1978	Hostess	98
1978	Kellogg's	13
1978	O-Pee-Chee	145
1978	RC Cola Cans	20
1978	SSPC 270	7
1978	Topps	485
1978	Wiffle Ball Discs	18
1978	Yankees Burger King	12
1978	Yankees Photo Album	4
1978	Yankees SSPC Diary	7
1979	Baseball Patches	19
1979	Kellogg's	37
1979	O-Pee-Chee	171
1979	Topps	335
1979	Yankees Burger King	12
1979	Yankees Picture Album	6
1980	O-Pee-Chee	328
1980	Topps	625
1981	All-Star Game Program Inserts	93
1981	Braves Police	10
1981	Donruss	219
1981	Fleer	252
1981	Fleer Sticker Cards	81
1981	O-Pee-Chee	155
1981	Topps	155

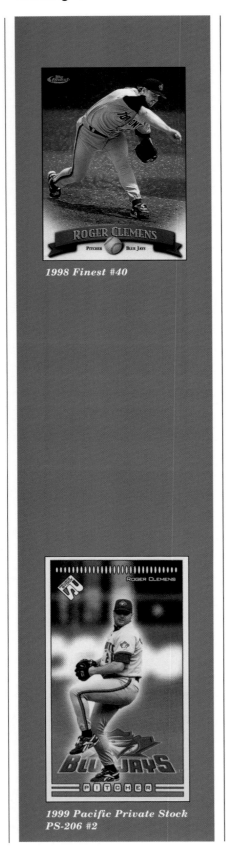

1998 Finest #40

1999 Pacific Private Stock PS-206 #2

Year	Set Name	Card No.
1981	Topps Stickers	147
1982	Braves Burger King Lids	6
1982	Braves Police	10
1982	Donruss	47
1982	Fleer	433
1982	Fleer Stamps	70
1982	Kellogg's	52
1982	O-Pee-Chee	320
1982	O-Pee-Chee	321
1982	Topps	320
1982	Topps	321
1982	Topps Sticker Variations	17
1982	Topps/O-Pee-Chee Stickers	17
1983	All-Star Game Program Inserts	92
1983	Braves Police	10
1983	Donruss	123
1983	Fleer	134
1983	Fleer Stamps	37
1983	Fleer Stickers	86
1983	O-Pee-Chee	11
1983	Topps	792
1983	Topps/O-Pee-Chee Stickers	212
1984	All-Star Game Program Inserts	2
1984	Braves Police	10
1984	Donruss	537
1984	Donruss Action All-Stars	29
1984	Fleer	175
1984	Fun Foods Pins	123
1984	Nestle 792	50
1984	O-Pee-Chee	50
1984	Topps	50
1984	Topps Rub Downs	13
1984	Topps Tiffany	50
1984	Topps/O-Pee-Chee Stickers	28
1985	Braves Hostess	7
1985	Braves Police	10
1985	Donruss	287
1985	Fleer	322
1985	Leaf/Donruss	168
1985	O-Pee-Chee	187
1985	Topps	518
1985	Topps Tiffany	518
1985	Topps/O-Pee-Chee Stickers	29
1986	Braves Police	10
1986	Donruss	618
1986	Fleer	512
1986	Topps	293
1986	Topps Tiffany	293
1987	Fleer	513
1987	Fleer Glossy	513
1987	O-Pee-Chee	204
1987	Topps	777
1987	Topps Tiffany	777
1989	London Tigers ProCards	1378
1991	Greenville Braves Classic/Best	25
1991	Greenville Braves Line Drive	224
1991	Greenville Braves ProCards	3018
1991	Line Drive AA	224
1991	Upper Deck Sheets	6
1992	Action Packed ASG	55
1992	Richmond Braves Bleacher Bums	5
1992	Richmond Braves Bob's Camera	26
1992	Richmond Braves Fleer/ProCards	391
1992	Richmond Braves Richmond Comix	3
1992	Richmond Braves SkyBox	449
1992	Yankees WIZ 70s	32
1992	Yankees WIZ 80s	30
1992	Yankees WIZ All-Stars	9
1997-98	Fleer Million Dollar Moments	37
1997-98	Fleer Million Dollar Moments Redemption	37

Roger Clemens

Year	Set Name	Card No.
1984	Fleer Update	27
1984	Pawtucket Red Sox TCMA	22

Year	Set Name	Card No.
1984-89	O'Connell and Son Ink	242
1985	Donruss	273
1985	Fleer	155
1985	Fleer Star Stickers	123
1985	Leaf/Donruss	99
1985	Topps	181
1985	Topps Tiffany	181
1986	Donruss	172
1986	Donruss Highlights	5
1986	Donruss Highlights	6
1986	Donruss Highlights	17
1986	Donruss Highlights	18
1986	Donruss Highlights	26
1986	Fleer	345
1986	Fleer Mini	73
1986	Fleer Sluggers/Pitchers	7
1986	O-Pee-Chee	98
1986	Topps	661
1986	Topps Tiffany	661
1987	Burger King All-Pro	4
1987	Classic Game	84
1987	Classic Update Yellow	114
1987	Donruss	2
1987	Donruss	276
1987	Donruss All-Star Box	PC14
1987	Donruss All-Stars	8
1987	Donruss Pop-Ups	8
1987	Donruss Super DK's	2
1987	Drake's	31
1987	Fleer	32
1987	Fleer	634
1987	Fleer	640
1987	Fleer All-Stars	11
1987	Fleer Award Winners	9
1987	Fleer Baseball All-Stars	10
1987	Fleer Exciting Stars	11
1987	Fleer Game Winners	10
1987	Fleer Glossy	32
1987	Fleer Glossy	634
1987	Fleer Glossy	640
1987	Fleer Glossy	WS3
1987	Fleer Hottest Stars	10
1987	Fleer League Leaders	10
1987	Fleer Limited Edition	9
1987	Fleer Mini	20
1987	Fleer Record Setters	4
1987	Fleer Sluggers/Pitchers	10
1987	Fleer Sticker Cards	24
1987	Fleer World Series	3
1987	General Mills Booklets	2B
1987	Kay-Bee	10
1987	Key Food Discs	2
1987	Kraft Foods	45
1987	Leaf/Donruss	2
1987	Leaf/Donruss	190
1987	M and M's Star Lineup	7
1987	MSA Iced Tea Discs	2
1987	MSA Jiffy Pop Discs	12
1987	O-Pee-Chee	340
1987	Our Own Discs	2
1987	Ralston Purina	10
1987	Red Foley Sticker Book	70
1987	Red Sox Postcards	6
1987	Red Sox Sports Action Postcards	6
1987	Seven-Eleven Coins	E8
1987	Seven-Eleven Coins	M10
1987	Sportflics	10
1987	Sportflics	111
1987	Sportflics	159
1987	Sportflics	196
1987	Sportflics Dealer Panels	1
1987	Sportflics Team Preview	9
1987	Sports Illustrated Stickers	3
1987	Sports Reading	12
1987	Star Clemens	1
1987	Star Clemens	2
1987	Star Clemens	3

Year	Set Name	Card No.	Year	Set Name	Card No.	Year	Set Name	Card No.
1987	Star Clemens	4	1988	Star Clemens/Gooden	8	1990	All-American Baseball Team	8
1987	Star Clemens	5	1988	Star Clemens/Gooden	10	1990	Bowman	268
1987	Star Clemens	6	1988	Starting Lineup All-Stars	7	1990	Bowman Tiffany	268
1987	Star Clemens	7	1988	Starting Lineup Red Sox	6	1990	Classic Blue	51
1987	Star Clemens	8	1988	Tara Plaques	9	1990	Collect-A-Books	19
1987	Star Clemens	9	1988	Tetley Tea Discs	9	1990	Donruss	184
1987	Star Clemens	10	1988	Topps	70	1990	Donruss Best AL	58
1987	Star Clemens	11	1988	Topps	394	1990	Fleer	271
1987	Star Clemens	12	1988	Topps Big	118	1990	Fleer	627
1987	Star Clemens II	1	1988	Topps Cloth	23	1990	Fleer Baseball MVP's	8
1987	Star Clemens II	2	1988	Topps Cloth	24	1990	Fleer Baseball MVP's Canadian	8
1987	Star Clemens II	3	1988	Topps Coins	2	1990	Fleer Canadian	271
1987	Star Clemens II	4	1988	Topps Gallery of Champions	5	1990	Fleer Canadian	627
1987	Star Clemens II	5	1988	Topps Glossy Send-Ins	13	1990	Fleer Wax Box Cards	C3
1987	Stuart Panels	15	1988	Topps Mini Leaders	2	1990	Hottest 50 Players Stickers	7
1987	Topps	1	1988	Topps Revco League Leaders	28	1990	Leaf	12
1987	Topps	340	1988	Topps Tiffany	70	1990	M.V.P. Pins	10
1987	Topps	614	1988	Topps Tiffany	394	1990	MLBPA Baseball Buttons (Pins)	69
1987	Topps Coins	8	1988	Topps UK Minis	15	1990	O-Pee-Chee	245
1987	Topps Gallery of Champions	5	1988	Topps UK Minis Tiffany	15	1990	Panini Stickers	24
1987	Topps Glossy All-Stars	21	1988	Topps/O-Pee-Chee Sticker Backs	58	1990	Post	2
1987	Topps Glossy Send-Ins	5	1988	Topps/O-Pee-Chee Stickers	251	1990	Pubs.Int'l. Stickers	281
1987	Topps Mini Leaders	42	1988	Weis Market Discs	9	1990	Pubs.Int'l. Stickers	452
1987	Topps Tiffany	1	1988	Woolworth's	11	1990	Red Foley Sticker Book	18
1987	Topps Tiffany	340	1989	Bowman	26	1990	Red Sox Pepsi	6
1987	Topps Tiffany	614	1989	Bowman Tiffany	26	1990	Score	310
1987	Topps/O-Pee-Chee Stickers	2	1989	Cadaco Ellis Discs	9	1990	Score 100 Superstars	79
1987	Topps/O-Pee-Chee Stickers	3	1989	Cereal Superstars	7	1990	Score McDonald's	18
1987	Topps/O-Pee-Chee Stickers	154	1989	Classic Travel Orange	119	1990	Sportflics	149
1987	Topps/O-Pee-Chee Stickers	244	1989	Donruss	280	1990	Sunflower Seeds	18
1987	Weis Market Discs	2	1989	Donruss All-Stars	14	1990	Topps	245
1987	Woolworth's	7	1989	Donruss Baseball's Best	65	1990	Topps Big	22
1988	Bazooka	4	1989	Fleer	85	1990	Topps Doubleheaders	11
1988	Chef Boyardee	23	1989	Fleer Baseball All-Stars	7	1990	Topps Mini Leaders	4
1988	Classic Blue	217	1989	Fleer Baseball MVP's	8	1990	Topps Stickers	255
1988	Classic Red	158	1989	Fleer Exciting Stars	6	1990	Topps Tiffany	245
1988	Donruss	51	1989	Fleer For The Record	2	1990	Topps TV All-Stars	25
1988	Donruss Baseball's Best	57	1989	Fleer Glossy	85	1990	Topps TV Red Sox	8
1988	Donruss Team Book Red Sox	51	1989	Fleer Heroes of Baseball	8	1990	U.S. Playing Card All-Stars	1S
1988	Drake's	30	1989	Fleer League Leaders	5	1990	Upper Deck	57
1988	Fleer	349	1989	Fleer Superstars	9	1990	Upper Deck	323
1988	Fleer All-Stars	4	1989	K-Mart	20	1990	Windwalker Discs	3
1988	Fleer Award Winners	6	1989	Kay-Bee	7	1990	Wonder Bread Stars	2
1988	Fleer Baseball All-Stars	8	1989	Key Food Discs	8	1990-93	Topps Magazine	26
1988	Fleer Baseball MVP's	6	1989	MSA Holsum Discs	16	1991	Baseball's Best Aces of the Mound	4
1988	Fleer Exciting Stars	10	1989	MSA Iced Tea Discs	8	1991	Bowman	118
1988	Fleer Glossy	349	1989	Nissen	16	1991	Cadaco Ellis Discs	9
1988	Fleer Hottest Stars	7	1989	O-Pee-Chee	121	1991	Classic Game	149
1988	Fleer League Leaders	6	1989	Our Own Tea Discs	8	1991	Classic I	T18
1988	Fleer Mini	5	1989	Panini Stickers	249	1991	Classic II	T65
1988	Fleer Record Setters	7	1989	Panini Stickers	270	1991	Classic II	T97
1988	Fleer Sluggers/Pitchers	9	1989	Red Foley Sticker Book	23	1991	Collect-A-Books	1
1988	Fleer Sticker Cards	7	1989	Score	350	1991	Donruss	9
1988	Fleer Superstars	9	1989	Score	350A	1991	Donruss	81
1988	Fleer Team Leaders	5	1989	Score Hottest 100 Stars	90	1991	Donruss	395
1988	Grenada Baseball Stamps	47	1989	Score Scoremasters	20	1991	Donruss Super DK's	9
1988	Houston Show	13	1989	Sportflics	3	1991	Fleer	90
1988	K-Mart	7	1989	Tetley Tea Discs	8	1991	Fleer All-Stars	10
1988	Key Food Discs	9	1989	Topps	405	1991	Fleer Pro-Visions	9
1988	King-B Discs	20	1989	Topps	450	1991	Jimmy Dean	18
1988	Leaf/Donruss	56	1989	Topps Baseball Talk/LJN	58	1991	Leaf	174
1988	MSA Iced Tea Discs	9	1989	Topps Big	42	1991	Leaf	488
1988	MSA Jiffy Pop Discs	6	1989	Topps Cap'n Crunch	18	1991	Major League Collector Pins	8
1988	Nestle	1	1989	Topps Coins	37	1991	MSA Holsum Discs	13
1988	O-Pee-Chee	70	1989	Topps Doubleheaders All-Stars	9	1991	O-Pee-Chee	530
1988	Our Own Tea Discs	9	1989	Topps Glossy Send-Ins	23	1991	O-Pee-Chee Premier	23
1988	Panini Stickers	21	1989	Topps Hills Team MVP's	8	1991	Panini Canadian Top 15	63
1988	Red Foley Sticker Book	13	1989	Topps Mini Leaders	46	1991	Panini Canadian Top 15	69
1988	Score	110	1989	Topps Tiffany	405	1991	Panini Canadian Top 15	80
1988	Score Glossy	110	1989	Topps Tiffany	450	1991	Panini Canadian Top 15	94
1988	Score Young Superstars II	23	1989	Topps UK Minis	16	1991	Panini French Stickers	271
1988	Sportflics	207	1989	Topps/O-Pee-Chee Sticker Backs	25	1991	Panini Stickers	215
1988	Sportflics Gamewinners	20	1989	Topps/O-Pee-Chee Stickers	259	1991	Pepsi Superstar	6
1988	Star Clemens/Gooden	1	1989	TV Sports Mailbags	63	1991	Petro-Canada Standups	3
1988	Star Clemens/Gooden	2	1989	Upper Deck	195	1991	Post	12
1988	Star Clemens/Gooden	4	1989	Weis Market Discs	8	1991	Post Canadian	18
1988	Star Clemens/Gooden	6	1989-91	Sports Illustrated For Kids I	60	1991	Red Foley Stickers	20

1997 Score Premium Stock #181

1997 Donruss Signature Series Millenium Marks Autograph

Year	Set Name	Card No.	Year	Set Name	Card No.
1991	Red Sox Pepsi	5	1992	Pinnacle Rookie Idols	4
1991	Red Sox Postcards	7	1992	Pinnacle Team Pinnacle	1
1991	Score	399	1992	Post	16
1991	Score	655	1992	Post Canadian	10
1991	Score	684	1992	Red Foley Stickers	26
1991	Score	850	1992	Red Sox Dunkin' Donuts	9
1991	Score 100 Superstars	50	1992	Score	21
1991	Seven-Eleven 3-D Coins National	3	1992	Score	790
1991	Seven-Eleven Coins	F3	1992	Score 100 Superstars	74
1991	Seven-Eleven Coins	T4	1992	Score Coke/Hardees Discs	5
1991	Seven-Eleven Coins	NE3	1992	Score Impact Players	57
1991	SilverStar Holograms	6	1992	Seven-Eleven Coins	3
1991	Stadium Club	309	1992	Sports Stars Collector Coins	9
1991	Stadium Club Members Only	12	1992	Stadium Club	80
1991	Starline Prototypes	3	1992	Stadium Club	593
1991	Starshots Pinback Badges	9	1992	Stadium Club Dome	29
1991	Studio	14	1992	Stadium Club Members Only	11
1991	Studio Previews	2	1992	Studio	132
1991	Topps	530	1992	Texas Longhorns	8
1991	Topps Cracker Jack I	22	1992	Topps	150
1991	Topps Desert Shield	530	1992	Topps	405
1991	Topps Micro	530	1992	Topps Gold	150
1991	Topps Stand-Ups	9	1992	Topps Gold	405
1991	Topps Tiffany	530	1992	Topps Gold Winners	150
1991	Topps Triple Headers	A2	1992	Topps Gold Winners	405
1991	U.S. Playing Card All-Stars	10H	1992	Topps Kids	67
1991	Ultra	31	1992	Topps McDonald's	10
1991	Upper Deck	655	1992	Topps Micro	150
1992	Bowman	691	1992	Topps Micro	405
1992	Classic Game	189	1992	Triple Play	216
1992	Classic I	T26	1992	Ultra	15
1992	Classic I	NNO	1992	Ultra Award Winners	6
1992	Classic II	T61	1992	Upper Deck	545
1992	Colla All-Star Game	19	1992	Upper Deck	641
1992	Colla All-Stars Promos	19	1992	Upper Deck FanFest	19
1992	Donruss	244	1992	Upper Deck FanFest Gold	19
1992	Donruss Bonus Cards	BC3	1992	Upper Deck Team MVP Holograms	16
1992	Donruss Cracker Jack I	17	1992-94	Highland Mint Mint-Cards Topps	13
1992	Donruss McDonald's	10	1992-94	Highland Mint Mint-Cards Topps	14
1992	Fleer	37	1992-97	Sports Illustrated For Kids II	36
1992	Fleer Citgo The Performer	6	1992-98	Highland Mint Mint-Coins	30
1992	Fleer Clemens	1	1992-98	Highland Mint Mint-Coins	31
1992	Fleer Clemens	2	1993	Bowman	635
1992	Fleer Clemens	3	1993	Cadaco Discs	11
1992	Fleer Clemens	4	1993	Classic Game	21
1992	Fleer Clemens	5	1993	Diamond Marks	25
1992	Fleer Clemens	6	1993	Donruss	119
1992	Fleer Clemens	7	1993	Donruss Diamond Kings	DK3
1992	Fleer Clemens	8	1993	Donruss MVPs	15
1992	Fleer Clemens	9	1993	Donruss Previews	13
1992	Fleer Clemens	10	1993	Duracell Power Players I	1
1992	Fleer Clemens	11	1993	Finest	104
1992	Fleer Clemens	12	1993	Finest Jumbos	104
1992	Fleer Clemens	13	1993	Finest Refractors	104
1992	Fleer Clemens	14	1993	Flair	160
1992	Fleer Clemens	15	1993	Fleer	177
1992	Fleer Clemens	AU0	1993	Fleer	348
1992	Fleer Clemens	NNO	1993	Fleer	717
1992	Fleer Smoke 'n Heat	S4	1993	Fleer Atlantic	5
1992	French's	2	1993	Fleer Fruit of the Loom	12
1992	High 5	7	1993	Fleer Team Leaders	AL4
1992	High 5 Superstars	8	1993	Fun Pack	14
1992	Jimmy Dean	10	1993	Fun Pack	23
1992	King-B Discs	9	1993	Fun Pack	29
1992	L and K Decals	6	1993	Fun Pack	161
1992	Leaf	19	1993	Fun Pack	162
1992	Leaf Black Gold	19	1993	Hostess	27
1992	MooTown Snackers	4	1993	Humpty Dumpty Canadian	3
1992	Mr. Turkey Superstars	7	1993	Jimmy Dean	7
1992	MVP Pins	5	1993	King-B Discs	21
1992	O-Pee-Chee	150	1993	Kraft	5
1992	O-Pee-Chee Premier	105	1993	Leaf	279
1992	Pacific Ryan Texas Express II	200	1993	Leaf Gold All-Stars	R20
1992	Panini Stickers	92	1993	Leaf Heading for the Hall	6
1992	Panini Stickers	146	1993	Metz Baking	5
1992	Pepsi Diet MSA	1	1993	MSA Ben's Super Pitchers Discs	12
1992	Pinnacle	95	1993	O-Pee-Chee	259

Year	Set Name	Card No.
1993	O-Pee-Chee Premier Star Performers	18
1993	O-Pee-Chee Premier Star Performers Foil	18
1993	Pacific Jugadores Calientes	4
1993	Pacific Spanish	30
1993	Panini Stickers	90
1993	Pinnacle	25
1993	Pinnacle Cooperstown	18
1993	Pinnacle Cooperstown Dufex	18
1993	Post	4
1993	Post Canadian	3
1993	Red Foley Stickers	20
1993	Red Sox Postcards	6
1993	Red Sox Winter Haven Police	8
1993	Score	7
1993	Score Franchise	2
1993	Select	14
1993	Select Aces	1
1993	Select Chase Stars	21
1993	Select Dufex Insert Promos	2
1993	Select Stat Leaders	62
1993	Select Stat Leaders	75
1993	Select Stat Leaders	79
1993	Select Stat Leaders	87
1993	SP	199
1993	Stadium Club	220
1993	Stadium Club	748
1993	Stadium Club First Day Issue	220
1993	Stadium Club First Day Issue	748
1993	Stadium Club Members Only Parallel	220
1993	Stadium Club Members Only Parallel	748
1993	Stadium Club Murphy	97
1993	Studio	22
1993	Studio Heritage	3
1993	Topps	4
1993	Topps	409
1993	Topps Black Gold	27
1993	Topps Commanders of the Hill	3
1993	Topps Full Shots	15
1993	Topps Gold	4
1993	Topps Gold	409
1993	Topps Inagural Rockies	4
1993	Topps Inagural Rockies	409
1993	Topps Inaugural Marlins	4
1993	Topps Inaugural Marlins	409
1993	Topps Micro	4
1993	Topps Micro	409
1993	Triple Play	118
1993	Triple Play Action	14
1993	Triple Play Nicknames	2
1993	U.S. Playing Cards Aces	11S
1993	Ultra	508
1993	Ultra Strikeout Kings	1
1993	Upper Deck	48
1993	Upper Deck	135
1993	Upper Deck	630
1993	Upper Deck Clutch Performers	R7
1993	Upper Deck Diamond Gallery	21
1993	Upper Deck Future Heroes	57
1993	Upper Deck Gold	48
1993	Upper Deck Gold	135
1993	Upper Deck Gold	630
1993	Upper Deck On Deck	D9
1994	Bowman	475
1994	Bowman's Best	R37
1994	Bowman's Best	X100
1994	Bowman's Best Refractors	R37
1994	Bowman's Best Refractors	X100
1994	Church's Hometown Stars	13
1994	Church's Hometown Stars Gold	13
1994	Collector's Choice	322
1994	Collector's Choice	348
1994	Collector's Choice	550
1994	Collector's Choice Gold Signature	322
1994	Collector's Choice Gold Signature	348
1994	Collector's Choice Gold Signature	550
1994	Collector's Choice Silver Signature	322
1994	Collector's Choice Silver Signature	348

Year	Set Name	Card No.
1994	Collector's Choice Silver Signature	550
1994	Collector's Choice Team vs. Team	3
1994	Donruss	356
1994	Donruss	600
1994	Donruss Special Edition	356
1994	Finest	217
1994	Finest Jumbos	217
1994	Finest Refractors	217
1994	Flair	261
1994	Fleer	26
1994	Fleer Extra Bases	16
1994	Fleer Extra Bases Game Breakers	7
1994	Fleer Extra Bases Pitchers Duel	1
1994	Fleer Smoke 'n Heat	1
1994	Fleer Sunoco	7
1994	Fleer Update Diamond Tribute	4
1994	Fun Pack	21
1994	Fun Pack	207
1994	Leaf	255
1994	Leaf Limited	7
1994	O-Pee-Chee	67
1994	O-Pee-Chee All-Star Redemptions	18
1994	O-Pee-Chee Jumbo All-Stars	18
1994	Oscar Mayer Round-Ups	3
1994	Pacific	49
1994	Panini Stickers	26
1994	Pinnacle	25
1994	Pinnacle Artist's Proofs	25
1994	Pinnacle Museum Collection	25
1994	Pinnacle The Naturals	25
1994	Red Foley's Magazine Inserts	31
1994	Score	25
1994	Score Gold Rush	25
1994	Select	61
1994	Select Crown Contenders	CC3
1994	SP	152
1994	SP Die Cuts	152
1994	SP Holoviews	5
1994	SP Holoviews Die Cuts	5
1994	Sportflics	15
1994	Stadium Club	534
1994	Stadium Club	650
1994	Stadium Club First Day Issue	534
1994	Stadium Club First Day Issue	650
1994	Stadium Club Golden Rainbow	534
1994	Stadium Club Golden Rainbow	650
1994	Stadium Club Members Only Parallel	534
1994	Stadium Club Members Only Parallel	650
1994	Studio	159
1994	Sucker Saver	20
1994	Topps	720
1994	Topps Gold	720
1994	Topps Spanish	720
1994	Topps Superstar Samplers	10
1994	Triple Play	201
1994	Ultra	11
1994	Upper Deck	450
1994	Upper Deck All-Star Jumbos	21
1994	Upper Deck All-Star Jumbos Gold	21
1994	Upper Deck Diamond Collection	E2
1994	Upper Deck Electric Diamond	450
1994-95	Pro Mags	11
1995	Bazooka	9
1995	Bowman	293
1995	Bowman's Best	R23
1995	Bowman's Best Refractors	R23
1995	Classic $10 Phone Cards	9
1995	Collector's Choice	410
1995	Collector's Choice Gold Signature	410
1995	Collector's Choice SE	190
1995	Collector's Choice SE Gold Signature	190
1995	Collector's Choice SE Silver Signature	190
1995	Collector's Choice Silver Signature	410
1995	Denny's Holograms	6
1995	Donruss	427
1995	Donruss Press Proofs	427
1995	Donruss Top of the Order	19

Year	Set Name	Card No.
1995	Emotion	10
1995	Finest	185
1995	Finest Flame Throwers	FT2
1995	Finest Refractors	185
1995	Flair	10
1995	Fleer	26
1995	Fleer Team Leaders	2
1995	Fleer Update Headliners	7
1995	Leaf	255
1995	Leaf Limited	48
1995	Pacific	34
1995	Pacific Prisms	12
1995	Panini Stickers	14
1995	Pinnacle	2
1995	Pinnacle Artist's Proofs	2
1995	Pinnacle FanFest	2
1995	Pinnacle Gate Attractions	GA13
1995	Pinnacle Museum Collection	2
1995	Pinnacle Red Hot	RH18
1995	Pinnacle White Hot	WH18
1995	ProMint	5
1995	Red Foley	3
1995	Score	118
1995	Score Double Gold Champs	GC7
1995	Score Gold Rush	118
1995	Score Hall of Gold	HG15
1995	Score Platinum Team Sets	118
1995	Select	72
1995	Select Artist's Proofs	72
1995	Select Certified	88
1995	Select Certified Mirror Gold	88
1995	SP	127
1995	SP Championship	122
1995	SP Championship Die Cuts	122
1995	SP Silver	127
1995	SP Special FX	2
1995	Sportflix	51
1995	Sportflix Artist's Proofs	51
1995	Stadium Club	10
1995	Stadium Club First Day Issue	10
1995	Stadium Club Members Only Parallel	10
1995	Stadium Club Members Only Parallel	RL32
1995	Stadium Club Ring Leaders	RL32
1995	Stadium Club Super Team Division Winners	RS10
1995	Stadium Club Super Team World Series	10
1995	Stadium Club Virtual Reality	5
1995	Stadium Club Virtual Reality Members Only	5
1995	Studio	16
1995	Studio Gold Series	16
1995	Studio Platinum Series	16
1995	Summit	41
1995	Summit	190
1995	Summit Nth Degree	41
1995	Summit Nth Degree	190
1995	Topps	360
1995	Topps Cyberstats	192
1995	Topps D3	9
1995	Topps Embossed	106
1995	Topps Embossed Golden Idols	106
1995	Topps League Leaders	LL23
1995	U.S. Playing Cards Aces	10S
1995	UC3	95
1995	UC3	141
1995	UC3 Artist's Proofs	95
1995	UC3 Artist's Proofs	141
1995	Ultra	10
1995	Ultra Gold Medallion	10
1995	Ultra Strikeout Kings	2
1995	Ultra Strikeout Kings Gold Medallion	2
1995	Upper Deck	159
1995	Upper Deck	J159
1995	Upper Deck Autographs	1
1995	Upper Deck Electric Diamond	159
1995	Upper Deck Electric Diamond Gold	159
1995	Upper Deck Special Edition	212
1995	Upper Deck Special Edition Gold	212

Year	Set Name	Card No.
1995	Upper Deck/GTS Phone Cards	MLB9
1995	Zenith	91
1996	Bazooka	62
1996	Bowman	89
1996	Bowman Foil	89
1996	Bowman's Best	33
1996	Bowman's Best Atomic Refractors	33
1996	Bowman's Best Refractors	33
1996	Circa	10
1996	Circa Rave	10
1996	Collector's Choice	60
1996	Collector's Choice	419
1996	Collector's Choice Gold Signature	60
1996	Collector's Choice Gold Signature	419
1996	Collector's Choice Silver Signature	60
1996	Collector's Choice Silver Signature	419
1996	Donruss	539
1996	Donruss Press Proofs	539
1996	Donruss Showdown	4
1996	Emotion-XL	12
1996	Finest	S46
1996	Finest Refractors	S46
1996	Flair	16
1996	Fleer	25
1996	Fleer Smoke 'n Heat	2
1996	Fleer Tiffany	25
1996	King-B Discs	1
1996	Leaf	69
1996	Leaf Limited	2
1996	Leaf Limited Gold	2
1996	Leaf Preferred	19
1996	Leaf Preferred Press Proofs	19
1996	Leaf Preferred Steel	63
1996	Leaf Preferred Steel Gold	63
1996	Leaf Press Proofs Bronze	69
1996	Leaf Press Proofs Gold	69
1996	Leaf Press Proofs Silver	69
1996	Leaf Signature	28
1996	Leaf Signature Extended Autographs	32
1996	Leaf Signature Extended Autographs Century Marks	3
1996	Leaf Signature Press Proofs Gold	28
1996	Leaf Signature Press Proofs Platinum	28
1996	Metal Universe	13
1996	Metal Universe Platinum	13
1996	Pacific	258
1996	Pacific Prisms	P79
1996	Pacific Prisms Flame Throwers	FT3
1996	Pacific Prisms Gold	P79
1996	Panini Stickers	136
1996	Pinnacle	247
1996	Pinnacle Aficionado	9
1996	Pinnacle Aficionado Artist's Proofs	9
1996	Pinnacle Aficionado First Pitch Preview	9
1996	Pinnacle Aficionado Promos	9
1996	Pinnacle Foil	247
1996	Pinnacle Starburst	147
1996	Pinnacle Starburst Artist's Proofs	147
1996	Pro Stamps	110
1996	Red Sox Fleer	3
1996	Score	333
1996	Score Dugout Collection	B58
1996	Score Dugout Collection Artist's Proofs	B58
1996	Select	20
1996	Select Artist's Proofs	20
1996	Select Certified	8
1996	Select Certified Artist's Proofs	8
1996	Select Certified Certified Blue	8
1996	Select Certified Certified Red	8
1996	Select Certified Interleague Preview	5
1996	Select Certified Mirror Blue	8
1996	Select Certified Mirror Gold	8
1996	Select Certified Mirror Red	8
1996	Select Team Nucleus	8
1996	SP	39
1996	SP Marquee Matchup Die Cuts	19
1996	SP Marquee Matchups	MM19
1996	SP Special FX	38
1996	SP Special FX Die Cuts	38
1996	Sportflix	58
1996	Sportflix Artist's Proofs	58
1996	SPx	9
1996	SPx Gold	9
1996	Stadium Club	25
1996	Stadium Club Extreme Players Bronze	25
1996	Stadium Club Extreme Players Gold	25
1996	Stadium Club Extreme Players Silver	25
1996	Stadium Club Megaheroes	MH8
1996	Stadium Club Members Only Parallel	25
1996	Stadium Club Members Only Parallel	M4
1996	Stadium Club Members Only Parallel	MH8
1996	Stadium Club Metalists	M4
1996	Studio	11
1996	Studio Press Proofs Bronze	11
1996	Studio Press Proofs Gold	11
1996	Studio Press Proofs Silver	11
1996	Summit	101
1996	Summit	152
1996	Summit Above and Beyond	101
1996	Summit Above and Beyond	152
1996	Summit Artist's Proofs	101
1996	Summit Artist's Proofs	152
1996	Summit Foil	101
1996	Summit Foil	152
1996	Topps	197
1996	Topps Chrome	65
1996	Topps Chrome Masters of the Game	17
1996	Topps Chrome Masters of the Game Refractors	17
1996	Topps Chrome Refractors	65
1996	Topps Classic Confrontations	CC13
1996	Topps Gallery	174
1996	Topps Gallery Photo Gallery	PG8
1996	Topps Gallery Players Private Issue	174
1996	Topps Laser	52
1996	Topps Laser Stadium Stars	10
1996	Topps Masters of the Game	17
1996	Ultra	16
1996	Ultra Gold Medallion	16
1996	Upper Deck	20
1996	Upper Deck	374
1996	Upper Deck Diamond Destiny	DD11
1996	Upper Deck Diamond Destiny Gold	DD11
1996	Upper Deck Diamond Destiny Silver	DD11
1996	Upper Deck Predictor Hobby	H11
1996	Upper Deck Predictor Hobby Exchange	H11
1996	Upper Deck V.J. Lovero Showcase	VJ13
1996	Zenith	83
1996	Zenith Artist's Proofs	83
1996	Zenith Mozaics	9
1997	Blue Jays Bookmarks	2
1997	Blue Jays Copi Quik Interleague	1
1997	Blue Jays Oh Henry	5
1997	Blue Jays Sizzler	6
1997	Blue Jays Sizzler	31
1997	Blue Jays Sun	3
1997	Bowman	64
1997	Bowman Chrome	46
1997	Bowman Chrome International	46
1997	Bowman Chrome International Refractors	46
1997	Bowman Chrome Refractors	46
1997	Bowman International	64
1997	Bowman's Best	86
1997	Bowman's Best Atomic Refractors	86
1997	Bowman's Best Refractor	86
1997	Circa	21
1997	Circa Rave	21
1997	Clemens A and P	1
1997	Clemens The Fan	1
1997	Collector's Choice	61
1997	Collector's Choice	500
1997	Collector's Choice New Frontier	NF17
1997	Collector's Choice The Big Show	10
1997	Collector's Choice	
1997	The Big Show World Headquarters	10
1997	Collector's Choice Toast of the Town	T30
1997	Denny's Holograms	13
1997	Donruss	27
1997	Donruss	273
1997	Donruss	428
1997	Donruss Dominators	11
1997	Donruss Elite	40
1997	Donruss Elite Gold Stars	40
1997	Donruss Gold Press Proofs	27
1997	Donruss Gold Press Proofs	273
1997	Donruss Gold Press Proofs	428
1997	Donruss Limited	110
1997	Donruss Limited	124
1997	Donruss Limited	165
1997	Donruss Limited Exposure	110
1997	Donruss Limited Exposure	124
1997	Donruss Limited Exposure	165
1997	Donruss Limited Exposure Non-Glossy	124
1997	Donruss Preferred	52
1997	Donruss Preferred Cut to the Chase	52
1997	Donruss Preferred Tin Boxes	4
1997	Donruss Preferred Tin Boxes Gold	4
1997	Donruss Preferred Tin Packs	4
1997	Donruss Preferred Tin Packs Gold	4
1997	Donruss Preferred Tins Fanfest	4
1997	Donruss Signature	11
1997	Donruss Signature Autographs Century	26
1997	Donruss Signature Autographs Millenium	26
1997	Donruss Signature Notable Nicknames	3
1997	Donruss Signature Platinum Press Proofs	11
1997	Donruss Silver Press Proofs	27
1997	Donruss Silver Press Proofs	273
1997	Donruss Silver Press Proofs	428
1997	Donruss Team Sets MVP's	17
1997	Donruss VxP 1.0	48
1997	E-X2000	49
1997	E-X2000 Credentials	49
1997	E-X2000 Essential Credentials	49
1997	E-X2000 Hall or Nothing	7
1997	Finest	233
1997	Finest	344
1997	Finest Embossed	344
1997	Finest Embossed Refractors	344
1997	Finest Refractors	233
1997	Finest Refractors	344
1997	Flair Showcase Legacy Collection	21
1997	Flair Showcase Masterpieces	A21
1997	Flair Showcase Masterpieces	B21
1997	Flair Showcase Masterpieces	C21
1997	Flair Showcase Row 0	21
1997	Flair Showcase Row 1	21
1997	Flair Showcase Row 2	21
1997	Fleer	19
1997	Fleer	569
1997	Fleer Decade of Excellence	3
1997	Fleer Decade of Excellence Rare Traditions	3
1997	Fleer Tiffany	19
1997	Fleer Tiffany	569
1997	King-B Discs	8
1997	Leaf	208
1997	Leaf	366
1997	Leaf Fractal Matrix	208
1997	Leaf Fractal Matrix	366
1997	Leaf Fractal Matrix Die Cuts	208
1997	Leaf Fractal Matrix Die Cuts	366
1997	Leaf Get-A-Grip	11
1997	Leaf Gold Stars	13
1997	Metal Universe	20
1997	New Pinnacle	21
1997	New Pinnacle Artist's Proof	21
1997	New Pinnacle Keeping the Pace	10
1997	New Pinnacle Museum Collection	21
1997	New Pinnacle Press Plates	21
1997	New Pinnacle Press Plates	K10
1997	Pacific	35
1997	Pacific Light Blue	35

Year	Set Name	Card No.
1997	Pacific Prisms	14
1997	Pacific Prisms Gems of the Diamond	GD18
1997	Pacific Prisms Light Blue	14
1997	Pacific Prisms Platinum	14
1997	Pacific Prisms Sluggers and Hurlers	SH2B
1997	Pacific Silver	35
1997	Phillies Copi Quik	5
1997	Pinnacle	55
1997	Pinnacle All-Star FanFest Promos	1
1997	Pinnacle Artist's Proofs	PP55
1997	Pinnacle Cardfrontations	13
1997	Pinnacle Certified	39
1997	Pinnacle Certified	138
1997	Pinnacle Certified Lasting Impressions	11
1997	Pinnacle Certified Mirror Black	39
1997	Pinnacle Certified Mirror Black	138
1997	Pinnacle Certified Mirror Blue	39
1997	Pinnacle Certified Mirror Blue	138
1997	Pinnacle Certified Mirror Gold	39
1997	Pinnacle Certified Mirror Gold	138
1997	Pinnacle Certified Mirror Red	39
1997	Pinnacle Certified Mirror Red	138
1997	Pinnacle Certified Red	39
1997	Pinnacle Certified Red	138
1997	Pinnacle FanFest	FF19
1997	Pinnacle Inside	36
1997	Pinnacle Inside Club Edition	36
1997	Pinnacle Inside Diamond Edition	36
1997	Pinnacle Inside Dueling Dugouts	15
1997	Pinnacle Museum Collection	55
1997	Pinnacle Press Plate Previews	55
1997	Pinnacle Totally Certified Platinum Blue	39
1997	Pinnacle Totally Certified Platinum Blue	138
1997	Pinnacle Totally Certified Platinum Gold	39
1997	Pinnacle Totally Certified Platinum Gold	138
1997	Pinnacle Totally Certified Platinum Red	39
1997	Pinnacle Totally Certified Platinum Red	138
1997	Pinnacle Totally Certified Samples	39
1997	Pinnacle X-Press	54
1997	Pinnacle X-Press	148
1997	Pinnacle X-Press Men of Summer	54
1997	Pinnacle X-Press Men of Summer	148
1997	Pinnacle X-Press Metal Works	20
1997	Pinnacle X-Press Metal Works Gold	20
1997	Pinnacle X-Press Metal Works Silver	20
1997	Red Sox Score	8
1997	Red Sox Score Platinum	8
1997	Red Sox Score Premier	8
1997	Score	181
1997	Score	430
1997	Score	525
1997	Score Artist's Proofs White Border	181
1997	Score Artist's Proofs White Border	430
1997	Score Artist's Proofs White Border	525
1997	Score Premium Stock	181
1997	Score Reserve Collection	430
1997	Score Reserve Collection	525
1997	Score Showcase Series	181
1997	Score Showcase Series	430
1997	Score Showcase Series	525
1997	Score Showcase Series Artist's Proofs	181
1997	Score Showcase Series Artist's Proofs	430
1997	Score Showcase Series Artist's Proofs	525
1997	Select	24
1997	Select Artist's Proof	24
1997	Select Company	24
1997	Select Registered Gold	24
1997	Select Tools of the Trade	22
1997	Select Tools of the Trade Mirror Blue	22
1997	SP	180
1997	SP Inside Info	24
1997	SP Special FX	24
1997	SP SPx Force Autographs	5
1997	Sports Illustrated	30
1997	Sports Illustrated	133
1997	Sports Illustrated	171
1997	Sports Illustrated Extra Edition	30

Year	Set Name	Card No.
1997	Sports Illustrated Extra Edition	133
1997	Sports Illustrated Extra Edition	171
1997	SPx	50
1997	SPx Bronze	50
1997	SPx Gold	50
1997	SPx Grand Finale	50
1997	SPx Silver	50
1997	SPx Steel	50
1997	Stadium Club	209
1997	Stadium Club Instavision	I4
1997	Stadium Club Matrix	209
1997	Stadium Club Members Only Parallel	209
1997	Stadium Club Members Only Parallel	I4
1997	Strat-O-Matic All-Stars	15
1997	Studio	17
1997	Studio Press Proof Gold	17
1997	Studio Press Proof Silver	17
1997	Topps	370
1997	Topps Chrome	126
1997	Topps Chrome Refractors	126
1997	Topps Gallery	41
1997	Topps Gallery Player's Private Issue	41
1997	Topps Stars	50
1997	Topps Stars Always Mint	50
1997	Topps Stars Promos	PP2
1997	UD3	21
1997	Ultra	13
1997	Ultra	377
1997	Ultra Gold Medallion	13
1997	Ultra Gold Medallion	377
1997	Ultra Platinum Medallion	13
1997	Ultra Platinum Medallion	377
1997	Upper Deck	26
1997	Upper Deck	520
1997	Upper Deck Award Winner Jumbos	11
1997	Upper Deck Memorable Moments	B8
1997	Upper Deck Predictor	30
1997	Upper Deck Predictor Exchange	30
1997	Upper Deck Star Attractions	6
1997	Zenith	19
1997	Zenith 8 x 10	12
1997	Zenith 8x10 Dufex	12
1997	Zenith Z-Team	9
1997-98	Fleer Million Dollar Moments	12
1997-98	Fleer Million Dollar Moments Redemption	12
1997-98	Topps Members Only 55	14
1998	Bowman	38
1998	Bowman Chrome	38
1998	Bowman Chrome Golden Anniversary	38
1998	Bowman Chrome Golden Anniversary Refractors	38
1998	Bowman Chrome International	38
1998	Bowman Chrome International Refractors	38
1998	Bowman Chrome Refractors	38
1998	Bowman Golden Anniversary	38
1998	Bowman International	38
1998	Bowman's Best	48
1998	Bowman's Best Atomic Refractors	48
1998	Bowman's Best Refractors	48
1998	Circa Thunder	21
1998	Circa Thunder Boss	3
1998	Circa Thunder Limited Access	2
1998	Circa Thunder Quick Strike	2
1998	Circa Thunder Rave	21
1998	Circa Thunder Rave Review	3
1998	Circa Thunder Super Rave	21
1998	Collector's Choice	2
1998	Collector's Choice	257
1998	Collector's Choice	258
1998	Collector's Choice	259
1998	Collector's Choice	277
1998	Collector's Choice	530
1998	Collector's Choice Blowups 5x7	530
1998	Collector's Choice Cover Glory 5x7	2
1998	Collector's Choice Evolution Revolution	ER28
1998	Collector's Choice Golden Jubilee 5x7	277
1998	Collector's Choice Mini Bobbing Heads	29

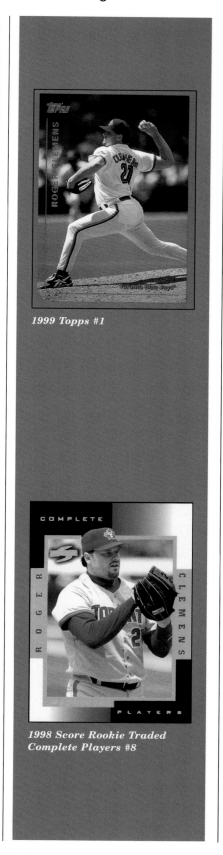

1999 Topps #1

1998 Score Rookie Traded Complete Players #8

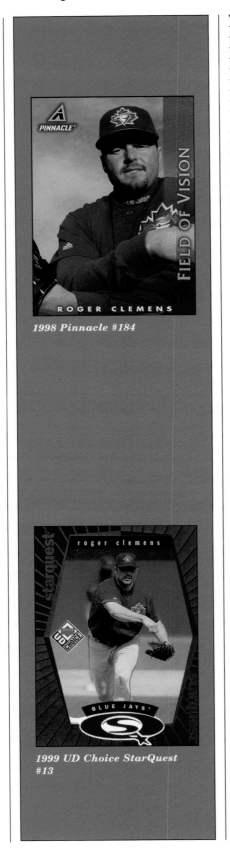

1998 Pinnacle #184

1999 UD Choice StarQuest #13

Year	Set Name	Card No.
1998	Collector's Choice Retail Jumbos	2
1998	Collector's Choice StarQuest Double	4
1998	Collector's Choice StarQuest Home Run	4
1998	Collector's Choice StarQuest Single	4
1998	Collector's Choice StarQuest Triple	4
1998	Collector's Choice Stick 'Ums	29
1998	Crown Royale	142
1998	Crown Royale Firestone on Baseball	25
1998	Crown Royale Firestone on Baseball Autographed	25
1998	Crown Royale Pillars of the Game	25
1998	Donruss	23
1998	Donruss	382
1998	Donruss	418
1998	Donruss Collections Donruss	23
1998	Donruss Collections Elite	414
1998	Donruss Collections Elite	531
1998	Donruss Collections Leaf	366
1998	Donruss Collections Preferred	565
1998	Donruss Collections Preferred	732
1998	Donruss Collections Samples	23
1998	Donruss Crusade Green	48
1998	Donruss Crusade Purple	48
1998	Donruss Crusade Red	48
1998	Donruss Diamond Kings	14
1998	Donruss Diamond Kings Canvas	14
1998	Donruss Dominators	1
1998	Donruss Elite	14
1998	Donruss Elite	131
1998	Donruss Elite Aspirations	14
1998	Donruss Elite Aspirations	131
1998	Donruss Elite Craftsmen	21
1998	Donruss Elite Master Craftsmen	21
1998	Donruss Elite Status	14
1998	Donruss Elite Status	131
1998	Donruss FANtasy Team	17
1998	Donruss FANtasy Team Die Cuts	17
1998	Donruss Gold Press Proofs	23
1998	Donruss Gold Press Proofs	382
1998	Donruss Gold Press Proofs	418
1998	Donruss Preferred	15
1998	Donruss Preferred	182
1998	Donruss Preferred Gold Boxes	14
1998	Donruss Preferred Great X-Pectations	8
1998	Donruss Preferred Great X-Pectations Die Cuts	8
1998	Donruss Preferred Great X-Pectations Samples	8
1998	Donruss Preferred Green Boxes	14
1998	Donruss Preferred Precious Metals	15
1998	Donruss Preferred Seating	15
1998	Donruss Preferred Seating	182
1998	Donruss Preferred Tin Packs	14
1998	Donruss Preferred Tin Packs Double-Wide	7
1998	Donruss Preferred Tin Packs Gold	14
1998	Donruss Preferred Tin Packs Silver	14
1998	Donruss Preferred Title Waves	3
1998	Donruss Prized Collections Donruss	23
1998	Donruss Prized Collections Elite	414
1998	Donruss Prized Collections Elite	531
1998	Donruss Prized Collections Leaf	366
1998	Donruss Prized Collections Preferred	565
1998	Donruss Prized Collections Preferred	732
1998	Donruss Signature	21
1998	Donruss Signature Autographs Century	25
1998	Donruss Signature Autographs Millenium	25
1998	Donruss Signature Proofs	21
1998	Donruss Silver Press Proofs	23
1998	Donruss Silver Press Proofs	382
1998	Donruss Silver Press Proofs	418
1998	E-X2001	4
1998	E-X2001 Destination Cooperstown	4
1998	E-X2001 Essential Credentials Future	4
1998	E-X2001 Essential Credentials Now	4
1998	Finest	40
1998	Finest Mystery Finest 2	M9
1998	Finest Mystery Finest 2	M11

Year	Set Name	Card No.
1998	Finest Mystery Finest 2	M12
1998	Finest Mystery Finest 2	M34
1998	Finest Mystery Finest 2 Refractors	M9
1998	Finest Mystery Finest 2 Refractors	M11
1998	Finest Mystery Finest 2 Refractors	M12
1998	Finest Mystery Finest 2 Refractors	M34
1998	Finest No-Protectors	40
1998	Finest No-Protectors Refractors	40
1998	Finest Oversize	A7
1998	Finest Oversize Refractors	A7
1998	Finest Refractors	40
1998	Finest The Man	TM19
1998	Finest The Man Refractors	TM19
1998	Flair Showcase Legacy Collection	21
1998	Flair Showcase Legacy Collection Masterpieces	21
1998	Flair Showcase Perfect 10	10
1998	Flair Showcase Row 0	21
1998	Flair Showcase Row 1	21
1998	Flair Showcase Row 2	21
1998	Flair Showcase Row 3	21
1998	Fleer	21
1998	Fleer	301
1998	Fleer	311
1998	Fleer	579
1998	Fleer Decade of Excellence	3
1998	Fleer Decade of Excellence Rare Traditions	3
1998	Fleer Diamond Ink	2
1998	Fleer Diamond Skills Commemorative Sheet	NNO
1998	Fleer Diamond Standouts	3
1998	Fleer Diamond Tribute	DT2
1998	Fleer In The Clutch	IC3
1998	Fleer Power Game	5
1998	Fleer Update	U3
1998	Fleer Vintage '63	62
1998	Fleer Vintage '63 Classic	62
1998	Fleer Zone	3
1998	Leaf	167
1998	Leaf Crusade Green	48
1998	Leaf Crusade Purple	48
1998	Leaf Crusade Red	48
1998	Leaf Fractal Diamond Axis	167
1998	Leaf Fractal Foundations	167
1998	Leaf Fractal Materials	167
1998	Leaf Fractal Materials Die Cuts	167
1998	Leaf Fractal Materials Samples	167
1998	Leaf Fractal Materials Z2 Axis	167
1998	Leaf Fractal Matrix	167
1998	Leaf Fractal Matrix Die Cuts	167
1998	Leaf Heading for the Hall	6
1998	Leaf Heading for the Hall Samples	6
1998	Leaf Rookies and Stars	40
1998	Leaf Rookies and Stars	158
1998	Leaf Rookies and Stars Extreme Measures	7
1998	Leaf Rookies and Stars Extreme Measures Die Cuts	7
1998	Leaf Rookies and Stars Great American Heroes	12
1998	Leaf Rookies and Stars Great American Heroes Samples	12
1998	Leaf Rookies and Stars Leaf MVP's	9
1998	Leaf Rookies and Stars Leaf MVP's Pennant Edition	9
1998	Leaf Rookies and Stars Longevity	40
1998	Leaf Rookies and Stars Longevity	158
1998	Leaf Rookies and Stars Longevity Holographic	40
1998	Leaf Rookies and Stars Longevity Holographic	158
1998	Leaf Rookies and Stars Standing Ovations	8
1998	Leaf Rookies and Stars Standing Ovations Samples	8
1998	Leaf Rookies and Stars Ticket Masters	14
1998	Leaf Rookies and Stars Ticket Masters Die Cuts	14
1998	Leaf Rookies and Stars True Blue	40

Year	Set Name	Card No.
1998	Leaf Rookies and Stars True Blue	158
1998	Metal Universe	167
1998	Metal Universe	205
1998	Metal Universe Precious Metal Gems	167
1998	Metal Universe Precious Metal Gems	205
1998	Pacific	215
1998	Pacific Aurora	92
1998	Pacific Aurora Hardball Cel-Fusions	19
1998	Pacific Aurora Pennant Fever	21
1998	Pacific Aurora Pennant Fever Copper	21
1998	Pacific Aurora Pennant Fever Platinum Blue	21
1998	Pacific Aurora Pennant Fever Red	21
1998	Pacific Aurora Pennant Fever Silver	21
1998	Pacific Cramer's Choice	10
1998	Pacific Gold Crown Die Cuts	35
1998	Pacific Invincible	73
1998	Pacific Invincible Cramer's Choice Dark Blue	10
1998	Pacific Invincible Cramer's Choice Gold	10
1998	Pacific Invincible Cramer's Choice Green	10
1998	Pacific Invincible Cramer's Choice Light Blue	10
1998	Pacific Invincible Cramer's Choice Purple	10
1998	Pacific Invincible Cramer's Choice Red	10
1998	Pacific Invincible Gems of the Diamond	110
1998	Pacific Invincible Interleague Players	14A
1998	Pacific Invincible Photoengravings	17
1998	Pacific Invincible Platinum Blue	73
1998	Pacific Invincible Silver	73
1998	Pacific Invincible Team Checklists	28
1998	Pacific Omega	245
1998	Pacific Omega Face To Face	4
1998	Pacific Omega Online Inserts	19
1998	Pacific Omega Red	245
1998	Pacific Online	755
1998	Pacific Online	780
1998	Pacific Online Red	755
1998	Pacific Online Red	780
1998	Pacific Online Web Cards	755
1998	Pacific Online Web Cards	780
1998	Pacific Paramount	111
1998	Pacific Paramount Copper	111
1998	Pacific Paramount Gold	111
1998	Pacific Paramount Holographic Silver	111
1998	Pacific Paramount Inaugural	42
1998	Pacific Paramount Platinum Blue	111
1998	Pacific Paramount Red	111
1998	Pacific Paramount Team Checklists	14
1998	Pacific Platinum Blue	215
1998	Pacific Red Threatt	215
1998	Pacific Silver	215
1998	Pacific Team Checklists	14
1998	Pinnacle	184
1998	Pinnacle Artist's Proofs	PP87
1998	Pinnacle Epix	E16
1998	Pinnacle Epix Game Emerald	E17
1998	Pinnacle Epix Game Orange	E17
1998	Pinnacle Epix Game Purple	E17
1998	Pinnacle Epix Moment Emerald	E17
1998	Pinnacle Epix Moment Orange	E17
1998	Pinnacle Epix Moment Purple	E17
1998	Pinnacle Epix Player Emerald	E17
1998	Pinnacle Epix Player Orange	E17
1998	Pinnacle Epix Player Purple	E17
1998	Pinnacle Epix Season Emerald	E17
1998	Pinnacle Epix Season Orange	E17
1998	Pinnacle Epix Season Purple	E17
1998	Pinnacle Inside	86
1998	Pinnacle Inside Behind the Numbers	13
1998	Pinnacle Inside Cans	1
1998	Pinnacle Inside Cans Gold	1
1998	Pinnacle Inside Club Edition	86
1998	Pinnacle Inside Diamond Edition	86
1998	Pinnacle Inside Stand-Up Guys	12AB
1998	Pinnacle Inside Stand-Up Guys	12CD
1998	Pinnacle Inside Stand-Up Guys Samples	12AB
1998	Pinnacle Inside Stand-Up Guys Samples	12CD
1998	Pinnacle Mint	5
1998	Pinnacle Mint Bronze	5
1998	Pinnacle Mint Coins Brass	5
1998	Pinnacle Mint Coins Brass Artist's Proofs	5
1998	Pinnacle Mint Coins Gold Plated	5
1998	Pinnacle Mint Coins Gold Plated Artist's Proofs	5
1998	Pinnacle Mint Coins Nickel	5
1998	Pinnacle Mint Coins Nickel Artist's Proofs	5
1998	Pinnacle Mint Coins Solid Gold Redemption	5
1998	Pinnacle Mint Coins Solid Silver	5
1998	Pinnacle Mint Gold	5
1998	Pinnacle Mint Mint Gems	3
1998	Pinnacle Mint Mint Gems Coins	3
1998	Pinnacle Mint Silver	5
1998	Pinnacle Museum Collection	PP87
1998	Pinnacle Performers	15
1998	Pinnacle Performers Peak Performers	15
1998	Pinnacle Plus	6
1998	Pinnacle Plus	194
1998	Pinnacle Plus All-Star Epix	16
1998	Pinnacle Plus All-Star Epix Emerald	16
1998	Pinnacle Plus All-Star Epix Purple	16
1998	Pinnacle Plus Artist's Proofs	PP3
1998	Pinnacle Plus Gold Artist's Proofs	PP3
1998	Pinnacle Plus Lasting Memories	7
1998	Pinnacle Plus Mirror Artist's Proofs	PP3
1998	Pinnacle Plus Team Pinnacle	12
1998	Pinnacle Plus Team Pinnacle Gold	12
1998	Pinnacle Plus Team Pinnacle Mirror	12
1998	Pinnacle Power Pack Jumbos	3
1998	Pinnacle Power Pack Jumbos Samples	3
1998	Pinnacle Press Plates	184
1998	Pinnacle Press Plates	E16
1998	Pinnacle Press Plates	S8
1998	Pinnacle Press Plates	S9
1998	Pinnacle Press Plates	S10
1998	Pinnacle Press Plates	S11
1998	Pinnacle Press Plates	S12
1998	Pinnacle Press Plates	S13
1998	Pinnacle Spellbound	8
1998	Pinnacle Spellbound	9
1998	Pinnacle Spellbound	10
1998	Pinnacle Spellbound	11
1998	Pinnacle Spellbound	12
1998	Pinnacle Spellbound	13
1998	Pinnacle Uncut	184
1998	Revolution	148
1998	Revolution Shadow Series	148
1998	Revolution Showstoppers	20
1998	Score	49
1998	Score All Score Team	17
1998	Score Artist's Proofs	PP131
1998	Score Epix	E16
1998	Score First Pitch	15
1998	Score Rookie Traded	8
1998	Score Rookie Traded Artist's Proofs	PP8
1998	Score Rookie Traded Artist's Proofs 1 of 1's	PP8
1998	Score Rookie Traded Complete Players	8A
1998	Score Rookie Traded Complete Players	8B
1998	Score Rookie Traded Complete Players	8C
1998	Score Rookie Traded Complete Players Samples	8A
1998	Score Rookie Traded Complete Players Samples	8B
1998	Score Rookie Traded Complete Players Samples	8C
1998	Score Rookie Traded Showcase Series	PP8
1998	Score Showcase Series	PP131
1998	SkyBox Dugout Axcess	88
1998	SkyBox Dugout Axcess	138
1998	SkyBox Dugout Axcess Autograph Redemptions	2
1998	SkyBox Dugout Axcess Dishwashers	D8
1998	SkyBox Dugout Axcess Inside Axcess	88
1998	SkyBox Dugout Axcess Inside Axcess	138
1998	SP Authentic	195
1998	SP Authentic Chirography	RC
1998	SP Authentic Sheer Dominance	SD35
1998	SP Authentic Sheer Dominance Gold	SD35
1998	SP Authentic Sheer Dominance Titanium	SD35
1998	Sports Illustrated	26
1998	Sports Illustrated	179
1998	Sports Illustrated	193
1998	Sports Illustrated Extra Edition	26
1998	Sports Illustrated Extra Edition	179
1998	Sports Illustrated Extra Edition	193
1998	Sports Illustrated First Edition	26
1998	Sports Illustrated First Edition	179
1998	Sports Illustrated First Edition	193
1998	Sports Illustrated Opening Day Mini Posters	OD30
1998	Sports Illustrated Then and Now	53
1998	Sports Illustrated Then and Now	72
1998	Sports Illustrated Then and Now Autograph Redemptions	1
1998	Sports Illustrated Then and Now Autographs	1
1998	Sports Illustrated Then and Now Covers	C8
1998	Sports Illustrated Then and Now Extra Edition	53
1998	Sports Illustrated Then and Now Extra Edition	72
1998	Sports Illustrated Then and Now Road to Cooperstown	RC2
1998	Sports Illustrated World Series Fever	52
1998	Sports Illustrated World Series Fever Extra Edition	52
1998	Sports Illustrated World Series Fever First Edition	52
1998	Sports Illustrated World Series Fever Reggie Jackson's Picks	9
1998	SPx Finite	140
1998	SPx Finite	170
1998	SPx Finite	180
1998	SPx Finite	213
1998	SPx Finite Radiance	140
1998	SPx Finite Radiance	170
1998	SPx Finite Radiance	180
1998	SPx Finite Radiance	213
1998	SPx Finite Spectrum	140
1998	SPx Finite Spectrum	170
1998	SPx Finite Spectrum	180
1998	SPx Finite Spectrum	213
1998	Stadium Club	101
1998	Stadium Club Co-Signers	CS31
1998	Stadium Club Co-Signers	CS32
1998	Stadium Club Co-Signers	CS33
1998	Stadium Club First Day Issue	101
1998	Stadium Club Never Compromise	NC9
1998	Stadium Club One Of A Kind	101
1998	Stadium Club Printing Plates	101
1998	Studio	202
1998	Studio Freeze Frame	25
1998	Studio Freeze Frame Die Cuts	25
1998	Studio Gold Press Proofs	202
1998	Studio Masterstrokes	5
1998	Studio Portraits 8 x 10	21
1998	Studio Portraits 8 x 10 Gold Proofs	21
1998	Studio Silver Press Proofs	202
1998	Topps	300
1998	Topps	475
1998	Topps Chrome	300
1998	Topps Chrome	475
1998	Topps Chrome HallBound	HB4
1998	Topps Chrome HallBound Refractors	HB4
1998	Topps Chrome Milestones	MS2
1998	Topps Chrome Milestones Refractors	MS2
1998	Topps Chrome Refractors	300
1998	Topps Chrome Refractors	475
1998	Topps Devil Rays	300
1998	Topps Devil Rays	475
1998	Topps Diamondbacks	300
1998	Topps Diamondbacks	475
1998	Topps Focal Points	FP9
1998	Topps Gallery	40
1998	Topps Gallery Awards Gallery	AG3

Trading Card Checklist

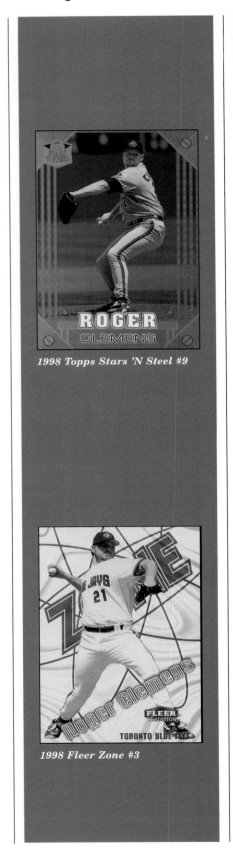

1998 Topps Stars 'N Steel #9

1998 Fleer Zone #3

Year	Set Name	Card No.
1998	Topps Gallery Gallery Proofs	40
1998	Topps Gallery Original Printing Plates	40
1998	Topps Gallery Player's Private Issue	40
1998	Topps Gallery Player's Private Issue Auction	40
1998	Topps Gold Label Class 1	21
1998	Topps Gold Label Class 1 Black	21
1998	Topps Gold Label Class 1 One to One	21
1998	Topps Gold Label Class 1 Red	21
1998	Topps Gold Label Class 2	21
1998	Topps Gold Label Class 2 Black	21
1998	Topps Gold Label Class 2 One to One	21
1998	Topps Gold Label Class 2 Red	21
1998	Topps Gold Label Class 3	21
1998	Topps Gold Label Class 3 Black	21
1998	Topps Gold Label Class 3 One to One	21
1998	Topps Gold Label Class 3 Red	21
1998	Topps HallBound	HB4
1998	Topps Milestones	MS2
1998	Topps Minted in Cooperstown	300
1998	Topps Minted in Cooperstown	475
1998	Topps Opening Day	127
1998	Topps Stars	136
1998	Topps Stars 'N Steel	9
1998	Topps Stars 'N Steel Gold	9
1998	Topps Stars 'N Steel Gold Holographic	9
1998	Topps Stars Bronze	136
1998	Topps Stars Gold	136
1998	Topps Stars Gold Rainbow	136
1998	Topps Stars Silver	136
1998	Topps SuperChrome	20
1998	Topps SuperChrome Refractors	20
1998	Topps Tek	21
1998	Topps Tek Diffractors	21
1998	Topps Tek Pre-Production	21
1998	UD3	80
1998	UD3	170
1998	UD3	260
1998	UD3 Die Cuts	80
1998	UD3 Die Cuts	170
1998	UD3 Die Cuts	260
1998	Ultra	3
1998	Ultra	213
1998	Ultra	492
1998	Ultra Diamond Immortals	14
1998	Ultra Double Trouble	19
1998	Ultra Gold Medallion	3
1998	Ultra Gold Medallion	213
1998	Ultra Gold Medallion	492
1998	Ultra Masterpieces	3
1998	Ultra Masterpieces	213
1998	Ultra Masterpieces	492
1998	Ultra Platinum Medallion	3
1998	Ultra Platinum Medallion	213
1998	Ultra Platinum Medallion	492
1998	Ultra Top 30	9
1998	Ultra Win Now	18
1998	Upper Deck	17
1998	Upper Deck	137
1998	Upper Deck	451
1998	Upper Deck	530
1998	Upper Deck	534
1998	Upper Deck	603
1998	Upper Deck 10th Anniversary Preview	3
1998	Upper Deck 10th Anniversary Preview Retail	3
1998	Upper Deck 5 x 7 Blow Ups	530
1998	Upper Deck All-Star Credentials	AS21
1998	Upper Deck Amazing Greats	AG21
1998	Upper Deck Amazing Greats Die Cuts	AG21
1998	Upper Deck Clearly Dominant	CD21
1998	Upper Deck Retro	99
1998	Upper Deck Retro Quantum Leap	Q11
1998	Upper Deck Retro Time Capsule	TC26
1998	Upper Deck Retrospectives	9
1998	Upper Deck Special F/X	10
1998	Upper Deck Unparalleled	9
1998	Zenith	32
1998	Zenith 5 x 7	45
1998	Zenith 5 x 7 Gold Impulse	45
1998	Zenith 5 x 7 Impulse	45
1998	Zenith Epix	E16
1998	Zenith Z-Gold	32
1998	Zenith Z-Silver	32
1998	Zenith Z-Team	9
1998	Zenith Z-Team 5 x 7	9
1998	Zenith Z-Team Gold	9
1999	Aurora	195
1999	Finest	80
1999	Finest	111
1999	Finest Gold Refractors	80
1999	Finest Gold Refractors	111
1999	Finest Peel and Reveal Common	11
1999	Finest Peel and Reveal Rare	11
1999	Finest Peel and Reveal Uncommon	11
1999	Finest Refractors	80
1999	Finest Refractors	111
1999	Finest Split Screen	S10
1999	Finest Split Screen Dual Refractors	S10
1999	Finest Team Finest Blue	TF7
1999	Finest Team Finest Blue Refractors	TF7
1999	Finest Team Finest Gold	TF7
1999	Finest Team Finest Gold Refractors	TF7
1999	Finest Team Finest Red	TF7
1999	Finest Team Finest Red Refractors	TF7
1999	Fleer	30
1999	Fleer Date With Destiny	2
1999	Fleer Diamond Magic	2
1999	Fleer Golden Memories	3
1999	Fleer Starting 9	30
1999	Fleer Vintage '61	30
1999	Fleer Warning Track	30
1999	Metal Universe	206
1999	Metal Universe	296
1999	Metal Universe Gem Masters	206
1999	Metal Universe Gem Masters	296
1999	Metal Universe Precious Metal Gems	206
1999	Metal Universe Precious Metal Gems	296
1999	Pacific	436
1999	Pacific	436A
1999	Pacific Crown Collection	292
1999	Pacific Crown Collection Platinum Blue	292
1999	Pacific Gold Crown Die Cuts	19
1999	Pacific Paramount	158
1999	Pacific Paramount Copper	158
1999	Pacific Paramount Holographic Silver	158
1999	Pacific Paramount Personal Bests	22
1999	Pacific Paramount Platinum Blue	158
1999	Pacific Paramount Team Checklists	20
1999	Pacific Platinum Blue	436
1999	Pacific Platinum Blue	436A
1999	Pacific Prism	147
1999	Pacific Prism Holographic Blue	147
1999	Pacific Prism Holographic Gold	147
1999	Pacific Prism Holographic Mirror	147
1999	Pacific Prism Holographic Purple	147
1999	Pacific Private Stock	2
1999	Pacific Private Stock Exclusive	2
1999	Pacific Private Stock Platinum	2
1999	Pacific Private Stock Preferred	2
1999	Pacific Private Stock PS-206	2
1999	Pacific Private Stock PS-206 Red	2
1999	Pacific Private Stock Vintage	2
1999	Pacific Red	436
1999	Pacific Red	436A
1999	Pacific Team Checklists	14
1999	Pacific Timelines	11
1999	SkyBox Thunder	265
1999	SkyBox Thunder In Depth	ID3
1999	SkyBox Thunder Rant	265
1999	SkyBox Thunder Rave	265
1999	SkyBox Thunder Super Rave	265
1999	SP Authentic	60
1999	SP Authentic Reflections	R30
1999	Sports Illustrated	14
1999	Sports Illustrated	15

Year	Set Name	Card No.
1999	Sports Illustrated	16
1999	Sports Illustrated	19
1999	Sports Illustrated	23
1999	Sports Illustrated	162
1999	Sports Illustrated Diamond Dominators	2
1999	Sports Illustrated Headliners	15
1999	Stadium Club	96
1999	Stadium Club First Day Issue	96
1999	Stadium Club Never Compromise	NC8
1999	Stadium Club One of a Kind	96
1999	Stadium Club Printing Plates	96
1999	Topps	1
1999	Topps	203
1999	Topps	232
1999	Topps Autographs	A1
1999	Topps Chrome	1
1999	Topps Chrome	203
1999	Topps Chrome	232
1999	Topps Chrome Refractors	1
1999	Topps Chrome Refractors	203
1999	Topps Chrome Refractors	232
1999	Topps MVP Promotion	1
1999	Topps Opening Day	2
1999	Topps Opening Day	161
1999	Topps Oversize	1
1999	Topps Power Brokers	PB19
1999	Topps Power Brokers Refractors	PB19
1999	Topps Pre-Production	PP1
1999	Topps Stars 'N Steel	12
1999	Topps Stars 'N Steel Gold	12
1999	Topps Stars 'N Steel Gold Domed Holographic	12
1999	Topps SuperChrome	1
1999	Topps SuperChrome	32
1999	Topps SuperChrome Refractors	1
1999	Topps SuperChrome Refractors	32
1999	UD Choice	41
1999	UD Choice	155
1999	UD Choice Blow Up	5
1999	UD Choice Blow Up Cover Glory	8
1999	UD Choice Prime Choice Reserve	41
1999	UD Choice Prime Choice Reserve	155
1999	UD Choice StarQuest	13
1999	UD Choice StarQuest Double	13
1999	UD Choice StarQuest Home Run	13
1999	UD Choice StarQuest Triple	13
1999	UD Ionix	59
1999	UD Ionix	89
1999	UD Ionix Cyber	C15
1999	UD Ionix Hyper	H15
1999	UD Ionix Reciprocal	59
1999	UD Ionix Reciprocal	89
1999	Ultra	190
1999	Ultra Gold Medallion	190
1999	Ultra Masterpieces	190
1999	Ultra Platinum Medallion	190
1999	Upper Deck	223
1999	Upper Deck 10th Anniversary Team	X30
1999	Upper Deck 10th Anniversary Team Double	X30
1999	Upper Deck 10th Anniversary Team Home Run	X30
1999	Upper Deck 10th Anniversary Team Triple	X30
1999	Upper Deck Black Diamond	88
1999	Upper Deck Black Diamond Dominance	D21
1999	Upper Deck Black Diamond Dominance Emerald	D21
1999	Upper Deck Black Diamond Double	88
1999	Upper Deck Black Diamond Mystery Numbers	M10
1999	Upper Deck Black Diamond Mystery Numbers Emerald	M10
1999	Upper Deck Black Diamond Quadruple	88
1999	Upper Deck Black Diamond Triple	88
1999	Upper Deck Crowning Glory	CG1
1999	Upper Deck Crowning Glory Double	CG1
1999	Upper Deck Crowning Glory Home Run	CG1
1999	Upper Deck Crowning Glory Triple	CG1
1999	Upper Deck Exclusives Level 1	223
1999	Upper Deck Exclusives Level 2	223
1999	Upper Deck Immaculate Perception	I4
1999	Upper Deck Immaculate Perception Double	I4
1999	Upper Deck Immaculate Perception +Home Run	I4
1999	Upper Deck Immaculate Perception Triple	I4
1999	Upper Deck Ovation	47
1999	Upper Deck Ovation Curtain Calls	R5
1999	Upper Deck Ovation Major Production	S20
1999	Upper Deck Ovation Standing Ovation	47
1999	Upper Deck Wonder Years	W5
1999	Upper Deck Wonder Years Double	W5
1999	Upper Deck Wonder Years Home Run	W5
1999	Upper Deck Wonder Years Triple	W5

Bucky Dent

Year	Set Name	Card No.
1974	O-Pee-Chee	582
1974	Topps	582
1975	O-Pee-Chee	299
1975	SSPC Puzzle Back	8
1975	Topps	299
1975	Topps Mini	299
1976	Hostess	119
1976	O-Pee-Chee	154
1976	SSPC	143
1976	Topps	154
1977	Burger Chef Discs	81
1977	Hostess	91
1977	O-Pee-Chee	122
1977	Topps	29
1977	Yankees Burger King	14
1978	Kellogg's	2
1978	O-Pee-Chee	164
1978	SSPC 270	24
1978	Topps	335
1978	Yankees Burger King	15
1978	Yankees Photo Album	6
1978	Yankees SSPC Diary	24
1979	Hostess	131
1979	O-Pee-Chee	254
1979	Topps	485
1979	Yankees Burger King	14
1979	Yankees Picture Album	9
1980	O-Pee-Chee	33
1980	Topps	60
1980	Yankees Photo Album	5
1981	All-Star Game Program Inserts	21
1981	Donruss	465
1981	Fleer	80
1981	Fleer Sticker Cards	110
1981	Kellogg's	7
1981	MSA Mini Discs	11
1981	O-Pee-Chee	164
1981	Perma-Graphic All-Stars	12
1981	Topps	650
1981	Topps Stickers	110
1981	Topps Super Home Team	62
1981	Yankees Photo Album	4
1982	Donruss	209
1982	Fleer	33
1982	Fleer	629
1982	O-Pee-Chee	240
1982	O-Pee-Chee	241
1982	O-Pee-Chee	298
1982	On Deck Discs	11
1982	Topps	240
1982	Topps	241
1982	Topps	550
1982	Yankees Photo Album	5
1983	Fleer	566
1983	O-Pee-Chee	279
1983	Rangers Affiliated Food	7
1983	Topps	565

Year	Set Name	Card No.
1983	Topps/O-Pee-Chee Stickers	122
1984	Donruss	300
1984	Fleer	417
1984	Nestle 792	331
1984	O-Pee-Chee	331
1984	Topps	331
1984	Topps Tiffany	331
1984	Topps/O-Pee-Chee Stickers	362
1987	Columbus Clippers Police	6
1987	Columbus Clippers ProCards	1
1987	Columbus Clippers TCMA	23
1988	Columbus Clippers CMC	25
1988	Columbus Clippers Police	25
1988	Columbus Clippers ProCards	306
1989	Columbus Clippers CMC	25
1989	Columbus Clippers Police	25
1989	Columbus Clippers ProCards	755
1989	Columbus Clippers ProCards	757
1989	Swell Baseball Greats	72
1989	Triple A All-Stars ProCards	AAA21
1990	O-Pee-Chee	519
1990	Topps	519
1990	Topps Tiffany	519
1990	Topps TV Yankees	1
1992	Yankees WIZ 70s	43
1992	Yankees WIZ 80s	43
1992	Yankees WIZ All-Stars	16
1993	Rangers Keebler	124
1993	Upper Deck All-Time Heroes	40
1994	Upper Deck All-Time Heroes	18
1994	Upper Deck All-Time Heroes	28
1994	Upper Deck All-Time Heroes 125th	18
1994	Upper Deck All-Time Heroes 125th	28
1995	Rangers Crayola	7
1996	Rangers Dr Pepper	6
1996	Rangers Mother's	28
1997	Rangers Dr Pepper	6
1997	Rangers Mother's	28
1997-98	Fleer Million Dollar Moments	43
1997-98	Fleer Million Dollar Moments Redemption	43
1998	Sports Illustrated World Series Fever	24
1998	Sports Illustrated World Series Fever Extra Edition	24
1998	Sports Illustrated World Series Fever First Edition	24

Bill Dickey

Year	Set Name	Card No.
1930	Schutter-Johnson R332	11
1931-32	Exhibits Four-in-One	25
1932	U.S. Caramel R328	6
1933	Butterfinger Canadian V94	13
1933	Exhibits Four-in-One	13
1933	George C. Miller R300	9
1933	Goudey Canadian V353	19
1933	Goudey R319	19
1933	Tatoo Orbit Self Develop R308	161
1934	Baby Ruth Gum	16
1934	Butterfinger Premiums R310	16
1934	Exhibits Four-in-One W463-4	13
1934-36	Batter-Up R318	30
1934-36	Batter-Up R318	117
1934-36	Diamond Stars R327	11
1934-36	Diamond Stars R327	103
1935	Exhibits Four-in-One W463-5	13
1935	Goudey Puzzle R321	4D
1935	Goudey Puzzle R321	7D
1935	Goudey Puzzle R321	12D
1936	Goudey Wide Pen Premiums R314	A27
1936	National Chicle Fine Pen Premiums R313	109
1936	R312 Pastel Photos	8
1936	S and S WG8	14
1936	Wheaties BB5	9
1936	World Wide Gum V355	34
1937	O-Pee-Chee Batter Ups V300	119

Trading Card Checklist

Year	Set Name	Card No.
1937	Wheaties BB6	1
1938	Baseball Tabs	6
1938	Clopay Foto-Fun R329	22
1938	Exhibits Four-in-One	13
1939	Goudey Premiums R303A	12
1939	Goudey Premiums R303B	5
1939	Play Ball R334	30
1939	World Wide Gum Trimmed Premiums V351B	12
1939-46	Exhibits Salutation	12A
1939-46	Exhibits Salutation	12B
1940	Play Ball R335	7
1940	Wheaties M4	3
1941	Double Play R330	65
1941	Play Ball R336	70
1943	MP and Co. R302-1	8
1943	Yankees Stamps	8
1946-49	Sports Exchange W603	1-1B
1947-66	PM10 Stadium Pins 1 3/4'	42
1948	Swell Sport Thrills	6
1949	Yankees Team Issue	7
1950	Yankees Team Issue	8
1950-56	Callahan HOF W576	26
1951	Bowman	290
1951	R423 Small Strip	22
1952	Topps	400
1953-63	Artvue Hall of Fame Postcards	28
1960	Nu-Card Hi-Lites	34
1960	Topps	465
1961	Golden Press	27
1961	Nu-Card Scoops	434
1963	Bazooka ATG	40
1963	Hall of Fame Busts	4
1967	Topps Venezuelan	140
1968	SCFS Old Timers	7
1968	Sports Memorabilia All-Time Greats	8
1968	Yankees Photos SCFC	84
1972	TCMA's the 30's	19
1973	Seven-Eleven Trading Cups	18
1975	TCMA Guam	9
1975	Yankee Dynasty 1936-39 TCMA	12
1975	Yankee Dynasty 1936-39 TCMA	51
1975	Yankees All-Time Team TCMA	1
1976	Rowe Exhibits	4
1976	Shakey's Pizza	71
1977	Shakey's Pizza	9
1977	TCMA The War Years	55
1977-84	Galasso Glossy Greats	68
1977-84	Galasso Glossy Greats	188
1980	Marchant Exhibits HOF	9
1980	Yankees Greats TCMA	8
1980-83	Pacific Legends	44
1980-87	SSPC HOF	71
1980-96	Perez-Steele Hall of Fame Postcards	71
1981	San Diego Sports Collectors	18
1981	San Diego Sports Collectors	19
1982	Diamond Classics	23
1982	TCMA Greatest Hitters	38
1983	Big League Collectibles Original All-Stars	15
1983	Conlon Marketcom	9
1983	Donruss HOF Heroes	26
1983	TCMA Playball 1942	3
1983	Topps Reprint 52	400
1983	Yankee A-S Fifty Years	9
1983	Yankee Yearbook Insert TCMA	10
1985	Feg Murray's Cartoon Greats	4
1986	Sportflics Decade Greats	13
1986	TCMA	16
1987	Hygrade All-Time Greats	14
1988	Conlon American All-Stars	8
1989	Perez-Steele Celebration Postcards	12
1990	Yankees Monument Park Rini Postcards	7
1990-97	Perez-Steele Great Moments	37
1992	Conlon TSN	474
1992	Megacards Ruth	158
1992	Yankees WIZ All-Stars	17
1992	Yankees WIZ HOF	8
1993	Conlon TSN	755
1993	Conlon TSN	869
1994	Conlon TSN	1086
1994	Conlon TSN Burgundy	1086
1994	Conlon TSN Color Inserts	36
1995	Conlon TSN Prototypes	1475
1995	Megacards Ruth	5

Whitey Ford

Year	Set Name	Card No.
1947-65	PM10 Stadium Pins 2 1/8'	14
1947-66	Exhibits	73A
1947-66	Exhibits	73B
1947-66	Exhibits	73C
1947-66	PM10 Stadium Pins 1 3/4'	60
1951	Berk Ross	D5
1951	Bowman	1
1953	Bowman Color	153
1953	Topps	207
1953-55	Dormand	115
1954	Bowman	177
1954	New York Journal American	46
1954	Red Man	AL16
1954	Topps	37
1955	Armour Coins	6
1955	Bowman	59
1955	Red Man	AL3
1956	Topps	240
1956	Yankees Jay Publishing	6
1956	Yankees Team Issue	8
1957	Topps	25
1957	Yankees Jay Publishing	5
1958	Jay Publishing All-Stars	5
1958	Topps	320
1958	Yankees Jay Publishing	4
1959	Armour Coins	8
1959	Topps	430
1959	Yoo-Hoo	2
1960	Armour Coins	10
1960	Topps	35
1960	Topps Tattoos	15
1960	Topps Venezuelan	35
1960	Yankees Jay Publishing	3
1961	Post	6A
1961	Post	6B
1961	Topps	160
1961	Topps	311
1961	Topps	586
1961	Topps Stamps Inserts	193
1961	Yankees Jay Publishing	4
1962	Bazooka	41
1962	Exhibit Stat Back	11
1962	Jello	9
1962	Post	9
1962	Post Canadian	9A
1962	Post Canadian	9B
1962	Salada Plastic Coins	8
1962	Shirriff Plastic Coins	8
1962	Topps	57
1962	Topps	59
1962	Topps	235
1962	Topps	310
1962	Topps	315
1962	Topps	475
1962	Topps Bucks	26
1962	Topps Stamps Inserts	85
1962	Topps Venezuelan	57
1962	Topps Venezuelan	59
1962	Yankees Jay Publishing	6
1963	Baseball Magazine M118	25
1963	Exhibit Stat Back	22
1963	Jello	19
1963	Post	19
1963	Topps	6
1963	Topps	142
1963	Topps	446
1963	Yankees Jay Publishing	3
1963-67	Yankee Requena K Postcards	7
1964	Auravision Records	6
1964	Challenge The Yankees	8
1964	Topps	4
1964	Topps	380
1964	Topps Coins Inserts	139
1964	Topps Giants	7
1964	Topps Venezuelan	4
1964	Wheaties Stamps	15
1964	Yankees Jay Publishing	4
1965	Challenge The Yankees	6
1965	Topps	330
1966	Dexter Press	1
1966	O-Pee-Chee	160
1966	Topps	160
1966	Topps Rub-Offs Inserts	32
1966	Topps Venezuelan	160
1966	Yankees Team Issue	3
1967	Nassau Health Ford	1
1967	O-Pee-Chee	5
1967	Topps	5
1967	Topps Venezuelan	178
1968	Laughlin World Series	58
1970	Fleer World Series	58
1971	Fleer World Series	59
1974	New York News This Day in Sports	18
1974	Syracuse Chiefs Team Issue	30
1975	SSPC 42	33
1975	Syracuse Chiefs Team Issue	5
1975	TCMA All-Time Greats	10
1975	Yankees All-Time Team TCMA	3
1976	Galasso Baseball's Great Hall of Fame	9
1976	Shakey's Pizza	144
1976	UPI Superstars	3
1977-84	Galasso Glossy Greats	25
1978	TCMA 60'S I	21
1979	Baseball Greats	73
1980	Yankees Greats TCMA	10
1980-87	SSPC HOF	144
1980-96	Perez-Steele Hall of Fame Postcards	144
1981	TCMA 60's II	450
1982	Cracker Jack	3
1982	TCMA Greatest Pitchers	3
1983	Diamond Classics Series 2	83
1983	MLBPA Pins	7
1983	Tigers Al Kaline Story	16
1983	Yankee A-S Fifty Years	13
1983	Yankee A-S Fifty Years	14
1983	Yankee Yearbook Insert TCMA	17
1983	Yankees 1961	11
1984	ASA Willie Mays 90	24
1984	Fifth National Convention Tickets	6
1984-89	O'Connell and Son Ink	5
1985	George Steinbrenner Menu	3
1985	Woolworth's	11
1986	Sportflics Decade Greats	44
1986	Sports Design J.D. McCarthy	24
1986	TCMA Superstars Simon	9
1987	Hygrade All-Time Greats	17
1987	Nestle Dream Team	21
1987	Yankees 1961 TCMA	7
1989	Bowman Reprint Inserts	3
1989	Bowman Reprint Inserts Tiffany	3
1989	HOF Sticker Book	70
1989	Kahn's Cooperstown	4
1989	Pacific Legends II	210
1989	Swell Baseball Greats	50
1989	Topps Baseball Talk/LJN	31
1989	Yankee Citgo All-Time Greats	1
1990	AGFA	16
1990	Swell Baseball Greats	8
1990	Yankees 61 Ron Lewis	11
1990-97	Perez-Steele Great Moments	5
1991	MDA All-Stars	10
1991	Topps Archives 1953	207
1991	Yankees Rini Postcards 1961 3	10

Year	Set Name	Card No.
1992	Bazooka Quadracard '53 Archives	12
1992	Front Row Ford	1
1992	Front Row Ford	2
1992	Front Row Ford	3
1992	Front Row Ford	4
1992	Front Row Ford	5
1992	Pinnacle Mantle	25
1992	St. Vincent HOF Heroes Stamps	4
1992	Yankees WIZ 60s	42
1992	Yankees WIZ All-Stars	21
1992	Yankees WIZ HOF	10
1993	Action Packed ASG	116
1993	Action Packed ASG 24K	50G
1993	Ted Williams	62
1993	Upper Deck All-Time Heroes	52
1993	Upper Deck All-Time Heroes	140
1993	Upper Deck All-Time Heroes	152
1993	Upper Deck All-Time Heroes	158
1993	Yoo-Hoo	6
1993-97	Bleachers	9
1994	Topps Archives 1954	37
1994	Topps Archives 1954 Gold	37
1994	Upper Deck All-Time Heroes	146
1994	Upper Deck All-Time Heroes	157
1994	Upper Deck All-Time Heroes 125th	146
1994	Upper Deck All-Time Heroes 125th	157
1995	Eagle Ballpark Legends	6
1995	SP Championship	105
1995	SP Championship Die Cuts	105
1995	Upper Deck Sonic Heroes of Baseball	1
1998	Sports Illustrated World Series Fever Autumn Excellence	5
1998	Sports Illustrated World Series Fever Autumn Excellence Gold	5
1998	Topps Stars Rookie Reprints	2
1998	Topps Stars Rookie Reprints Autographs	2
1999	Topps Hall of Fame Collection	HOF8

Lefty Gomez

Year	Set Name	Card No.
1929	Zeenuts	131
1932	U.S. Caramel R328	31
1932-34	"Orbit Gum Pins ""Numbered"""	120
1933	Butterfinger Canadian V94	20
1933	Cracker Jack Pins	8
1933	Delong R333	14
1933	Goudey R319	216
1933	Tatoo Orbit Self Develop R308	151
1934	Baby Ruth Gum	27
1934	Butterfinger Premiums R310	26
1934	Exhibits Four-in-One W463-4	13
1934-36	Batter-Up R318	23
1934-36	Batter-Up R318	86
1935	Exhibits Four-in-One W463-5	13
1935	Goudey Premiums R309-2	11
1936	Exhibits Four-in-One W463-6	13
1936	Goudey B/W R322	14
1936	Goudey Wide Pen Premiums R314	A39
1936	National Chicle Fine Pen Premiums R313	32
1936	National Chicle Fine Pen Premiums R313	92
1936	R312 Pastel Photos	34
1936	Wheaties BB5	1
1936	World Wide Gum V355	56
1936-38	Overland Candy R301	18
1937	Exhibits Four-in-One W463-7	13
1938	Baseball Tabs	12
1938	Clopay Foto-Fun R329	30
1938	Exhibits Four-in-One	13
1938	Our National Game Tabs	12
1939	Goudey Premiums R303A	17
1939	Goudey Premiums R303B	9
1939	Play Ball R334	48
1939	Wheaties BB12	3
1939	World Wide Gum Trimmed Premiums V351B	17
1939-46	Exhibits Salutation	20

Year	Set Name	Card No.
1940	Play Ball R335	6
1941	Double Play R330	61
1941	Play Ball R336	72
1942	Gillette Razor Label	1
1947-66	PM10 Stadium Pins 1 3/4'	72
1948	Babe Ruth Story	24
1960	Fleer	54
1961	Fleer	34
1972	Laughlin Great Feats	18
1972	TCMA's the 30's	32
1972	TCMA's the 30's	81
1975	Shakey's Pizza	3
1975	Yankee Dynasty 1936-39 TCMA	18
1976	Rowe Exhibits	4
1976	Shakey's Pizza	129
1977-84	Galasso Glossy Greats	76
1977-84	Galasso Glossy Greats	185
1977-84	Galasso Glossy Greats	265
1979	Diamond Greats	11
1980	Marchant Exhibits HOF	13
1980-83	Pacific Legends	117
1980-87	SSPC HOF	129
1980-96	Perez-Steele Hall of Fame Postcards	129
1981	Conlon TSN	44
1981	Diamond Stars Continuation Den's	118
1982	TCMA Greatest Pitchers	20
1983	Big League Collectibles Original All-Stars	4
1983	Conlon Marketcom	22
1983	Yankee A-S Fifty Years	16
1986	Conlon Series 1	45
1986	Sportflics Decade Greats	9
1987	Conlon Series 2	2
1988	Conlon American All-Stars	12
1988	Conlon Series 5	15
1989	HOF Sticker Book	76
1989	Perez-Steele Celebration Postcards	16
1989	Yankee Citgo All-Time Greats	3
1990	Swell Baseball Greats	84
1990	Yankees Monument Park Rini Postcards	8
1990-97	Perez-Steele Great Moments	44
1991	Conlon TSN	67
1991	Homers Cookies Classics	3
1991	Swell Baseball Greats	129
1991-92	Conlon TSN Prototypes	662
1992	Conlon TSN	536
1992	Conlon TSN All-Star Program	662G
1992	Yankees WIZ All-Stars	23
1992	Yankees WIZ HOF	12
1993	Action Packed ASG	105
1993	Action Packed ASG 24K	39G
1993	Conlon TSN	662
1994	Conlon TSN	1063
1994	Conlon TSN	1088
1994	Conlon TSN Burgundy	1063
1994	Conlon TSN Burgundy	1088
1996	NoirTech Satchel Paige	12

Ron Guidry

Year	Set Name	Card No.
1976	O-Pee-Chee	599
1976	Topps	599
1977	Topps	656
1977	Yankees Burger King	11
1977-79	Sportscaster	6102
1978	Hostess	25
1978	Papa Gino's Discs	28
1978	SSPC 270	17
1978	Topps	135
1978	Yankees Burger King	4
1978	Yankees Photo Album	9
1978	Yankees SSPC Diary	17
1979	Baseball Patches	36
1979	Hostess	89
1979	Kellogg's	11
1979	O-Pee-Chee	264

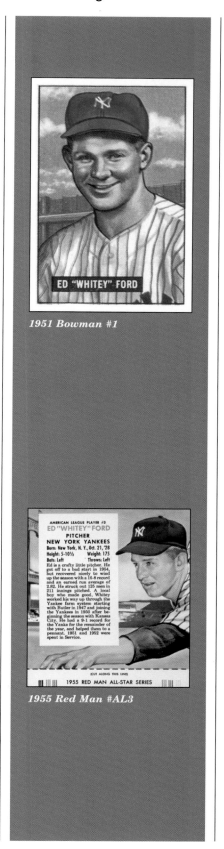

1951 Bowman #1

1955 Red Man #AL3

Trading Card Checklist

Year	Set Name	Card No.
1979	Sports Legends	4
1979	Topps	5
1979	Topps	7
1979	Topps	202
1979	Topps	500
1979	Topps Comics	13
1979	Yankees Burger King	4
1979	Yankees Picture Album	15
1980	Burger King Pitch/Hit/Run	4
1980	Kellogg's	4
1980	O-Pee-Chee	157
1980	Topps	207
1980	Topps	300
1980	Topps Super	7
1980	Yankees Photo Album	9
1981	All-Star Game Program Inserts	82
1981	Donruss	227
1981	Fleer	88
1981	Fleer Sticker Cards	76
1981	Kellogg's	45
1981	O-Pee-Chee	250
1981	Topps	250
1981	Topps Stickers	112
1981	Topps Super Home Team	64
1981	Yankees Photo Album	8
1982	Donruss	548
1982	Donruss	558
1982	Fleer	38
1982	Fleer Stamps	120
1982	Kellogg's	26
1982	O-Pee-Chee	9
1982	O-Pee-Chee	10
1982	Squirt	9
1982	Topps	9
1982	Topps	10
1982	Wilson Sporting Goods	3
1982	Yankees Photo Album	10
1983	Donruss	17
1983	Donruss	31
1983	Donruss Action All-Stars	15
1983	Fleer	383
1983	Fleer Stamps	73
1983	Fleer Stickers	47
1983	O-Pee-Chee	104
1983	Topps	440
1983	Topps/O-Pee-Chee Stickers	102
1983	Yankees Photo Album	10
1983	Yankees Roy Rogers Discs	4
1984	Donruss	173
1984	Donruss Action All-Stars	51
1984	Fleer	127
1984	Fun Foods Pins	96
1984	Milton Bradley	12
1984	MLBPA Pencils	5
1984	Nestle 792	110
1984	Nestle 792	406
1984	Nestle 792	486
1984	Nestle 792	717
1984	Nestle Dream Team	10
1984	O-Pee-Chee	110
1984	O-Pee-Chee	204
1984	Ralston Purina	31
1984	Seven-Eleven Coins	E16
1984	Topps	110
1984	Topps	406
1984	Topps	486
1984	Topps	717
1984	Topps Cereal	31
1984	Topps Glossy Send-Ins	14
1984	Topps Rub Downs	11
1984	Topps Super	17
1984	Topps Tiffany	110
1984	Topps Tiffany	406
1984	Topps Tiffany	486
1984	Topps Tiffany	717
1984	Topps/O-Pee-Chee Stickers	194
1984	Topps/O-Pee-Chee Stickers	318
1984-89	O'Connell and Son Ink	45
1985	All-Star Game Program Inserts	77
1985	Donruss	214
1985	Fleer	129
1985	Leaf/Donruss	237
1985	O-Pee-Chee	388
1985	Police Mets/Yankees	Y3
1985	Subway Discs	11
1985	Thom McAn Discs	11
1985	Topps	790
1985	Topps Rub Downs	11
1985	Topps Tiffany	790
1985	Topps/O-Pee-Chee Stickers	313
1985	Yankees TCMA Postcards	12
1986	Baseball Star Buttons	51
1986	Donruss	103
1986	Drake's	32
1986	Fleer	106
1986	Fleer Mini	22
1986	Fleer Sluggers/Pitchers	14
1986	Fleer Sticker Cards	48
1986	Leaf/Donruss	36
1986	O-Pee-Chee	109
1986	O-Pee-Chee Box Bottoms	H
1986	Seven-Eleven Coins	C6
1986	Seven-Eleven Coins	E6
1986	Seven-Eleven Coins	S6
1986	Seven-Eleven Coins	W6
1986	Sportflics	18
1986	Sportflics	59
1986	Sportflics	149
1986	Sportflics	179
1986	Sportflics	185
1986	Sportflics Decade Greats	71
1986	Topps	610
1986	Topps	721
1986	Topps 3-D	9
1986	Topps Glossy Send-Ins	12
1986	Topps Mini Leaders	26
1986	Topps Super	28
1986	Topps Tiffany	610
1986	Topps Tiffany	721
1986	Topps Wax Box Cards	H
1986	Topps/O-Pee-Chee Stickers	302
1986	Topps/O-Pee-Chee Tattoos	14
1986	Yankees TCMA	9
1987	Classic Game	68
1987	Donruss	93
1987	Fleer	100
1987	Fleer Award Winners	16
1987	Fleer Glossy	100
1987	Leaf/Donruss	101
1987	O-Pee-Chee	375
1987	Red Foley Sticker Book	54
1987	Sportflics	83
1987	Topps	375
1987	Topps Tiffany	375
1987	Topps/O-Pee-Chee Stickers	301
1988	Donruss	175
1988	Donruss Team Book Yankees	175
1988	Fleer	207
1988	Fleer Glossy	207
1988	Fleer Stickers Wax Box Cards	S3
1988	Leaf/Donruss	180
1988	O-Pee-Chee	127
1988	Score	310
1988	Score Glossy	310
1988	Starting Lineup Yankees	5
1988	Topps	535
1988	Topps Big	50
1988	Topps Tiffany	535
1988	Topps/O-Pee-Chee Sticker Backs	61
1988	Topps/O-Pee-Chee Stickers	296
1989	Score	342
1989	Topps	255
1989	Topps Baseball Talk/LJN	110
1989	Topps Tiffany	255
1989	Upper Deck	307
1989	Yankees Score Nat West	28
1990	HOF Sticker Book	97
1991	Upper Deck Sheets	16
1992	Yankees WIZ 70s	60
1992	Yankees WIZ 80s	72
1992	Yankees WIZ All-Stars	27

Elston Howard

Year	Set Name	Card No.
1947-65	PM10 Stadium Pins 2 1/8'	17
1947-66	Exhibits	101
1947-66	PM10 Stadium Pins 1 3/4'	90
1953-55	Dormand	139
1955	Bowman	68
1955-62	Don Wingfield	26
1956	Topps	208
1956	Yankees Jay Publishing	7
1956	Yankees Team Issue	10
1957	Topps	82
1957	Yankees Jay Publishing	6
1958	Topps	275
1958	Yankees Jay Publishing	5
1959	Topps	395
1960	Topps	65
1960	Topps Venezuelan	65
1960	Yankees Jay Publishing	4
1961	Post	2A
1961	Post	2B
1961	Topps	495
1961	Topps Stamps Inserts	194
1961	Yankees Jay Publishing	6
1962	Jello	8
1962	Post	8
1962	Post Canadian	8
1962	Salada Plastic Coins	95
1962	Shirriff Plastic Coins	95
1962	Topps	51
1962	Topps	400
1962	Topps	473
1962	Topps Bucks	37
1962	Topps Stamps Inserts	86
1962	Topps Venezuelan	51
1962	Yankees Jay Publishing	8
1963	Jello	18
1963	Kahn's	15
1963	Post	18
1963	Salada Metal Coins	45
1963	Topps	60
1963	Topps	306
1963	Yankees Jay Publishing	5
1963-67	Yankee Requena K Postcards	8
1964	Bazooka	29
1964	Challenge The Yankees	12
1964	Topps	100
1964	Topps Coins Inserts	23
1964	Topps Coins Inserts	135
1964	Topps Giants	21
1964	Topps Stamps	72
1964	Topps Stand Ups	33
1964	Topps Venezuelan	100
1964	Wheaties Stamps	21
1964	Yankees Jay Publishing	5
1965	Bazooka	29
1965	Challenge The Yankees	10
1965	O-Pee-Chee	1
1965	Topps	1
1965	Topps	450
1966	Topps	405
1966	Yankees Team Issue	4
1967	Ashland Oil	2
1967	Coke Caps All-Stars	25
1967	Coke Caps All-Stars AL	29
1967	Coke Caps Yankees and Mets	V9
1967	Dexter Press	99

Year	Set Name	Card No.
1967	O-Pee-Chee	25
1967	Topps	25
1967	Topps Venezuelan	255
1968	Coke Caps Red Sox	18
1968	O-Pee-Chee	167
1968	Topps	167
1968	Topps Venezuelan	167
1970	Yankees Photos SCFC	16
1973	O-Pee-Chee	116
1973	Topps	116A
1973	Topps	116B
1974	Syracuse Chiefs Team Issue	11
1975	O-Pee-Chee	201
1975	Syracuse Chiefs Team Issue	6
1975	Topps	201
1975	Topps Mini	201
1976	SSPC	619
1978	TCMA 60'S I	236
1979	Diamond Greats	24
1979	Elston Howard Sausage	1
1979	TCMA 50'S	271
1981	Red Sox Boston Globe	86
1981	TCMA 60's II	474
1982	K-Mart	3
1983	Yankees 1961	4
1984-89	O'Connell and Son Ink	109
1985	George Steinbrenner Menu	4
1986	Sportflics Decade Greats	49
1987	Sports Cube Game	3
1987	Yankees 1961 TCMA	5
1988	Pacific Legends I	19A
1988	Pacific Legends I	19B
1990	Yankees 61 Ron Lewis	4
1990	Yankees Monument Park Rini Postcards	4
1991	Yankees Rini Postcards 1961 2	12
1992	Yankees WIZ 60s	56
1992	Yankees WIZ All-Stars	31
1994	Ted Williams	59
1994	Ted Williams Memories	M26
1994	Topps Archives 1954	253
1994	Topps Archives 1954 Gold	253
1998	Bowman Chrome Reprints	8
1998	Bowman Chrome Reprints Refractors	8

Waite Hoyt

Year	Set Name	Card No.
1920	Gassler's American Maid Bread D381-1	10
1921	Koester's Bread World Series Issue D383	36
1921	Neilson's V61	44
1921-22	E121 Series of 120	46
1921-23	National Caramel E220	47
1922	E120	64
1922	W572	46
1922	W575	60
1922	William Paterson V89	32
1923	Maple Crispette V117	7
1923	W501	32
1923	W503	11
1923	W515	8
1923	Willards Chocolates V100	67
1926	Sport Company of America	22
1928	Star Player Candy E-Unc.	38
1928	W502	30
1928	W513	62
1928	W560 Playing Cards	H11
1928	Yuenglings	30
1929	Portraits and Action R316	43
1929-30	Exhibits Four-in-One	25
1930	W554	7
1931-32	Exhibits Four-in-One	24
1933	Butterfinger Canadian V94	28
1933	Goudey Canadian V353	60
1933	Goudey R319	60
1934	Baby Ruth Gum	36
1934	Butterfinger Premiums R310	35

Year	Set Name	Card No.
1934	Diamond Match Co. Silver Border	94
1935	Goudey Puzzle R321	1E
1935	Goudey Puzzle R321	3C
1935	Goudey Puzzle R321	5C
1935	Goudey Puzzle R321	14C
1935-36	Diamond Match Co. Series 3 Type 1	78
1936	Goudey Wide Pen Premiums R314	A55
1936	National Chicle Fine Pen Premiums R313	46
1936	World Wide Gum V355	39
1940	Play Ball R335	118
1956-65	Reds Burger Beer	7
1959-64	Reds Burger Beer Photos	5
1960	Fleer	69
1961	Fleer	44
1968	Laughlin World Series	18
1971	Fleer World Series	19
1973	TCMA All-Time Greats	8
1974	A's 1929-31 TCMA	12
1975	Yankees 1927 TCMA	11
1976	Shakey's Pizza	114
1977-84	Galasso Glossy Greats	117
1978	Dexter Hall of Fame Postcards	22
1979	Diamond Greats	32
1979	Yankees 1927 TCMA	14
1980-87	SSPC HOF	113
1980-96	Perez-Steele Hall of Fame Postcards	113
1982	Diamond Classics	28
1982	Ohio Hall of Fame	7
1984	Yankees 1927 Galasso	18
1984-89	O'Connell and Son Ink	111
1985	Feg Murray's Cartoon Greats	11
1986	Conlon Series 1	26
1987	Yankees 1927 TCMA	4
1989	Dodgers Smokey Greats	10
1989	HOF Sticker Book	71
1990	Dodgers Target	366
1991	Conlon TSN	115
1992	Conlon TSN	468
1992	Megacards Ruth	157
1992	Yankees WIZ HOF	16
1993	Conlon TSN	757
1993	Diamond Stars Extension Set	137

Catfish Hunter

Year	Set Name	Card No.
1965	Topps	526
1966	O-Pee-Chee	36
1966	Topps	36
1966	Topps Venezuelan	36
1967	Coke Caps Athletics	15
1967	Topps	369
1967	Topps Giant Stand Ups	23
1968	Bazooka	2
1968	Topps	385
1968	Topps Action Stickers	10A
1968	Topps Plaks	5
1968	Topps Posters	5
1969	A's Jack in the Box	8
1969	Milton Bradley	124
1969	MLB Official Stamps	87
1969	Topps	235
1969	Topps Stamps	216
1969	Topps Team Posters	21
1970	Dayton Daily News M137	75
1970	MLB Official Stamps	259
1970	Topps	565
1971	Bazooka Numbered Test	48
1971	Bazooka Unnumbered	18
1971	Milk Duds	10
1971	MLB Official Stamps	516
1971	O-Pee-Chee	45
1971	Topps	45
1971	Topps Coins Inserts	80
1971	Topps Tattoos	74
1972	Kellogg's	22

1998 Bowman Chrome Reprints #8

1978 Topps #135

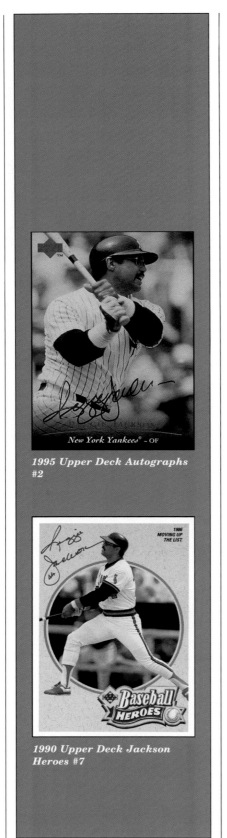

1995 Upper Deck Autographs #2

1990 Upper Deck Jackson Heroes #7

Year	Set Name	Card No.
1972	Milton Bradley	157
1972	O-Pee-Chee	330
1972	Topps	330
1973	A's Postcards	29
1973	Kellogg's 2D	20
1973	O-Pee-Chee	235
1973	O-Pee-Chee	344
1973	Topps	235
1973	Topps	344
1973	Topps Candy Lids	21
1973-74	Linnett Portraits	140
1974	Kellogg's	44
1974	O-Pee-Chee	196
1974	O-Pee-Chee	339
1974	Topps	7
1974	Topps	339
1974	Topps Deckle Edge	6
1974	Topps Stamps	225
1975	Blank Back Discs	3
1975	Hostess	148
1975	Kellogg's	44A
1975	Kellogg's	44B
1975	O-Pee-Chee	230
1975	O-Pee-Chee	310
1975	O-Pee-Chee	311
1975	SSPC Samples	2
1975	Topps	230
1975	Topps	310
1975	Topps	311
1975	Topps Mini	230
1975	Topps Mini	310
1975	Topps Mini	311
1975	Yankees SSPC	1
1976	Blankback Discs	21
1976	Buchman Discs	21
1976	Carousel Discs	21
1976	Crane Discs	21
1976	Dairy Isle Discs	21
1976	Hostess	141
1976	Isaly Discs	21
1976	Kellogg's	5
1976	Laughlin Diamond Jubilee	7
1976	O-Pee-Chee	100
1976	O-Pee-Chee	200
1976	O-Pee-Chee	202
1976	Orbakers Discs	21
1976	Red Barn Discs	21
1976	Safelon Discs	21
1976	Safelon Superstar Lunch Bags	3
1976	Safelon Superstar Lunch Bags	7
1976	Safelon Superstar Lunch Bags	10
1976	Safelon Superstar Lunch Bags	11
1976	Safelon Superstar Lunch Bags	12
1976	SSPC	425
1976	SSPC	593A
1976	SSPC	593B
1976	Topps	100
1976	Topps	200
1976	Topps	202
1976	Towne Club Discs	21
1977	Burger Chef Discs	178
1977	Chilly Willie Discs	32
1977	Customized Discs	32
1977	Dairy Isle Discs	32
1977	Detroit Caesars Discs	32
1977	Holiday Inn Discs	32
1977	Hostess	79
1977	MSA Discs	32
1977	O-Pee-Chee	10
1977	RC Cola Cans	30
1977	Saga Discs	32
1977	Topps	280
1977	Topps Cloth Stickers	21
1977	Wendy's Discs	32
1977	Yankees Burger King	4
1977	Zip'z Discs	32
1977-79	Sportscaster	1409

Year	Set Name	Card No.
1977-79	Sportscaster	1410
1978	O-Pee-Chee	69
1978	RC Cola Cans	58
1978	SSPC 270	23
1978	Topps	460
1978	Wiffle Ball Discs	31
1978	Yankees Burger King	7
1978	Yankees SSPC Diary	23
1979	O-Pee-Chee	352
1979	Topps	670
1979	Yankees Burger King	6
1979	Yankees Picture Album	19
1980-87	SSPC HOF	198
1980-96	Perez-Steele Hall of Fame Postcards	198
1982	TCMA Greatest Pitchers	25
1983	MLBPA Pins	10
1983	Yankee A-S Fifty Years	20
1986	A's Greats TCMA	9
1986	Sportflics Decade Greats	63
1987	A's Mother's	6
1987	Donruss Highlights	19
1988	Pacific Legends I	16
1988	Topps Glossy All-Stars	11
1989	HOF Sticker Book	82
1989	Pacific Legends II	193
1989	Perez-Steele Celebration Postcards	18
1989	Swell Baseball Greats	10
1990	Pacific Legends	68
1990-97	Perez-Steele Great Moments	62
1991	Upper Deck Sheets	7
1991	Upper Deck Sheets	16
1992	A's Unocal 76 Pins	3
1992	A's Unocal 76 Pins	4
1992	Pinnacle	587
1992	Upper Deck Sheets	27
1992	Yankees WIZ 70s	77
1992	Yankees WIZ All-Stars	32
1992	Yankees WIZ HOF	18
1993	Action Packed ASG	126
1993	Action Packed ASG 24K	60G
1993	MCI Ambassadors	8
1993	Nabisco All-Star Autographs	3
1994	Ted Williams	68
1995	Jimmy Dean All-Time Greats	2
1998	Donruss Signature Significant Signatures	4

Reggie Jackson

Year	Set Name	Card No.
1969	A's Jack in the Box	9
1969	Milton Bradley	127
1969	Rawlings	1
1969	Topps	260
1969	Topps Decals Inserts	19
1969	Topps Super	28
1969	Topps Team Posters	21
1970	Dayton Daily News M137	31
1970	Kellogg's	32
1970	Milton Bradley	11
1970	MLB Official Stamps	260
1970	O-Pee-Chee	64
1970	O-Pee-Chee	66
1970	O-Pee-Chee	140
1970	O-Pee-Chee	459
1970	Topps	64
1970	Topps	66
1970	Topps	140
1970	Topps	459
1970	Topps Booklets	10
1970	Topps Candy Lid	10
1970	Topps Super	28
1970	Transogram Statues	11B
1971	All-Star Baseball Album	10
1971	Bazooka Numbered Test	18
1971	Bazooka Unnumbered	3
1971	MLB Official Stamps	517

Year	Set Name	Card No.	Year	Set Name	Card No.	Year	Set Name	Card No.
1971	MLB Official Stamps	562	1976	Safelon Discs	22A	1981	Topps Stickers	245
1971	O-Pee-Chee	20	1976	Safelon Discs	22B	1981	Topps Super Home Team	65
1971	Topps	20	1976	SSPC	494	1981	Topps Super National	8
1971	Topps Coins Inserts	108	1976	Topps	194	1982	Donruss	535
1971	Topps Greatest Moments	47	1976	Topps	500	1982	Donruss	575
1971	Topps Super	38	1976	Towne Club Discs	22A	1982	Drake's	19
1971	Topps Tattoos	21	1976	Towne Club Discs	22B	1982	Fleer	39
1972	A's Postcards	14	1977	Burger Chef Discs	176	1982	Fleer	646
1972	Kellogg's	20	1977	Chilly Willie Discs	33	1982	Fleer	646B
1972	Milton Bradley	159	1977	Customized Discs	33	1982	Fleer Stamps	110
1972	O-Pee-Chee	90	1977	Dairy Isle Discs	33	1982	Fleer Stamps	112
1972	O-Pee-Chee	435	1977	Detroit Caesars Discs	33	1982	K-Mart	23
1972	O-Pee-Chee	436	1977	Holiday Inn Discs	33	1982	Kellogg's	14
1972	Seven-Eleven Trading Cups	21	1977	Hostess	3	1982	O-Pee-Chee	300
1972	Topps	90	1977	MSA Discs	33	1982	O-Pee-Chee	301
1972	Topps	435	1977	O-Pee-Chee	200	1982	O-Pee-Chee	377
1972	Topps	436	1977	Pepsi Glove Discs	34	1982	On Deck Discs	18
1973	Kellogg's 2D	22	1977	Saga Discs	33	1982	Perma-Graphic All-Stars	7
1973	O-Pee-Chee	255	1977	Topps	10	1982	Perma-Graphic Credit Cards	20
1973	Seven-Eleven Trading Cups	34	1977	Topps Cloth Stickers	22	1982	Perma-Graphic Credit Cards Gold	20
1973	Topps	255	1977	Wendy's Discs	33	1982	Perma-Graphics All-Stars Gold	7
1973	Topps Candy Lids	22	1977	Yankees Burger King	17	1982	Squirt	5
1973	Topps Comics	8	1977	Zip'z Discs	33	1982	Topps	300
1973	Topps Pin-Ups	8	1977-79	Sportscaster	1409	1982	Topps	301
1973-74	Linnett Portraits	141	1978	Hostess	47	1982	Topps	551
1974	A's Postcards	52	1978	Kellogg's	40	1982	Topps Sticker Variations	216
1974	Kellogg's	20	1978	O-Pee-Chee	110	1982	Topps Traded	47T
1974	Laughlin All-Star Games	71	1978	O-Pee-Chee	242	1982	Topps/O-Pee-Chee Stickers	216
1974	O-Pee-Chee	130	1978	Papa Gino's Discs	26	1983	All-Star Game Program Inserts	56
1974	O-Pee-Chee	202	1978	Pepsi	32	1983	Donruss	3
1974	O-Pee-Chee	203	1978	RC Cola Cans	81	1983	Donruss	115
1974	O-Pee-Chee	338	1978	SSPC 270	26	1983	Donruss Action All-Stars	3A
1974	O-Pee-Chee	470	1978	Topps	7	1983	Donruss Action All-Stars	3B
1974	O-Pee-Chee	477	1978	Topps	200	1983	Drake's	12
1974	Topps	130	1978	Topps	413	1983	Fleer	93
1974	Topps	202	1978	Wiffle Ball Discs	32	1983	Fleer	640
1974	Topps	203	1978	Yankees Burger King	21	1983	Fleer	645
1974	Topps	338	1978	Yankees SSPC Diary	26	1983	Fleer Stamps	90
1974	Topps	470	1979	Baseball Patches	42	1983	Fleer Stickers	32
1974	Topps	477	1979	Hostess	120	1983	Kellogg's	3
1974	Topps Deckle Edge	61	1979	Kellogg's	46	1983	O-Pee-Chee	56
1974	Topps Puzzles	6	1979	O-Pee-Chee	374	1983	O-Pee-Chee	219
1974	Topps Stamps	226	1979	Topps	700	1983	O-Pee-Chee	390
1975	Hostess	88	1979	Topps Comics	12	1983	Perma-Graphic Credit Cards	27
1975	Kellogg's	54	1979	Yankees Burger King	21	1983	Perma-Graphic Credit Cards Gold	27
1975	O-Pee-Chee	211	1979	Yankees Picture Album	20	1983	Seven-Eleven Coins	5
1975	O-Pee-Chee	300	1980	Burger King Pitch/Hit/Run	17	1983	Topps	390
1975	O-Pee-Chee	461	1980	Kellogg's	26	1983	Topps	500
1975	SSPC 42	11	1980	O-Pee-Chee	314	1983	Topps	501
1975	SSPC Puzzle Back	12	1980	Topps	600	1983	Topps	702
1975	Topps	211	1980	Topps Super	6	1983	Topps Foldouts	2
1975	Topps	300	1980-96	Perez-Steele Hall of Fame Postcards	216	1983	Topps Glossy Send-Ins	39
1975	Topps	461	1981	Accel Reggie Jackson	1	1983	Topps Sticker Boxes	4
1975	Topps Mini	211	1981	Accel Reggie Jackson	2	1983	Topps/O-Pee-Chee Stickers	5
1975	Topps Mini	300	1981	Accel Reggie Jackson	3	1983	Topps/O-Pee-Chee Stickers	17
1975	Topps Mini	461	1981	All-Star Game Program Inserts	53	1983	Topps/O-Pee-Chee Stickers	41
1976	Blankback Discs	22A	1981	Donruss	228	1983	Topps/O-Pee-Chee Stickers	163
1976	Blankback Discs	22B	1981	Donruss	348	1983-96	Kellogg's Cereal Boxes	15
1976	Buchman Discs	22A	1981	Donruss	468	1984	All-Star Game Program Inserts	145
1976	Buchman Discs	22B	1981	Drake's	10	1984	Angels Smokey	11
1976	Carousel Discs	22A	1981	Fleer	79	1984	Dodgers Union Oil	10
1976	Carousel Discs	22B	1981	Fleer	650	1984	Donruss	57
1976	Crane Discs	22A	1981	Fleer	650B	1984	Donruss Action All-Stars	36
1976	Crane Discs	22B	1981	Fleer Sticker Cards	115	1984	Donruss Champions	9
1976	Dairy Isle Discs	22A	1981	Fleer Sticker Cards	126	1984	Drake's	15
1976	Dairy Isle Discs	22B	1981	Kellogg's	3	1984	Fleer	520
1976	Hostess	146	1981	MSA Mini Discs	18	1984	Fun Foods Pins	16
1976	Isaly Discs	22A	1981	O-Pee-Chee	370	1984	Galasso Reggie Jackson	1
1976	Isaly Discs	22B	1981	Perma-Graphic All-Stars	14	1984	Galasso Reggie Jackson	2
1976	Kellogg's	8	1981	Perma-Graphic Credit Cards	7	1984	Galasso Reggie Jackson	3
1976	O-Pee-Chee	194	1981	Squirt	5	1984	Galasso Reggie Jackson	4
1976	O-Pee-Chee	500	1981	Tigers Detroit News	120	1984	Galasso Reggie Jackson	5
1976	Orbakers Discs	22A	1981	Topps	2	1984	Galasso Reggie Jackson	6
1976	Orbakers Discs	22B	1981	Topps	400	1984	Galasso Reggie Jackson	7
1976	Orioles Postcards	22	1981	Topps Scratchoffs	3	1984	Galasso Reggie Jackson	8
1976	Red Barn Discs	22A	1981	Topps Stickers	11	1984	Galasso Reggie Jackson	9
1976	Red Barn Discs	22B	1981	Topps Stickers	107	1984	Galasso Reggie Jackson	10

Trading Card Checklist

Year	Set Name	Card No.	Year	Set Name	Card No.	Year	Set Name	Card No.
1984	Galasso Reggie Jackson	11	1985	Star Reggie Jackson	18	1987	Topps Traded	52T
1984	Galasso Reggie Jackson	12	1985	Star Reggie Jackson	19	1987	Topps Traded Tiffany	52T
1984	Galasso Reggie Jackson	13	1985	Star Reggie Jackson	20	1987	Woolworth's	4
1984	Galasso Reggie Jackson	14	1985	Star Reggie Jackson	21	1988	Fleer	283
1984	Galasso Reggie Jackson	15	1985	Star Reggie Jackson	22	1988	Fleer Glossy	283
1984	Galasso Reggie Jackson	16	1985	Star Reggie Jackson	23	1988	Grenada Baseball Stamps	3
1984	Galasso Reggie Jackson	17	1985	Star Reggie Jackson	24	1988	Panini Stickers	175
1984	Galasso Reggie Jackson	18	1985	Topps	200	1988	Score	500
1984	Galasso Reggie Jackson	19	1985	Topps 3-D	14	1988	Score	501
1984	Galasso Reggie Jackson	20	1985	Topps Glossy All-Stars	19	1988	Score	502
1984	Galasso Reggie Jackson	21	1985	Topps Glossy Send-Ins	15	1988	Score	503
1984	Galasso Reggie Jackson	22	1985	Topps Rub Downs	27	1988	Score	504
1984	Galasso Reggie Jackson	23	1985	Topps Super	29	1988	Score Glossy	500
1984	Galasso Reggie Jackson	24	1985	Topps Tiffany	200	1988	Score Glossy	501
1984	Galasso Reggie Jackson	25	1985	Topps/O-Pee-Chee Stickers	187	1988	Score Glossy	502
1984	Galasso Reggie Jackson	26	1985	Topps/O-Pee-Chee Stickers	220	1988	Score Glossy	503
1984	Galasso Reggie Jackson	27	1986	Angels Smokey	2	1988	Score Glossy	504
1984	Galasso Reggie Jackson	28	1986	Burger King All-Pro	12	1988	Sportflics	120
1984	Galasso Reggie Jackson	29	1986	Donruss	377	1988	Starting Lineup A's	8
1984	Galasso Reggie Jackson	30	1986	Donruss Highlights	10	1989	Angels Smokey	15
1984	Milton Bradley	14	1986	Dorman's Cheese	11	1989	Pacific Legends II	111
1984	MLBPA Pencils	3	1986	Drake's	3	1989	Topps Baseball Talk/LJN	9
1984	Nestle 792	100	1986	Fleer	160	1990	Baseball Wit	42
1984	Nestle 792	711	1986	Fleer Future Hall of Famers	6	1990	HOF Sticker Book	88
1984	Nestle 792	712	1986	Fleer Limited Edition	26	1990	Upper Deck Jackson Heroes	1
1984	Nestle 792	713	1986	Fleer Mini	32	1990	Upper Deck Jackson Heroes	2
1984	O-Pee-Chee	100	1986	Fleer Sluggers/Pitchers	18	1990	Upper Deck Jackson Heroes	3
1984	Ralston Purina	19	1986	Fleer Sticker Cards	65	1990	Upper Deck Jackson Heroes	4
1984	Seven-Eleven Coins	W12	1986	General Mills Booklets	2G	1990	Upper Deck Jackson Heroes	5
1984	Topps	100	1986	Leaf/Donruss	173	1990	Upper Deck Jackson Heroes	6
1984	Topps	711	1986	Meadow Gold Blank Back	7	1990	Upper Deck Jackson Heroes	7
1984	Topps	712	1986	Meadow Gold Stat Back	6	1990	Upper Deck Jackson Heroes	8
1984	Topps	713	1986	MSA Jiffy Pop Discs	8	1990	Upper Deck Jackson Heroes	9
1984	Topps Cereal	19	1986	O-Pee-Chee	394	1990	Upper Deck Jackson Heroes	AU1
1984	Topps Gallery of Champions	6	1986	O-Pee-Chee Box Bottoms	I	1990	Upper Deck Jackson Heroes	NNO0
1984	Topps Rub Downs	27	1986	Quaker Granola	26	1990	Upper Deck Sheets	2
1984	Topps Super	21	1986	Seven-Eleven Coins	W9	1990-97	Perez-Steele Great Moments	104
1984	Topps Tiffany	100	1986	Sportflics	37	1991	A's Mother's	28
1984	Topps Tiffany	711	1986	Sportflics	57	1991	Baseball's Best Record Breakers	8
1984	Topps Tiffany	712	1986	Sportflics	61	1991	Foul Ball	32
1984	Topps Tiffany	713	1986	Sportflics	71	1991	Orioles Crown	217
1984	Topps/O-Pee-Chee Stickers	102B	1986	Sportflics	147	1991	Upper Deck Comic Ball Promos	4
1984	Topps/O-Pee-Chee Stickers	231	1986	Sportflics	150	1991	Upper Deck Heroes of Baseball 5x7	1
1984-89	O'Connell and Son Ink	21	1986	Sportflics Decade Greats	53	1991	Upper Deck Sheets	1
1984-89	O'Connell and Son Ink	95	1986	Topps	700	1991	Upper Deck Sheets	5
1985	All-Star Game Program Inserts	59	1986	Topps 3-D	13	1991	Upper Deck Sheets	11
1985	Angels Smokey	2	1986	Topps Glossy Send-Ins	2	1991	Upper Deck Sheets	12
1985	Angels Straw Hat	8	1986	Topps Super	35	1992	A's Unocal 76 Pins	2
1985	Circle K	13	1986	Topps Tiffany	700	1992	A's Unocal 76 Pins	5
1985	Donruss	57	1986	Topps Wax Box Cards	I	1992	TV Sports Mailbag/Photo File 500 Home Run Club	4
1985	Donruss Action All-Stars	39	1986	Topps/O-Pee-Chee Stickers	177	1992	Upper Deck FanFest	46
1985	Drake's	17	1986	Topps/O-Pee-Chee Tattoos	17	1992	Upper Deck FanFest Gold	46
1985	Fleer	303	1986	True Value	13	1992	Upper Deck Heroes Highlights	HI5
1985	Fleer	639	1986	Woolworth's	15	1992	Upper Deck Sheets	4
1985	Fleer Limited Edition	14	1987	A's Mother's	5	1992	Upper Deck Sheets	17
1985	General Mills Stickers	19	1987	A's Mother's	27	1992	Upper Deck Sheets	27
1985	Leaf/Donruss	170	1987	A's Smokey Colorgrams	7	1992	Upper Deck Sheets	34
1985	O-Pee-Chee	200	1987	Classic Game	24	1992	Yankees WIZ 70s	79
1985	Seven-Eleven Coins	C12	1987	Donruss	210	1992	Yankees WIZ 80s	89
1985	Seven-Eleven Coins	W13	1987	Donruss Opening Day	22	1992	Yankees WIZ All-Stars	33
1985	Star Reggie Jackson	1	1987	Fleer	84	1993	Fun Pack	28
1985	Star Reggie Jackson	2	1987	Fleer Glossy	84	1993	Upper Deck All-Time Heroes	72
1985	Star Reggie Jackson	3	1987	Fleer Update	49	1993	Upper Deck All-Time Heroes	135
1985	Star Reggie Jackson	4	1987	Fleer Update Glossy	49	1993	Upper Deck All-Time Heroes	165
1985	Star Reggie Jackson	5	1987	General Mills Booklets	3E	1993	Upper Deck All-Time Heroes Preview	2
1985	Star Reggie Jackson	6	1987	K-Mart	16	1993	Upper Deck All-Time Heroes Preview	3
1985	Star Reggie Jackson	7	1987	Leaf/Donruss	201	1993	Upper Deck All-Time Heroes Preview	4
1985	Star Reggie Jackson	8	1987	O-Pee-Chee	300	1993	Upper Deck Clark Reggie Jackson	C1
1985	Star Reggie Jackson	9	1987	Red Foley Sticker Book	108	1993	Upper Deck Clark Reggie Jackson	C2
1985	Star Reggie Jackson	10	1987	Sportflics	44	1993	Upper Deck Clark Reggie Jackson	C3
1985	Star Reggie Jackson	11	1987	Sportflics Team Preview	23	1993	Upper Deck Fifth Anniversary	A9
1985	Star Reggie Jackson	12	1987	Topps	300	1993	Upper Deck Fifth Anniversary Jumbo	A9
1985	Star Reggie Jackson	13	1987	Topps	312	1993	Upper Deck Jackson Heroes Jumbo	1
1985	Star Reggie Jackson	14	1987	Topps Coins	15	1993	Upper Deck Jackson Heroes Jumbo	2
1985	Star Reggie Jackson	15	1987	Topps Glossy Send-Ins	54	1993	Upper Deck Jackson Heroes Jumbo	3
1985	Star Reggie Jackson	16	1987	Topps Tiffany	300	1993	Upper Deck Jackson Heroes Jumbo	4
1985	Star Reggie Jackson	17	1987	Topps Tiffany	312			

Year	Set Name	Card No.
1993	Upper Deck Jackson Heroes Jumbo	5
1993	Upper Deck Jackson Heroes Jumbo	6
1993	Upper Deck Jackson Heroes Jumbo	7
1993	Upper Deck Jackson Heroes Jumbo	8
1993	Upper Deck Jackson Heroes Jumbo	9
1993	Upper Deck Sheets	1
1993	Upper Deck Sheets	3
1993	Upper Deck Sheets	18
1993	Upper Deck Sheets	20
1993	Upper Deck Sheets	23
1993	Upper Deck Then And Now	TN16
1994	Ted Williams 500 Club	2
1994	Upper Deck All-Time Heroes	9
1994	Upper Deck All-Time Heroes	44
1994	Upper Deck All-Time Heroes	107
1994	Upper Deck All-Time Heroes	122
1994	Upper Deck All-Time Heroes	167
1994	Upper Deck All-Time Heroes	210
1994	Upper Deck All-Time Heroes	P44
1994	Upper Deck All-Time Heroes 125th	9
1994	Upper Deck All-Time Heroes 125th	44
1994	Upper Deck All-Time Heroes 125th	107
1994	Upper Deck All-Time Heroes 125th	122
1994	Upper Deck All-Time Heroes 125th	167
1994	Upper Deck All-Time Heroes 125th	210
1994	Upper Deck All-Time Heroes Autographs	2
1994	Upper Deck Sheets	5
1994	Upper Deck Sheets	8
1994	Upper Deck: The American Epic	75
1994	Upper Deck: The American Epic Little Debbies	LD15
1995	Eagle Ballpark Legends	2
1995	SP Championship	109
1995	SP Championship Classic Performances	CP1
1995	SP Championship Classic Performances Die Cuts	CP1
1995	SP Championship Die Cuts	109
1995	Upper Deck Autographs	2
1995	Upper Deck Sonic Heroes of Baseball	10
1995	Upper Deck Sports Drink Jackson	1
1995	Upper Deck Sports Drink Jackson	2
1995	Upper Deck Sports Drink Jackson	3
1997	Arizona State Baseball Greats	12
1997	Donruss Signature Notable Nicknames	4
1997	Donruss Signature Significant Signatures	11A
1997	Donruss Signature Significant Signatures	11B
1997	St. Vincent HOF Heroes Stamps	9
1998	Sports Illustrated World Series Fever	10
1998	Sports Illustrated World Series Fever Autumn Excellence	4
1998	Sports Illustrated World Series Fever Autumn Excellence Gold	4
1998	Sports Illustrated World Series Fever Extra Edition	10
1998	Sports Illustrated World Series Fever First Edition	10

Derek Jeter

Year	Set Name	Card No.
1992	Classic Draft Picks	6
1992	Classic Draft Picks Foil Bonus	BC6
1992	Classic/Best	402
1992	Classic/Best Blue Bonus	BC22
1992	Front Row Draft Picks	55
1992	Front Row Draft Picks Promo Sheet	55
1992	Gulf Coast Yankees Fleer/ProCards	3797
1992	High School Prospects Little Sun	2
1992	High School Prospects Little Sun	NNO
1992	Upper Deck Minors	5
1992-98	Highland Mint Mint-Coins	50
1992-98	Highland Mint Mint-Coins	51
1992-98	Highland Mint Mint-Coins	52
1993	Bowman	511
1993	Classic/Best	91
1993	Classic/Best	AU4

Year	Set Name	Card No.
1993	Classic/Best Gold	115
1993	Classic/Best Insert Cards	4
1993	Classic/Best Promos	1
1993	Excel	210
1993	Greensboro Hornets Classic/Best	1
1993	Greensboro Hornets Fleer/ProCards	893
1993	Pinnacle	457
1993	Score	489
1993	Select	360
1993	South Atlantic League All-Stars Fleer/ProCards	21
1993	SP	279
1993	Stadium Club Murphy	117
1993	Topps	98
1993	Topps Gold	98
1993	Topps Inagural Rockies	98
1993	Topps Inaugural Marlins	98
1993	Topps Micro	98
1993	Upper Deck	449
1993	Upper Deck Gold	449
1993-97	Bleachers	18
1994	Action Packed	43
1994	Albany-Colonie Yankees Team Issue	2
1994	Bowman	376
1994	Bowman	633
1994	Bowman's Best	B2
1994	Bowman's Best	X95
1994	Bowman's Best Refractors	B2
1994	Bowman's Best Refractors	X95
1994	Classic	60
1994	Classic Cream of the Crop	C17
1994	Classic Tri-Cards	T55
1994	Classic/Best Gold	83
1994	Classic/Best Gold Acetates	SH3
1994	Collector's Choice	644
1994	Collector's Choice Gold Signature	644
1994	Collector's Choice Silver Signature	644
1994	Excel	106
1994	Excel League Leaders	10
1994	Florida State League All-Stars Fleer/ProCards	FSL22
1994	Signature Rookies	35
1994	Signature Rookies Hottest Prospects	S4
1994	Signature Rookies Hottest Prospects Mail-In Promos	S4
1994	Signature Rookies Signatures	35
1994	Tampa Yankees Classic	1
1994	Tampa Yankees Fleer/ProCards	2393
1994	Ted Williams	124
1994	Ted Williams Dan Gardiner Collection	DG3
1994	Topps	158
1994	Topps Gold	158
1994	Topps Spanish	158
1994	Upper Deck	550
1994	Upper Deck All-Time Heroes Next In Line	7
1994	Upper Deck Electric Diamond	550
1994	Upper Deck Minors	185
1995	Action Packed	1
1995	Action Packed	10
1995	Action Packed	67
1995	Action Packed 24K Gold	6G
1995	Action Packed 24K Gold	AU1
1995	Action Packed 24K Gold	AU2
1995	Bowman	229
1995	Bowman Gold Foil	229
1995	Bowman's Best	B1
1995	Bowman's Best Refractors	B1
1995	Collector's Choice	15
1995	Collector's Choice Gold Signature	15
1995	Collector's Choice SE	2
1995	Collector's Choice SE Gold Signature	2
1995	Collector's Choice SE Silver Signature	2
1995	Collector's Choice Silver Signature	15
1995	Columbus Clippers Milk Caps Team Issue	13
1995	Columbus Clippers Police	14
1995	Columbus Clippers Team Issue	14
1995	Emotion	60

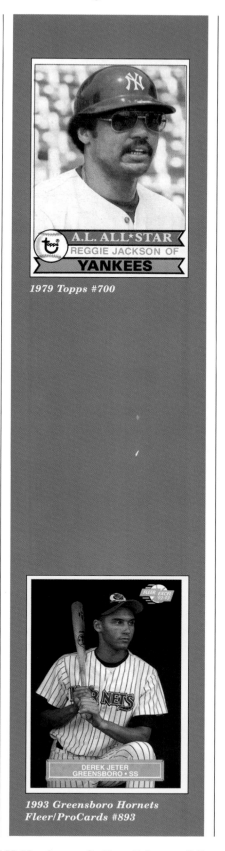

1979 Topps #700

1993 Greensboro Hornets Fleer/ProCards #893

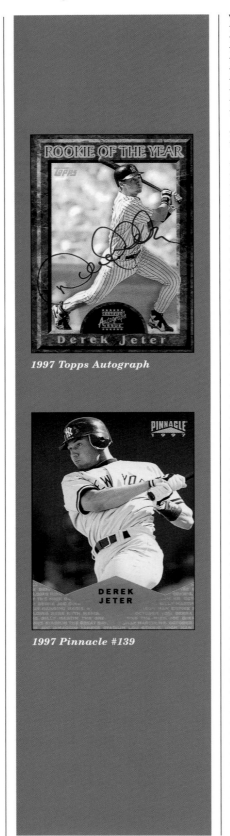

1997 Topps Autograph

1997 Pinnacle #139

Year	Set Name	Card No.
1995	Excel	97
1995	Excel All-Stars	5
1995	Finest	279
1995	Finest Refractors	279
1995	Fleer Major League Prospects	7
1995	Select Certified	122
1995	Select Certified Mirror Gold	122
1995	Signature Rookies Future Dynasty	FD3
1995	Signature Rookies Future Dynasty Signatures	FD3
1995	Signature Rookies Old Judge Star Squad	3
1995	Signature Rookies Old Judge Star Squad Signatures	3
1995	SP	181
1995	SP Championship	20
1995	SP Championship Die Cuts	20
1995	SP Silver	181
1995	Stadium Club Crystal Ball	CB14
1995	Stadium Club Members Only Parallel	CB14
1995	Topps	199
1995	Ultra Golden Prospects	7
1995	Ultra Golden Prospects Gold Medallion	7
1995	Upper Deck	225
1995	Upper Deck Electric Diamond	225
1995	Upper Deck Electric Diamond Gold	225
1995	Upper Deck Minor League Autographs	7
1995	Upper Deck Minors	1
1995	Upper Deck Minors	165
1995	Upper Deck Minors Future Stock	1
1995	Upper Deck Minors Future Stock	165
1995	Upper Deck Minors Top 10 Prospect	1
1995	Upper Deck Predictor Award Winner Exchange	H14
1995	Upper Deck Predictor Award Winners	H14
1995	Upper Deck Special Edition	5
1995	Upper Deck Special Edition Gold	5
1995	Zenith	134
1995	Zenith Rookie Roll Call	2
1996	Bazooka	80
1996	Bowman	112
1996	Bowman Foil	112
1996	Bowman's Best	79
1996	Bowman's Best Atomic Refractors	79
1996	Bowman's Best Cuts	3
1996	Bowman's Best Cuts Atomic Refractors	3
1996	Bowman's Best Cuts Refractors	3
1996	Bowman's Best Previews	BBP15
1996	Bowman's Best Previews Atomic Refractors	BBP15
1996	Bowman's Best Previews Refractors	BBP15
1996	Bowman's Best Refractors	79
1996	Circa	65
1996	Circa Rave	65
1996	Collector's Choice	231
1996	Collector's Choice Gold Signature	231
1996	Collector's Choice Silver Signature	231
1996	Donruss	491
1996	Donruss Press Proofs	491
1996	Emotion-XL	90
1996	Finest	B92
1996	Finest	S350
1996	Finest Refractors	B92
1996	Finest Refractors	S350
1996	Flair	129
1996	Fleer	184
1996	Fleer Tiffany	184
1996	Fleer Update	U226
1996	Fleer Update Tiffany	U226
1996	Leaf	211
1996	Leaf Limited Rookies	4
1996	Leaf Limited Rookies Gold	4
1996	Leaf Preferred	116
1996	Leaf Preferred Press Proofs	116
1996	Leaf Preferred Staremaster	3
1996	Leaf Preferred Steel	40
1996	Leaf Preferred Steel Gold	40
1996	Leaf Press Proofs Bronze	211

Year	Set Name	Card No.
1996	Leaf Press Proofs Gold	211
1996	Leaf Press Proofs Silver	211
1996	Leaf Signature	67
1996	Leaf Signature Autographs	118
1996	Leaf Signature Autographs Gold	118
1996	Leaf Signature Autographs Silver	118
1996	Leaf Signature Extended Autographs	89
1996	Leaf Signature Extended Autographs Century Marks	11
1996	Leaf Signature Press Proofs Platinum	67
1996	Metal Universe	87
1996	Metal Universe Mining For Gold	6
1996	Metal Universe Platinum	87
1996	MLB Pins	16
1996	Pacific	383
1996	Pinnacle	171
1996	Pinnacle	279
1996	Pinnacle Aficionado	163
1996	Pinnacle Aficionado Artist's Proofs	163
1996	Pinnacle Aficionado Slick Picks	18
1996	Pinnacle First Rate	13
1996	Pinnacle Foil	279
1996	Pinnacle Project Stardom	2
1996	Pinnacle Starburst	97
1996	Pinnacle Starburst	179
1996	Pinnacle Starburst Artist's Proofs	97
1996	Pinnacle Starburst Artist's Proofs	179
1996	Pinnacle Team Spirit	3
1996	Pinnacle Team Tomorrow	9
1996	Score	240
1996	Score	384
1996	Score Diamond Aces	11
1996	Score Dugout Collection	A106
1996	Score Dugout Collection	B109
1996	Score Dugout Collection Artist's Proofs	A106
1996	Score Dugout Collection Artist's Proofs	B109
1996	Score Future Franchise	3
1996	Score Numbers Game	26
1996	Score Reflexions	10
1996	Score Samples	240
1996	Select	161
1996	Select Artist's Proofs	161
1996	Select Certified	100
1996	Select Certified Artist's Proofs	100
1996	Select Certified Certified Blue	100
1996	Select Certified Certified Red	100
1996	Select Certified Interleague Preview	6
1996	Select Certified Mirror Blue	100
1996	Select Certified Mirror Gold	100
1996	Select Certified Mirror Red	100
1996	Select Certified Select Few	2
1996	SP	135
1996	SP Marquee Matchup Die Cuts	4
1996	SP Marquee Matchups	MM3
1996	SP Special FX	48
1996	SP Special FX Die Cuts	48
1996	Sportflix	139
1996	Sportflix Artist's Proofs	139
1996	Sportflix Double Take	9
1996	Sportflix Rookie Jumbos	6
1996	SPx	43
1996	SPx Gold	43
1996	Stadium Club	123
1996	Stadium Club	260
1996	Stadium Club Extreme Players Bronze	123
1996	Stadium Club Extreme Players Gold	123
1996	Stadium Club Extreme Players Silver	123
1996	Studio	33
1996	Studio Press Proofs Bronze	33
1996	Studio Press Proofs Gold	33
1996	Studio Press Proofs Silver	33
1996	Summit	154
1996	Summit	171
1996	Summit Above and Beyond	154
1996	Summit Above and Beyond	171
1996	Summit Artist's Proofs	154
1996	Summit Artist's Proofs	171

Year	Set Name	Card No.	Year	Set Name	Card No.	Year	Set Name	Card No.
1996	Summit Ballparks	6	1997	Collector's Choice Big Shots Gold Signatures	13	1997	Fleer Goudey Greats	4
1996	Summit Foil	154	1997	Collector's Choice New Frontier	NF29	1997	Fleer Goudey Greats Foil	4
1996	Summit Foil	171	1997	Collector's Choice Teams	NY5	1997	Fleer Headliners	8
1996	Team Out	39	1997	Collector's Choice The Big Show	34	1997	Fleer Rookie Sensations	7
1996	Topps	219	1997	Collector's Choice The Big Show		1997	Fleer Soaring Stars	5
1996	Topps Big Cards	4		World Headquarters	34	1997	Fleer Soaring Stars Glowing	5
1996	Topps Chrome	80	1997	Collector's Choice Toast of the Town	T19	1997	Fleer Tiffany	168
1996	Topps Chrome Refractors	80	1997	Cracker Jack	5	1997	Fleer Tiffany	703
1996	Topps Gallery	143	1997	Denny's Holograms	14	1997	Fleer Tiffany	739
1996	Topps Gallery Players Private Issue	143	1997	Donruss	49	1997	Leaf	165
1996	Topps Laser	82	1997	Donruss	415	1997	Leaf	200
1996	Topps Laser Bright Spots	2	1997	Donruss Armed and Dangerous	11	1997	Leaf	358
1996	Topps Laser Bright Spots	13	1997	Donruss Elite	24	1997	Leaf Banner Season	14
1996	Ultra	386	1997	Donruss Elite Gold Stars	24	1997	Leaf Fractal Matrix	165
1996	Ultra Checklists	B5	1997	Donruss Elite Passing the Torch	11	1997	Leaf Fractal Matrix	200
1996	Ultra Checklists Gold Medallion	B5	1997	Donruss Elite Passing the Torch	12	1997	Leaf Fractal Matrix	358
1996	Ultra Gold Medallion	386	1997	Donruss Elite Passing the Torch Autographs	11	1997	Leaf Fractal Matrix Die Cuts	165
1996	Ultra Golden Prospects	8	1997	Donruss Elite Passing the Torch Autographs	12	1997	Leaf Fractal Matrix Die Cuts	200
1996	Ultra Golden Prospects Gold Medallion	8	1997	Donruss Elite Turn of the Century	7	1997	Leaf Fractal Matrix Die Cuts	358
1996	Upper Deck	156	1997	Donruss Elite Turn of the Century	P7	1997	Leaf Get-A-Grip	14
1996	Upper Deck Blue Chip Prospects	BC17	1997	Donruss Elite Turn of the Century Die Cuts	7	1997	Leaf Gold Stars	7
1996	Upper Deck Diamond Destiny	DD28	1997	Donruss Franchise Features	14	1997	Leaf Leagues of the Nation	4
1996	Upper Deck Diamond Destiny Gold	DD28	1997	Donruss Gold Press Proofs	49	1997	Leaf Statistical Standouts	12
1996	Upper Deck Diamond Destiny Silver	DD28	1997	Donruss Gold Press Proofs	415	1997	Metal Universe	118
1996	Upper Deck Predictor Hobby	H25	1997	Donruss Limited	22	1997	Metal Universe Magnetic Field	5
1996	Upper Deck Predictor Hobby Exchange	H25	1997	Donruss Limited	83	1997	Metal Universe Platinum Portraits	4
1996	Upper Deck V.J. Lovero Showcase	VJ3	1997	Donruss Limited	116	1997	New Pinnacle	53
1996	Zenith	93	1997	Donruss Limited Exposure	22	1997	New Pinnacle Artist's Proof	53
1996	Zenith	147	1997	Donruss Limited Exposure	83	1997	New Pinnacle Interleague Encounter	6
1996	Zenith Artist's Proofs	93	1997	Donruss Limited Exposure	116	1997	New Pinnacle Keeping the Pace	9
1996	Zenith Artist's Proofs	147	1997	Donruss Limited Exposure Non-Glossy	22	1997	New Pinnacle Museum Collection	53
1997	Bowman	1	1997	Donruss Limited Fabric of the Game	61	1997	New Pinnacle Press Plates	53
1997	Bowman Certified Black Ink Autographs	CA41	1997	Donruss Power Alley	24	1997	New Pinnacle Press Plates	I6A
1997	Bowman Certified Blue Ink Autographs	CA41	1997	Donruss Power Alley Die Cuts	24	1997	New Pinnacle Press Plates	K9
1997	Bowman Certified Blue Ink Autographs	CA41B	1997	Donruss Preferred	125	1997	Pacific	152
1997	Bowman Certified Gold Ink Autographs	CA41	1997	Donruss Preferred	184	1997	Pacific Baerga Softball	9
1997	Bowman Certified Green Ink Jeter		1997	Donruss Preferred Precious Metals	21	1997	Pacific Card-Supials	13
	Autograph	CA41	1997	Donruss Preferred Staremasters	7	1997	Pacific Card-Supials Minis	13
1997	Bowman Chrome	1	1997	Donruss Preferred Staremasters Samples	7	1997	Pacific Fireworks Die Cuts	7
1997	Bowman Chrome International	1	1997	Donruss Preferred Tin Boxes	8	1997	Pacific Gold Crown Die Cuts	11
1997	Bowman Chrome International Refractors	1	1997	Donruss Preferred Tin Boxes Gold	8	1997	Pacific Light Blue	152
1997	Bowman Chrome Refractors	1	1997	Donruss Preferred Tin Packs	8	1997	Pacific Prisms	51
1997	Bowman International	1	1997	Donruss Preferred Tin Packs Gold	8	1997	Pacific Prisms Gate Attractions	GA9
1997	Bowman's Best	82	1997	Donruss Preferred Tins Fanfest	8	1997	Pacific Prisms Light Blue	51
1997	Bowman's Best Atomic Refractors	82	1997	Donruss Signature	51	1997	Pacific Prisms Platinum	51
1997	Bowman's Best Autographs	82	1997	Donruss Signature Autographs Century	64	1997	Pacific Prisms Sizzling Lumber	SL4A
1997	Bowman's Best Autographs Atomic Refractor	82	1997	Donruss Signature Autographs Millenium	64	1997	Pacific Prisms Sluggers and Hurlers	SH5A
1997	Bowman's Best Autographs Refractor	82	1997	Donruss Signature Platinum Press Proofs	51	1997	Pacific Silver	152
1997	Bowman's Best Best Cuts	BC1	1997	Donruss Silver Press Proofs	49	1997	Pinnacle	139
1997	Bowman's Best Best Cuts Atomic Refractor	BC1	1997	Donruss Silver Press Proofs	415	1997	Pinnacle Artist's Proofs	PP139
1997	Bowman's Best Best Cuts Refractor	BC1	1997	Donruss Team Sets	123	1997	Pinnacle Certified	51
1997	Bowman's Best Jumbo	82	1997	Donruss Team Sets Pennant Edition	123	1997	Pinnacle Certified	141
1997	Bowman's Best Jumbo Atomic Refractor	82	1997	Donruss VxP 1.0	22	1997	Pinnacle Certified Certified Gold Team	3
1997	Bowman's Best Jumbo Refractor	82	1997	E-X2000	33	1997	Pinnacle Certified Certified Mirror Gold Team	3
1997	Bowman's Best Mirror Image	MI1	1997	E-X2000 Credentials	33	1997	Pinnacle Certified Certified Team	3
1997	Bowman's Best Mirror Image		1997	E-X2000 Essential Credentials	33	1997	Pinnacle Certified Mirror Black	51
	Atomic Refractor	MI1	1997	E-X2000 Star Date 2000	7	1997	Pinnacle Certified Mirror Black	141
1997	Bowman's Best Mirror Image		1997	Finest	15	1997	Pinnacle Certified Mirror Blue	51
	Atomic Refractor Inverted	MI1	1997	Finest	166	1997	Pinnacle Certified Mirror Blue	141
1997	Bowman's Best Mirror Image Inverted	MI1	1997	Finest	310	1997	Pinnacle Certified Mirror Gold	51
1997	Bowman's Best Mirror Image Refractor	MI1	1997	Finest Embossed	166	1997	Pinnacle Certified Mirror Gold	141
1997	Bowman's Best Mirror Image Refractor		1997	Finest Embossed	310	1997	Pinnacle Certified Mirror Red	51
	Inverted	MI1	1997	Finest Embossed Refractors	166	1997	Pinnacle Certified Mirror Red	141
1997	Bowman's Best Preview Atomic Refractor	4	1997	Finest Embossed Refractors	310	1997	Pinnacle Certified Red	51
1997	Bowman's Best Preview Refractor	4	1997	Finest Promos	15	1997	Pinnacle Certified Red	141
1997	Bowman's Best Previews	4	1997	Finest Refractors	15	1997	Pinnacle Home/Away	17
1997	Bowman's Best Refractor	82	1997	Finest Refractors	166	1997	Pinnacle Home/Away	18
1997	Circa	200	1997	Finest Refractors	310	1997	Pinnacle Inside	87
1997	Circa Boss	8	1997	Flair Showcase Diamond Cuts	13	1997	Pinnacle Inside	148
1997	Circa Fast Track	3	1997	Flair Showcase Hot Gloves	6	1997	Pinnacle Inside Cans	16
1997	Circa Icons	4	1997	Flair Showcase Legacy Collection	2	1997	Pinnacle Inside Club Edition	87
1997	Circa Limited Access	7	1997	Flair Showcase Row 0	2	1997	Pinnacle Inside Club Edition	148
1997	Circa Rave	200	1997	Flair Showcase Row 1	2	1997	Pinnacle Inside Diamond Edition	87
1997	Collector's Choice	180	1997	Flair Showcase Row 2	2	1997	Pinnacle Inside Diamond Edition	148
1997	Collector's Choice	331	1997	Fleer	168	1997	Pinnacle Inside Dueling Dugouts	11
1997	Collector's Choice All-Star Connection	40	1997	Fleer	703	1997	Pinnacle Mint	16
1997	Collector's Choice Big Shots	13	1997	Fleer	739	1997	Pinnacle Mint Bronze	16

Trading Card Checklist

Year	Set Name	Card No.
1997	Pinnacle Mint Coins Brass	16
1997	Pinnacle Mint Coins Gold Redemption	16
1997	Pinnacle Mint Coins Gold-Plated	16
1997	Pinnacle Mint Coins Nickel	16
1997	Pinnacle Mint Coins Solid Silver	16
1997	Pinnacle Mint Gold	16
1997	Pinnacle Mint Silver	16
1997	Pinnacle Museum Collection	139
1997	Pinnacle Press Plate Previews	139
1997	Pinnacle Totally Certified Platinum Blue	51
1997	Pinnacle Totally Certified Platinum Blue	141
1997	Pinnacle Totally Certified Platinum Gold	51
1997	Pinnacle Totally Certified Platinum Gold	141
1997	Pinnacle Totally Certified Platinum Red	51
1997	Pinnacle Totally Certified Platinum Red	141
1997	Pinnacle X-Press	32
1997	Pinnacle X-Press Melting Pot	19
1997	Pinnacle X-Press Melting Pot Samples	19
1997	Pinnacle X-Press Men of Summer	32
1997	Pinnacle X-Press Metal Works	5
1997	Pinnacle X-Press Metal Works Gold	5
1997	Pinnacle X-Press Metal Works Silver	5
1997	Score	35
1997	Score	545
1997	Score Artist's Proofs White Border	35
1997	Score Artist's Proofs White Border	545
1997	Score Heart of the Order	16
1997	Score Premium Stock	35
1997	Score Reserve Collection	545
1997	Score Showcase Series	35
1997	Score Showcase Series	545
1997	Score Showcase Series Artist's Proofs	35
1997	Score Showcase Series Artist's Proofs	545
1997	Score Stand and Deliver	9
1997	Select	60
1997	Select	148
1997	Select Artist's Proof	60
1997	Select Artist's Proof	148
1997	Select Registered Gold	60
1997	Select Registered Gold	148
1997	Select Rookie Revolution	2
1997	Select Tools of the Trade	25
1997	Select Tools of the Trade Mirror Blue	25
1997	SP	125
1997	SP Game Film	GF6
1997	SP Inside Info	17
1997	SP Marquee Matchups	MM10
1997	SP Special FX	16
1997	SP SPx Force	6
1997	SP SPx Force Autographs	6
1997	Sports Illustrated	62
1997	Sports Illustrated	128
1997	Sports Illustrated	179
1997	Sports Illustrated Extra Edition	62
1997	Sports Illustrated Extra Edition	128
1997	Sports Illustrated Extra Edition	179
1997	Sports Illustrated Great Shots	16
1997	SPx	36
1997	SPx Bound for Glory	13
1997	SPx Bronze	36
1997	SPx Cornerstones of the Game	10
1997	SPx Gold	36
1997	SPx Grand Finale	36
1997	SPx Silver	36
1997	SPx Steel	36
1997	Stadium Club	55
1997	Stadium Club Co-Signers	CO1
1997	Stadium Club Instavision	I17
1997	Stadium Club Matrix	55
1997	Stadium Club Members Only Parallel	I17
1997	Stadium Club Members Only Parallel	M1
1997	Stadium Club Members Only Parallel	PG19
1997	Stadium Club Members Only Parallel	PL13
1997	Stadium Club Millennium	M1
1997	Stadium Club Patent Leather	PL13
1997	Stadium Club Pure Gold	PG19
1997	Studio	91
1997	Studio Hard Hats	13
1997	Studio Master Strokes	1
1997	Studio Master Strokes 8x10	1
1997	Studio Portraits 8x10	10
1997	Studio Press Proof Gold	91
1997	Studio Press Proof Silver	91
1997	Topps	13
1997	Topps	NNO
1997	Topps Awesome Impact	AI7
1997	Topps Chrome	7
1997	Topps Chrome Diamond Duos	DD2
1997	Topps Chrome Diamond Duos Refractors	DD2
1997	Topps Chrome Refractors	7
1997	Topps Gallery	161
1997	Topps Gallery Gallery of Heroes	GH1
1997	Topps Gallery Peter Max Serigraphs	1
1997	Topps Gallery Peter Max Signature Series Serigraphs	1
1997	Topps Gallery Photo Gallery	PG6
1997	Topps Gallery Player's Private Issue	161
1997	Topps Gallery Promos	PP2
1997	Topps Hobby Masters	HM18
1997	Topps Screenplays/Tins	9
1997	Topps Stars Future All-Stars	FAS1
1997	UD3	55
1997	UD3 Generation Next	GN15
1997	UD3 Superb Signatures	4
1997	Ultra	99
1997	Ultra Baseball Rules	3
1997	Ultra Checklists	B9
1997	Ultra Double Trouble	7
1997	Ultra Fame Game	7
1997	Ultra Gold Medallion	99
1997	Ultra Hitting Machines	7
1997	Ultra Leather Shop	4
1997	Ultra Platinum Medallion	99
1997	Ultra Rookie Reflections	5
1997	Ultra Starring Role	9
1997	Ultra Top 30	9
1997	Ultra Top 30 Gold Medallion	9
1997	Upper Deck	421
1997	Upper Deck	440
1997	Upper Deck Award Winner Jumbos	18
1997	Upper Deck Blue Chip Prospects	BC2
1997	Upper Deck Home Team Heroes	HT2
1997	Upper Deck Hot Commodities	HC3
1997	Upper Deck Memorable Moments	B3
1997	Upper Deck Predictor	19
1997	Upper Deck Predictor Exchange	19
1997	Upper Deck Rock Solid Foundation	RS3
1997	Upper Deck Ticket To Stardom	TS5
1997	Yankees Score	3
1997	Yankees Score Platinum	3
1997	Yankees Score Premier	3
1997	Zenith	17
1997	Zenith 8 x 10	17
1997	Zenith 8x10 Dufex	17
1997	Zenith the Big Picture	17
1997	Zenith V-2	7
1997	Zenith Z-Team	7
1997-98	Fleer Million Dollar Moments	2
1997-98	Fleer Million Dollar Moments Redemption	2
1997-98	Topps Members Only 55	25
1998	Bowman	224
1998	Bowman Chrome	224
1998	Bowman Chrome Golden Anniversary	224
1998	Bowman Chrome Golden Anniversary Refractors	224
1998	Bowman Chrome International	224
1998	Bowman Chrome International Refractors	224
1998	Bowman Chrome Refractors	224
1998	Bowman Chrome Reprints	38
1998	Bowman Chrome Reprints Refractors	38
1998	Bowman Golden Anniversary	224
1998	Bowman International	224
1998	Bowman Minor League MVP's	MVP6
1998	Bowman's Best	77
1998	Bowman's Best Atomic Refractors	77
1998	Bowman's Best Refractors	77
1998	Circa Thunder	2
1998	Circa Thunder Boss	9
1998	Circa Thunder Limited Access	8
1998	Circa Thunder Rave	2
1998	Circa Thunder Rave Review	9
1998	Circa Thunder Super Rave	2
1998	Collector's Choice	450
1998	Collector's Choice Blowups 5x7	450
1998	Collector's Choice Mini Bobbing Heads	19
1998	Collector's Choice StarQuest	SQ53
1998	Collector's Choice StarQuest Double	6
1998	Collector's Choice StarQuest Home Run	6
1998	Collector's Choice StarQuest Single	6
1998	Collector's Choice StarQuest Triple	6
1998	Collector's Choice Stick 'Ums	19
1998	Crown Royale	94
1998	Crown Royale All-Stars	5
1998	Crown Royale Diamond Knights	15
1998	Donruss	100
1998	Donruss	165
1998	Donruss	367
1998	Donruss	404
1998	Donruss Collections Donruss	100
1998	Donruss Collections Donruss	165
1998	Donruss Collections Elite	408
1998	Donruss Collections Elite	525
1998	Donruss Collections Leaf	363
1998	Donruss Collections Preferred	559
1998	Donruss Collections Preferred	726
1998	Donruss Collections Samples	100
1998	Donruss Collections Samples	165
1998	Donruss Crusade Green	32
1998	Donruss Crusade Purple	32
1998	Donruss Crusade Red	32
1998	Donruss Days	12
1998	Donruss Diamond Kings	10
1998	Donruss Diamond Kings Canvas	10
1998	Donruss Elite	8
1998	Donruss Elite	125
1998	Donruss Elite Aspirations	8
1998	Donruss Elite Aspirations	125
1998	Donruss Elite Craftsmen	8
1998	Donruss Elite Inserts	4
1998	Donruss Elite Master Craftsmen	8
1998	Donruss Elite Status	8
1998	Donruss Elite Status	125
1998	Donruss FANtasy Team	18
1998	Donruss FANtasy Team Die Cuts	18
1998	Donruss Gold Press Proofs	100
1998	Donruss Gold Press Proofs	165
1998	Donruss Gold Press Proofs	367
1998	Donruss Gold Press Proofs	404
1998	Donruss MLB 99	6
1998	Donruss Preferred	9
1998	Donruss Preferred	176
1998	Donruss Preferred Gold Boxes	9
1998	Donruss Preferred Great X-Pectations	21
1998	Donruss Preferred Great X-Pectations Die Cuts	21
1998	Donruss Preferred Great X-Pectations Samples	21
1998	Donruss Preferred Green Boxes	9
1998	Donruss Preferred Precious Metals	9
1998	Donruss Preferred Seating	9
1998	Donruss Preferred Seating	176
1998	Donruss Preferred Tin Packs	9
1998	Donruss Preferred Tin Packs Double-Wide	5
1998	Donruss Preferred Tin Packs Gold	9
1998	Donruss Preferred Tin Packs Silver	9
1998	Donruss Preferred Title Waves	10
1998	Donruss Prized Collections Donruss	100
1998	Donruss Prized Collections Donruss	165
1998	Donruss Prized Collections Elite	408
1998	Donruss Prized Collections Elite	525
1998	Donruss Prized Collections Leaf	363

Year	Set Name	Card No.
1998	Donruss Prized Collections Preferred	559
1998	Donruss Prized Collections Preferred	726
1998	Donruss Production Line On-Base	20
1998	Donruss Signature	2
1998	Donruss Signature Autographs Century	63
1998	Donruss Signature Autographs Millenium	64
1998	Donruss Signature Proofs	2
1998	Donruss Silver Press Proofs	100
1998	Donruss Silver Press Proofs	165
1998	Donruss Silver Press Proofs	367
1998	Donruss Silver Press Proofs	404
1998	E-X2001	7
1998	E-X2001 Destination Cooperstown	13
1998	E-X2001 Essential Credentials Future	7
1998	E-X2001 Essential Credentials Now	7
1998	Finest	92
1998	Finest Mystery Finest 1	M12
1998	Finest Mystery Finest 1	M15
1998	Finest Mystery Finest 1	M18
1998	Finest Mystery Finest 1	M19
1998	Finest Mystery Finest 1 Refractors	M12
1998	Finest Mystery Finest 1 Refractors	M15
1998	Finest Mystery Finest 1 Refractors	M18
1998	Finest Mystery Finest 1 Refractors	M19
1998	Finest Mystery Finest 2	M14
1998	Finest Mystery Finest 2	M16
1998	Finest Mystery Finest 2	M18
1998	Finest Mystery Finest 2 Refractors	M14
1998	Finest Mystery Finest 2 Refractors	M16
1998	Finest Mystery Finest 2 Refractors	M18
1998	Finest Mystery Finest Oversize	2
1998	Finest Mystery Finest Oversize Refractors	2
1998	Finest No-Protectors	92
1998	Finest No-Protectors Refractors	92
1998	Finest Refractors	92
1998	Finest Stadium Stars	SS7
1998	Finest The Man	TM9
1998	Finest The Man Refractors	TM9
1998	Flair Showcase Legacy Collection	14
1998	Flair Showcase Legacy Collection Masterpieces	14
1998	Flair Showcase Row 0	14
1998	Flair Showcase Row 1	14
1998	Flair Showcase Row 2	14
1998	Flair Showcase Row 3	14
1998	Fleer	2
1998	Fleer	343
1998	Fleer	586
1998	Fleer Diamond Skills Commemorative Sheet	NNO
1998	Fleer Diamond Standouts	9
1998	Fleer In The Clutch	IC9
1998	Fleer Vintage '63	38
1998	Fleer Vintage '63 Classic	38
1998	Leaf	164
1998	Leaf Fractal Diamond Axis	164
1998	Leaf Fractal Foundations	164
1998	Leaf Fractal Materials	164
1998	Leaf Fractal Materials Die Cuts	164
1998	Leaf Fractal Materials Z2 Axis	164
1998	Leaf Fractal Matrix	164
1998	Leaf Fractal Matrix Die Cuts	164
1998	Leaf Rookies and Stars	34
1998	Leaf Rookies and Stars	152
1998	Leaf Rookies and Stars Crosstraining	10
1998	Leaf Rookies and Stars Greatest Hits	9
1998	Leaf Rookies and Stars Longevity	34
1998	Leaf Rookies and Stars Longevity	152
1998	Leaf Rookies and Stars Longevity Holographic	34
1998	Leaf Rookies and Stars Longevity Holographic	152
1998	Leaf Rookies and Stars Major League Hard Drives	11
1998	Leaf Rookies and Stars Major League Hard Drives Samples	11
1998	Leaf Rookies and Stars Ticket Masters	6

Year	Set Name	Card No.
1998	Leaf Rookies and Stars Ticket Masters Die Cuts	6
1998	Leaf Rookies and Stars True Blue	34
1998	Leaf Rookies and Stars True Blue	152
1998	Leaf State Representatives	18
1998	Leaf Statistical Standouts	23
1998	Leaf Statistical Standouts Die Cuts	23
1998	Metal Universe	199
1998	Metal Universe	208
1998	Metal Universe All-Galactic Team	9
1998	Metal Universe Platinum Portraits	7
1998	Metal Universe Precious Metal Gems	199
1998	Metal Universe Precious Metal Gems	208
1998	Metal Universe Titanium	9
1998	Metal Universe Universal Language	9
1998	Pacific	151
1998	Pacific Aurora	58
1998	Pacific Aurora Cubes	11
1998	Pacific Aurora Hardball Cel-Fusions	11
1998	Pacific Aurora On Deck Laser Cuts	11
1998	Pacific Aurora Pennant Fever	2
1998	Pacific Aurora Pennant Fever Copper	2
1998	Pacific Aurora Pennant Fever Platinum Blue	2
1998	Pacific Aurora Pennant Fever Red	2
1998	Pacific Aurora Pennant Fever Silver	2
1998	Pacific Gold Crown Die Cuts	22
1998	Pacific Invincible	52
1998	Pacific Invincible Gems of the Diamond	73
1998	Pacific Invincible Interleague Players	8A
1998	Pacific Invincible Photoengravings	9
1998	Pacific Invincible Platinum Blue	52
1998	Pacific Invincible Silver	52
1998	Pacific Invincible Team Checklists	19
1998	Pacific Omega	165
1998	Pacific Omega Online Inserts	10
1998	Pacific Omega Prisms	7
1998	Pacific Omega Red	165
1998	Pacific Online	505A
1998	Pacific Online	505B
1998	Pacific Online Red	505A
1998	Pacific Online Red	505B
1998	Pacific Online Web Cards	505A
1998	Pacific Online Web Cards	505B
1998	Pacific Paramount	69
1998	Pacific Paramount Copper	69
1998	Pacific Paramount Fielder's Choice	11
1998	Pacific Paramount Gold	69
1998	Pacific Paramount Holographic Silver	69
1998	Pacific Paramount Inaugural	13
1998	Pacific Paramount Platinum Blue	69
1998	Pacific Paramount Red	69
1998	Pacific Paramount Special Delivery	13
1998	Pacific Paramount Team Checklists	9
1998	Pacific Platinum Blue	151
1998	Pacific Red Threatt	151
1998	Pacific Silver	151
1998	Pacific Team Checklists	10
1998	Pinnacle	64
1998	Pinnacle	185
1998	Pinnacle Artist's Proofs	PP57
1998	Pinnacle Artist's Proofs	PP88
1998	Pinnacle Epix	E8
1998	Pinnacle Epix Game Emerald	E8
1998	Pinnacle Epix Game Orange	E8
1998	Pinnacle Epix Game Purple	E8
1998	Pinnacle Epix Moment Emerald	E8
1998	Pinnacle Epix Moment Orange	E8
1998	Pinnacle Epix Moment Purple	E8
1998	Pinnacle Epix Player Emerald	E8
1998	Pinnacle Epix Player Orange	E8
1998	Pinnacle Epix Player Purple	E8
1998	Pinnacle Epix Season Emerald	E8
1998	Pinnacle Epix Season Orange	E8
1998	Pinnacle Epix Season Purple	E8
1998	Pinnacle Inside	2
1998	Pinnacle Inside	133
1998	Pinnacle Inside Behind the Numbers	14

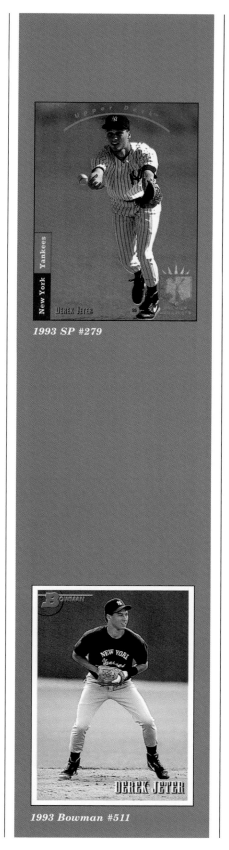

1993 SP #279

1993 Bowman #511

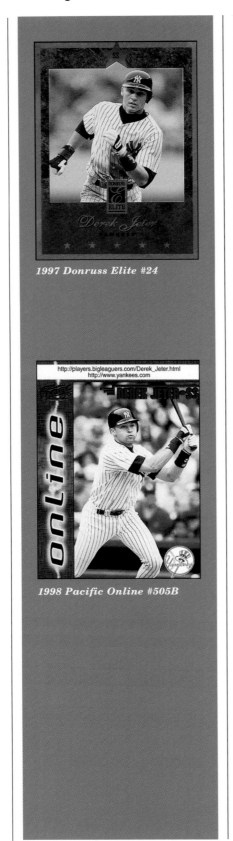

1997 Donruss Elite #24

1998 Pacific Online #505B

Year	Set Name	Card No.
1998	Pinnacle Inside Cans	9
1998	Pinnacle Inside Cans Gold	9
1998	Pinnacle Inside Club Edition	2
1998	Pinnacle Inside Club Edition	133
1998	Pinnacle Inside Diamond Edition	2
1998	Pinnacle Inside Diamond Edition	133
1998	Pinnacle Inside Stand-Up Guys	6AB
1998	Pinnacle Inside Stand-Up Guys	6CD
1998	Pinnacle Inside Stand-Up Guys	19AB
1998	Pinnacle Inside Stand-Up Guys	19CD
1998	Pinnacle Inside Stand-Up Guys Samples	6AB
1998	Pinnacle Inside Stand-Up Guys Samples	6CD
1998	Pinnacle Inside Stand-Up Guys Samples	19AB
1998	Pinnacle Inside Stand-Up Guys Samples	19CD
1998	Pinnacle Mint	9
1998	Pinnacle Mint Bronze	9
1998	Pinnacle Mint Coins Brass	9
1998	Pinnacle Mint Coins Brass Artist's Proofs	9
1998	Pinnacle Mint Coins Gold Plated	9
1998	Pinnacle Mint Coins Gold Plated Artist's Proofs	9
1998	Pinnacle Mint Coins Nickel	9
1998	Pinnacle Mint Coins Nickel Artist's Proofs	9
1998	Pinnacle Mint Coins Solid Gold Redemption	9
1998	Pinnacle Mint Coins Solid Silver	9
1998	Pinnacle Mint Gold	9
1998	Pinnacle Mint Silver	9
1998	Pinnacle Museum Collection	PP57
1998	Pinnacle Museum Collection	PP88
1998	Pinnacle Performers	9
1998	Pinnacle Performers	146
1998	Pinnacle Performers Launching Pad	3
1998	Pinnacle Performers Peak Performers	9
1998	Pinnacle Performers Peak Performers	146
1998	Pinnacle Plus All-Star Epix	8
1998	Pinnacle Plus All-Star Epix Emerald	8
1998	Pinnacle Plus All-Star Epix Purple	8
1998	Pinnacle Plus Lasting Memories	24
1998	Pinnacle Power Pack Jumbos	4
1998	Pinnacle Power Pack Jumbos Samples	4
1998	Pinnacle Press Plates	64
1998	Pinnacle Press Plates	185
1998	Pinnacle Press Plates	E8
1998	Pinnacle Snapshots	NYY4
1998	Pinnacle Snapshots	NYY9
1998	Pinnacle Uncut	185
1998	Revolution	99
1998	Revolution Prime Time Performers	6
1998	Revolution Shadow Series	99
1998	Revolution Showstoppers	11
1998	Score	22
1998	Score Artist's Proofs	PP7
1998	Score Complete Players	3A
1998	Score Complete Players	3B
1998	Score Complete Players	3C
1998	Score Complete Players Gold	3A
1998	Score Complete Players Gold	3B
1998	Score Complete Players Gold	3C
1998	Score Epix	E8
1998	Score First Pitch	7
1998	Score Rookie Traded	6
1998	Score Rookie Traded	262
1998	Score Rookie Traded Artist's Proofs	PP6
1998	Score Rookie Traded Artist's Proofs	PP155
1998	Score Rookie Traded Artist's Proofs 1 of 1's	PP6
1998	Score Rookie Traded Artist's Proofs 1 of 1's	PP155
1998	Score Rookie Traded Showcase Series	PP6
1998	Score Rookie Traded Showcase Series	PP155
1998	Score Rookie Traded Star Gazing	8
1998	Score Showcase Series	PP7
1998	Select Selected Samples	8
1998	SkyBox Dugout Axcess	73
1998	SkyBox Dugout Axcess	124
1998	SkyBox Dugout Axcess Double Header	DH4
1998	SkyBox Dugout Axcess Inside Axcess	73

Year	Set Name	Card No.
1998	SkyBox Dugout Axcess Inside Axcess	124
1998	SP Authentic	145
1998	SP Authentic Sheer Dominance	SD41
1998	SP Authentic Sheer Dominance Gold	SD41
1998	SP Authentic Sheer Dominance Titanium	SD41
1998	Sports Illustrated	64
1998	Sports Illustrated	148
1998	Sports Illustrated Covers	C2
1998	Sports Illustrated Editor's Choice	EC6
1998	Sports Illustrated Extra Edition	64
1998	Sports Illustrated Extra Edition	148
1998	Sports Illustrated First Edition	64
1998	Sports Illustrated First Edition	148
1998	Sports Illustrated Then and Now	93
1998	Sports Illustrated Then and Now Extra Edition	93
1998	Sports Illustrated Then and Now Great Shots	8
1998	Sports Illustrated World Series Fever	65
1998	Sports Illustrated World Series Fever Extra Edition	65
1998	Sports Illustrated World Series Fever First Edition	65
1998	SPx Finite	30
1998	SPx Finite	159
1998	SPx Finite	305
1998	SPx Finite Radiance	30
1998	SPx Finite Radiance	159
1998	SPx Finite Radiance	305
1998	SPx Finite Spectrum	30
1998	SPx Finite Spectrum	159
1998	SPx Finite Spectrum	305
1998	Stadium Club	241
1998	Stadium Club Co-Signers	CS2
1998	Stadium Club Co-Signers	CS4
1998	Stadium Club Co-Signers	CS6
1998	Stadium Club First Day Issue	241
1998	Stadium Club Never Compromise	NC10
1998	Stadium Club One Of A Kind	241
1998	Stadium Club Printing Plates	241
1998	Stadium Club Triumvirate Illuminator	T2A
1998	Stadium Club Triumvirate Illuminator	T14A
1998	Stadium Club Triumvirate Luminescent	T2A
1998	Stadium Club Triumvirate Luminescent	T14A
1998	Stadium Club Triumvirate Luminous	T2A
1998	Stadium Club Triumvirate Luminous	T14A
1998	Studio	163
1998	Studio Freeze Frame	2
1998	Studio Freeze Frame Die Cuts	2
1998	Studio Gold Press Proofs	163
1998	Studio Masterstrokes	12
1998	Studio MLB 99	6
1998	Studio Portraits 8 x 10	6
1998	Studio Portraits 8 x 10 Gold Proofs	6
1998	Studio Silver Press Proofs	163
1998	Topps	160
1998	Topps Baby Boomers	BB1
1998	Topps Chrome	160
1998	Topps Chrome Baby Boomers	BB1
1998	Topps Chrome Baby Boomers Refractors	BB1
1998	Topps Chrome Refractors	160
1998	Topps Devil Rays	160
1998	Topps Diamondbacks	160
1998	Topps Gallery	115
1998	Topps Gallery Gallery of Heroes	GH2
1998	Topps Gallery Gallery of Heroes Jumbos	GH2
1998	Topps Gallery Gallery Proofs	115
1998	Topps Gallery Original Printing Plates	115
1998	Topps Gallery Photo Gallery	PG3
1998	Topps Gallery Player's Private Issue	115
1998	Topps Gallery Player's Private Issue Auction	115
1998	Topps Gold Label Class 1	7
1998	Topps Gold Label Class 1 Black	7
1998	Topps Gold Label Class 1 One to One	7
1998	Topps Gold Label Class 1 Red	7
1998	Topps Gold Label Class 2	7
1998	Topps Gold Label Class 2 Black	7
1998	Topps Gold Label Class 2 One to One	7

Year	Set Name	Card No.	Year	Set Name	Card No.	Year	Set Name	Card No.
1998	Topps Gold Label Class 2 Red	7	1998	Zenith Samples Small	17	1999	Pacific Private Stock Preferred	8
1998	Topps Gold Label Class 3	7	1998	Zenith Z-Gold	17	1999	Pacific Private Stock PS-206	8
1998	Topps Gold Label Class 3 Black	7	1998	Zenith Z-Silver	17	1999	Pacific Private Stock PS-206 Red	8
1998	Topps Gold Label Class 3 One to One	7	1998	Zenith Z-Team	7	1999	Pacific Private Stock Vintage	8
1998	Topps Gold Label Class 3 Red	7	1998	Zenith Z-Team 5 x 7	7	1999	Pacific Red	294
1998	Topps Minted in Cooperstown	160	1998	Zenith Z-Team Gold	7	1999	Pacific Red	294A
1998	Topps Mystery Finest	ILM6	1999	Aurora	128	1999	Pacific Team Checklists	9
1998	Topps Mystery Finest Bordered	M8	1999	Aurora On Deck Laser-Cuts	18	1999	Pacific Timelines	6
1998	Topps Mystery Finest Bordered Refractors	M8	1999	Aurora Pennant Fever	12	1999	Pinheads	12
1998	Topps Mystery Finest Borderless	M8	1999	Aurora Pennant Fever Blue	18	1999	SkyBox Thunder	273
1998	Topps Mystery Finest Borderless Refractors	M8	1999	Aurora Pennant Fever Copper	18	1999	SkyBox Thunder Hip-No-Tized	H5
1998	Topps Mystery Finest Refractors	ILM6	1999	Aurora Pennant Fever Silver	18	1999	SkyBox Thunder Rant	273
1998	Topps Opening Day	83	1999	Aurora Styrotechs	12	1999	SkyBox Thunder Rave	273
1998	Topps Pre-Production	PP4	1999	Finest	90	1999	SkyBox Thunder Super Rave	273
1998	Topps Stars	33	1999	Finest	115	1999	SkyBox Thunder www.batterz.com	WB5
1998	Topps Stars 'N Steel	18	1999	Finest Gold Refractors	90	1999	SP Authentic	57
1998	Topps Stars 'N Steel Gold	18	1999	Finest Gold Refractors	115	1999	SP Authentic Epic Figures	E18
1998	Topps Stars 'N Steel Gold Holographic	18	1999	Finest Peel and Reveal Common	7	1999	SP Authentic Reflections	R18
1998	Topps Stars Bronze	33	1999	Finest Peel and Reveal Rare	7	1999	Sports Illustrated	152
1998	Topps Stars Gold	33	1999	Finest Peel and Reveal Uncommon	7	1999	Sports Illustrated Headliners	21
1998	Topps Stars Gold Rainbow	33	1999	Finest Refractors	90	1999	Stadium Club	65
1998	Topps Stars Silver	33	1999	Finest Refractors	115	1999	Stadium Club Co-Signers	CS4
1998	Topps SuperChrome	13	1999	Finest Split Screen	S3	1999	Stadium Club Co-Signers	CS10
1998	Topps SuperChrome Refractors	13	1999	Finest Split Screen Dual Refractors	S3	1999	Stadium Club Co-Signers	CS15
1998	Topps Tek	14	1999	Fleer	5	1999	Stadium Club Co-Signers	CS20
1998	Topps Tek Diffractors	14	1999	Fleer	585	1999	Stadium Club First Day Issue	65
1998	UD3	79	1999	Fleer	598	1999	Stadium Club Never Compromise	NC10
1998	UD3	169	1999	Fleer Diamond Magic	7	1999	Stadium Club One of a Kind	65
1998	UD3	259	1999	Fleer Starting 9	5	1999	Stadium Club Printing Plates	65
1998	UD3 Die Cuts	79	1999	Fleer Starting 9	585	1999	Stadium Club Triumvirate Illuminator	T4A
1998	UD3 Die Cuts	169	1999	Fleer Starting 9	598	1999	Stadium Club Triumvirate Luminescent	T4A
1998	UD3 Die Cuts	259	1999	Fleer Vintage '61	5	1999	Stadium Club Triumvirate Luminous	T4A
1998	Ultra	150	1999	Fleer Warning Track	5	1999	Topps	85
1998	Ultra	481	1999	Fleer Warning Track	585	1999	Topps	230
1998	Ultra Artistic Talents	6	1999	Fleer Warning Track	598	1999	Topps Chrome	85
1998	Ultra Back to the Future	3	1999	Metal Universe	97	1999	Topps Chrome	230
1998	Ultra Diamond Immortals	10	1999	Metal Universe	238	1999	Topps Chrome Early Road to the Hall	ER2
1998	Ultra Diamond Producers	6	1999	Metal Universe	281	1999	Topps Chrome Early Road to the Hall Refractors	ER2
1998	Ultra Double Trouble	5	1999	Metal Universe Boyz With The Wood	12	1999	Topps Chrome New Breed	NB9
1998	Ultra Fall Classics	6	1999	Metal Universe Diamond Soul	4	1999	Topps Chrome New Breed Refractors	NB9
1998	Ultra Gold Medallion	150	1999	Metal Universe Gem Masters	97	1999	Topps Chrome Refractors	85
1998	Ultra Gold Medallion	481	1999	Metal Universe Gem Masters	238	1999	Topps Chrome Refractors	230
1998	Ultra Kid Gloves	3	1999	Metal Universe Gem Masters	281	1999	Topps MVP Promotion	85
1998	Ultra Masterpieces	150	1999	Metal Universe Linchpins	7	1999	Topps New Breed	NB9
1998	Ultra Masterpieces	481	1999	Metal Universe Planet Metal	6	1999	Topps Opening Day	48
1998	Ultra Millennium Men	4	1999	Metal Universe Precious Metal Gems	97	1999	Topps Picture Perfect	P10
1998	Ultra Notables	20	1999	Metal Universe Precious Metal Gems	238	1999	Topps Pre-Production	PP3
1998	Ultra Platinum Medallion	150	1999	Metal Universe Precious Metal Gems	281	1999	Topps Stars 'N Steel	34
1998	Ultra Platinum Medallion	481	1999	Metal Universe Sample Sheet	NNOA	1999	Topps Stars 'N Steel Gold	34
1998	Ultra Prime Leather	6	1999	Metal Universe Sample Sheet	NNO	1999	Topps Stars 'N Steel Gold Domed Holographic	34
1998	Ultra Ticket Studs	11	1999	Pacific	294	1999	Topps SuperChrome	14
1998	Ultra Top 30	18	1999	Pacific	294A	1999	Topps SuperChrome Refractors	14
1998	Ultra Win Now	6	1999	Pacific Crown Collection	190	1999	UD Choice	33
1998	Upper Deck	141	1999	Pacific Crown Collection In The Cage	11	1999	UD Choice	115
1998	Upper Deck	450	1999	Pacific Crown Collection Platinum Blue	190	1999	UD Choice Blow Up	6
1998	Upper Deck	618	1999	Pacific Crown Collection Team Checklists	20	1999	UD Choice Blow Up Cover Glory	4
1998	Upper Deck 10th Anniversary Preview	41	1999	Pacific Dynagon Diamond	4	1999	UD Choice Mini Bobbing Head	B16
1998	Upper Deck 10th Anniversary Preview Retail	41	1999	Pacific Dynagon Diamond Titanium	4	1999	UD Choice Prime Choice Reserve	33
1998	Upper Deck 5 x 7 Blow Ups	450	1999	Pacific Gold Crown Die Cuts	10	1999	UD Choice Prime Choice Reserve	115
1998	Upper Deck All-Star Credentials	AS11	1999	Pacific Paramount	162	1999	UD Choice StarQuest	4
1998	Upper Deck Amazing Greats	AG2	1999	Pacific Paramount Copper	162	1999	UD Choice StarQuest Double	4
1998	Upper Deck Amazing Greats Die Cuts	AG2	1999	Pacific Paramount Fielder's Choice	12	1999	UD Choice StarQuest Home Run	4
1998	Upper Deck Blue Chip Prospects	BC15	1999	Pacific Paramount Holographic Silver	162	1999	UD Choice StarQuest Triple	4
1998	Upper Deck Clearly Dominant	CD2	1999	Pacific Paramount Personal Bests	23	1999	UD Ionix	41
1998	Upper Deck Destination Stardom	DS28	1999	Pacific Paramount Platinum Blue	162	1999	UD Ionix	78
1998	Upper Deck Retro	67	1999	Pacific Platinum Blue	294	1999	UD Ionix Cyber	C8
1998	Upper Deck Retro Groovy Kind of Glove	G24	1999	Pacific Platinum Blue	294A	1999	UD Ionix HoloGrFX	HG8
1998	Upper Deck Retro Quantum Leap	Q22	1999	Pacific Prism	100	1999	UD Ionix Hyper	H8
1998	Upper Deck Retro Time Capsule	TC13	1999	Pacific Prism Ahead of the Game	13	1999	UD Ionix Nitro	N8
1998	Yankees Score	2	1999	Pacific Prism Diamond Glory	13	1999	UD Ionix Reciprocal	41
1998	Yankees Score Platinum	2	1999	Pacific Prism Holographic Blue	100	1999	UD Ionix Reciprocal	78
1998	Zenith	17	1999	Pacific Prism Holographic Gold	100	1999	UD Ionix Warp Zone	WZ8
1998	Zenith 5 x 7	15	1999	Pacific Prism Holographic Mirror	100	1999	Ultra	30
1998	Zenith 5 x 7 Gold Impulse	15	1999	Pacific Prism Holographic Purple	100	1999	Ultra Damage Inc.	5
1998	Zenith 5 x 7 Impulse	15	1999	Pacific Private Stock	8	1999	Ultra Diamond Producers	10
1998	Zenith Epix	E8	1999	Pacific Private Stock Exclusive	8			
1998	Zenith Samples Large	Z15	1999	Pacific Private Stock Platinum	8			

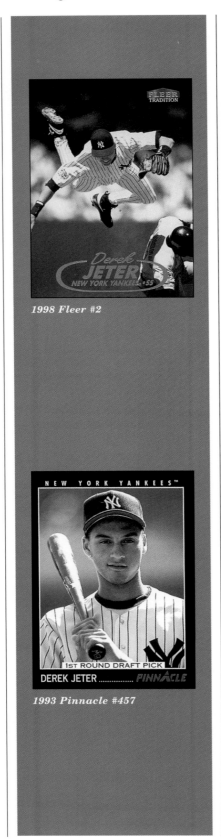

1998 Fleer #2

1993 Pinnacle #457

Year	Set Name	Card No.
1999	Ultra Gold Medallion	30
1999	Ultra Masterpieces	30
1999	Ultra Platinum Medallion	30
1999	Ultra RBI Kings	18
1999	Ultra The Book On	19
1999	Ultra Thunderclap	6
1999	Upper Deck	154
1999	Upper Deck 10th Anniversary Team	X25
1999	Upper Deck 10th Anniversary Team Double	X25
1999	Upper Deck 10th Anniversary Team Home Run	X25
1999	Upper Deck 10th Anniversary Team Triple	X25
1999	Upper Deck Black Diamond	56
1999	Upper Deck Black Diamond Dominance	D2
1999	Upper Deck Black Diamond Dominance Emerald	D2
1999	Upper Deck Black Diamond Double	56
1999	Upper Deck Black Diamond Mystery Numbers	M8
1999	Upper Deck Black Diamond Mystery Numbers Emerald	M8
1999	Upper Deck Black Diamond Quadruple	56
1999	Upper Deck Black Diamond Triple	56
1999	Upper Deck Exclusives Level 1	154
1999	Upper Deck Exclusives Level 2	154
1999	Upper Deck Immaculate Perception	I27
1999	Upper Deck Immaculate Perception Double	I27
1999	Upper Deck Immaculate Perception Home Run	I27
1999	Upper Deck Immaculate Perception Triple	I27
1999	Upper Deck Wonder Years	W12
1999	Upper Deck Wonder Years Double	W12
1999	Upper Deck Wonder Years Triple	W12
1999	Upper Deck Wonder Years Home Run	W12

Tommy John

Year	Set Name	Card No.
1964	Topps	146
1964	Topps Venezuelan	146
1965	O-Pee-Chee	208
1965	Topps	208
1966	Topps	486
1966	White Sox Team Issue	7
1967	Coke Caps White Sox	15
1967	Dexter Press	105
1967	Topps	609
1968	O-Pee-Chee	72
1968	Topps	72
1968	Topps Venezuelan	72
1969	Milton Bradley	133
1969	MLB Official Stamps	31
1969	Nabisco Team Flakes	11
1969	Topps	465
1969	Topps Stamps	155
1969	Topps Team Posters	11
1969	Transogram Statues	22
1969	White Sox Team Issue	6
1970	MLB Official Stamps	186
1970	O-Pee-Chee	180
1970	Topps	180
1970	White Sox Team Issue	7
1971	Kellogg's	74
1971	Milk Duds	11
1971	O-Pee-Chee	520
1971	Topps	520
1971	Topps Coins Inserts	56
1972	Milton Bradley	165
1972	O-Pee-Chee	264
1972	Topps	264
1973	O-Pee-Chee	258
1973	Topps	258
1974	O-Pee-Chee	451
1974	Topps	451
1975	O-Pee-Chee	47
1975	Topps	47

Year	Set Name	Card No.
1975	Topps Mini	47
1976	Dodgers Postcards	8
1976	O-Pee-Chee	416
1976	SSPC	69
1976	Topps	416
1977	Topps	128
1977-78	Dodgers Photos	5
1977-79	Sportscaster	3204
1978	Hostess	7
1978	Kellogg's	36
1978	RC Cola Cans	82
1978	SSPC 270	75
1978	Topps	375
1979	Baseball Patches	43
1979	O-Pee-Chee	129
1979	Topps	255
1979	Yankees Burger King	9
1979	Yankees Picture Album	21
1980	O-Pee-Chee	348
1980	Topps	690
1980	Topps Super	23
1980	Wilson Glove Tags	3
1980	Yankees Photo Album	13
1981	All-Star Game Program Inserts	84
1981	Donruss	107
1981	Fleer	81
1981	Fleer Sticker Cards	121
1981	Kellogg's	52
1981	O-Pee-Chee	96
1981	Topps	550
1981	Topps Scratchoffs	52
1981	Topps Stickers	2
1981	Topps Stickers	114
1981	Topps Stickers	250
1981	Topps Super Home Team	66
1981	Yankees Photo Album	10
1982	Donruss	409
1982	Donruss	558
1982	Fleer	40
1982	Fleer Stamps	115
1982	O-Pee-Chee	75
1982	Topps	75
1982	Topps	486
1982	Topps/O-Pee-Chee Stickers	214
1982	Wilson Sporting Goods	4
1982	Yankees Photo Album	12
1983	Donruss	570
1983	Fleer	95
1983	Fleer Stamps	92
1983	Fleer Stickers	25
1983	O-Pee-Chee	144
1983	O-Pee-Chee	196
1983	Seven-Eleven Coins	9
1983	Topps	735
1983	Topps	736
1983	Topps Foldouts	1
1984	Angels Smokey	13
1984	Donruss	301
1984	Donruss Champions	36
1984	Fleer	522
1984	Fun Foods Pins	92
1984	Nestle 792	415
1984	Nestle 792	715
1984	O-Pee-Chee	284
1984	Topps	415
1984	Topps	715
1984	Topps Rub Downs	28
1984	Topps Tiffany	415
1984	Topps Tiffany	715
1984	Topps/O-Pee-Chee Stickers	232
1985	Angels Smokey	23
1985	Donruss	423
1985	Fleer	304
1985	O-Pee-Chee	179
1985	Topps	179
1985	Topps Tiffany	179
1985	Topps/O-Pee-Chee Stickers	229

Year	Set Name	Card No.
1986	Fleer	422
1986	Fleer Update	57
1986	Topps	240
1986	Topps Tiffany	240
1986	Wilson Glove Tags	1
1986	Yankees TCMA	1
1987	Dodgers Smokey All-Stars	15
1987	Fleer	102
1987	Fleer Glossy	102
1987	O-Pee-Chee	236
1987	Topps	236
1987	Topps Tiffany	236
1988	Donruss	17
1988	Donruss	401
1988	Donruss Baseball's Best	220
1988	Donruss Super DK's	17
1988	Donruss Team Book Yankees	401
1988	Fleer	211
1988	Fleer Glossy	211
1988	Leaf/Donruss	17
1988	Leaf/Donruss	230
1988	Panini Stickers	148
1988	Score	240
1988	Score Glossy	240
1988	Sportflics	122
1988	Starting Lineup Yankees	7
1988	Topps	611
1988	Topps Tiffany	611
1989	Classic Light Blue	40
1989	Dodgers Smokey Greats	91
1989	Fleer	255
1989	Fleer Glossy	255
1989	Score	477
1989	Topps	359
1989	Topps Baseball Talk/LJN	139
1989	Topps Tiffany	359
1989	Topps/O-Pee-Chee Stickers	310
1989	Upper Deck	230
1990	Dodgers Target	386
1992	Dodgers Stamps Trak Auto	17
1992	Yankees WIZ 70s	80
1992	Yankees WIZ 80s	92
1992	Yankees WIZ All-Stars	34
1993	Action Packed ASG	157
1993	Upper Deck All-Time Heroes	75
1994	Ted Williams	12
1994	Upper Deck All-Time Heroes	78
1994	Upper Deck All-Time Heroes 125th	78
1995	Sonic/Pepsi Greats	5

Sparky Lyle

Year	Set Name	Card No.
1969	Milton Bradley	163
1969	Red Sox Arco Oil	7
1969	Red Sox Team Issue	7
1969	Topps	311
1970	MLB Official Stamps	160
1970	O-Pee-Chee	116
1970	Red Sox Color Photo Post Cards	7
1970	Topps	116
1971	MLB Official Stamps	324
1971	O-Pee-Chee	649
1971	Red Sox Team Issue	6
1971	Topps	649
1972	Milton Bradley	202
1972	O-Pee-Chee	259
1972	Topps	259
1973	Kellogg's 2D	15
1973	New York Sunday News M138	21
1973	O-Pee-Chee	68
1973	O-Pee-Chee	394
1973	Seven-Eleven Trading Cups	40
1973	Syracuse Chiefs Team Issue	14
1973	Topps	68
1973	Topps	394

Year	Set Name	Card No.
1973	Yankees	2
1973-74	Linnett Portraits	130
1974	Kellogg's	41
1974	O-Pee-Chee	66
1974	Syracuse Chiefs Team Issue	13
1974	Topps	66
1974	Topps Stamps	212
1975	Hostess	134
1975	Kellogg's	47
1975	O-Pee-Chee	485
1975	SSPC 42	28
1975	Syracuse Chiefs Team Issue	8
1975	Topps	485
1975	Topps Mini	485
1975	Yankees SSPC	22
1976	O-Pee-Chee	545
1976	SSPC	429
1976	Topps	545
1977	O-Pee-Chee	89
1977	Topps	598
1977	Yankees Burger King	10
1978	Hostess	68
1978	Kellogg's	43
1978	O-Pee-Chee	214
1978	O-Pee-Chee	237
1978	RC Cola Cans	84
1978	SSPC 270	11
1978	Topps	2
1978	Topps	35
1978	Yankees Burger King	9
1978	Yankees Photo Album	17
1978	Yankees SSPC Diary	11
1979	Hostess	143
1979	O-Pee-Chee	188
1979	Topps	365
1980	O-Pee-Chee	62
1980	Topps	115
1981	Donruss	284
1981	Fleer	17
1981	Fleer Sticker Cards	91
1981	O-Pee-Chee	337
1981	Red Sox Boston Globe	92
1981	Topps	719
1982	Donruss	189
1982	Fleer	247
1982	O-Pee-Chee	285
1982	Topps	285
1983	O-Pee-Chee	92
1983	O-Pee-Chee	208
1983	Topps	693
1983	Topps	694
1983	Yankee A-S Fifty Years	25
1990	Pacific Legends	93
1992	Yankees WIZ 70s	99
1992	Yankees WIZ All-Stars	42
1993	MCI Ambassadors	13
1993	Rangers Keebler	235
1994	MCI Ambassadors	1
1994	Ted Williams	60
1994	Ted Williams	138
1995	MCI Ambassadors	7
1995	Sonic/Pepsi Greats	7

Billy Martin

Year	Set Name	Card No.
1947-65	PM10 Stadium Pins 2 1/8'	24
1948	Signal Oil	17
1948	Smith's Clothing	17
1949	Remar Bread	17
1952	Berk Ross	38
1952	Topps	175
1953	Bowman Color	93
1953	Bowman Color	118
1953	Topps	86
1953-55	Dormand	130

Year	Set Name	Card No.
1954	Bowman	145
1954	Red Heart	19
1954	Topps	13
1956	Topps	181
1956	Yankees Jay Publishing	9
1956	Yankees Team Issue	15
1957	Topps	62
1957	Yankees Jay Publishing	11
1958	Topps	271
1959	Indians	10
1959	Kahn's	20
1959	Tigers Graphic Arts Service PC749	12
1959	Topps	295
1960	Kahn's	24
1960	Topps	173
1960	Topps Venezuelan	173
1961	Post	190A
1961	Post	190B
1961	Topps	89
1961	Topps Magic Rub-Offs	26
1962	Jello	84
1962	Post	84
1962	Post Canadian	84
1962	Salada Plastic Coins	43
1962	Shirriff Plastic Coins	43
1962	Topps	208
1969	Topps	547
1969	Twins Team Issue Color	7
1971	O-Pee-Chee	208
1971	Topps	208
1972	O-Pee-Chee	33
1972	O-Pee-Chee	34
1972	Topps	33
1972	Topps	34
1973	O-Pee-Chee	323
1973	Tigers Jewel	12
1973	Topps	323
1973-97	Book Promotional Cards	15
1974	O-Pee-Chee	379
1974	Topps	379
1975	O-Pee-Chee	511
1975	Rangers Postcards	21
1975	Topps	511
1975	Topps Mini	511
1976	SSPC	453
1976	Topps	17
1977	Topps	387
1977	Yankees Burger King	1
1977-79	Sportscaster	8309
1978	SSPC 270	14
1978	Topps	721
1978	Twins Frisz	10
1978	Yankees Burger King	1
1978	Yankees SSPC Diary	14
1979	TCMA 50'S	143
1979	Yankees Picture Album	24
1981	A's Granny Goose	1
1981	Donruss	479
1981	Fleer	581
1981	TCMA 60's II	364
1981	Tigers Detroit News	67
1981	Tigers Detroit News	107
1981	Topps	671
1982	A's Granny Goose	9
1982	Donruss	491
1982	Topps/O-Pee-Chee Stickers	115
1983	Donruss	575
1983	Tigers Al Kaline Story	15
1983	Tigers Al Kaline Story	16
1983	Tigers Al Kaline Story	43
1983	Topps	156
1983	Topps Reprint 52	175
1983	Topps Traded	66T
1983	Yankee A-S Fifty Years	28
1983	Yankee Yearbook Insert TCMA	5
1983	Yankees Photo Album	14
1984	Fleer	652

Year	Set Name	Card No.
1984	Nestle 792	81
1984	Topps	81
1984	Topps Tiffany	81
1984-89	O'Connell and Son Ink	65
1985	Police Mets/Yankees	Y6
1985	Topps Traded	78T
1985	Topps Traded Tiffany	78T
1986	TCMA Superstars Simon	17
1986	Topps	651
1986	Topps Tiffany	651
1987	A's Mother's	23
1990	Yankees Score Nat West	30
1991	Score Mantle	1
1991	Topps Archives 1953	86
1992	Bazooka Quadracard '53 Archives	8
1992	Pinnacle Mantle	26
1992	Yankees WIZ All-Stars	45
1992-93	Revolutionary Legends 1	13
1992-93	Revolutionary Legends 1	14
1992-93	Revolutionary Legends 1	15
1993	Action Packed ASG	140
1993	Rangers Keebler	245
1993	Upper Deck All-Time Heroes	88
1993	Upper Deck All-Time Heroes	141
1993	Upper Deck Sheets	25
1994	Ted Williams	61
1994	Topps Archives 1954	13
1994	Topps Archives 1954 Gold	13
1994	Upper Deck All-Time Heroes	99
1994	Upper Deck All-Time Heroes 125th	99

Tino Martinez

Year	Set Name	Card No.
1987	Pan Am Team USA Blue INDEP	19
1987	Pan Am Team USA Red BDK	1
1988	Topps Traded	66T
1988	Topps Traded Tiffany	66T
1989	Baseball America AA Prospects Best	AA6
1989	Bowman	211
1989	Bowman Tiffany	211
1989	Eastern League All-Stars ProCards	18
1989	Star	124
1989	Topps Big	93
1989	Williamsport Bills ProCards	635
1989	Williamsport Bills Star	13
1990	Bowman	484
1990	Bowman Tiffany	484
1990	Calgary Cannons CMC	12
1990	Calgary Cannons ProCards	659
1990	Fleer Update	119
1990	ProCards AAA	124
1990	Score	596
1990	Upper Deck	37
1990-93	Topps Magazine	46
1991	Bowman	257
1991	Calgary Cannons Line Drive	66
1991	Calgary Cannons ProCards	523
1991	Classic Game	150
1991	Classic I	T2
1991	Donruss	28
1991	Donruss Previews	6
1991	Fleer	458
1991	Leaf Previews	24
1991	Line Drive AAA	66
1991	Major League Collector Pins	7
1991	Mariners Country Hearth	10
1991	O-Pee-Chee	482
1991	O-Pee-Chee Premier	76
1991	Score	798
1991	Score Rookies	38
1991	Seven-Eleven Coins	NW12
1991	Stadium Club	179
1991	Studio	118
1991	Topps	482
1991	Topps Debut '90	99

Year	Set Name	Card No.
1991	Topps Desert Shield	482
1991	Topps Micro	482
1991	Topps Tiffany	482
1991	Triple A All-Stars ProCards	AAA5
1991	Ultra	341
1991	Upper Deck	553
1992	Bowman	483
1992	Bowman	626
1992	Classic Game	50
1992	Classic II	T42
1992	Donruss	410
1992	Donruss	525
1992	Fleer	287
1992	Leaf	329
1992	Leaf Black Gold	329
1992	Mariners Mother's	11
1992	MVP Pins	4
1992	O-Pee-Chee	481
1992	O-Pee-Chee Premier	64
1992	Pinnacle	123
1992	Pinnacle Team 2000	62
1992	ProCards	138
1992	Score	596
1992	Score 100 Rising Stars	51
1992	Score Hot Rookies	7
1992	Stadium Club	573
1992	Studio	236
1992	Topps	481
1992	Topps Gold	481
1992	Topps Gold Winners	481
1992	Topps Micro	481
1992	Triple Play	259
1992	Ultra	127
1992	Upper Deck	554
1993	Bowman	303
1993	Donruss	217
1993	Flair	274
1993	Fleer	310
1993	Leaf	406
1993	Mariners Mother's	17
1993	Mariners Stadium Club	18
1993	O-Pee-Chee	212
1993	Pacific Beisbol Amigos	11
1993	Pacific Spanish	289
1993	Panini Stickers	66
1993	Pinnacle	213
1993	Red Foley Stickers	58
1993	Score	76
1993	Select	246
1993	SP	134
1993	Stadium Club	273
1993	Stadium Club First Day Issue	273
1993	Stadium Club Members Only Parallel	273
1993	Studio	204
1993	Topps	232
1993	Topps Gold	232
1993	Topps Inagural Rockies	232
1993	Topps Inaugural Marlins	232
1993	Topps Micro	232
1993	Triple Play	35
1993	Ultra	623
1993	Upper Deck	287
1993	Upper Deck Gold	287
1994	Bowman	669
1994	Collector's Choice	191
1994	Collector's Choice Gold Signature	191
1994	Collector's Choice Silver Signature	191
1994	Donruss	296
1994	Finest	55
1994	Finest Refractors	55
1994	Flair	106
1994	Fleer	295
1994	Fleer Extra Bases	170
1994	Leaf	92
1994	Leaf Limited	69
1994	Mariners Mother's	16
1994	Pacific	577

Year	Set Name	Card No.
1994	Panini Stickers	122
1994	Pinnacle	129
1994	Pinnacle Artist's Proofs	129
1994	Pinnacle Museum Collection	129
1994	Score	59
1994	Score Gold Rush	59
1994	Select	163
1994	Stadium Club	60
1994	Stadium Club First Day Issue	60
1994	Stadium Club Golden Rainbow	60
1994	Stadium Club Members Only Parallel	60
1994	Studio	104
1994	Topps	693
1994	Topps Gold	693
1994	Topps Spanish	693
1994	Triple Play	130
1994	Ultra	121
1994	Upper Deck	94
1994	Upper Deck Electric Diamond	94
1995	Collector's Choice	283
1995	Collector's Choice Gold Signature	283
1995	Collector's Choice SE	127
1995	Collector's Choice SE Gold Signature	127
1995	Collector's Choice SE Silver Signature	127
1995	Collector's Choice Silver Signature	283
1995	Donruss	63
1995	Donruss Press Proofs	63
1995	Donruss Top of the Order	153
1995	Emotion	80
1995	Finest	51
1995	Finest Refractors	51
1995	Flair	83
1995	Fleer	273
1995	Leaf	90
1995	Leaf Limited	96
1995	Mariners Mother's	23
1995	Mariners Pacific	7
1995	Mariners Pacific	36
1995	Pacific	401
1995	Pinnacle	310
1995	Pinnacle Artist's Proofs	310
1995	Pinnacle Museum Collection	310
1995	Score	128
1995	Score Gold Rush	128
1995	Score Platinum Team Sets	128
1995	SP	191
1995	SP Silver	191
1995	Stadium Club	227
1995	Stadium Club First Day Issue	227
1995	Stadium Club Members Only Parallel	227
1995	Stadium Club Super Team Division Winners	M227
1995	Stadium Club Super Team World Series	227
1995	Stadium Club Virtual Reality	115
1995	Stadium Club Virtual Reality Members Only	115
1995	Studio	82
1995	Topps	377
1995	Topps Cyberstats	198
1995	Topps Embossed	73
1995	Topps Embossed Golden Idols	73
1995	Ultra	328
1995	Ultra Gold Medallion	328
1995	Upper Deck	99
1995	Upper Deck Electric Diamond	99
1995	Upper Deck Electric Diamond Gold	99
1995	Upper Deck Special Edition	256
1995	Upper Deck Special Edition Gold	256
1995	Zenith	103
1996	Bazooka	113
1996	Bowman	49
1996	Bowman Foil	49
1996	Bowman's Best	59
1996	Bowman's Best Atomic Refractors	59
1996	Bowman's Best Refractors	59
1996	Circa	66
1996	Circa Rave	66
1996	Collector's Choice	318

Year	Set Name	Card No.
1996	Collector's Choice	780
1996	Collector's Choice Gold Signature	318
1996	Collector's Choice Silver Signature	318
1996	Donruss	43
1996	Donruss Press Proofs	43
1996	Emotion-XL	91
1996	Finest	B260
1996	Finest	S357
1996	Finest Refractors	B260
1996	Finest Refractors	S357
1996	Flair	132
1996	Fleer	188
1996	Fleer Tiffany	188
1996	Fleer Update	U64
1996	Fleer Update Tiffany	U64
1996	Leaf Limited	4
1996	Leaf Limited Gold	4
1996	Leaf Preferred	7
1996	Leaf Preferred Press Proofs	7
1996	Leaf Signature	123
1996	Leaf Signature Press Proofs Gold	123
1996	Leaf Signature Press Proofs Platinum	123
1996	Metal Universe	89
1996	Metal Universe Platinum	89
1996	MLB Pins	20
1996	Pacific	404
1996	Pacific Estrellas Latinas	EL18
1996	Pacific Prisms	P134
1996	Pacific Prisms Gold	P134
1996	Panini Stickers	225
1996	Pinnacle	27
1996	Pinnacle	361
1996	Pinnacle Aficionado	64
1996	Pinnacle Aficionado Artist's Proofs	64
1996	Pinnacle Aficionado First Pitch Preview	64
1996	Pinnacle Aficionado Slick Picks	24
1996	Pinnacle Foil	361
1996	Pinnacle Starburst	13
1996	Pinnacle Starburst Artist's Proofs	13
1996	Score	354
1996	Score Dugout Collection	B79
1996	Score Dugout Collection Artist's Proofs	B79
1996	Select	104
1996	Select Artist's Proofs	104
1996	Select Certified	2
1996	Select Certified Artist's Proofs	2
1996	Select Certified Certified Blue	2
1996	Select Certified Certified Red	2
1996	Select Certified Mirror Blue	2
1996	Select Certified Mirror Gold	2
1996	Select Certified Mirror Red	2
1996	Sportflix	84
1996	Sportflix Artist's Proofs	84
1996	Stadium Club	185
1996	Stadium Club Members Only	24
1996	Stadium Club Members Only Parallel	185
1996	Studio	144
1996	Studio Press Proofs Bronze	144
1996	Studio Press Proofs Gold	144
1996	Studio Press Proofs Silver	144
1996	Summit	3
1996	Summit Above and Beyond	3
1996	Summit Artist's Proofs	3
1996	Summit Foil	3
1996	Topps	168
1996	Topps Chrome	48
1996	Topps Chrome Refractors	48
1996	Topps Laser	85
1996	Topps Road Warriors	RW10
1996	Ultra	129
1996	Ultra	390
1996	Ultra Gold Medallion	129
1996	Ultra Gold Medallion	390
1996	Upper Deck	503U
1996	Zenith	14
1996	Zenith Artist's Proofs	14
1997	Bowman	48

Year	Set Name	Card No.
1997	Bowman Chrome	38
1997	Bowman Chrome International	38
1997	Bowman Chrome International Refractors	38
1997	Bowman Chrome Refractors	38
1997	Bowman International	48
1997	Bowman's Best	66
1997	Bowman's Best Atomic Refractors	66
1997	Bowman's Best Refractor	66
1997	Circa	104
1997	Circa Rave	104
1997	Collector's Choice	181
1997	Collector's Choice Teams	NY6
1997	Donruss	55
1997	Donruss Elite	105
1997	Donruss Elite Gold Stars	105
1997	Donruss Gold Press Proofs	55
1997	Donruss Limited	56
1997	Donruss Limited	93
1997	Donruss Limited Exposure	56
1997	Donruss Limited Exposure	93
1997	Donruss Limited Exposure Non-Glossy	56
1997	Donruss Limited Fabric of the Game	35
1997	Donruss Preferred	79
1997	Donruss Preferred Cut to the Chase	79
1997	Donruss Signature	34
1997	Donruss Signature Autographs Century	86
1997	Donruss Signature Autographs Millenium	86
1997	Donruss Signature Platinum Press Proofs	34
1997	Donruss Silver Press Proofs	55
1997	Donruss Team Sets	124
1997	Donruss Team Sets Pennant Edition	124
1997	Donruss VxP 1.0	27
1997	Finest	204
1997	Finest Refractors	204
1997	Fleer	171
1997	Fleer Tiffany	171
1997	Leaf	254
1997	Leaf Fractal Matrix	254
1997	Leaf Fractal Matrix Die Cuts	254
1997	Leaf Leagues of the Nation	13
1997	Metal Universe	119
1997	New Pinnacle	66
1997	New Pinnacle Artist's Proof	66
1997	New Pinnacle Museum Collection	66
1997	New Pinnacle Press Plates	66
1997	Pacific	154
1997	Pacific Latinos of the Major Leagues	13
1997	Pacific Light Blue	154
1997	Pacific Prisms	52
1997	Pacific Prisms Light Blue	52
1997	Pacific Prisms Platinum	52
1997	Pacific Silver	154
1997	Phillies Copi Quik	17
1997	Pinnacle Inside	55
1997	Pinnacle Inside Club Edition	55
1997	Pinnacle Inside Diamond Edition	55
1997	Pinnacle X-Press	44
1997	Pinnacle X-Press	144
1997	Pinnacle X-Press Men of Summer	44
1997	Pinnacle X-Press Men of Summer	144
1997	Pinnacle X-Press Swing for the Fences	39
1997	Pinnacle X-Press Swing for the Fences Upgrade	3
1997	Score	208
1997	Score Artist's Proofs White Border	208
1997	Score Premium Stock	208
1997	Score Showcase Series	208
1997	Score Showcase Series Artist's Proofs	208
1997	SP	126
1997	Sports Illustrated	29
1997	Sports Illustrated	129
1997	Sports Illustrated Extra Edition	29
1997	Sports Illustrated Extra Edition	129
1997	Stadium Club	220
1997	Stadium Club Matrix	220
1997	Stadium Club Members Only Parallel	220
1997	Strat-O-Matic All-Stars	44

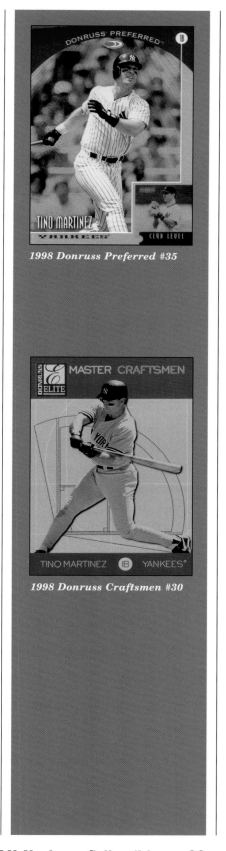

1998 Donruss Preferred #35

1998 Donruss Craftsmen #30

1998 Finest Power Zone #P18

1989 Star #124

Year	Set Name	Card No.	Year	Set Name	Card No.
1997	Studio	31	1998	Donruss Dominators	10
1997	Studio Press Proof Gold	31	1998	Donruss Elite	71
1997	Studio Press Proof Silver	31	1998	Donruss Elite	150
1997	Topps	187	1998	Donruss Elite Aspirations	71
1997	Topps Chrome	72	1998	Donruss Elite Aspirations	150
1997	Topps Chrome Refractors	72	1998	Donruss Elite Craftsmen	30
1997	Topps Gallery	89	1998	Donruss Elite Master Craftsmen	30
1997	Topps Gallery Player's Private Issue	89	1998	Donruss Elite Status	71
1997	Topps Stars	2	1998	Donruss Elite Status	150
1997	Topps Stars '97 All-Stars	AS3	1998	Donruss Gold Press Proofs	25
1997	Topps Stars Always Mint	2	1998	Donruss Gold Press Proofs	168
1997	Ultra	100	1998	Donruss Gold Press Proofs	358
1997	Ultra Gold Medallion	100	1998	Donruss Longball Leaders	3
1997	Ultra Platinum Medallion	100	1998	Donruss Preferred	35
1997	Upper Deck	123	1998	Donruss Preferred	194
1997	Upper Deck Star Attractions	8	1998	Donruss Preferred Seating	35
1997	Yankees Score	13	1998	Donruss Preferred Seating	194
1997	Yankees Score Platinum	13	1998	Donruss Prized Collections Donruss	25
1997	Yankees Score Premier	13	1998	Donruss Prized Collections Donruss	168
1997	Zenith	23	1998	Donruss Prized Collections Elite	471
1998	Bowman	43	1998	Donruss Prized Collections Elite	550
1998	Bowman Chrome	43	1998	Donruss Prized Collections Leaf	202
1998	Bowman Chrome Golden Anniversary	43	1998	Donruss Prized Collections Preferred	585
1998	Bowman Chrome Golden Anniversary Refractors	43	1998	Donruss Prized Collections Preferred	744
1998	Bowman Chrome International	43	1998	Donruss Production Line Power Index	19
1998	Bowman Chrome International Refractors	43	1998	Donruss Production Line Slugging	12
1998	Bowman Chrome Refractors	43	1998	Donruss Signature	69
1998	Bowman Chrome Reprints	12	1998	Donruss Signature Proofs	69
1998	Bowman Chrome Reprints Refractors	12	1998	Donruss Silver Press Proofs	25
1998	Bowman Golden Anniversary	43	1998	Donruss Silver Press Proofs	168
1998	Bowman International	43	1998	Donruss Silver Press Proofs	358
1998	Bowman Minor League MVP's	MVP8	1998	E-X2001	38
1998	Bowman's Best	65	1998	E-X2001 Cheap Seat Treats	4
1998	Bowman's Best Atomic Refractors	65	1998	E-X2001 Essential Credentials Future	38
1998	Bowman's Best Refractors	65	1998	E-X2001 Essential Credentials Now	38
1998	Circa Thunder	195	1998	Finest	9
1998	Circa Thunder Rave	195	1998	Finest Mystery Finest 1	M43
1998	Circa Thunder Super Rave	195	1998	Finest Mystery Finest 1	M46
1998	Circa Thunder Thunder Boomers	7	1998	Finest Mystery Finest 1	M48
1998	Collector's Choice	9	1998	Finest Mystery Finest 1	M50
1998	Collector's Choice	23	1998	Finest Mystery Finest 1 Refractors	M43
1998	Collector's Choice	180	1998	Finest Mystery Finest 1 Refractors	M46
1998	Collector's Choice Cover Glory 5x7	9	1998	Finest Mystery Finest 1 Refractors	M48
1998	Collector's Choice Crash the Game	CG26A	1998	Finest Mystery Finest 1 Refractors	M50
1998	Collector's Choice Crash the Game	CG26B	1998	Finest No-Protectors	9
1998	Collector's Choice Crash the Game	CG26C	1998	Finest No-Protectors Refractors	9
1998	Collector's Choice Crash the Game Exchange	CG26	1998	Finest Power Zone	P18
1998	Collector's Choice Crash the Game Instant Win	CG26	1998	Finest Refractors	9
1998	Collector's Choice Evolution Revolution	ER19	1998	Finest Stadium Stars	SS21
1998	Collector's Choice Golden Jubilee 5x7	276	1998	Flair Showcase Legacy Collection	60
1998	Collector's Choice Retail Jumbos	180	1998	Flair Showcase Legacy Collection Masterpieces	60
1998	Collector's Choice StarQuest	SQ45	1998	Flair Showcase Row 0	60
1998	Collector's Choice StarQuest	SQ87	1998	Flair Showcase Row 1	60
1998	Collector's Choice StarQuest Double	21	1998	Flair Showcase Row 2	60
1998	Collector's Choice StarQuest Home Run	21	1998	Flair Showcase Row 3	60
1998	Collector's Choice StarQuest Single	21	1998	Fleer	278
1998	Collector's Choice StarQuest Triple	21	1998	Fleer	331
1998	Collector's Choice Stick 'Ums	20	1998	Fleer Lumber Company	9
1998	Crown Royale	97	1998	Fleer Power Game	14
1998	Donruss	25	1998	Fleer Vintage '63	39
1998	Donruss	168	1998	Fleer Vintage '63 Classic	39
1998	Donruss	358	1998	Hamburger Helper	3
1998	Donruss Collections Donruss	25	1998	Leaf	2
1998	Donruss Collections Donruss	168	1998	Leaf Fractal Diamond Axis	2
1998	Donruss Collections Elite	471	1998	Leaf Fractal Foundations	2
1998	Donruss Collections Elite	550	1998	Leaf Fractal Materials	2
1998	Donruss Collections Leaf	202	1998	Leaf Fractal Materials Die Cuts	2
1998	Donruss Collections Preferred	585	1998	Leaf Fractal Materials Z2 Axis	2
1998	Donruss Collections Preferred	744	1998	Leaf Fractal Matrix	2
1998	Donruss Collections Samples	25	1998	Leaf Fractal Matrix Die Cuts	2
1998	Donruss Collections Samples	168	1998	Leaf Rookies and Stars	8
1998	Donruss Crusade Green	33	1998	Leaf Rookies and Stars Greatest Hits	11
1998	Donruss Crusade Purple	33	1998	Leaf Rookies and Stars Home Run Derby	1
1998	Donruss Crusade Red	33	1998	Leaf Rookies and Stars Longevity	8
			1998	Leaf Rookies and Stars Longevity Holographic	8
			1998	Leaf Rookies and Stars Ticket Masters	12

Year	Set Name	Card No.
1998	Leaf Rookies and Stars Ticket Masters Die Cuts	12
1998	Leaf Rookies and Stars True Blue	8
1998	Leaf State Representatives	13
1998	Metal Universe	122
1998	Metal Universe Precious Metal Gems	122
1998	Pacific	152
1998	Pacific Aurora	60
1998	Pacific Gold Crown Die Cuts	23
1998	Pacific Home Run Hitters	14
1998	Pacific In The Cage	11
1998	Pacific Invincible	53
1998	Pacific Invincible Gems of the Diamond	76
1998	Pacific Invincible Interleague Players	9A
1998	Pacific Invincible Photoengravings	10
1998	Pacific Invincible Platinum Blue	53
1998	Pacific Invincible Silver	53
1998	Pacific Invincible Team Checklists	19
1998	Pacific Latinos of the Major Leagues	26
1998	Pacific Omega	167
1998	Pacific Omega Red	167
1998	Pacific Online	508
1998	Pacific Online Red	508
1998	Pacific Online Web Cards	508
1998	Pacific Paramount	71
1998	Pacific Paramount Copper	71
1998	Pacific Paramount Gold	71
1998	Pacific Paramount Holographic Silver	71
1998	Pacific Paramount Inaugural	47
1998	Pacific Paramount Platinum Blue	71
1998	Pacific Paramount Red	71
1998	Pacific Platinum Blue	152
1998	Pacific Red Threatt	152
1998	Pacific Silver	152
1998	Pacific Team Checklists	10
1998	Pinnacle	189
1998	Pinnacle	198
1998	Pinnacle	199
1998	Pinnacle Artist's Proofs	PP92
1998	Pinnacle Hit It Here	7
1998	Pinnacle Hit It Here Samples	7
1998	Pinnacle Inside	77
1998	Pinnacle Inside Club Edition	77
1998	Pinnacle Inside Diamond Edition	77
1998	Pinnacle Inside Stand-Up Guys	19AB
1998	Pinnacle Inside Stand-Up Guys	19CD
1998	Pinnacle Inside Stand-Up Guys Samples	19AB
1998	Pinnacle Inside Stand-Up Guys Samples	19CD
1998	Pinnacle Mint	13
1998	Pinnacle Mint Bronze	13
1998	Pinnacle Mint Coins Brass	13
1998	Pinnacle Mint Coins Brass Artist's Proofs	13
1998	Pinnacle Mint Coins Gold Plated	13
1998	Pinnacle Mint Coins Gold Plated Artist's Proofs	13
1998	Pinnacle Mint Coins Nickel	13
1998	Pinnacle Mint Coins Nickel Artist's Proofs	13
1998	Pinnacle Mint Coins Solid Gold Redemption	13
1998	Pinnacle Mint Coins Solid Silver	13
1998	Pinnacle Mint Gold	13
1998	Pinnacle Mint Silver	13
1998	Pinnacle Museum Collection	PP92
1998	Pinnacle Performers	36
1998	Pinnacle Performers Big Bang	13
1998	Pinnacle Performers Big Bang Samples	13
1998	Pinnacle Performers Big Bang Seasonal Outburst	13
1998	Pinnacle Performers Peak Performers	36
1998	Pinnacle Performers Swing for the Fences	16
1998	Pinnacle Plus	12
1998	Pinnacle Plus Artist's Proofs	PP6
1998	Pinnacle Plus Gold Artist's Proofs	PP6
1998	Pinnacle Plus Mirror Artist's Proofs	PP6
1998	Pinnacle Plus Team Pinnacle	10
1998	Pinnacle Plus Team Pinnacle Gold	10
1998	Pinnacle Plus Team Pinnacle Mirror	10
1998	Pinnacle Plus Yardwork	6
1998	Pinnacle Power Pack Jumbos	8
1998	Pinnacle Power Pack Jumbos Samples	8
1998	Pinnacle Press Plates	189
1998	Pinnacle Press Plates	198
1998	Pinnacle Press Plates	199
1998	Pinnacle Press Plates	H7
1998	Pinnacle Snapshots	NYY8
1998	Pinnacle Snapshots	NYY11
1998	Revolution	101
1998	Revolution Shadow Series	101
1998	Score	42
1998	Score Artist's Proofs	PP127
1998	Score Rookie Traded	41
1998	Score Rookie Traded Artist's Proofs	PP41
1998	Score Rookie Traded Artist's Proofs 1 of 1's	PP41
1998	Score Rookie Traded Showcase Series	PP41
1998	Score Showcase Series	PP127
1998	SP Authentic	140
1998	SP Authentic Sheer Dominance	SD39
1998	SP Authentic Sheer Dominance Gold	SD39
1998	SP Authentic Sheer Dominance Titanium	SD39
1998	Sports Illustrated	86
1998	Sports Illustrated Extra Edition	86
1998	Sports Illustrated First Edition	86
1998	Sports Illustrated Then and Now	112
1998	Sports Illustrated Then and Now Extra Edition	112
1998	Sports Illustrated World Series Fever	99
1998	Sports Illustrated World Series Fever Extra Edition	99
1998	Sports Illustrated World Series Fever First Edition	99
1998	SPx Finite	44
1998	SPx Finite	105
1998	SPx Finite	160
1998	SPx Finite	236
1998	SPx Finite Radiance	44
1998	SPx Finite Radiance	105
1998	SPx Finite Radiance	160
1998	SPx Finite Radiance	236
1998	SPx Finite Spectrum	44
1998	SPx Finite Spectrum	105
1998	SPx Finite Spectrum	160
1998	SPx Finite Spectrum	236
1998	Stadium Club	202
1998	Stadium Club Bowman Previews	BP8
1998	Stadium Club Co-Signers	CS21
1998	Stadium Club Co-Signers	CS23
1998	Stadium Club Co-Signers	CS24
1998	Stadium Club First Day Issue	202
1998	Stadium Club One Of A Kind	202
1998	Stadium Club Playing With Passion	P8
1998	Stadium Club Printing Plates	202
1998	Stadium Club Triumvirate Illuminator	T2C
1998	Stadium Club Triumvirate Illuminator	T11B
1998	Stadium Club Triumvirate Luminescent	T2C
1998	Stadium Club Triumvirate Luminescent	T11B
1998	Stadium Club Triumvirate Luminous	T2C
1998	Stadium Club Triumvirate Luminous	T11B
1998	Studio	139
1998	Studio Gold Press Proofs	139
1998	Studio Hit Parade	14
1998	Studio Portraits 8 x 10	25
1998	Studio Portraits 8 x 10 Gold Proofs	25
1998	Studio Silver Press Proofs	139
1998	Topps	269
1998	Topps	284
1998	Topps	483
1998	Topps Chrome	269
1998	Topps Chrome	284
1998	Topps Chrome	483
1998	Topps Chrome Refractors	269
1998	Topps Chrome Refractors	284
1998	Topps Chrome Refractors	483
1998	Topps Devil Rays	269
1998	Topps Devil Rays	284
1998	Topps Devil Rays	483
1998	Topps Diamondbacks	269
1998	Topps Diamondbacks	284
1998	Topps Diamondbacks	483
1998	Topps Gallery	145
1998	Topps Gallery Gallery Proofs	145
1998	Topps Gallery Original Printing Plates	145
1998	Topps Gallery Player's Private Issue	145
1998	Topps Gallery Player's Private Issue Auction	145
1998	Topps Gold Label Class 1	95
1998	Topps Gold Label Class 1 Black	95
1998	Topps Gold Label Class 1 One to One	95
1998	Topps Gold Label Class 1 Red	95
1998	Topps Gold Label Class 2	95
1998	Topps Gold Label Class 2 Black	95
1998	Topps Gold Label Class 2 One to One	95
1998	Topps Gold Label Class 2 Red	95
1998	Topps Gold Label Class 3	95
1998	Topps Gold Label Class 3 Black	95
1998	Topps Gold Label Class 3 One to One	95
1998	Topps Gold Label Class 3 Red	95
1998	Topps Minted in Cooperstown	269
1998	Topps Minted in Cooperstown	284
1998	Topps Minted in Cooperstown	483
1998	Topps Mystery Finest	ILM8
1998	Topps Mystery Finest Bordered	M11
1998	Topps Mystery Finest Bordered Refractors	M11
1998	Topps Mystery Finest Borderless	M11
1998	Topps Mystery Finest Borderless Refractors	M11
1998	Topps Mystery Finest Refractors	ILM8
1998	Topps Opening Day	111
1998	Topps Stars	82
1998	Topps Stars 'N Steel	28
1998	Topps Stars 'N Steel Gold	28
1998	Topps Stars 'N Steel Gold Holographic	28
1998	Topps Stars Bronze	82
1998	Topps Stars Gold	82
1998	Topps Stars Gold Rainbow	82
1998	Topps Stars Silver	82
1998	Topps SuperChrome	16
1998	Topps SuperChrome Refractors	16
1998	Topps Tek	25
1998	Topps Tek Diffractors	25
1998	UD3	39
1998	UD3	129
1998	UD3	219
1998	UD3 Die Cuts	39
1998	UD3 Die Cuts	129
1998	UD3 Die Cuts	219
1998	Ultra	139
1998	Ultra Big Shots	13
1998	Ultra Double Trouble	5
1998	Ultra Gold Medallion	139
1998	Ultra Masterpieces	139
1998	Ultra Notables	13
1998	Ultra Platinum Medallion	139
1998	Upper Deck	1
1998	Upper Deck	12
1998	Upper Deck	244
1998	Upper Deck	460
1998	Upper Deck	606
1998	Upper Deck All-Star Credentials	AS24
1998	Upper Deck Amazing Greats	AG18
1998	Upper Deck Amazing Greats Die Cuts	AG18
1998	Upper Deck Clearly Dominant	CD24
1998	Upper Deck Retro	68
1998	Upper Deck Retro Big Boppers	BB11
1998	Upper Deck Retro Time Capsule	TC14
1998	Upper Deck Retrospectives	23
1998	Upper Deck Special F/X	5
1998	Upper Deck Special F/X Power Zone Power Driven	PZ9
1998	Upper Deck Tape Measure Titans	20
1998	Upper Deck Tape Measure Titans Gold	20
1998	Yankees Score	3

Year	Set Name	Card No.
1998	Yankees Score Platinum	3
1998	Zenith	42
1998	Zenith 5 x 7	47
1998	Zenith 5 x 7 Gold Impulse	47
1998	Zenith 5 x 7 Impulse	47
1998	Zenith Z-Gold	42
1998	Zenith Z-Silver	42
1999	Aurora	130
1999	Finest	5
1999	Finest Gold Refractors	5
1999	Finest Pre-Production	PP5
1999	Finest Refractors	5
1999	Fleer	268
1999	Fleer Starting 9	268
1999	Fleer Warning Track	268
1999	Metal Universe	60
1999	Metal Universe Gem Masters	60
1999	Metal Universe Precious Metal Gems	60
1999	Pacific	297
1999	Pacific Crown Collection	192
1999	Pacific Crown Collection Latinos of the Major Leagues	13
1999	Pacific Crown Collection Platinum Blue	192
1999	Pacific Paramount	164
1999	Pacific Paramount Copper	164
1999	Pacific Paramount Holographic Silver	164
1999	Pacific Paramount Platinum Blue	164
1999	Pacific Platinum Blue	297
1999	Pacific Prism	101
1999	Pacific Prism Holographic Blue	101
1999	Pacific Prism Holographic Gold	101
1999	Pacific Prism Holographic Mirror	101
1999	Pacific Prism Holographic Purple	101
1999	Pacific Private Stock	113
1999	Pacific Private Stock PS-206	113
1999	Pacific Private Stock PS-206 Red	113
1999	Pacific Red	297
1999	SkyBox Thunder	230
1999	SkyBox Thunder Rant	230
1999	SkyBox Thunder Rave	230
1999	SkyBox Thunder Super Rave	230
1999	SP Authentic	58
1999	SP Authentic Epic Figures	E19
1999	SP Authentic Reflections	R19
1999	Sports Illustrated	135
1999	Stadium Club Autographs	SCA4
1999	Stadium Club Triumvirate Illuminator	T4B
1999	Stadium Club Triumvirate Luminescent	T4B
1999	Stadium Club Triumvirate Luminous	T4B
1999	Topps	236
1999	Topps Chrome	236
1999	Topps Chrome Refractors	236
1999	Topps Opening Day	157
1999	UD Choice	119
1999	UD Choice Mini Bobbing Head	B18
1999	UD Choice Prime Choice Reserve	119
1999	UD Choice Yard Work	Y20
1999	UD Ionix	42
1999	UD Ionix	79
1999	UD Ionix Reciprocal	42
1999	UD Ionix Reciprocal	79
1999	Ultra	4
1999	Ultra Gold Medallion	4
1999	Ultra Masterpieces	4
1999	Ultra Platinum Medallion	4
1999	Ultra RBI Kings	28
1999	Upper Deck Black Diamond	58
1999	Upper Deck Black Diamond Dominance	D28
1999	Upper Deck Black Diamond Dominance Emerald	D28
1999	Upper Deck Black Diamond Double	58
1999	Upper Deck Black Diamond Quadruple	58
1999	Upper Deck Black Diamond Triple	58
1999	Upper Deck Ovation	15
1999	Upper Deck Ovation Standing Ovation	15
1999	Upper Deck Wonder Years	W18
1999	Upper Deck Wonder Years Double	W18

Year	Set Name	Card No.
1999	Upper Deck Wonder Years Home Run	W18
1999	Upper Deck Wonder Years Triple	W18

Don Mattingly

Year	Set Name	Card No.
1981	Nashville Sounds Team Issue	8
1982	Columbus Clippers Police	19
1982	Columbus Clippers TCMA	21
1984	Donruss	248
1984	Fleer	131
1984	Fun Foods Pins	77
1984	Nestle 792	8
1984	O-Pee-Chee	8
1984	Topps	8
1984	Topps Tiffany	8
1984	Topps/O-Pee-Chee Stickers	325
1984-89	O'Connell and Son Ink	103
1984-91	Topps Pewter Bonuses	3
1985	All-Star Game Program Inserts	6
1985	Donruss	7
1985	Donruss	295
1985	Donruss	651A
1985	Donruss	651B
1985	Donruss Action All-Stars	48
1985	Donruss Highlights	36
1985	Donruss Highlights	44
1985	Donruss Highlights	45
1985	Donruss Super DK's	7
1985	Drake's	19
1985	Fleer	133
1985	Fleer Limited Edition	20
1985	Fleer Star Stickers	4
1985	Fleer Star Stickers	37
1985	Leaf/Donruss	7
1985	Leaf/Donruss	140
1985	O-Pee-Chee	324
1985	Seven-Eleven Coins	E12
1985	Topps	665
1985	Topps 3-D	8
1985	Topps Gallery of Champions	6
1985	Topps Glossy Send-Ins	27
1985	Topps Rub Downs	22
1985	Topps Super	4
1985	Topps Tiffany	665
1985	Topps/O-Pee-Chee Stickers	171
1985	Topps/O-Pee-Chee Stickers	310
1985	Yankees TCMA Postcards	27
1986	Baseball Star Buttons	71
1986	Burger King All-Pro	19
1986	Donruss	173
1986	Donruss All-Stars	50
1986	Donruss Highlights	48
1986	Donruss Highlights	53
1986	Dorman's Cheese	13
1986	Drake's	7
1986	Fleer	109
1986	Fleer	627
1986	Fleer	639
1986	Fleer All-Stars	1
1986	Fleer League Leaders	22
1986	Fleer Limited Edition	27
1986	Fleer Mini	24
1986	Fleer Sluggers/Pitchers	21
1986	Fleer Sticker Cards	72
1986	Franklin Glove Tags	2
1986	Franklin Glove Tags	3
1986	General Mills Booklets	1D
1986	Kay-Bee	19
1986	Leaf/Donruss	103
1986	Meadow Gold Blank Back	8
1986	Meadow Gold Milk	5
1986	Meadow Gold Stat Back	5
1986	MSA Jiffy Pop Discs	6
1986	O-Pee-Chee	180
1986	O-Pee-Chee Box Bottoms	J

Year	Set Name	Card No.
1986	Quaker Granola	18
1986	Seven-Eleven Coins	C3
1986	Seven-Eleven Coins	E3
1986	Seven-Eleven Coins	S3
1986	Seven-Eleven Coins	W3
1986	Sportflics	2
1986	Sportflics	54
1986	Sportflics	75
1986	Sportflics	176
1986	Sportflics	179
1986	Sportflics	180
1986	Sportflics	183
1986	Sportflics	184
1986	Sportflics Decade Greats	65
1986	Topps	180
1986	Topps	712
1986	Topps 3-D	15
1986	Topps Gallery of Champions	6
1986	Topps Glossy Send-Ins	31
1986	Topps Mini Leaders	28
1986	Topps Super	1
1986	Topps Tiffany	180
1986	Topps Tiffany	712
1986	Topps Wax Box Cards	J
1986	Topps/O-Pee-Chee Stickers	296
1986	Topps/O-Pee-Chee Tattoos	7
1986	True Value	5
1986	Woolworth's	20
1986	Yankees TCMA	24
1987	Boardwalk and Baseball	32
1987	Burger King All-Pro	13
1987	Classic Game	10
1987	Classic Update Yellow	104
1987	Donruss	52
1987	Donruss All-Stars	33
1987	Donruss Highlights	17
1987	Donruss Highlights	23
1987	Donruss Highlights	48
1987	Donruss Opening Day	241
1987	Drake's	8
1987	Fleer	104
1987	Fleer	638
1987	Fleer All-Stars	1
1987	Fleer Award Winners	24
1987	Fleer Baseball All-Stars	26
1987	Fleer Exciting Stars	33
1987	Fleer Game Winners	26
1987	Fleer Glossy	104
1987	Fleer Glossy	638
1987	Fleer Hottest Stars	27
1987	Fleer League Leaders	28
1987	Fleer Limited Edition	26
1987	Fleer Mini	66
1987	Fleer Record Setters	20
1987	Fleer Sluggers/Pitchers	25
1987	Fleer Sticker Cards	74
1987	Fleer Sticker Cards	131
1987	Fleer Stickers Wax Box Cards	S8
1987	General Mills Booklets	2E
1987	Hostess Stickers	27
1987	K-Mart	28
1987	Kay-Bee	19
1987	Key Food Discs	6
1987	Kraft Foods	29
1987	Leaf/Donruss	150
1987	M and M's Star Lineup	11
1987	MSA Iced Tea Discs	6
1987	MSA Jiffy Pop Discs	6
1987	O-Pee-Chee	229
1987	Our Own Discs	6
1987	Ralston Purina	5
1987	Red Foley Sticker Book	106
1987	Seven-Eleven Coins	E12
1987	Sportflics	1
1987	Sportflics	75
1987	Sportflics	159
1987	Sportflics Dealer Panels	1

Year	Set Name	Card No.	Year	Set Name	Card No.
1987	Sportflics Team Preview	7	1988	CMC Mattingly	10
1987	Sports Illustrated Stickers	8	1988	CMC Mattingly	11
1987	Sports Reading	21	1988	CMC Mattingly	12
1987	Star Mattingly	1	1988	CMC Mattingly	13
1987	Star Mattingly	2	1988	CMC Mattingly	14
1987	Star Mattingly	3	1988	CMC Mattingly	15
1987	Star Mattingly	4	1988	CMC Mattingly	16
1987	Star Mattingly	5	1988	CMC Mattingly	17
1987	Star Mattingly	6	1988	CMC Mattingly	18
1987	Star Mattingly	7	1988	CMC Mattingly	19
1987	Star Mattingly	8	1988	CMC Mattingly	20
1987	Star Mattingly	9	1988	CMC Mattingly	P1
1987	Star Mattingly	10	1988	Donruss	217
1987	Star Mattingly	11	1988	Donruss All-Stars	1
1987	Star Mattingly	12	1988	Donruss Baseball's Best	1
1987	Star Mattingly Blankback	1	1988	Donruss Bonus MVP's	BC21
1987	Star Mattingly Blankback	2	1988	Donruss Pop-Ups	1
1987	Star Mattingly Blankback	3	1988	Donruss Team Book Yankees	217
1987	Star Mattingly Blankback	4	1988	Drake's	1
1987	Star Mattingly Blankback	5	1988	Fleer	214
1987	Star Mattingly Blankback	6	1988	Fleer Award Winners	23
1987	Star Sticker Mattingly	1	1988	Fleer Baseball All-Stars	23
1987	Star Sticker Mattingly	2	1988	Fleer Baseball MVP's	22
1987	Star Sticker Mattingly	3	1988	Fleer Exciting Stars	25
1987	Star Sticker Mattingly	4	1988	Fleer Glossy	214
1987	Star Sticker Mattingly	5	1988	Fleer Headliners	1
1987	Star Sticker Mattingly	6	1988	Fleer Hottest Stars	24
1987	Star Sticker Mattingly	7	1988	Fleer League Leaders	25
1987	Star Sticker Mattingly	8	1988	Fleer Mini	41
1987	Star Sticker Mattingly	9	1988	Fleer Record Setters	24
1987	Star Sticker Mattingly	10	1988	Fleer Sluggers/Pitchers	26
1987	Star Sticker Mattingly	11	1988	Fleer Sticker Cards	48
1987	Star Sticker Mattingly	12	1988	Fleer Superstars	22
1987	Star Sticker Mattingly	13	1988	Fleer Team Leaders	19
1987	Star Sticker Mattingly	14	1988	Grenada Baseball Stamps	14
1987	Star Sticker Mattingly	15	1988	K-Mart	15
1987	Star Sticker Mattingly	16	1988	Kay-Bee	16
1987	Star Sticker Mattingly	17	1988	Key Food Discs	3
1987	Star Sticker Mattingly	18	1988	King-B Discs	15
1987	Star Sticker Mattingly	19	1988	Leaf/Donruss	177
1987	Star Sticker Mattingly	20	1988	MSA Fantastic Sam's Discs	9
1987	Star Sticker Mattingly	21	1988	MSA Iced Tea Discs	3
1987	Star Sticker Mattingly	22	1988	Nestle	15
1987	Star Sticker Mattingly	23	1988	O-Pee-Chee	300
1987	Star Sticker Mattingly	24	1988	Our Own Tea Discs	3
1987	Stuart Panels	23	1988	Panini Stickers	152
1987	Topps	406	1988	Panini Stickers	155
1987	Topps	500	1988	Panini Stickers	227
1987	Topps	606	1988	Panini Stickers	430
1987	Topps	606A	1988	Red Foley Sticker Book	53
1987	Topps Coins	17	1988	Score	1
1987	Topps Gallery of Champions	7	1988	Score	650
1987	Topps Glossy Send-Ins	1	1988	Score	658
1987	Topps Mini Leaders	65	1988	Score Box Cards	2
1987	Topps Tiffany	406	1988	Score Glossy	1
1987	Topps Tiffany	500	1988	Score Glossy	650
1987	Topps Tiffany	606A	1988	Score Glossy	658
1987	Topps Tiffany	606B	1988	Score Young Superstars II	1
1987	Topps/O-Pee-Chee Stickers	294	1988	Sportflics	1
1987	Weis Market Discs	6	1988	Sportflics	222
1987	Woolworth's	15	1988	Sportflics Gamewinners	1
1988	Action Packed Test	5	1988	Star Mattingly	1
1988	Bazooka	11	1988	Star Mattingly	2
1988	Chef Boyardee	16	1988	Star Mattingly	3
1988	Classic Blue	211	1988	Star Mattingly	4
1988	Classic Blue	247	1988	Star Mattingly	5
1988	Classic Red	151	1988	Star Mattingly	6
1988	Classic Red	152	1988	Star Mattingly	7
1988	CMC Mattingly	1	1988	Star Mattingly	8
1988	CMC Mattingly	2	1988	Star Mattingly	9
1988	CMC Mattingly	3	1988	Star Mattingly	10
1988	CMC Mattingly	4	1988	Star Mattingly	11
1988	CMC Mattingly	5	1988	Star Mattingly/Schmidt	1
1988	CMC Mattingly	6	1988	Star Mattingly/Schmidt	3
1988	CMC Mattingly	7	1988	Star Mattingly/Schmidt	5
1988	CMC Mattingly	8	1988	Star Mattingly/Schmidt	7
1988	CMC Mattingly	9	1988	Star Mattingly/Schmidt	9

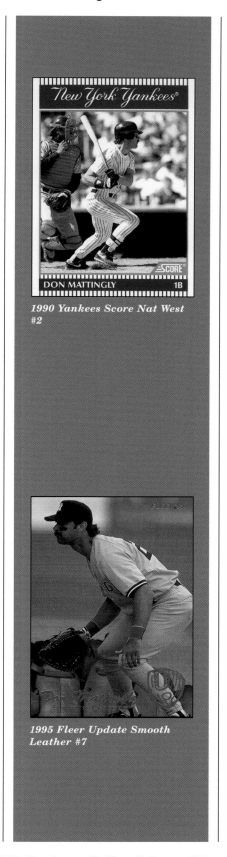

1990 Yankees Score Nat West #2

1995 Fleer Update Smooth Leather #7

Trading Card Checklist

1984 Donruss #248

1991 Fleer Pro-Visions #11

Year	Set Name	Card No.
1988	Star Mattingly/Schmidt	11
1988	Starting Lineup All-Stars	17
1988	Starting Lineup Yankees	8
1988	Tara Plaques	26
1988	Tetley Tea Discs	3
1988	Topps	2
1988	Topps	300
1988	Topps	386
1988	Topps Big	229
1988	Topps Cloth	67
1988	Topps Coins	19
1988	Topps Glossy All-Stars	2
1988	Topps Glossy Send-Ins	11
1988	Topps Mattingly World	1
1988	Topps Mini Leaders	27
1988	Topps Rite-Aid Team MVP's	22
1988	Topps Tiffany	2
1988	Topps Tiffany	300
1988	Topps Tiffany	386
1988	Topps UK Minis	45
1988	Topps UK Minis Tiffany	45
1988	Topps/O-Pee-Chee Sticker Backs	35
1988	Topps/O-Pee-Chee Stickers	3
1988	Topps/O-Pee-Chee Stickers	156
1988	Topps/O-Pee-Chee Stickers	299
1988	Weis Market Discs	3
1988	Woolworth's	4
1989	Bowman	176
1989	Bowman Tiffany	176
1989	Cadaco Ellis Discs	34
1989	Cereal Superstars	11
1989	Classic Light Blue	5
1989	Classic Travel Orange	106
1989	Donruss	26
1989	Donruss	74
1989	Donruss All-Stars	21
1989	Donruss Baseball's Best	1
1989	Donruss Super DK's	26
1989	Fleer	258
1989	Fleer Baseball All-Stars	28
1989	Fleer Baseball MVP's	26
1989	Fleer Exciting Stars	31
1989	Fleer For The Record	6
1989	Fleer Glossy	258
1989	Fleer Heroes of Baseball	26
1989	Fleer League Leaders	25
1989	Fleer Superstars	29
1989	K-Mart	12
1989	Kay-Bee	20
1989	Key Food Discs	1
1989	Master Bread Discs	6
1989	MSA Holsum Discs	4
1989	MSA Iced Tea Discs	1
1989	Nissen	4
1989	O-Pee-Chee	26
1989	Our Own Tea Discs	1
1989	Panini Stickers	404
1989	Red Foley Sticker Book	79
1989	Rini Postcards Mattingly 1	1
1989	Rini Postcards Mattingly 1	2
1989	Rini Postcards Mattingly 1	3
1989	Rini Postcards Mattingly 1	4
1989	Rini Postcards Mattingly 1	5
1989	Rini Postcards Mattingly 1	6
1989	Rini Postcards Mattingly 1	7
1989	Rini Postcards Mattingly 1	8
1989	Rini Postcards Mattingly 1	9
1989	Rini Postcards Mattingly 1	10
1989	Rini Postcards Mattingly 1	11
1989	Rini Postcards Mattingly 1	12
1989	Score	100
1989	Score Hottest 100 Stars	10
1989	Score Scoremasters	6
1989	Sportflics	50
1989	Tetley Tea Discs	1
1989	Topps	397
1989	Topps	700

Year	Set Name	Card No.
1989	Topps Baseball Talk/LJN	123
1989	Topps Batting Leaders	3
1989	Topps Big	50
1989	Topps Cap'n Crunch	8
1989	Topps Coins	43
1989	Topps Doubleheaders All-Stars	1
1989	Topps Doubleheaders Mets/Yankees Test	14
1989	Topps Glossy Send-Ins	51
1989	Topps Heads Up Test	19
1989	Topps Ritz Mattingly	1
1989	Topps Ritz Mattingly	2
1989	Topps Ritz Mattingly	3
1989	Topps Ritz Mattingly	4
1989	Topps Ritz Mattingly	5
1989	Topps Ritz Mattingly	6
1989	Topps Ritz Mattingly	7
1989	Topps Ritz Mattingly	8
1989	Topps Ritz Mattingly	9
1989	Topps Tiffany	397
1989	Topps Tiffany	700
1989	Topps UK Minis	49
1989	Topps/O-Pee-Chee Sticker Backs	2
1989	Topps/O-Pee-Chee Stickers	314
1989	TV Sports Mailbags	82
1989	Upper Deck	200
1989	Upper Deck	693
1989	Upper Deck Sheets	3
1989	Weis Market Discs	1
1989	Yankees Score Nat West	1
1989-91	Sports Illustrated For Kids I	37
1990	All-American Baseball Team	11
1990	Bowman	443
1990	Bowman Insert Lithographs	5
1990	Bowman Inserts	5
1990	Bowman Inserts Tiffany	5
1990	Bowman Tiffany	443
1990	Bowman Tiffany	A5
1990	Classic Blue	16
1990	Classic Yellow	T12
1990	Classic Yellow	NNO0
1990	Colla Mattingly	1
1990	Colla Mattingly	2
1990	Colla Mattingly	3
1990	Colla Mattingly	4
1990	Colla Mattingly	5
1990	Colla Mattingly	6
1990	Colla Mattingly	7
1990	Colla Mattingly	8
1990	Colla Mattingly	9
1990	Colla Mattingly	10
1990	Colla Mattingly	11
1990	Colla Mattingly	12
1990	Collect the Stars Baseball Magnetables	97
1990	Collect-A-Books	13
1990	Donruss	190
1990	Donruss Best AL	38
1990	Donruss Learning Series	12
1990	Fleer	447
1990	Fleer	626
1990	Fleer	638
1990	Fleer Award Winners	21
1990	Fleer Baseball All-Star Canadian	24
1990	Fleer Baseball All-Stars	24
1990	Fleer Baseball MVP's	23
1990	Fleer Baseball MVP's Canadian	23
1990	Fleer Canadian	447
1990	Fleer Canadian	626
1990	Fleer Canadian	638
1990	Fleer League Leaders	23
1990	Fleer League Leaders Canadian	23
1990	Fleer League Standouts	2
1990	Fleer Wax Box Cards	C19
1990	Good Humor Ice Cream Big League Sticks	13
1990	HOF Sticker Book	90
1990	Hottest 50 Players Stickers	25
1990	K-Mart	17
1990	Kay-Bee	18

Year	Set Name	Card No.
1990	King-B Discs	14
1990	Leaf	69
1990	M.V.P. Pins	68
1990	MLBPA Baseball Buttons (Pins)	63
1990	MSA Iced Tea Discs	14
1990	O-Pee-Chee	200
1990	Panini Stickers	125
1990	Post	1
1990	Pubs.Int'l. Stickers	291
1990	Pubs.Int'l. Stickers	540
1990	Red Foley Sticker Book	59
1990	Score	1
1990	Score 100 Superstars	10
1990	Sportflics	150
1990	Starline Long John Silver	1
1990	Starline Long John Silver	28
1990	Starline Long John Silver	35
1990	Sunflower Seeds	8
1990	Topps	200
1990	Topps Ames All-Stars	18
1990	Topps Batting Leaders	4
1990	Topps Big	85
1990	Topps Coins	21
1990	Topps Doubleheaders	43
1990	Topps Glossy Send-Ins	11
1990	Topps Heads Up	19
1990	Topps Hills Hit Men	3
1990	Topps Mini Leaders	24
1990	Topps Sticker Backs	34
1990	Topps Stickers	308
1990	Topps Tiffany	200
1990	Topps TV All-Stars	17
1990	Topps TV Yankees	25
1990	Upper Deck	191
1990	Wonder Bread Stars	6
1990	Yankees Score Nat West	2
1990-93	Topps Magazine	17
1991	Baseball's Best Hit Men	14
1991	Baseball's Best Record Breakers	11
1991	Bowman	178
1991	Cadaco Ellis Discs	36
1991	Classic Game	98
1991	Classic I	T33
1991	Classic III	T56
1991	Coke Mattingly	1
1991	Coke Mattingly	2
1991	Coke Mattingly	3
1991	Coke Mattingly	4
1991	Coke Mattingly	5
1991	Coke Mattingly	6
1991	Coke Mattingly	7
1991	Coke Mattingly	8
1991	Coke Mattingly	9
1991	Coke Mattingly	10
1991	Coke Mattingly	11
1991	Coke Mattingly	12
1991	Coke Mattingly	13
1991	Coke Mattingly	14
1991	Coke Mattingly	15
1991	Denny's Holograms	8
1991	Donruss	107
1991	Fleer	673
1991	Fleer Pro-Visions	11
1991	Leaf	425
1991	Leaf Previews	22
1991	Major League Collector Pins	1
1991	MooTown Snackers	15
1991	O-Pee-Chee	100
1991	O-Pee-Chee Premier	77
1991	Panini French Stickers	324
1991	Panini Stickers	267
1991	Pepsi Superstar	11
1991	Petro-Canada Standups	19
1991	Playball Mattingly	26
1991	Playball Mattingly	27
1991	Playball Mattingly	28
1991	Playball Mattingly	29
1991	Playball Mattingly	30
1991	Playball Mattingly	44
1991	Playball Mattingly	45
1991	Playball Mattingly	46
1991	Playball Mattingly	47
1991	Playball Mattingly	48
1991	Playball Mattingly Gold	4
1991	Playball Mattingly Gold	5
1991	Post	29
1991	Red Foley Stickers	61
1991	Rini Postcards Mattingly II	1
1991	Rini Postcards Mattingly II	2
1991	Rini Postcards Mattingly II	3
1991	Rini Postcards Mattingly II	4
1991	Rini Postcards Mattingly II	5
1991	Rini Postcards Mattingly II	6
1991	Rini Postcards Mattingly II	7
1991	Rini Postcards Mattingly II	8
1991	Rini Postcards Mattingly II	9
1991	Rini Postcards Mattingly II	10
1991	Rini Postcards Mattingly II	11
1991	Rini Postcards Mattingly II	12
1991	Score	23
1991	Score	856
1991	Score 100 Superstars	23
1991	Seven-Eleven 3-D Coins National	11
1991	Seven-Eleven Coins	NE11
1991	Simon and Schuster More Little Big Leaguers	28
1991	Stadium Club	21
1991	Stadium Club Pre-Production	25
1991	Starshots Pinback Badges	29
1991	Studio	97
1991	Topps	100
1991	Topps	100A
1991	Topps Cracker Jack I	7
1991	Topps Desert Shield	100
1991	Topps Micro	100
1991	Topps Stand-Ups	24
1991	Topps Tiffany	100
1991	Topps Triple Headers	A10
1991	Ultra	239
1991	Upper Deck	354
1992	Bowman	340
1992	Classic Game	105
1992	Classic I	T58
1992	Classic II	T49
1992	Colla Promos	11
1992	Donruss	596
1992	Donruss Cracker Jack I	36
1992	Fleer	237
1992	Fleer Citgo The Performer	16
1992	Fleer Team Leaders	1
1992	French's	11
1992	High 5	89
1992	Hit The Books Bookmarks	21
1992	Jimmy Dean	8
1992	L and K Decals	21
1992	Leaf	57
1992	Leaf Black Gold	57
1992	Leaf Gold Previews	22
1992	Leaf Previews	22
1992	Mattingly's #23 Restaurant	1
1992	Mr. Turkey Superstars	16
1992	MVP Pins	1
1992	NewSport	15
1992	O-Pee-Chee	300
1992	O-Pee-Chee Premier	92
1992	Panini Stickers	135
1992	Pinnacle	23
1992	Pinnacle	584
1992	Post	3
1992	Red Foley Stickers	61
1992	Score	23
1992	Score 100 Superstars	23
1992	Score/Pinnacle Promo Panels	7
1992	Seven-Eleven Coins	2
1992	Sports Stars Collector Coins	32
1992	Stadium Club	420
1992	Star Promos	7
1992	Studio	216
1992	Studio Heritage	BC5
1992	Studio Previews	9
1992	Topps	300
1992	Topps Gold	300
1992	Topps Gold Winners	300
1992	Topps Kids	84
1992	Topps Micro	300
1992	Topps Micro	G300
1992	Triple Play	159
1992	Triple Play Previews	4
1992	Ultra	105
1992	Ultra Award Winners	19
1992	Upper Deck	356
1992	Upper Deck FanFest	31
1992	Upper Deck FanFest Gold	31
1992	Upper Deck Sheets	1
1992	Upper Deck Team MVP Holograms	33
1992	Yankees WIZ 80s	111
1992	Yankees WIZ All-Stars	46
1992-94	Highland Mint Mint-Cards Topps	22
1992-94	Highland Mint Mint-Cards Topps	23
1992-98	Highland Mint Mint-Coins	70
1992-98	Highland Mint Mint-Coins	71
1993	Bowman	595
1993	Cadaco Discs	40
1993	Classic Game	59
1993	Diamond Marks	71
1993	Donruss	264
1993	Donruss	609
1993	Donruss Elite	24
1993	Donruss Elite Dominators	6
1993	Donruss Elite Dominators	AU6
1993	Donruss Elite Supers	6
1993	Donruss MVPs	5
1993	Donruss Previews	18
1993	Duracell Power Players I	19
1993	Finest	98
1993	Finest Jumbos	98
1993	Finest Promo Refractors	98
1993	Finest Promos	98
1993	Finest Refractors	98
1993	Flair	249
1993	Fleer	281
1993	Fleer Atlantic	14
1993	Fleer Fruit of the Loom	43
1993	Fun Pack	208
1993	Hostess	28
1993	Jimmy Dean	6
1993	Kraft	9
1993	Leaf	237
1993	Leaf Gold All-Stars	R2
1993	Metz Baking	14
1993	O-Pee-Chee	103
1993	O-Pee-Chee Premier	46
1993	Pacific Spanish	208
1993	Panini Stickers	154
1993	Pinnacle	23
1993	Pinnacle	470
1993	Pinnacle Cooperstown	14
1993	Pinnacle Cooperstown Dufex	14
1993	Pinnacle Slugfest	23
1993	Post	12
1993	Red Foley Stickers	59
1993	Score	23
1993	Score Franchise	10
1993	Select	24
1993	Select Samples	24
1993	Select Stat Leaders	14
1993	SP	265
1993	Stadium Club	557
1993	Stadium Club First Day Issue	557

Trading Card Checklist

Year	Set Name	Card No.	Year	Set Name	Card No.	Year	Set Name	Card No.
1993	Stadium Club Inserts	B2	1994	Select	23	1995	Pacific Gold Prisms	10
1993	Stadium Club Members Only Parallel	557	1994	SP	198	1995	Pacific Prisms	97
1993	Stadium Club Members Only Parallel	MB2	1994	SP Die Cuts	198	1995	Panini Stickers	38
1993	Studio	193	1994	SP Holoviews	25	1995	Pinnacle	21
1993	Topps	32	1994	SP Holoviews Die Cuts	25	1995	Pinnacle	295
1993	Topps Gold	32	1994	SP Previews	ER4	1995	Pinnacle Artist's Proofs	21
1993	Topps Inagural Rockies	32	1994	Sportflics	127	1995	Pinnacle Artist's Proofs	295
1993	Topps Inaugural Marlins	32	1994	Sportflics Movers	MM9	1995	Pinnacle FanFest	3
1993	Topps Micro	32	1994	Stadium Club	195	1995	Pinnacle Gate Attractions	GA12
1993	Topps Micro	P32	1994	Stadium Club First Day Issue	195	1995	Pinnacle Museum Collection	21
1993	Topps Pre-Production	32	1994	Stadium Club Golden Rainbow	195	1995	Pinnacle Museum Collection	295
1993	Triple Play	120	1994	Stadium Club Members Only Parallel	195	1995	Pinnacle Red Hot	RH10
1993	Triple Play Action	19	1994	Stadium Club Members Only Parallel	ST24	1995	Pinnacle White Hot	WH10
1993	Ultra	244	1994	Stadium Club Super Teams	ST24	1995	ProMint	9
1993	Ultra Award Winners	12	1994	Stadium Club Team	181	1995	Red Foley	27
1993	Upper Deck	47	1994	Stadium Club Team Finest	7	1995	Score	239
1993	Upper Deck	134	1994	Stadium Club Team First Day Issue	181	1995	Score	564
1993	Upper Deck Clutch Performers	R14	1994	Studio	215	1995	Score Double Gold Champs	GC5
1993	Upper Deck Diamond Gallery	28	1994	Studio Heritage	4	1995	Score Gold Rush	239
1993	Upper Deck Gold	47	1994	Studio Series Stars	10	1995	Score Gold Rush	564
1993	Upper Deck Gold	134	1994	Studio Series Stars Gold	10	1995	Score Hall of Gold	HG22
1993	Upper Deck Iooss Collection	WI26	1994	Topps	600	1995	Score Platinum Team Sets	239
1993	Upper Deck Iooss Collection Jumbo	WI26	1994	Topps Gold	600	1995	Score Platinum Team Sets	564
1993	Upper Deck Then And Now	TN13	1994	Topps Spanish	600	1995	Score Rules	SR25
1993	Yankees Stadium Club	1	1994	Topps Superstar Samplers	27	1995	Score Rules Jumbos	SR25
1993-97	Bleachers	25	1994	Triple Play	276	1995	Select	101
1994	Bowman	25	1994	Triple Play Promos	9	1995	Select Artist's Proofs	101
1994	Bowman	386	1994	Ultra	400	1995	Select Big Sticks	BS5
1994	Bowman's Best	R45	1994	Ultra Award Winners	2	1995	Select Certified	21
1994	Bowman's Best Refractors	R45	1994	Upper Deck	90	1995	Select Certified Gold Team	8
1994	Collector's Choice	192	1994	Upper Deck	290	1995	Select Certified Mirror Gold	21
1994	Collector's Choice	355	1994	Upper Deck All-Star Jumbos	8	1995	SP	175
1994	Collector's Choice Gold Signature	192	1994	Upper Deck All-Star Jumbos Gold	8	1995	SP Championship	171
1994	Collector's Choice Gold Signature	355	1994	Upper Deck Diamond Collection	E8	1995	SP Championship	175
1994	Collector's Choice Silver Signature	192	1994	Upper Deck Electric Diamond	90	1995	SP Championship Die Cuts	171
1994	Collector's Choice Silver Signature	355	1994	Upper Deck Electric Diamond	290	1995	SP Championship Die Cuts	175
1994	Collector's Choice Team vs. Team	3	1994	Yoo-Hoo	10	1995	SP Championship Fall Classic	5
1994	Donruss	340	1994-95	Pro Mags	88	1995	SP Championship Fall Classic Die Cuts	5
1994	Donruss Anniversary '84	8	1995	Bazooka	47	1995	SP Silver	175
1994	Donruss Diamond Kings	DK16	1995	Bowman	282	1995	SP Special FX	15
1994	Donruss Diamond Kings Jumbo	DK16	1995	Bowman's Best	R46	1995	Sportflix	13
1994	Donruss MVPs	24	1995	Bowman's Best Refractors	R46	1995	Sportflix Artist's Proofs	13
1994	Donruss Promos	9	1995	Classic $10 Phone Cards	38	1995	Sportflix Hammer Team	HT8
1994	Donruss Special Edition	340	1995	Collector's Choice	510	1995	Sportflix ProMotion	PM9
1994	Donruss Spirit of the Game	9	1995	Collector's Choice Gold Signature	510	1995	Stadium Club	212
1994	Donruss Spirit of the Game Jumbos	9	1995	Collector's Choice SE	240	1995	Stadium Club	381
1994	Finest	392	1995	Collector's Choice SE Gold Signature	240	1995	Stadium Club First Day Issue	212
1994	Finest Refractors	392	1995	Collector's Choice SE Silver Signature	240	1995	Stadium Club Members Only Parallel	212
1994	Flair	84	1995	Collector's Choice Silver Signature	510	1995	Stadium Club Members Only Parallel	381
1994	Flair Hot Gloves	6	1995	Denny's Holograms	15	1995	Stadium Club Members Only Parallel	RL33
1994	Flair Infield Power	4	1995	Donruss	55	1995	Stadium Club Members Only Parallel	SS5
1994	Fleer	239	1995	Donruss	220	1995	Stadium Club Ring Leaders	RL33
1994	Fleer Extra Bases	133	1995	Donruss	440	1995	Stadium Club Super Skills	SS5
1994	Fleer Extra Bases Game Breakers	17	1995	Donruss Press Proofs	55	1995	Stadium Club Super Team World Series	212
1994	Fleer Sunoco	17	1995	Donruss Press Proofs	220	1995	Stadium Club Super Team World Series	381
1994	Fleer Team Leaders	10	1995	Donruss Press Proofs	440	1995	Stadium Club Virtual Reality	200
1994	Fleer Update Diamond Tribute	6	1995	Donruss Top of the Order	120	1995	Stadium Club Virtual Reality Members Only	200
1994	Fun Pack	123	1995	Emotion	62	1995	Studio	3
1994	Fun Pack	200	1995	Finest	126	1995	Studio Gold Series	3
1994	Leaf	121	1995	Finest Refractors	126	1995	Studio Platinum Series	3
1994	Leaf Gamers	4	1995	Flair	66	1995	Summit	21
1994	Leaf Gold Stars	6	1995	Flair Hot Gloves	8	1995	Summit	181
1994	Leaf Limited	56	1995	Fleer	76	1995	Summit Big Bang	BB8
1994	Leaf Promos	5	1995	Fleer Team Leaders	10	1995	Summit Nth Degree	21
1994	O-Pee-Chee	54	1995	Fleer Update Smooth Leather	7	1995	Summit Nth Degree	181
1994	Pacific	430	1995	Leaf	303	1995	Topps	399
1994	Pacific Silver Prisms	10	1995	Leaf 300 Club	15	1995	Topps Cyberstats	200
1994	Pacific Silver Prisms Circular	10	1995	Leaf Cornerstones	3	1995	Topps D3	37
1994	Panini Stickers	102	1995	Leaf Gold Stars	6	1995	Topps Embossed	115
1994	Pinnacle	23	1995	Leaf Great Gloves	10	1995	Topps Embossed Golden Idols	115
1994	Pinnacle Artist's Proofs	23	1995	Leaf Limited	55	1995	UC3	20
1994	Pinnacle Museum Collection	23	1995	Leaf Limited Bat Patrol	21	1995	UC3	139
1994	Post	2	1995	Leaf Limited Gold	12	1995	UC3 Artist's Proofs	20
1994	Red Foley's Magazine Inserts	17	1995	Leaf Statistical Standouts	3	1995	UC3 Artist's Proofs	139
1994	Score	23	1995	Megacards Ruth	13	1995	UC3 Cyclone Squad	CS11
1994	Score Dream Team	3	1995	National Packtime 2	5	1995	UC3 In Motion	IM9
1994	Score Gold Rush	23	1995	Pacific	299	1995	Ultra	311
1994	Score Gold Stars	49						

Year	Set Name	Card No.
1995	Ultra Award Winners	2
1995	Ultra Award Winners Gold Medallion	2
1995	Ultra Gold Medallion	311
1995	Upper Deck	210
1995	Upper Deck Electric Diamond	210
1995	Upper Deck Electric Diamond Gold	210
1995	Upper Deck Predictor Award Winner Exchange	H22
1995	Upper Deck Predictor Award Winners	H22
1995	Upper Deck Predictor League Leaders	R53
1995	Upper Deck Predictor League Leaders Exchange	R53
1995	Upper Deck Special Edition	145
1995	Upper Deck Special Edition Gold	145
1995	Upper Deck Steal of a Deal	SD13
1995	Upper Deck/GTS Phone Cards	MLB11
1995	Zenith	29
1995	Zenith Z-Team	17
1996	Bazooka	23
1996	Collector's Choice	100
1996	Collector's Choice	237
1996	Collector's Choice	368T
1996	Collector's Choice Gold Signature	100
1996	Collector's Choice Gold Signature	237
1996	Collector's Choice Silver Signature	100
1996	Collector's Choice Silver Signature	237
1996	Collector's Choice You Make the Play	23
1996	Collector's Choice You Make the Play	23A
1996	Collector's Choice You Make the Play Gold Signature	23
1996	Collector's Choice You Make the Play Gold Signature	23A
1996	Donruss	301
1996	Donruss Diamond Kings	16
1996	Donruss Hit List	15
1996	Donruss Press Proofs	301
1996	Fleer	189
1996	Fleer Team Leaders	10
1996	Fleer Tiffany	189
1996	Metal Universe	90
1996	Metal Universe Platinum	90
1996	Metal Universe Promo Sheet	90
1996	Pacific	376
1996	Pacific Gold Crown Die Cuts	DC4
1996	Pacific Hometowns	HP5
1996	Pacific Milestones	M2
1996	Pacific October Moments	OM15
1996	Pacific Prisms	P119
1996	Pacific Prisms Gold	P119
1996	Pacific Prisms Red Hot Stars	RH18
1996	Panini Stickers	151
1996	Pinnacle	99
1996	Pinnacle	157
1996	Pinnacle	307
1996	Pinnacle Essence of the Game	15
1996	Pinnacle Foil	307
1996	Pinnacle Starburst	37
1996	Pinnacle Starburst	84
1996	Pinnacle Starburst	192
1996	Pinnacle Starburst Artist's Proofs	37
1996	Pinnacle Starburst Artist's Proofs	84
1996	Pinnacle Starburst Artist's Proofs	192
1996	Pro Mags Die Cuts	18
1996	Score	8
1996	Score	377
1996	Score Dugout Collection	A8
1996	Score Dugout Collection	B102
1996	Score Dugout Collection Artist's Proofs	A8
1996	Score Dugout Collection Artist's Proofs	B102
1996	Score Numbers Game	23
1996	Score Reflextions	5
1996	Sportflix ProMotion	12
1996	Stadium Club	73
1996	Stadium Club Extreme Players Bronze	73
1996	Stadium Club Extreme Players Gold	73
1996	Stadium Club Extreme Players Silver	73
1996	Stadium Club Members Only Parallel	73

Year	Set Name	Card No.
1996	Topps	185
1996	Topps Chrome	56
1996	Topps Chrome Masters of the Game	13
1996	Topps Chrome Masters of the Game Refractors	13
1996	Topps Chrome Refractors	56
1996	Topps Masters of the Game	13
1996	Topps Profiles	AL17
1996	Ultra	101
1996	Ultra Gold Medallion	101
1996	Upper Deck	154
1997	Donruss Signature Significant Signatures	14
1998	Donruss Signature Significant Signatures	10

Johnny Mize

Year	Set Name	Card No.
1936	R312 Pastel Photos	17
1936-38	Overland Candy R301	35
1938	Clopay Foto-Fun R329	62
1938	Exhibits Four-in-One	8
1939-46	Exhibits Salutation	44A
1939-46	Exhibits Salutation	44B
1940	Wheaties M4	6A
1940	Wheaties M4	6B
1941	Cardinals W754	18
1941	Double Play R330	39
1941	Double Play R330	99
1942	Gillette Razor Label	1
1943	MP and Co. R302-1	17
1946-49	Sports Exchange W603	6-3
1947	Homogenized Bond	34
1947	Tip Top	131
1948	Bowman	4
1948	Giants Team Issue	18
1948-49	Blue Tint R346	30
1949	Bowman	85A
1949	Bowman	85B
1949	Eureka Stamps	120
1949	Giants Team Issue	20
1949	Leaf	46
1950	Bowman	139
1951	Berk Ross	A7
1951	Bowman	50
1951	R423 Small Strip	70
1951	Topps Blue Backs	50
1951-52	Fischer Baking Labels	19
1952	Berk Ross	42
1952	Bowman	145
1952	Topps	129
1953	Bowman B/W	15
1953	Northland Bread Labels	19
1953	Red Man	AL18
1953	Topps	77
1953-55	Dormand	112
1958	Jay Publishing All-Time Greats	8
1960	Fleer	38
1961	Fleer	63
1966	Cardinals Coins	3
1967	Topps Venezuelan	182
1968	Laughlin World Series	49
1970	Fleer World Series	49
1970	Sports Cards for Collectors Old-Timer Postcards	25
1971	Fleer World Series	50
1972	Laughlin Great Feats	17
1972	Topps Test 53	8
1973	Sports Scoop HOF Candidates	12
1973	Sports Scoop HOF Candidates	13
1973	Sports Scoop HOF Candidates	14
1973-97	Book Promotional Cards	9
1974	Laughlin All-Star Games	47
1975-76	Johnny Mize	1
1975-76	Johnny Mize	2
1975-76	Johnny Mize	3
1975-76	Johnny Mize	4

1992 Ultra Award Winners #19

1951 Bowman #50

Year	Set Name	Card No.
1975-76	Johnny Mize	5
1975-76	Johnny Mize	6
1975-76	Johnny Mize	7
1975-76	Johnny Mize	8
1975-76	Johnny Mize	9
1975-76	Johnny Mize	10
1975-76	Johnny Mize	11
1975-76	Johnny Mize	12
1975-76	Johnny Mize	13
1975-76	Johnny Mize	14
1975-76	Johnny Mize	15
1975-76	Johnny Mize	16
1975-76	Johnny Mize	17
1975-76	Johnny Mize	18
1975-76	Johnny Mize	19
1975-76	Johnny Mize	20
1976	Galasso Baseball's Great Hall of Fame	19
1976	Taylor/Schmierer Bowman 47	15
1977	Shakey's Pizza	B
1978	Atlanta Convention	18
1979	Diamond Greats	39
1980-83	Pacific Legends	49
1980-87	SSPC HOF	176
1980-96	Perez-Steele Hall of Fame Postcards	176
1982	Diamond Classics	24
1982	TCMA Greatest Sluggers	25
1983	ASA Johnny Mize	1
1983	ASA Johnny Mize	2
1983	ASA Johnny Mize	3
1983	ASA Johnny Mize	4
1983	ASA Johnny Mize	5
1983	ASA Johnny Mize	6
1983	ASA Johnny Mize	7
1983	ASA Johnny Mize	8
1983	ASA Johnny Mize	9
1983	ASA Johnny Mize	10
1983	ASA Johnny Mize	11
1983	ASA Johnny Mize	12
1983	Donruss HOF Heroes	10
1983	TCMA Playball 1942	31
1983	Topps Reprint 52	129
1983	Yankee A-S Fifty Years	29
1984-89	O'Connell and Son Ink	58
1985	Big League Collectibles 30s	16
1985	Circle K	32
1985	Donruss HOF Sluggers	4
1985	TCMA Photo Classics	17
1985	Ultimate Baseball Card	12
1986	Sportflics Decade Greats	24
1988	Pacific Legends I	63
1989	HOF Sticker Book	3
1989	Pacific Legends II	180
1989	Perez-Steele Celebration Postcards	32
1989	Swell Baseball Greats	55
1990	Swell Baseball Greats	90
1990-92	Perez-Steele Master Works	31
1990-92	Perez-Steele Master Works	32
1990-92	Perez-Steele Master Works	33
1990-92	Perez-Steele Master Works	34
1990-92	Perez-Steele Master Works	35
1990-97	Perez-Steele Great Moments	23
1991	Conlon TSN	53
1991	Swell Baseball Greats	62
1991	Topps Archives 1953	77
1992	Action Packed ASG	13
1992	Action Packed ASG 24K	13G
1992	Bazooka Quadracard '53 Archives	9
1992	Cardinals McDonald's/Pacific	3
1992	Conlon TSN	435
1992	Conlon TSN	628
1992	Yankees WIZ All-Stars	49
1992	Yankees WIZ HOF	24
1993	Action Packed ASG Coke/Amoco	13
1993	Conlon TSN	918
1993	Diamond Stars Extension Set	145
1993	Metallic Images	13
1993	Ted Williams	66
1993	Ted Williams	129

Year	Set Name	Card No.
1993	Ted Williams	145
1993	Ted Williams Locklear Collection	4
1993	Upper Deck All-Time Heroes	96
1994	Conlon TSN	1126
1994	Conlon TSN Burgundy	1126
1994	Conlon TSN Color Inserts	28
1994	Upper Deck All-Time Heroes	48
1994	Upper Deck All-Time Heroes	161
1994	Upper Deck All-Time Heroes 125th	48
1994	Upper Deck All-Time Heroes 125th	161

Thurman Munson

Year	Set Name	Card No.
1970	O-Pee-Chee	189
1970	Topps	189
1970	Yankee Clinic Day Postcards	9
1970	Yankees Photos SCFC	27
1971	Milk Duds	19
1971	MLB Official Stamps	497
1971	O-Pee-Chee	5
1971	Topps	5
1971	Topps	275
1971	Topps Coins Inserts	118
1971	Topps Greatest Moments	1
1971	Topps Tattoos	83
1971	Yankee Clinic Day Postcards	12
1971	Yankees Arco Oil	8
1972	O-Pee-Chee	441
1972	O-Pee-Chee	442
1972	Topps	441
1972	Topps	442
1972	Yankees Schedules	3
1973	New York Sunday News M138	14
1973	O-Pee-Chee	142
1973	Seven-Eleven Trading Cups	50
1973	Syracuse Chiefs Team Issue	19
1973	Topps	142
1973	Topps Candy Lids	34
1973-74	Linnett Portraits	132
1974	O-Pee-Chee	340
1974	Syracuse Chiefs Team Issue	18
1974	Topps	238
1974	Topps	340
1974	Topps Deckle Edge	7
1974	Topps Stamps	215
1975	Hostess	138
1975	O-Pee-Chee	20
1975	SSPC Puzzle Back	18
1975	Syracuse Chiefs Team Issue	13
1975	Topps	20
1975	Topps Mini	20
1975	Yankees SSPC	5
1976	Blankback Discs	41
1976	Buchman Discs	41
1976	Carousel Discs	41
1976	Crane Discs	41
1976	Dairy Isle Discs	41
1976	Hostess	16
1976	Hostess Twinkie	16
1976	Isaly Discs	41
1976	Kellogg's	53
1976	O-Pee-Chee	192
1976	O-Pee-Chee	650
1976	Orbakers Discs	41
1976	Red Barn Discs	41
1976	Safelon Discs	41
1976	SSPC	433
1976	Topps	192
1976	Topps	650
1976	Towne Club Discs	41
1977	Burger Chef Discs	177
1977	Chilly Willie Discs	49
1977	Customized Discs	49
1977	Dairy Isle Discs	49
1977	Detroit Caesars Discs	49
1977	Holiday Inn Discs	49

Year	Set Name	Card No.
1977	Hostess	5
1977	Kellogg's	23
1977	MSA Discs	49
1977	O-Pee-Chee	30
1977	Pepsi Glove Discs	36
1977	RC Cola Cans	46
1977	Saga Discs	49
1977	Topps	170
1977	Topps Cloth Stickers	32
1977	Wendy's Discs	49
1977	Yankees Burger King	2
1977	Yankees Nedicks Cups	3
1977	Zip'z Discs	49
1977-79	Sportscaster	2005
1978	Hostess	150
1978	Kellogg's	30
1978	O-Pee-Chee	200
1978	Papa Gino's Discs	27
1978	RC Cola Cans	15
1978	Saga Discs	7
1978	SSPC 270	1
1978	Tastee-Freez Discs	7
1978	Topps	60
1978	Wiffle Ball Discs	53
1978	Yankees Burger King	2
1978	Yankees Photo Album	18
1978	Yankees SSPC Diary	1
1979	Baseball Patches	59
1979	Hostess	26
1979	O-Pee-Chee	157
1979	Topps	310
1979	Yankees Burger King	2
1979	Yankees Picture Album	25
1980	Laughlin Famous Feats	13
1982	K-Mart	29
1982	Ohio Hall of Fame	50
1983	Franchise Brooks Robinson	39
1984-85	Sports Design Products West	15
1984-89	O'Connell and Son Ink	32
1984-89	O'Connell and Son Ink	158
1985	George Steinbrenner Menu	7
1986	Sportflics Decade Greats	62
1986	TCMA Superstars Simon	31
1987	Sports Cube Game	3
1988	Pacific Legends I	34
1989	Yankees Score Nat West	32
1990	Rini Postcards Munson	1
1990	Rini Postcards Munson	2
1990	Rini Postcards Munson	3
1990	Rini Postcards Munson	4
1990	Rini Postcards Munson	5
1990	Rini Postcards Munson	6
1990	Rini Postcards Munson	7
1990	Rini Postcards Munson	8
1990	Rini Postcards Munson	9
1990	Rini Postcards Munson	10
1990	Rini Postcards Munson	11
1990	Rini Postcards Munson	12
1990	Yankees Monument Park Rini Postcards	3
1991	Collect-A-Books	22
1991	Line Drive	38
1991	Swell Baseball Greats	149
1992	Pinnacle Rookie Idols	10
1992	Yankees WIZ 60s	92
1992	Yankees WIZ 70s	118
1992	Yankees WIZ All-Stars	50
1993	Action Packed ASG	161
1993	Upper Deck Sheets	20
1994	Ted Williams	62
1994	Yoo-Hoo	11

Graig Nettles

Year	Set Name	Card No.
1969	O-Pee-Chee	99
1969	Topps	99A
1969	Topps	99B

Year	Set Name	Card No.
1970	Indians	9
1970	O-Pee-Chee	491
1970	Topps	491
1971	MLB Official Stamps	380
1971	O-Pee-Chee	324
1971	Topps	324
1972	Topps	590
1973	New York Sunday News M138	12
1973	O-Pee-Chee	498
1973	Syracuse Chiefs Team Issue	21
1973	Topps	498
1973	Yankees	4
1973-74	Linnett Portraits	134
1974	O-Pee-Chee	251
1974	Syracuse Chiefs Team Issue	20
1974	Topps	251
1974	Topps Stamps	217
1975	Hostess	24
1975	Hostess Twinkie	24
1975	O-Pee-Chee	160
1975	Syracuse Chiefs Team Issue	14
1975	Topps	160
1975	Topps Mini	160
1975	Yankees SSPC	20
1976	Hostess	81
1976	O-Pee-Chee	169
1976	SSPC	437
1976	Topps	169
1977	Burger Chef Discs	174
1977	Hostess	116
1977	O-Pee-Chee	2
1977	O-Pee-Chee	217
1977	Topps	2
1977	Topps	20
1977	Yankees Burger King	15
1978	Hostess	132
1978	O-Pee-Chee	10
1978	RC Cola Cans	88
1978	SSPC 270	25
1978	Topps	250
1978	Wiffle Ball Discs	54
1978	Yankees Burger King	14
1978	Yankees Photo Album	19
1978	Yankees SSPC Diary	25
1979	Baseball Patches	61
1979	Hostess	110
1979	O-Pee-Chee	240
1979	Topps	460
1979	Yankees Burger King	15
1979	Yankees Picture Album	28
1980	Kellogg's	18
1980	O-Pee-Chee	359
1980	Topps	710
1980	Topps Super	21
1980	Yankees Photo Album	18
1981	All-Star Game Program Inserts	36
1981	Donruss	105
1981	Fleer	87A
1981	Fleer	87B
1981	Fleer Sticker Cards	72
1981	O-Pee-Chee	365
1981	Topps	365
1981	Topps Super Home Team	69
1981	Yankees Photo Album	18
1982	Donruss	335
1982	Drake's	26
1982	Fleer	46
1982	Fleer Stamps	119
1982	Fleer Stamps	238
1982	Louisville Slugger	4
1982	O-Pee-Chee	21
1982	O-Pee-Chee	62
1982	Topps	505
1982	Topps	506
1982	Topps Sticker Variations	215
1982	Topps/O-Pee-Chee Stickers	215
1982	Yankees Photo Album	19
1983	All-Star Game Program Inserts	36

Year	Set Name	Card No.
1983	Donruss	83
1983	Fleer	391
1983	Fleer Stamps	137
1983	Fleer Stickers	38
1983	O-Pee-Chee	207
1983	O-Pee-Chee	293
1983	Topps	635
1983	Topps	636
1983	Topps Foldouts	2
1983	Topps/O-Pee-Chee Stickers	13
1983	Yankees Photo Album	18
1983	Yankees Roy Rogers Discs	7
1984	All-Star Game Program Inserts	33
1984	Donruss	518
1984	Donruss Champions	12
1984	Fleer	135
1984	Fleer Update	82
1984	Fun Foods Pins	66
1984	Nestle 792	175
1984	Nestle 792	712
1984	Nestle 792	713
1984	O-Pee-Chee	175
1984	Padres Mother's	22
1984	Topps	175
1984	Topps	712
1984	Topps	713
1984	Topps Tiffany	175
1984	Topps Tiffany	712
1984	Topps Tiffany	713
1984	Topps Traded	83T
1984	Topps Traded Tiffany	83T
1984	Topps/O-Pee-Chee Stickers	326
1984-89	O'Connell and Son Ink	196
1985	All-Star Game Program Inserts	123
1985	Donruss	234
1985	Fleer	42
1985	Leaf/Donruss	177
1985	O-Pee-Chee	35
1985	Padres Mother's	4
1985	Topps	35
1985	Topps Tiffany	35
1985	Topps/O-Pee-Chee Stickers	155
1986	Donruss	478
1986	Donruss All-Stars	6
1986	Donruss Pop-Ups	6
1986	Fleer	332
1986	General Mills Booklets	5E
1986	O-Pee-Chee	151
1986	Seven-Eleven Coins	W11
1986	Sportflics	91
1986	Topps	450
1986	Topps Glossy All-Stars	15
1986	Topps Tiffany	450
1986	Topps/O-Pee-Chee Stickers	106
1986	Topps/O-Pee-Chee Stickers	151
1986	Topps/O-Pee-Chee Tattoos	7
1987	Braves Smokey	15
1987	Fleer	426
1987	Fleer Glossy	426
1987	O-Pee-Chee	205
1987	Red Foley Sticker Book	87
1987	Topps	205
1987	Topps Tiffany	205
1987	Topps Traded	85T
1987	Topps Traded Tiffany	85T
1988	Alaska Goldpanners All-Time AS '60s Team	
Issue		4
1988	Expos Postcards	23
1988	San Diego State Aztecs All-Time Greats	13
1988	Score	440
1988	Score Glossy	440
1988	Score Rookie/Traded	25T
1988	Score Rookie/Traded Glossy	25T
1988	Topps	574
1988	Topps Tiffany	574
1989	San Diego State All-Time Greats	12
1989	Score	277
1989-90	Pacific Senior League	115

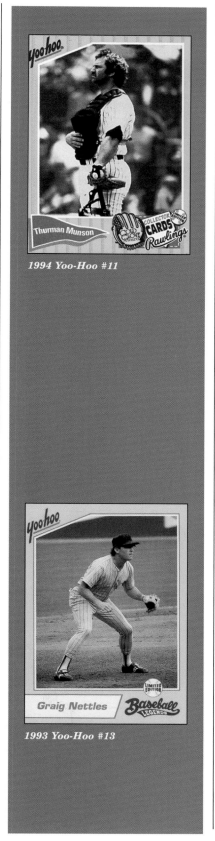

1994 Yoo-Hoo #11

1993 Yoo-Hoo #13

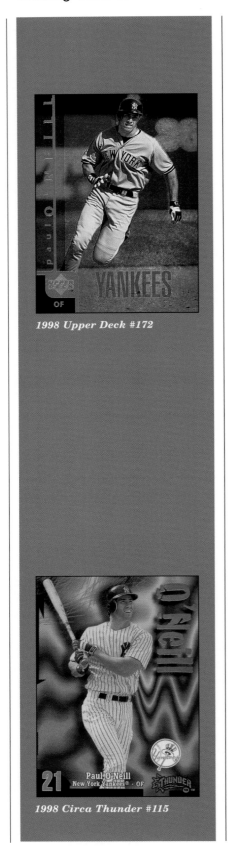

1998 Upper Deck #172

1998 Circa Thunder #115

Year	Set Name	Card No.
1989-90	Pacific Senior League	132
1989-90	Pacific Senior League	158
1989-90	T/M Senior League	82
1989-90	Topps Senior League	25
1990	Elite Senior League	43
1991	Foul Ball	25
1991	Line Drive	26
1991	Swell Baseball Greats	67
1992	Kodak Celebration Denver	3
1992	MCI Ambassadors	6
1992	MVP 2 Highlights	19
1992	MVP Game	7
1992	Yankees WIZ 70s	122
1992	Yankees WIZ All-Stars	53
1993	Action Packed ASG	162
1993	MCI Ambassadors	13
1993	Ted Williams	68
1993	Upper Deck Sheets	11
1993	Upper Deck Sheets	13
1993	Yoo-Hoo	13
1994	Upper Deck All-Time Heroes	148
1994	Upper Deck All-Time Heroes 125th	148
1995	Padres Mother's	28
1995	Sonic/Pepsi Greats	10

Paul O'Neill

Year	Set Name	Card No.
1982	Cedar Rapids Reds TCMA	21
1983	Tampa Tarpons TCMA	19
1986	Donruss	37
1986	Fleer	646
1987	Fleer Update	94
1987	Fleer Update Glossy	94
1987	Reds Kahn's	21
1987	Sportflics Rookies I	17
1987	Sportflics Team Preview	4
1988	Donruss	433
1988	Fleer Update	85
1988	Fleer Update Glossy	85
1988	Red Foley Sticker Book	64
1988	Reds Kahn's	21
1988	Score	304
1988	Score Glossy	304
1988	Starting Lineup Reds	14
1988	Topps	204
1988	Topps Cloth	80
1988	Topps Tiffany	204
1989	Bowman	313
1989	Bowman Tiffany	313
1989	Cedar Rapids Reds All-Decade Best	5
1989	Donruss	360
1989	Donruss Baseball's Best	230
1989	Fleer	166
1989	Fleer Glossy	166
1989	O-Pee-Chee	187
1989	Panini Stickers	77
1989	Reds Kahn's	21
1989	Score	206
1989	Score Young Superstars II	5
1989	Topps	604
1989	Topps Big	39
1989	Topps Tiffany	604
1989	TV Sports Mailbags	44
1989	Upper Deck	428
1990	Bowman	49
1990	Bowman Tiffany	49
1990	Cedar Rapids Reds All Decade Best	5
1990	Classic Blue	117
1990	Donruss	198
1990	Donruss Best NL	39
1990	Fleer	427
1990	Fleer Canadian	427
1990	Leaf	70
1990	O-Pee-Chee	332
1990	Panini Stickers	245

Year	Set Name	Card No.
1990	Pubs.Int'l. Stickers	36
1990	Red Foley Sticker Book	71
1990	Reds Kahn's	20
1990	Score	295
1990	Score 100 Superstars	17
1990	Sportflics	4
1990	Topps	332
1990	Topps Big	30
1990	Topps Stickers	141
1990	Topps Tiffany	332
1990	Upper Deck	161
1991	Bowman	685
1991	Donruss	583
1991	Fleer	76
1991	Leaf	219
1991	O-Pee-Chee	122
1991	Panini French Stickers	133
1991	Panini Stickers	120
1991	Reds Kahn's	21
1991	Reds Pepsi	15
1991	Score	227
1991	Stadium Club	218
1991	Studio	169
1991	Topps	122
1991	Topps Desert Shield	122
1991	Topps Micro	122
1991	Topps Tiffany	122
1991	U.S. Playing Card All-Stars	2C
1991	Ultra	100
1991	Upper Deck	133
1992	Bowman	267
1992	Denny's Holograms	11
1992	Donruss	63
1992	Fleer	415
1992	Leaf	99
1992	Leaf Black Gold	99
1992	O-Pee-Chee	61
1992	Panini Stickers	266
1992	Pinnacle	154
1992	Reds Kahn's	21
1992	Score	57
1992	Score 100 Superstars	58
1992	Score Impact Players	66
1992	Stadium Club	175
1992	Stadium Club Dome	135
1992	Studio	25
1992	Topps	61
1992	Topps Gold	61
1992	Topps Gold Winners	61
1992	Topps Kids	41
1992	Topps Micro	61
1992	Triple Play	162
1992	Ultra	194
1992	Upper Deck	464
1992	Upper Deck Home Run Heroes	HR15
1992-97	Sports Illustrated For Kids II	391
1993	Bowman	75
1993	Donruss	696
1993	Finest	170
1993	Finest Refractors	170
1993	Flair	251
1993	Fleer	39
1993	Fleer Final Edition	250
1993	Leaf	379
1993	O-Pee-Chee	218
1993	O-Pee-Chee Premier	14
1993	Pacific Spanish	560
1993	Panini Stickers	151
1993	Pinnacle	446
1993	Score	439
1993	Select	86
1993	Select Rookie/Traded	21T
1993	SP	266
1993	Stadium Club	717
1993	Stadium Club First Day Issue	717
1993	Stadium Club Members Only Parallel	717
1993	Studio	140

Year	Set Name	Card No.
1993	Topps	276
1993	Topps Gold	276
1993	Topps Inagural Rockies	276
1993	Topps Inaugural Marlins	276
1993	Topps Micro	276
1993	Topps Traded	84T
1993	Ultra	599
1993	Upper Deck	796
1993	Upper Deck Gold	796
1993	Upper Deck Home Run Heroes	HR27
1993	Yankees Stadium Club	14
1994	Bowman	249
1994	Bowman's Best	R31
1994	Bowman's Best Refractors	R31
1994	Collector's Choice	218
1994	Collector's Choice Gold Signature	218
1994	Collector's Choice Silver Signature	218
1994	Donruss	50
1994	Donruss Special Edition	50
1994	Finest	69
1994	Finest Refractors	69
1994	Flair	86
1994	Fleer	243
1994	Fleer Extra Bases	136
1994	Fun Pack	67
1994	Leaf	108
1994	Leaf Limited	57
1994	O-Pee-Chee	229
1994	Pacific	433
1994	Panini Stickers	103
1994	Pinnacle	280
1994	Pinnacle Artist's Proofs	280
1994	Pinnacle Museum Collection	280
1994	Score	15
1994	Score Gold Rush	15
1994	Select	8
1994	SP	199
1994	SP Die Cuts	199
1994	Sportflics	147
1994	Stadium Club	74
1994	Stadium Club First Day Issue	74
1994	Stadium Club Golden Rainbow	74
1994	Stadium Club Members Only Parallel	74
1994	Stadium Club Team	199
1994	Stadium Club Team First Day Issue	199
1994	Studio	216
1994	Studio Editor's Choice	7
1994	Topps	546
1994	Topps Gold	546
1994	Topps Spanish	546
1994	Triple Play	277
1994	Ultra	99
1994	Upper Deck	186
1994	Upper Deck Electric Diamond	186
1995	Bazooka	45
1995	Bazooka Red Hot	RH10
1995	Bowman	356
1995	Bowman's Best	R66
1995	Bowman's Best Refractors	R66
1995	Classic $10 Phone Cards	39
1995	Collector's Choice	72
1995	Collector's Choice Gold Signature	72
1995	Collector's Choice SE	243
1995	Collector's Choice SE Gold Signature	243
1995	Collector's Choice SE Silver Signature	243
1995	Collector's Choice Silver Signature	72
1995	Donruss	284
1995	Donruss Diamond Kings	DK7
1995	Donruss Dominators	9
1995	Donruss Elite	50
1995	Donruss Press Proofs	284
1995	Donruss Top of the Order	122
1995	Emotion	64
1995	Finest	181
1995	Finest Bronze	5
1995	Finest Refractors	181
1995	Flair	67
1995	Fleer	78
1995	Fleer All-Stars	18
1995	Fleer League Leaders	1
1995	Kraft	10
1995	Leaf	80
1995	Leaf Checklists	4
1995	Leaf Limited	76
1995	Pacific	301
1995	Pacific Prisms	98
1995	Panini Stickers	89
1995	Panini Stickers	122
1995	Pinnacle	245
1995	Pinnacle Artist's Proofs	245
1995	Pinnacle Museum Collection	245
1995	Pinnacle Performers	PP17
1995	Post Canadian	7
1995	Score	41
1995	Score Gold Rush	41
1995	Score Hall of Gold	HG26
1995	Score Platinum Team Sets	41
1995	Score Rules	SR21
1995	Score Rules Jumbos	SR21
1995	Select	131
1995	Select Artist's Proofs	131
1995	Select Certified	65
1995	Select Certified Mirror Gold	65
1995	SP	178
1995	SP Championship	173
1995	SP Championship Die Cuts	173
1995	SP Silver	178
1995	Sportflix	58
1995	Sportflix Artist's Proofs	58
1995	Stadium Club	124
1995	Stadium Club	519
1995	Stadium Club Clear Cut	CC22
1995	Stadium Club First Day Issue	124
1995	Stadium Club Members Only	35
1995	Stadium Club Members Only Parallel	124
1995	Stadium Club Members Only Parallel	519
1995	Stadium Club Members Only Parallel	CC22
1995	Stadium Club Members Only Parallel	RL20
1995	Stadium Club Members Only Parallel	SS13
1995	Stadium Club Ring Leaders	RL20
1995	Stadium Club Super Skills	SS13
1995	Stadium Club Super Team World Series	124
1995	Stadium Club Super Team World Series	519
1995	Stadium Club Virtual Reality	63
1995	Stadium Club Virtual Reality Members Only	63
1995	Studio	162
1995	Summit	77
1995	Summit Nth Degree	77
1995	Topps	426
1995	Topps Cyberstats	224
1995	Topps D3	26
1995	Topps Embossed	72
1995	Topps Embossed Golden Idols	72
1995	Topps League Leaders	LL26
1995	U.S. Playing Cards Aces	12D
1995	UC3	68
1995	UC3 Artist's Proofs	68
1995	Ultra	84
1995	Ultra All-Stars	14
1995	Ultra All-Stars Gold Medallion	14
1995	Ultra Gold Medallion	84
1995	Ultra League Leaders	1
1995	Ultra League Leaders Gold Medallion	1
1995	Ultra On-Base Leaders	9
1995	Ultra On-Base Leaders Gold Medallion	9
1995	Upper Deck	208
1995	Upper Deck Electric Diamond	208
1995	Upper Deck Electric Diamond Gold	208
1995	Upper Deck Predictor League Leaders	R24
1995	Upper Deck Predictor League Leaders Exchange	R24
1995	Upper Deck Special Edition	141
1995	Upper Deck Special Edition Gold	141
1995	Zenith	80
1996	Bazooka	128
1996	Bowman	34
1996	Bowman Foil	34
1996	Bowman's Best	37
1996	Bowman's Best Atomic Refractors	37
1996	Bowman's Best Refractors	37
1996	Circa	67
1996	Circa Access	10
1996	Circa Boss	17
1996	Circa Rave	67
1996	Collector's Choice	635
1996	Collector's Choice Gold Signature	635
1996	Collector's Choice Silver Signature	635
1996	Donruss	404
1996	Donruss Press Proofs	404
1996	Emotion-XL	92
1996	Finest	B93
1996	Finest	S182
1996	Finest	S242
1996	Finest Refractors	B93
1996	Finest Refractors	S182
1996	Finest Refractors	S242
1996	Flair	133
1996	Fleer	192
1996	Fleer Tiffany	192
1996	Leaf	13
1996	Leaf Limited	44
1996	Leaf Limited Gold	44
1996	Leaf Preferred	50
1996	Leaf Preferred Press Proofs	50
1996	Leaf Press Proofs Bronze	13
1996	Leaf Press Proofs Gold	13
1996	Leaf Press Proofs Silver	13
1996	Leaf Signature	31
1996	Leaf Signature Press Proofs Gold	31
1996	Leaf Signature Press Proofs Platinum	31
1996	Liberty Sports	2
1996	Metal Universe	91
1996	Metal Universe Platinum	91
1996	MLB Pins	24
1996	Pacific	384
1996	Pacific Prisms	P121
1996	Pacific Prisms Gold	P121
1996	Panini Stickers	154
1996	Pinnacle	237
1996	Pinnacle Aficionado	17
1996	Pinnacle Aficionado Artist's Proofs	17
1996	Pinnacle Aficionado First Pitch Preview	17
1996	Pinnacle Foil	237
1996	Pinnacle Starburst	137
1996	Pinnacle Starburst Artist's Proofs	137
1996	Pro Stamps	138
1996	Score	296
1996	Score Dugout Collection	B21
1996	Score Dugout Collection Artist's Proofs	B21
1996	Select	92
1996	Select Artist's Proofs	92
1996	Select Certified	49
1996	Select Certified Artist's Proofs	49
1996	Select Certified Certified Blue	49
1996	Select Certified Certified Red	49
1996	Select Certified Interleague Preview	21
1996	Select Certified Mirror Blue	49
1996	Select Certified Mirror Gold	49
1996	Select Certified Mirror Red	49
1996	SP	132
1996	Sportflix	81
1996	Sportflix Artist's Proofs	81
1996	Stadium Club	212
1996	Stadium Club	272
1996	Stadium Club Extreme Players Bronze	272
1996	Stadium Club Extreme Players Gold	272
1996	Stadium Club Extreme Players Silver	272
1996	Stadium Club Members Only Parallel	212
1996	Stadium Club Members Only Parallel	272
1996	Studio	110
1996	Studio Press Proofs Bronze	110

Trading Card Checklist

Year	Set Name	Card No.
1996	Studio Press Proofs Gold	110
1996	Studio Press Proofs Silver	110
1996	Summit	104
1996	Summit Above and Beyond	104
1996	Summit Artist's Proofs	104
1996	Summit Foil	104
1996	Topps	284
1996	Topps Chrome	114
1996	Topps Chrome Refractors	114
1996	Topps Gallery	153
1996	Topps Gallery Players Private Issue	153
1996	Topps Laser	75
1996	Topps Profiles	AL7
1996	Ultra	103
1996	Ultra Gold Medallion	103
1996	Upper Deck	155
1996	Zenith	45
1996	Zenith Artist's Proofs	45
1996	Zenith Mozaics	22
1997	Bowman	260
1997	Bowman Chrome	82
1997	Bowman Chrome International	82
1997	Bowman Chrome International Refractors	82
1997	Bowman Chrome Refractors	82
1997	Bowman International	260
1997	Circa	359
1997	Circa Rave	359
1997	Collector's Choice	401
1997	Collector's Choice Teams	NY12
1997	Donruss	35
1997	Donruss Gold Press Proofs	35
1997	Donruss Limited	125
1997	Donruss Limited	182
1997	Donruss Limited Exposure	125
1997	Donruss Limited Exposure	182
1997	Donruss Limited Exposure Non-Glossy	182
1997	Donruss Preferred	64
1997	Donruss Preferred Cut to the Chase	64
1997	Donruss Signature Autographs	74
1997	Donruss Signature Autographs Century	92
1997	Donruss Signature Autographs Millenium	92
1997	Donruss Silver Press Proofs	35
1997	Donruss Team Sets	122
1997	Donruss Team Sets Pennant Edition	122
1997	Finest	87
1997	Finest Refractors	87
1997	Flair Showcase Legacy Collection	121
1997	Flair Showcase Masterpieces	A121
1997	Flair Showcase Masterpieces	B121
1997	Flair Showcase Masterpieces	C121
1997	Flair Showcase Row 0	121
1997	Flair Showcase Row 1	121
1997	Flair Showcase Row 2	121
1997	Fleer	174
1997	Fleer Tiffany	174
1997	Leaf	92
1997	Leaf Fractal Matrix	92
1997	Leaf Fractal Matrix Die Cuts	92
1997	Metal Universe	120
1997	New Pinnacle	8
1997	New Pinnacle Artist's Proof	8
1997	New Pinnacle Museum Collection	8
1997	New Pinnacle Press Plates	8
1997	Pacific	155
1997	Pacific Light Blue	155
1997	Pacific Silver	155
1997	Pinnacle X-Press	43
1997	Pinnacle X-Press Men of Summer	43
1997	Score	150
1997	Score Artist's Proofs White Border	150
1997	Score Premium Stock	150
1997	Score Showcase Series	150
1997	Score Showcase Series Artist's Proofs	150
1997	Stadium Club	32
1997	Stadium Club Matrix	32
1997	Stadium Club Members Only Parallel	32
1997	Studio	117
1997	Studio Press Proof Gold	117
1997	Studio Press Proof Silver	117
1997	Topps	247
1997	Topps Chrome	88
1997	Topps Chrome Refractors	88
1997	Topps Gallery	45
1997	Topps Gallery Player's Private Issue	45
1997	Topps Stars	83
1997	Topps Stars '97 All-Stars	AS18
1997	Topps Stars Always Mint	83
1997	Ultra	339
1997	Ultra Gold Medallion	339
1997	Ultra Platinum Medallion	339
1997	Upper Deck	126
1997	Yankees Score	9
1997	Yankees Score Platinum	9
1997	Yankees Score Premier	9
1998	Bowman	241
1998	Bowman Chrome	241
1998	Bowman Chrome Golden Anniversary	241
1998	Bowman Chrome Golden Anniversary Refractors	241
1998	Bowman Chrome International	241
1998	Bowman Chrome International Refractors	241
1998	Bowman Chrome Refractors	241
1998	Bowman Golden Anniversary	241
1998	Bowman International	241
1998	Bowman's Best	55
1998	Bowman's Best Atomic Refractors	55
1998	Bowman's Best Refractors	55
1998	Circa Thunder	115
1998	Circa Thunder Rave	115
1998	Circa Thunder Super Rave	115
1998	Collector's Choice	444
1998	Crown Royale	98
1998	Donruss	78
1998	Donruss Collections Donruss	78
1998	Donruss Collections Leaf	317
1998	Donruss Collections Preferred	642
1998	Donruss Collections Samples	78
1998	Donruss Gold Press Proofs	78
1998	Donruss Preferred	92
1998	Donruss Preferred Seating	92
1998	Donruss Prized Collections Donruss	78
1998	Donruss Prized Collections Leaf	317
1998	Donruss Prized Collections Preferred	642
1998	Donruss Signature Autographs	63
1998	Donruss Signature Autographs Century	83
1998	Donruss Signature Autographs Millenium	84
1998	Donruss Silver Press Proofs	78
1998	Finest	62
1998	Finest No-Protectors	62
1998	Finest No-Protectors Refractors	62
1998	Finest Refractors	62
1998	Fleer	167
1998	Fleer Decade of Excellence	11
1998	Fleer Decade of Excellence Rare Traditions	11
1998	Fleer Vintage '63	40
1998	Fleer Vintage '63 Classic	40
1998	Leaf	118
1998	Leaf Fractal Diamond Axis	118
1998	Leaf Fractal Foundations	118
1998	Leaf Fractal Materials	118
1998	Leaf Fractal Materials Die Cuts	118
1998	Leaf Fractal Materials Z2 Axis	118
1998	Leaf Fractal Matrix	118
1998	Leaf Fractal Matrix Die Cuts	118
1998	Leaf Rookies and Stars	92
1998	Leaf Rookies and Stars Longevity	92
1998	Leaf Rookies and Stars Longevity Holographic	92
1998	Leaf Rookies and Stars True Blue	92
1998	Metal Universe	144
1998	Metal Universe Precious Metal Gems	144
1998	Pacific	154
1998	Pacific Aurora	61
1998	Pacific Omega	168
1998	Pacific Omega Red	168
1998	Pacific Online	511
1998	Pacific Online Red	511
1998	Pacific Online Web Cards	511
1998	Pacific Paramount	72
1998	Pacific Paramount Copper	72
1998	Pacific Paramount Gold	72
1998	Pacific Paramount Holographic Silver	72
1998	Pacific Paramount Platinum Blue	72
1998	Pacific Paramount Red	72
1998	Pacific Platinum Blue	154
1998	Pacific Red Threatt	154
1998	Pacific Silver	154
1998	Pinnacle Plus	104
1998	Pinnacle Snapshots	NYY17
1998	Revolution	102
1998	Revolution Shadow Series	102
1998	Score	116
1998	Score Artist's Proofs	PP47
1998	Score Rookie Traded	164
1998	Score Rookie Traded Artist's Proofs	PP93
1998	Score Rookie Traded Artist's Proofs 1 of 1's	PP93
1998	Score Rookie Traded Showcase Series	PP93
1998	Score Showcase Series	PP47
1998	SP Authentic	146
1998	Sports Illustrated World Series Fever	104
1998	Sports Illustrated World Series Fever Extra Edition	104
1998	Sports Illustrated World Series Fever First Edition	104
1998	Sports Illustrated World Series Fever Reggie Jackson's Picks	1
1998	SPx Finite	107
1998	SPx Finite Radiance	107
1998	SPx Finite Spectrum	107
1998	Stadium Club	104
1998	Stadium Club First Day Issue	104
1998	Stadium Club One Of A Kind	104
1998	Stadium Club Printing Plates	104
1998	Studio	130
1998	Studio Gold Press Proofs	130
1998	Studio Silver Press Proofs	130
1998	Topps	322
1998	Topps Chrome	322
1998	Topps Chrome Refractors	322
1998	Topps Devil Rays	322
1998	Topps Diamondbacks	322
1998	Topps Gallery	149
1998	Topps Gallery Gallery Proofs	149
1998	Topps Gallery Original Printing Plates	149
1998	Topps Gallery Player's Private Issue	149
1998	Topps Gallery Player's Private Issue Auction	149
1998	Topps Gold Label Class 1	33
1998	Topps Gold Label Class 1 Black	33
1998	Topps Gold Label Class 1 One to One	33
1998	Topps Gold Label Class 1 Red	33
1998	Topps Gold Label Class 2	33
1998	Topps Gold Label Class 2 Black	33
1998	Topps Gold Label Class 2 One to One	33
1998	Topps Gold Label Class 2 Red	33
1998	Topps Gold Label Class 3	33
1998	Topps Gold Label Class 3 Black	33
1998	Topps Gold Label Class 3 One to One	33
1998	Topps Gold Label Class 3 Red	33
1998	Topps Minted in Cooperstown	322
1998	Topps Opening Day	148
1998	Topps Stars	18
1998	Topps Stars Bronze	18
1998	Topps Stars Gold	18
1998	Topps Stars Gold Rainbow	18
1998	Topps Stars Silver	18
1998	Topps Tek	37
1998	Topps Tek Diffractors	37
1998	Ultra	47
1998	Ultra Gold Medallion	47
1998	Ultra Masterpieces	47

Year	Set Name	Card No.
1998	Ultra Platinum Medallion	47
1998	Upper Deck	172
1998	Upper Deck Retro	69
1998	Upper Deck Special F/X	93
1998	Yankees Score	10
1998	Yankees Score Platinum	10
1999	Finest	51
1999	Finest Gold Refractors	51
1999	Finest Refractors	51
1999	Fleer	286
1999	Fleer Starting 9	286
1999	Fleer Warning Track	286
1999	Metal Universe	230
1999	Metal Universe Gem Masters	230
1999	Metal Universe Precious Metal Gems	230
1999	Pacific	299
1999	Pacific Crown Collection	194
1999	Pacific Crown Collection Platinum Blue	194
1999	Pacific Paramount	165
1999	Pacific Paramount Copper	165
1999	Pacific Paramount Holographic Silver	165
1999	Pacific Paramount Platinum Blue	165
1999	Pacific Platinum Blue	299
1999	Pacific Private Stock	123
1999	Pacific Private Stock PS-206	123
1999	Pacific Private Stock PS-206 Red	123
1999	Pacific Red	299
1999	SkyBox Thunder	200
1999	SkyBox Thunder Rant	200
1999	SkyBox Thunder Rave	200
1999	SkyBox Thunder Super Rave	200
1999	Stadium Club	19
1999	Stadium Club First Day Issue	19
1999	Stadium Club One of a Kind	19
1999	Stadium Club Printing Plates	19
1999	Topps Opening Day	133
1999	Topps Stars 'N Steel	25
1999	Topps Stars 'N Steel Gold	25
1999	Topps Stars 'N Steel Gold Domed Holographic	25
1999	UD Choice	118
1999	UD Choice Prime Choice Reserve	118
1999	Ultra RBI Kings	25
1999	Upper Deck	156
1999	Upper Deck Exclusives Level 1	156
1999	Upper Deck Exclusives Level 2	156

Andy Pettitte

Year	Set Name	Card No.
1992	Classic/Best	286
1992	Greensboro Hornets Classic/Best	1
1992	Greensboro Hornets Fleer/ProCards	777
1992-97	Sports Illustrated For Kids II	561
1993	Bowman	103
1993	Classic/Best Gold	117
1993	Excel	214
1993	Prince William Cannons Classic/Best	19
1993	South Atlantic League All-Stars Play II	31
1994	Albany Yankees Fleer/ProCards	1438
1994	Bowman	493
1994	Classic	28
1994	Excel	111
1995	Bowman	257
1995	Bowman Gold Foil	257
1995	Bowman's Best	B50
1995	Bowman's Best Refractors	B50
1995	Columbus Clippers Milk Caps Team Issue	12
1995	Columbus Clippers Police	23
1995	Columbus Clippers Team Issue	23
1995	Emotion	65
1995	Excel	101
1995	Flair	287
1995	Fleer Update	27
1995	Select	163
1995	Select Artist's Proofs	163

Year	Set Name	Card No.
1995	Select Certified	96
1995	Select Certified Mirror Gold	96
1995	Stadium Club	565
1995	Stadium Club Members Only Parallel	565
1995	Stadium Club Super Team World Series	565
1995	Summit	168
1995	Summit Nth Degree	168
1995	Topps	640
1995	Upper Deck	493
1995	Upper Deck Minors	176
1995	Upper Deck Minors Future Stock	176
1996	Bowman's Best	24
1996	Bowman's Best Atomic Refractors	24
1996	Bowman's Best Refractors	24
1996	Circa	68
1996	Circa Rave	68
1996	Collector's Choice	234
1996	Collector's Choice Gold Signature	234
1996	Collector's Choice Silver Signature	234
1996	Donruss	74
1996	Donruss Press Proofs	74
1996	Emotion-XL	93
1996	Finest	B122
1996	Finest Refractors	B122
1996	Flair	134
1996	Fleer	194
1996	Fleer Rookie Sensations	14
1996	Fleer Tiffany	194
1996	Leaf	185
1996	Leaf Limited	81
1996	Leaf Limited Gold	81
1996	Leaf Preferred	72
1996	Leaf Preferred Press Proofs	72
1996	Leaf Press Proofs Bronze	185
1996	Leaf Press Proofs Gold	185
1996	Leaf Press Proofs Silver	185
1996	Leaf Signature	54
1996	Leaf Signature Autographs	181
1996	Leaf Signature Autographs Gold	181
1996	Leaf Signature Autographs Silver	181
1996	Leaf Signature Extended Autographs	158
1996	Leaf Signature Extended Autographs Century Marks	23
1996	Leaf Signature Press Proofs Gold	54
1996	Leaf Signature Press Proofs Platinum	54
1996	Metal Universe	92
1996	Metal Universe Mining For Gold	11
1996	Metal Universe Platinum	92
1996	Pacific	371
1996	Panini Stickers	152
1996	Panini Stickers	242
1996	Pinnacle	103
1996	Pinnacle	291
1996	Pinnacle Foil	291
1996	Score	396
1996	Select	103
1996	Select Artist's Proofs	103
1996	Select Certified	91
1996	Select Certified Artist's Proofs	91
1996	Select Certified Certified Blue	91
1996	Select Certified Certified Red	91
1996	Select Certified Mirror Blue	91
1996	Select Certified Mirror Gold	91
1996	Select Certified Mirror Red	91
1996	SP	130
1996	Stadium Club	436
1996	Stadium Club Extreme Players Bronze	436
1996	Stadium Club Extreme Players Gold	436
1996	Stadium Club Extreme Players Silver	436
1996	Stadium Club Members Only	50
1996	Stadium Club Members Only Parallel	436
1996	Team Out	63
1996	Topps	378
1996	Topps Gallery	104
1996	Topps Gallery Players Private Issue	104
1996	Ultra	104
1996	Ultra Gold Medallion	104

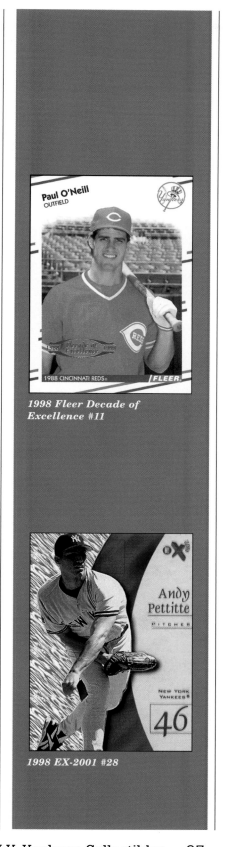

1998 Fleer Decade of Excellence #11

1998 EX-2001 #28

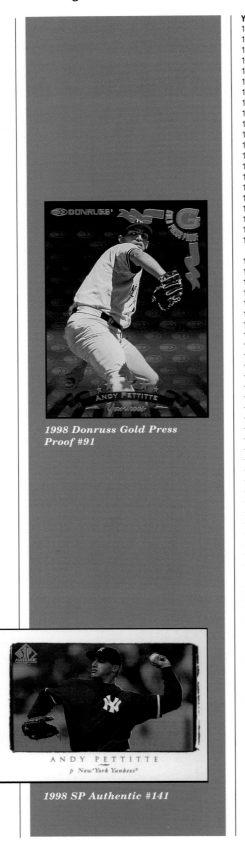

1998 Donruss Gold Press Proof #91

1998 SP Authentic #141

Year	Set Name	Card No.
1996	Upper Deck	144
1996	Zenith	88
1996	Zenith Artist's Proofs	88
1997	Bowman	248
1997	Bowman Chrome	72
1997	Bowman Chrome International	72
1997	Bowman Chrome International Refractors	72
1997	Bowman Chrome Refractors	72
1997	Bowman International	248
1997	Bowman's Best	21
1997	Bowman's Best Atomic Refractors	21
1997	Bowman's Best Refractor	21
1997	Circa	149
1997	Circa Fast Track	6
1997	Circa Rave	149
1997	Collector's Choice	60
1997	Collector's Choice	404
1997	Collector's Choice All-Star Connection	18
1997	Collector's Choice Teams	NY10
1997	Collector's Choice The Big Show	35
1997	Collector's Choice The Big Show World Headquarters	35
1997	Collector's Choice Toast of the Town	T20
1997	Cracker Jack	16
1997	Donruss	82
1997	Donruss	424
1997	Donruss Elite	14
1997	Donruss Elite Gold Stars	14
1997	Donruss Gold Press Proofs	82
1997	Donruss Gold Press Proofs	424
1997	Donruss Limited	34
1997	Donruss Limited	135
1997	Donruss Limited	177
1997	Donruss Limited Exposure	34
1997	Donruss Limited Exposure	135
1997	Donruss Limited Exposure	177
1997	Donruss Limited Exposure Non-Glossy	34
1997	Donruss Preferred	20
1997	Donruss Preferred Cut to the Chase	20
1997	Donruss Signature	74
1997	Donruss Signature Autographs Century	98
1997	Donruss Signature Autographs Millenium	98
1997	Donruss Signature Platinum Press Proofs	74
1997	Donruss Silver Press Proofs	82
1997	Donruss Silver Press Proofs	424
1997	Donruss Team Sets	126
1997	Donruss Team Sets Pennant Edition	126
1997	Donruss VxP 1.0	37
1997	E-X2000	34
1997	E-X2000 Credentials	34
1997	E-X2000 Essential Credentials	34
1997	E-X2000 Star Date 2000	3
1997	Finest	287
1997	Finest Embossed	287
1997	Finest Embossed Refractors	287
1997	Finest Refractors	287
1997	Flair Showcase Legacy Collection	46
1997	Flair Showcase Masterpieces	A46
1997	Flair Showcase Masterpieces	B46
1997	Flair Showcase Masterpieces	C46
1997	Flair Showcase Row 0	46
1997	Flair Showcase Row 1	46
1997	Flair Showcase Row 2	46
1997	Fleer	175
1997	Fleer	711
1997	Fleer Team Leaders	10
1997	Fleer Tiffany	175
1997	Fleer Tiffany	711
1997	Fleer Zone	13
1997	Leaf	136
1997	Leaf	198
1997	Leaf Fractal Matrix	136
1997	Leaf Fractal Matrix	198
1997	Leaf Fractal Matrix Die Cuts	136
1997	Leaf Fractal Matrix Die Cuts	198
1997	Leaf Get-A-Grip	3
1997	Leaf Gold Stars	12

Year	Set Name	Card No.
1997	Metal Universe	121
1997	Metal Universe Platinum Portraits	8
1997	New Pinnacle	24
1997	New Pinnacle Artist's Proof	24
1997	New Pinnacle Keeping the Pace	15
1997	New Pinnacle Museum Collection	24
1997	New Pinnacle Press Plates	24
1997	New Pinnacle Press Plates	K15
1997	Pacific	156
1997	Pacific Card-Supials	14
1997	Pacific Card-Supials Minis	14
1997	Pacific Cramer's Choice	4
1997	Pacific Fireworks Die Cuts	8
1997	Pacific Gold Crown Die Cuts	12
1997	Pacific Light Blue	156
1997	Pacific Prisms	53
1997	Pacific Prisms Gate Attractions	GA10
1997	Pacific Prisms Light Blue	53
1997	Pacific Prisms Platinum	53
1997	Pacific Prisms Sluggers and Hurlers	SH5B
1997	Pacific Silver	156
1997	Pinnacle	14
1997	Pinnacle All-Star FanFest Promos	5
1997	Pinnacle Artist's Proofs	PP14
1997	Pinnacle Cardfrontations	5
1997	Pinnacle Certified	92
1997	Pinnacle Certified Certified Gold Team	17
1997	Pinnacle Certified Certified Mirror Gold Team	17
1997	Pinnacle Certified Certified Team	17
1997	Pinnacle Certified Mirror Black	92
1997	Pinnacle Certified Mirror Blue	92
1997	Pinnacle Certified Mirror Gold	92
1997	Pinnacle Certified Mirror Red	92
1997	Pinnacle Certified Red	92
1997	Pinnacle FanFest	FF17
1997	Pinnacle Inside	52
1997	Pinnacle Inside Cans	12
1997	Pinnacle Inside Club Edition	52
1997	Pinnacle Inside Diamond Edition	52
1997	Pinnacle Inside Dueling Dugouts	16
1997	Pinnacle Museum Collection	14
1997	Pinnacle Press Plate Previews	14
1997	Pinnacle Team Pinnacle	9
1997	Pinnacle Team Pinnacle	10
1997	Pinnacle Totally Certified Platinum Blue	92
1997	Pinnacle Totally Certified Platinum Gold	92
1997	Pinnacle Totally Certified Platinum Red	92
1997	Pinnacle X-Press	2
1997	Pinnacle X-Press Men of Summer	2
1997	Pinnacle X-Press Metal Works	17
1997	Pinnacle X-Press Metal Works Gold	17
1997	Pinnacle X-Press Metal Works Silver	17
1997	Score	82
1997	Score	518
1997	Score All-Star Fanfest	17
1997	Score Artist's Proofs White Border	82
1997	Score Artist's Proofs White Border	518
1997	Score Premium Stock	82
1997	Score Reserve Collection	518
1997	Score Showcase Series	82
1997	Score Showcase Series	518
1997	Score Showcase Series Artist's Proofs	82
1997	Score Showcase Series Artist's Proofs	518
1997	Score Stand and Deliver	10
1997	Select	58
1997	Select Artist's Proof	58
1997	Select Company	58
1997	Select Registered Gold	58
1997	Select Tools of the Trade	2
1997	Select Tools of the Trade Mirror Blue	2
1997	SP	128
1997	SP Special FX	34
1997	Sports Illustrated	66
1997	Sports Illustrated	130
1997	Sports Illustrated Extra Edition	66
1997	Sports Illustrated Extra Edition	130
1997	SPx	35

Year	Set Name	Card No.
1997	SPx Bronze	35
1997	SPx Gold	35
1997	SPx Grand Finale	35
1997	SPx Silver	35
1997	SPx Steel	35
1997	Stadium Club	46
1997	Stadium Club Co-Signers	CO1
1997	Stadium Club Instavision	I13
1997	Stadium Club Matrix	46
1997	Stadium Club Members Only Parallel	46
1997	Stadium Club Members Only Parallel	I13
1997	Studio	5
1997	Studio Master Strokes	6
1997	Studio Master Strokes 8x10	6
1997	Studio Press Proof Gold	5
1997	Studio Press Proof Silver	5
1997	Topps	60
1997	Topps All-Stars	AS17
1997	Topps Chrome	20
1997	Topps Chrome All-Stars	AS17
1997	Topps Chrome All-Stars Refractors	AS17
1997	Topps Chrome Refractors	20
1997	Topps Chrome Season's Best	17
1997	Topps Chrome Season's Best Refractors	17
1997	Topps Gallery	160
1997	Topps Gallery Photo Gallery	PG14
1997	Topps Gallery Player's Private Issue	160
1997	Topps Season's Best	SB17
1997	UD3	54
1997	UD3 Generation Next	GN12
1997	Ultra	102
1997	Ultra Double Trouble	7
1997	Ultra Fame Game	13
1997	Ultra Gold Medallion	102
1997	Ultra Platinum Medallion	102
1997	Ultra Season Crowns	7
1997	Ultra Top 30	15
1997	Ultra Top 30 Gold Medallion	15
1997	Upper Deck	68
1997	Upper Deck	122
1997	Upper Deck	254
1997	Upper Deck	266
1997	Upper Deck	380
1997	Upper Deck Award Winner Jumbos	9
1997	Upper Deck Blue Chip Prospects	BC17
1997	Upper Deck Rock Solid Foundation	RS9
1997	Yankees McDonald's Pins	3
1997	Yankees Score	5
1997	Yankees Score Platinum	5
1997	Yankees Score Premier	5
1997	Zenith	21
1997-98	Fleer Million Dollar Moments	48
1997-98	Fleer Million Dollar Moments Redemption	48
1998	Bowman	3
1998	Bowman Chrome	3
1998	Bowman Chrome Golden Anniversary	3
1998	Bowman Chrome Golden Anniversary Refractors	3
1998	Bowman Chrome International	3
1998	Bowman Chrome International Refractors	3
1998	Bowman Chrome Refractors	3
1998	Bowman Chrome Reprints	37
1998	Bowman Chrome Reprints Refractors	37
1998	Bowman Golden Anniversary	3
1998	Bowman International	3
1998	Bowman's Best	39
1998	Bowman's Best Atomic Refractors	39
1998	Bowman's Best Refractors	39
1998	Circa Thunder	276
1998	Circa Thunder Rave	276
1998	Circa Thunder Super Rave	276
1998	Collector's Choice	445
1998	Collector's Choice StarQuest	SQ32
1998	Donruss	91
1998	Donruss	379
1998	Donruss Collections Donruss	91
1998	Donruss Collections Elite	424

Year	Set Name	Card No.
1998	Donruss Collections Leaf	331
1998	Donruss Collections Preferred	578
1998	Donruss Collections Preferred	740
1998	Donruss Collections Samples	91
1998	Donruss Crusade Green	34
1998	Donruss Crusade Purple	34
1998	Donruss Crusade Red	34
1998	Donruss Diamond Kings	7
1998	Donruss Diamond Kings Canvas	7
1998	Donruss Elite	24
1998	Donruss Elite Aspirations	24
1998	Donruss Elite Status	24
1998	Donruss Gold Press Proofs	91
1998	Donruss Gold Press Proofs	379
1998	Donruss Preferred	28
1998	Donruss Preferred	190
1998	Donruss Preferred Seating	28
1998	Donruss Preferred Seating	190
1998	Donruss Preferred Title Waves	14
1998	Donruss Prized Collections Donruss	91
1998	Donruss Prized Collections Elite	424
1998	Donruss Prized Collections Leaf	331
1998	Donruss Prized Collections Preferred	578
1998	Donruss Prized Collections Preferred	740
1998	Donruss Signature	72
1998	Donruss Signature Autographs Century	91
1998	Donruss Signature Autographs Millenium	92
1998	Donruss Signature Proofs	72
1998	Donruss Silver Press Proofs	91
1998	Donruss Silver Press Proofs	379
1998	E-X2001	28
1998	E-X2001 Essential Credentials Future	28
1998	E-X2001 Essential Credentials Now	28
1998	Finest	270
1998	Finest No-Protectors	270
1998	Finest No-Protectors Refractors	270
1998	Finest Refractors	270
1998	Flair Showcase Legacy Collection	43
1998	Flair Showcase Legacy Collection Masterpieces	43
1998	Flair Showcase Row 0	43
1998	Flair Showcase Row 1	43
1998	Flair Showcase Row 2	43
1998	Flair Showcase Row 3	43
1998	Fleer	144
1998	Fleer	308
1998	Fleer	592
1998	Fleer Vintage '63	41
1998	Fleer Vintage '63 Classic	41
1998	Leaf	132
1998	Leaf Crusade Green	34
1998	Leaf Crusade Purple	34
1998	Leaf Crusade Red	34
1998	Leaf Fractal Diamond Axis	132
1998	Leaf Fractal Foundations	132
1998	Leaf Fractal Materials	132
1998	Leaf Fractal Materials Die Cuts	132
1998	Leaf Fractal Materials Z2 Axis	132
1998	Leaf Fractal Matrix	132
1998	Leaf Fractal Matrix Die Cuts	132
1998	Leaf Rookies and Stars	1
1998	Leaf Rookies and Stars	190
1998	Leaf Rookies and Stars Longevity	1
1998	Leaf Rookies and Stars Longevity	190
1998	Leaf Rookies and Stars Longevity Holographic	1
1998	Leaf Rookies and Stars Longevity Holographic	190
1998	Leaf Rookies and Stars Ticket Masters	6
1998	Leaf Rookies and Stars Ticket Masters Die Cuts	6
1998	Leaf Rookies and Stars True Blue	1
1998	Leaf Rookies and Stars True Blue	190
1998	Leaf State Representatives	25
1998	Leaf Statistical Standouts	17
1998	Leaf Statistical Standouts Die Cuts	17
1998	Metal Universe	192
1998	Metal Universe Precious Metal Gems	192

Year	Set Name	Card No.
1998	Pacific	155
1998	Pacific Aurora	62
1998	Pacific Invincible	54
1998	Pacific Invincible Platinum Blue	54
1998	Pacific Invincible Silver	54
1998	Pacific Invincible Team Checklists	19
1998	Pacific Omega	169
1998	Pacific Omega Red	169
1998	Pacific Online	512
1998	Pacific Online Red	512
1998	Pacific Online Web Cards	512
1998	Pacific Paramount	73
1998	Pacific Paramount Copper	73
1998	Pacific Paramount Gold	73
1998	Pacific Paramount Holographic Silver	73
1998	Pacific Paramount Platinum Blue	73
1998	Pacific Paramount Red	73
1998	Pacific Platinum Blue	155
1998	Pacific Red Threatt	155
1998	Pacific Silver	155
1998	Pinnacle	29
1998	Pinnacle Artist's Proofs	PP29
1998	Pinnacle Inside	32
1998	Pinnacle Inside Club Edition	32
1998	Pinnacle Inside Diamond Edition	32
1998	Pinnacle Inside Stand-Up Guys	19AB
1998	Pinnacle Inside Stand-Up Guys	19CD
1998	Pinnacle Inside Stand-Up Guys Samples	19AB
1998	Pinnacle Inside Stand-Up Guys Samples	19CD
1998	Pinnacle Mint	16
1998	Pinnacle Mint Bronze	16
1998	Pinnacle Mint Coins Brass	16
1998	Pinnacle Mint Coins Brass Artist's Proofs	16
1998	Pinnacle Mint Coins Gold Plated	16
1998	Pinnacle Mint Coins Gold Plated Artist's Proofs	16
1998	Pinnacle Mint Coins Nickel	16
1998	Pinnacle Mint Coins Nickel Artist's Proofs	16
1998	Pinnacle Mint Coins Solid Gold Redemption	16
1998	Pinnacle Mint Coins Solid Silver	16
1998	Pinnacle Mint Gold	16
1998	Pinnacle Mint Silver	16
1998	Pinnacle Museum Collection	PP29
1998	Pinnacle Performers	29
1998	Pinnacle Performers Peak Performers	29
1998	Pinnacle Press Plates	29
1998	Pinnacle Snapshots	NYY1
1998	Pinnacle Snapshots	NYY5
1998	Score	57
1998	Score Artist's Proofs	PP20
1998	Score Rookie Traded	23
1998	Score Rookie Traded Artist's Proofs	PP23
1998	Score Rookie Traded Artist's Proofs 1 of 1's	PP23
1998	Score Rookie Traded Showcase Series	PP23
1998	Score Showcase Series	PP20
1998	SkyBox Dugout Axcess	75
1998	SkyBox Dugout Axcess Dishwashers	D9
1998	SkyBox Dugout Axcess Inside Axcess	75
1998	SP Authentic	141
1998	Sports Illustrated	100
1998	Sports Illustrated	143
1998	Sports Illustrated Extra Edition	100
1998	Sports Illustrated Extra Edition	143
1998	Sports Illustrated First Edition	100
1998	Sports Illustrated First Edition	143
1998	Sports Illustrated Then and Now	120
1998	Sports Illustrated Then and Now Extra Edition	120
1998	Sports Illustrated World Series Fever	109
1998	Sports Illustrated World Series Fever Extra Edition	109
1998	Sports Illustrated World Series Fever First Edition	109
1998	SPx Finite	108
1998	SPx Finite Radiance	108
1998	SPx Finite Spectrum	108

Trading Card Checklist

Year	Set Name	Card No.
1998	Stadium Club	117
1998	Stadium Club Co-Signers	CS20
1998	Stadium Club Co-Signers	CS22
1998	Stadium Club Co-Signers	CS24
1998	Stadium Club First Day Issue	117
1998	Stadium Club One Of A Kind	117
1998	Stadium Club Printing Plates	117
1998	Studio	41
1998	Studio Gold Press Proofs	41
1998	Studio Portraits 8 x 10	29
1998	Studio Portraits 8 x 10 Gold Proofs	29
1998	Studio Silver Press Proofs	41
1998	Topps	337
1998	Topps Baby Boomers	BB13
1998	Topps Chrome	337
1998	Topps Chrome Baby Boomers	BB13
1998	Topps Chrome Baby Boomers Refractors	BB13
1998	Topps Chrome Refractors	337
1998	Topps Devil Rays	337
1998	Topps Diamondbacks	337
1998	Topps Gallery	129
1998	Topps Gallery Gallery Proofs	129
1998	Topps Gallery Original Printing Plates	129
1998	Topps Gallery Player's Private Issue	129
1998	Topps Gallery Player's Private Issue Auction	129
1998	Topps Minted in Cooperstown	337
1998	Topps Opening Day	164
1998	Topps Stars	76
1998	Topps Stars Bronze	76
1998	Topps Stars Gold	76
1998	Topps Stars Gold Rainbow	76
1998	Topps Stars Silver	76
1998	Topps SuperChrome	35
1998	Topps SuperChrome Refractors	35
1998	Ultra	175
1998	Ultra Double Trouble	15
1998	Ultra Gold Medallion	175
1998	Ultra Masterpieces	175
1998	Ultra Platinum Medallion	175
1998	Upper Deck	170
1998	Upper Deck 10th Anniversary Preview	7
1998	Upper Deck 10th Anniversary Preview Retail	7
1998	Upper Deck Amazing Greats	AG16
1998	Upper Deck Amazing Greats Die Cuts	AG16
1998	Upper Deck Blue Chip Prospects	BC12
1998	Upper Deck Retro	70
1998	Upper Deck Special F/X	92
1998	Yankees Score	5
1998	Yankees Score Platinum	5
1998	Zenith	27
1998	Zenith 5 x 7	24
1998	Zenith 5 x 7 Gold Impulse	24
1998	Zenith 5 x 7 Impulse	24
1998	Zenith Z-Gold	27
1998	Zenith Z-Silver	27
1999	Fleer	275
1999	Fleer Starting 9	275
1999	Fleer Warning Track	275
1999	Metal Universe	217
1999	Metal Universe Gem Masters	217
1999	Metal Universe Precious Metal Gems	217
1999	Pacific	300
1999	Pacific Platinum Blue	300
1999	Pacific Red	300
1999	SkyBox Thunder	172
1999	SkyBox Thunder Rant	172
1999	SkyBox Thunder Rave	172
1999	SkyBox Thunder Super Rave	172
1999	Sports Illustrated	86
1999	Topps	74
1999	Topps	239
1999	Topps Chrome	74
1999	Topps Chrome	239
1999	Topps Chrome Refractors	74
1999	Topps Chrome Refractors	239
1999	Topps MVP Promotion	74
1999	Topps Opening Day	42
1999	Upper Deck	157
1999	Upper Deck Exclusives Level 1	157
1999	Upper Deck Exclusives Level 2	157

Tim Raines

Year	Set Name	Card No.
1979	Memphis Chicks TCMA	20
1981	Donruss	538
1981	Expos Postcards	9
1981	O-Pee-Chee	136
1981	Topps	479
1981	Topps Traded	816
1982	Donruss	214
1982	Expos Hygrade Meats	16
1982	Expos Postcards	31
1982	Expos Zellers	3
1982	FBI Discs	17
1982	Fleer	202
1982	Fleer	207
1982	Fleer Stamps	31
1982	Kellogg's	53
1982	O-Pee-Chee	70
1982	O-Pee-Chee Posters	17
1982	Perma-Graphic All-Stars	13
1982	Perma-Graphic Credit Cards	6
1982	Perma-Graphic Credit Cards Gold	6
1982	Perma-Graphics All-Stars Gold	13
1982	Topps	3
1982	Topps	70
1982	Topps	164
1982	Topps/O-Pee-Chee Stickers	7
1982	Topps/O-Pee-Chee Stickers	62
1982	Topps/O-Pee-Chee Stickers	116
1983	All-Star Game Program Inserts	158
1983	Donruss	540
1983	Expos Postcards	23
1983	Expos Stuart	9
1983	Fleer	292
1983	Fleer Stamps	155
1983	Fleer Stickers	265
1983	O-Pee-Chee	227
1983	O-Pee-Chee	352
1983	Perma-Graphic All-Stars	14
1983	Perma-Graphic All-Stars Gold	14
1983	Topps	403
1983	Topps	595
1983	Topps	704
1983	Topps/O-Pee-Chee Stickers	210
1983	Topps/O-Pee-Chee Stickers	253
1984	All-Star Game Program Inserts	66
1984	Donruss	299
1984	Expos Postcards	22
1984	Expos Stuart	20
1984	Expos Stuart	36
1984	Expos Stuart	37
1984	Fleer	281
1984	Fleer	631
1984	Fleer Stickers	51
1984	Fleer Stickers	88
1984	Fun Foods Pins	41
1984	Nestle 792	134
1984	Nestle 792	370
1984	Nestle 792	390
1984	Nestle Dream Team	17
1984	O-Pee-Chee	370
1984	O-Pee-Chee	390
1984	Seven-Eleven Coins	E20
1984	Topps	134
1984	Topps	370
1984	Topps	390
1984	Topps Glossy All-Stars	17
1984	Topps Glossy Send-Ins	37
1984	Topps Rub Downs	23
1984	Topps Sticker Boxes	4
1984	Topps Tiffany	134
1984	Topps Tiffany	370
1984	Topps Tiffany	390
1984	Topps/O-Pee-Chee Stickers	91
1984	Topps/O-Pee-Chee Stickers	179
1984	Topps/O-Pee-Chee Stickers	201
1985	All-Star Game Program Inserts	157
1985	Donruss	299
1985	Donruss Action All-Stars	1
1985	Drake's	24
1985	Expos Postcards	17
1985	Fleer	405
1985	Fleer Limited Edition	26
1985	Fleer Star Stickers	42
1985	Fleer Star Stickers	58
1985	Leaf/Donruss	218
1985	Leaf/Donruss	252
1985	O-Pee-Chee	277
1985	O-Pee-Chee Posters	7
1985	Seven-Eleven Coins	S12
1985	Topps	630
1985	Topps 3-D	17
1985	Topps Rub Downs	9
1985	Topps Super	15
1985	Topps Tiffany	630
1985	Topps/O-Pee-Chee Stickers	82
1985	Topps/O-Pee-Chee Stickers	282
1985	Topps/OPC Minis	630
1986	Donruss	177
1986	Donruss All-Stars	20
1986	Drake's	15
1986	Expos Provigo Panels	7
1986	Expos Provigo Posters	1
1986	Fleer	256
1986	Fleer	632
1986	Fleer League Leaders	33
1986	Fleer Mini	54
1986	Fleer Sticker Cards	92
1986	General Mills Booklets	6E
1986	Leaf/Donruss	108
1986	O-Pee-Chee	280
1986	Quaker Granola	10
1986	Seven-Eleven Coins	E12
1986	Sportflics	11
1986	Sportflics	127
1986	Sportflics	144
1986	Sportflics Decade Greats	74
1986	Topps	280
1986	Topps Glossy Send-Ins	15
1986	Topps Mini Leaders	49
1986	Topps Super	42
1986	Topps Tiffany	280
1986	Topps/O-Pee-Chee Stickers	75
1986	Topps/O-Pee-Chee Tattoos	17
1987	Boardwalk and Baseball	24
1987	Classic Game	29
1987	Donruss	56
1987	Donruss All-Stars	36
1987	Donruss Highlights	7
1987	Donruss Highlights	16
1987	Expos Postcards	21
1987	Fleer	328
1987	Fleer	642
1987	Fleer All-Stars	12
1987	Fleer Baseball All-Stars	34
1987	Fleer Exciting Stars	34
1987	Fleer Glossy	328
1987	Fleer Glossy	642
1987	Fleer Mini	85
1987	Fleer Record Setters	30
1987	Fleer Sluggers/Pitchers	32
1987	Fleer Sticker Cards	94
1987	General Mills Booklets	5E
1987	Kay-Bee	25
1987	Leaf/Donruss	149
1987	O-Pee-Chee	30
1987	Red Foley Sticker Book	39
1987	Sportflics	34

Year	Set Name	Card No.
1987	Sportflics	152
1987	Sportflics	197
1987	Sportflics	199
1987	Sportflics Dealer Panels	1
1987	Sportflics Superstar Discs	15
1987	Star Raines	1
1987	Star Raines	2
1987	Star Raines	3
1987	Star Raines	4
1987	Star Raines	5
1987	Star Raines	6
1987	Star Raines	7
1987	Star Raines	8
1987	Star Raines	9
1987	Star Raines	10
1987	Star Raines	11
1987	Star Raines	12
1987	Stuart Panels	7
1987	Topps	30
1987	Topps Gallery of Champions	8
1987	Topps Glossy Send-Ins	48
1987	Topps Mini Leaders	17
1987	Topps Tiffany	30
1987	Topps/O-Pee-Chee Stickers	85
1987	Woolworth's	11
1988	Bazooka	15
1988	Classic Red	168
1988	Donruss	2
1988	Donruss	345
1988	Donruss All-Stars	57
1988	Donruss All-Stars	62
1988	Donruss Baseball's Best	180
1988	Donruss Bonus MVP's	BC18
1988	Donruss Super DK's	2
1988	Drake's	2
1988	Expos Postcards	27
1988	Fleer	193
1988	Fleer	631
1988	Fleer Award Winners	30
1988	Fleer Baseball All-Stars	31
1988	Fleer Baseball MVP's	27
1988	Fleer Exciting Stars	31
1988	Fleer Glossy	193
1988	Fleer Glossy	631
1988	Fleer Headliners	6
1988	Fleer Hottest Stars	31
1988	Fleer League Leaders	31
1988	Fleer Mini	90
1988	Fleer Record Setters	30
1988	Fleer Sticker Cards	97
1988	Fleer Superstars	29
1988	Fleer Team Leaders	27
1988	Grenada Baseball Stamps	51
1988	K-Mart	19
1988	Kay-Bee	24
1988	Leaf/Donruss	2
1988	Leaf/Donruss	114
1988	Leaf/Donruss	211
1988	MSA Fantastic Sam's Discs	16
1988	MSA Hostess Discs	11
1988	MSA Jiffy Pop Discs	14
1988	Nestle	31
1988	O-Pee-Chee	243
1988	Panini Stickers	325
1988	Panini Stickers	330
1988	Score	3
1988	Score	649
1988	Score Glossy	3
1988	Score Glossy	649
1988	Sportflics	2
1988	Starting Lineup All-Stars	23
1988	Starting Lineup Expos	13
1988	Tara Plaques	32
1988	Topps	403
1988	Topps	720
1988	Topps Big	116
1988	Topps Coins	49

Year	Set Name	Card No.
1988	Topps Glossy Send-Ins	12
1988	Topps Mini Leaders	57
1988	Topps Revco League Leaders	5
1988	Topps Rite-Aid Team MVP's	6
1988	Topps Tiffany	403
1988	Topps Tiffany	720
1988	Topps UK Minis	58
1988	Topps UK Minis Tiffany	58
1988	Topps/O-Pee-Chee Sticker Backs	20
1988	Topps/O-Pee-Chee Stickers	76
1989	Bowman	369
1989	Bowman Tiffany	369
1989	Cereal Superstars	6
1989	Classic Light Blue	42
1989	Donruss	97
1989	Donruss Baseball's Best	258
1989	Expos Postcards	24
1989	Fleer	391
1989	Fleer Glossy	391
1989	K-Mart	27
1989	Kay-Bee	25
1989	O-Pee-Chee	87
1989	Panini Stickers	125
1989	Red Foley Sticker Book	91
1989	Score	40
1989	Score Hottest 100 Stars	95
1989	Sportflics	150
1989	Topps	81
1989	Topps	560
1989	Topps Baseball Talk/LJN	80
1989	Topps Batting Leaders	7
1989	Topps Big	73
1989	Topps Coins	22
1989	Topps Glossy Send-Ins	53
1989	Topps Tiffany	81
1989	Topps Tiffany	560
1989	Topps UK Minis	61
1989	Topps/O-Pee-Chee Stickers	77
1989	TV Sports Mailbags	13
1989	Upper Deck	402
1989	Upper Deck Sheets	2
1989-91	Sports Illustrated For Kids I	178
1990	Bowman	118
1990	Bowman Tiffany	118
1990	Classic Blue	118
1990	Donruss	216
1990	Donruss Best NL	104
1990	Donruss Bonus MVP's	BC7
1990	Expos Postcards	28
1990	Fleer	359
1990	Fleer Baseball MVP's	30
1990	Fleer Baseball MVP's Canadian	30
1990	Fleer Canadian	359
1990	Good Humor Ice Cream Big League Sticks	16
1990	Hottest 50 Players Stickers	32
1990	Kay-Bee	24
1990	King-B Discs	6
1990	Leaf	212
1990	M.V.P. Pins	61
1990	MSA Holsum Discs	2
1990	O-Pee-Chee	180
1990	Panini Stickers	283
1990	Pubs.Int'l. Stickers	186
1990	Score	409
1990	Score 100 Superstars	75
1990	Sportflics	69
1990	Starline Long John Silver	23
1990	Starline Long John Silver	39
1990	Sunflower Seeds	14
1990	Superstar Action Marbles	16
1990	Topps	180
1990	Topps Ames All-Stars	17
1990	Topps Batting Leaders	7
1990	Topps Big	154
1990	Topps Coins	54
1990	Topps Doubleheaders	50
1990	Topps Glossy Send-Ins	38

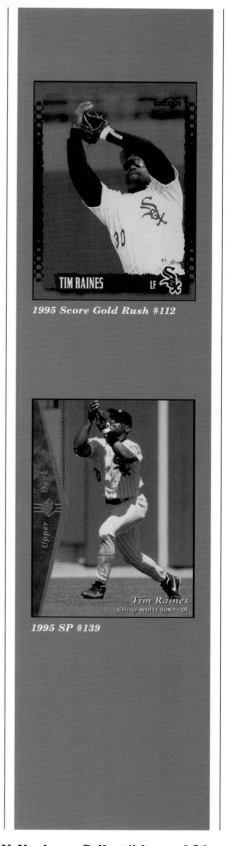

1995 Score Gold Rush #112

1995 SP #139

1995 Pacific #95

1997 Circa #292

Year	Set Name	Card No.	Year	Set Name	Card No.
1990	Topps Mini Leaders	63	1993	SP	259
1990	Topps Sticker Backs	18	1993	Stadium Club	43
1990	Topps Stickers	69	1993	Stadium Club First Day Issue	43
1990	Topps Tiffany	180	1993	Stadium Club Members Only Parallel	43
1990	Topps TV All-Stars	55	1993	Studio	215
1990	Upper Deck	29	1993	Topps	675
1990	Upper Deck	177	1993	Topps Gold	675
1991	Baseball's Best Hit Men	16	1993	Topps Inagural Rockies	675
1991	Bowman	362	1993	Topps Inaugural Marlins	675
1991	Classic Game	174	1993	Topps Micro	675
1991	Classic II	T9	1993	Triple Play	108
1991	Denny's Holograms	26	1993	U.S. Playing Cards Aces	6H
1991	Donruss	457	1993	Ultra	178
1991	Fleer	244	1993	Upper Deck	597
1991	Fleer Update	15	1993	Upper Deck Gold	597
1991	Leaf	413	1993	White Sox Kodak	24
1991	O-Pee-Chee	360	1993	White Sox Stadium Club	5
1991	O-Pee-Chee Premier	97	1994	Bowman	127
1991	Panini French Stickers	143	1994	Collector's Choice	385
1991	Panini Stickers	63	1994	Collector's Choice Gold Signature	385
1991	Red Foley Stickers	75	1994	Collector's Choice Silver Signature	385
1991	Score	35	1994	Donruss	220
1991	Score 100 Superstars	89	1994	Donruss	258
1991	Score Rookie/Traded	10T	1994	Finest	192
1991	Stadium Club	523	1994	Finest Refractors	192
1991	Starline Prototypes	4	1994	Flair	35
1991	Studio	37	1994	Fleer	93
1991	Studio Previews	4	1994	Fleer Extra Bases	52
1991	Topps	360	1994	Leaf	116
1991	Topps Cracker Jack I	3	1994	Leaf Limited	23
1991	Topps Desert Shield	360	1994	O-Pee-Chee	228
1991	Topps Micro	360	1994	Pacific	136
1991	Topps Tiffany	360	1994	Pinnacle	462
1991	Topps Traded	94T	1994	Pinnacle Artist's Proofs	462
1991	Topps Traded Tiffany	94T	1994	Pinnacle Museum Collection	462
1991	Ultra	81	1994	Score	379
1991	Upper Deck	143	1994	Score Gold Rush	379
1991	Upper Deck	773	1994	Select	92
1991	White Sox Kodak	30	1994	Stadium Club	350
1992	Bowman	204	1994	Stadium Club	525
1992	Classic Game	99	1994	Stadium Club First Day Issue	350
1992	Donruss	312	1994	Stadium Club First Day Issue	525
1992	Fleer	97	1994	Stadium Club Golden Rainbow	350
1992	Leaf	37	1994	Stadium Club Golden Rainbow	525
1992	Leaf Black Gold	37	1994	Stadium Club Members Only Parallel	350
1992	O-Pee-Chee	426	1994	Stadium Club Members Only Parallel	525
1992	Panini Stickers	131	1994	Stadium Club Team	136
1992	Pinnacle	178	1994	Stadium Club Team First Day Issue	136
1992	Pinnacle	605	1994	Studio	208
1992	Red Foley Stickers	78	1994	Sucker Saver	4
1992	Score	635	1994	Topps	243
1992	Stadium Club	426	1994	Topps Gold	243
1992	Studio	156	1994	Topps Spanish	243
1992	Topps	426	1994	Triple Play	268
1992	Topps Gold	426	1994	Ultra	341
1992	Topps Gold Winners	426	1994	Upper Deck	254
1992	Topps Kids	104	1994	Upper Deck All-Star Jumbos	42
1992	Topps Micro	426	1994	Upper Deck All-Star Jumbos Gold	42
1992	Triple Play	107	1994	Upper Deck Electric Diamond	254
1992	Ultra	43	1994	White Sox Kodak	25
1992	Upper Deck	575	1994-95	Pro Mags	27
1992	White Sox Kodak	30	1995	Bowman	291
1993	Bowman	499	1995	Collector's Choice	495
1993	Donruss	565	1995	Collector's Choice Gold Signature	495
1993	Expos Donruss McDonald's	6	1995	Collector's Choice Silver Signature	495
1993	Finest	183	1995	Donruss	75
1993	Finest Refractors	183	1995	Donruss Press Proofs	75
1993	Fleer	209	1995	Donruss Top of the Order	53
1993	Fun Pack	201	1995	Emotion	28
1993	Leaf	420	1995	Finest	187
1993	O-Pee-Chee	290	1995	Finest Refractors	187
1993	Pacific Spanish	75	1995	Flair	248
1993	Panini Stickers	140	1995	Fleer	127
1993	Pinnacle	53	1995	Leaf	208
1993	Red Foley Stickers	77	1995	Leaf Limited	94
1993	Score	658	1995	Pacific	95
1993	Select	236	1995	Score	112

Year	Set Name	Card No.
1995	Score Gold Rush	112
1995	Score Platinum Team Sets	112
1995	SP	139
1995	SP Championship	139
1995	SP Championship Die Cuts	139
1995	SP Silver	139
1995	Stadium Club	302
1995	Stadium Club	410
1995	Stadium Club Members Only Parallel	302
1995	Stadium Club Members Only Parallel	410
1995	Stadium Club Members Only Parallel	RL12
1995	Stadium Club Ring Leaders	RL12
1995	Stadium Club Super Team World Series	302
1995	Stadium Club Super Team World Series	410
1995	Stadium Club Virtual Reality	158
1995	Stadium Club Virtual Reality Members Only	158
1995	Studio	148
1995	Topps	77
1995	Topps Cyberstats	54
1995	Topps Embossed	130
1995	Topps Embossed Golden Idols	130
1995	Ultra	33
1995	Ultra Gold Medallion	33
1995	Upper Deck	198
1995	Upper Deck Electric Diamond	198
1995	Upper Deck Electric Diamond Gold	198
1995	Upper Deck Special Edition	157
1995	Upper Deck Special Edition Gold	157
1995	White Sox Kodak	26
1996	Collector's Choice	95
1996	Collector's Choice	779
1996	Collector's Choice Gold Signature	95
1996	Collector's Choice Silver Signature	95
1996	Donruss	384
1996	Donruss Press Proofs	384
1996	Emotion-XL	94
1996	Finest	B224
1996	Finest Refractors	B224
1996	Flair	135
1996	Fleer	75
1996	Fleer Tiffany	75
1996	Fleer Update	U66
1996	Fleer Update Tiffany	U66
1996	Leaf Signature	136
1996	Leaf Signature Press Proofs Gold	136
1996	Leaf Signature Press Proofs Platinum	136
1996	Metal Universe	93
1996	Metal Universe Platinum	93
1996	MLB Pins	28
1996	Pacific	284
1996	Panini Stickers	174
1996	Pinnacle	364
1996	Pinnacle Foil	364
1996	Score	449
1996	Stadium Club	418
1996	Stadium Club Extreme Players Bronze	418
1996	Stadium Club Extreme Players Gold	418
1996	Stadium Club Extreme Players Silver	418
1996	Stadium Club Members Only Parallel	418
1996	Studio	59
1996	Studio Press Proofs Bronze	59
1996	Studio Press Proofs Gold	59
1996	Studio Press Proofs Silver	59
1996	Topps	272
1996	Topps Chrome Masters of the Game	7
1996	Topps Chrome Masters of the Game Refractors	7
1996	Topps Masters of the Game	7
1996	Ultra	43
1996	Ultra	393
1996	Ultra Gold Medallion	43
1996	Ultra Gold Medallion	393
1996	Upper Deck	111
1996	Upper Deck	409
1997	Circa	292
1997	Circa Rave	292
1997	Collector's Choice	182

Year	Set Name	Card No.
1997	Collector's Choice Teams	NY7
1997	Fleer	503
1997	Fleer Tiffany	503
1997	Leaf	274
1997	Leaf Fractal Matrix	274
1997	Leaf Fractal Matrix Die Cuts	274
1997	Pacific	157
1997	Pacific Light Blue	157
1997	Pacific Silver	157
1997	Score	391
1997	Score Artist's Proofs White Border	391
1997	Score Reserve Collection	391
1997	Score Showcase Series	391
1997	Score Showcase Series Artist's Proofs	391
1997	Topps	334
1997	Ultra	461
1997	Ultra Gold Medallion	461
1997	Ultra Platinum Medallion	461
1997	Upper Deck	443
1998	Collector's Choice	192
1998	Donruss Collections Leaf	300
1998	Donruss Prized Collections Leaf	300
1998	Fleer	437
1998	Leaf	101
1998	Leaf Fractal Diamond Axis	101
1998	Leaf Fractal Foundations	101
1998	Leaf Fractal Materials	101
1998	Leaf Fractal Materials Die Cuts	101
1998	Leaf Fractal Materials Z2 Axis	101
1998	Leaf Fractal Matrix	101
1998	Leaf Fractal Matrix Die Cuts	101
1998	Pacific Online	514
1998	Pacific Online Red	514
1998	Pacific Online Web Cards	514
1998	Pinnacle Snapshots	NYY6
1998	Upper Deck	449
1999	Fleer	535
1999	Fleer Starting 9	535
1999	Fleer Warning Track	535
1999	Pacific	302
1999	Pacific Paramount	173
1999	Pacific Paramount Copper	173
1999	Pacific Paramount Holographic Silver	173
1999	Pacific Paramount Platinum Blue	173
1999	Pacific Platinum Blue	302
1999	Pacific Red	302

Bobby Richardson

Year	Set Name	Card No.
1947-66	Exhibits	186
1957	Topps	286
1958	Topps	101A
1958	Topps	101B
1959	Topps	76
1959	Topps	237
1959	Topps Venezuelan	76
1960	Topps	405
1961	Nu-Card Scoops	415
1961	Post	8A
1961	Post	8B
1961	Topps	180
1961	Topps	308
1961	Topps Dice Game	13
1961	Yankees Jay Publishing	10
1962	Jello	2
1962	Post	2
1962	Post Canadian	2
1962	Salada Plastic Coins	64
1962	Shirriff Plastic Coins	64
1962	Topps	65
1962	Topps Stamps Inserts	90
1962	Topps Venezuelan	65
1962	Yankees Jay Publishing	11
1962-66	American Tract Society	43A
1962-66	American Tract Society	43B

Year	Set Name	Card No.
1962-66	American Tract Society	43C
1962-66	American Tract Society	43D
1963	Fleer	25
1963	Jello	13
1963	Kahn's	26
1963	Post	13
1963	Salada Metal Coins	52
1963	Topps	173
1963	Topps	420
1963	Topps Stick-Ons Inserts	33
1963	Yankees Jay Publishing	10
1963-67	Yankee Requena K Postcards	14
1964	Challenge The Yankees	21
1964	Topps	190
1964	Topps Coins Inserts	72
1964	Topps Coins Inserts	123
1964	Topps Stamps	12
1964	Topps Stand Ups	60
1964	Topps Venezuelan	190
1964	Wheaties Stamps	38
1964	Yankees Jay Publishing	10
1965	Challenge The Yankees	20
1965	MacGregor Staff	9
1965	O-Pee-Chee	115
1965	Topps	115
1965	Topps Embossed Inserts	65
1965	Topps Transfers Inserts	26
1966	Topps	490
1966	Topps Rub-Offs Inserts	77
1966	Yankees Team Issue	10
1970	Fleer World Series	61
1977-84	Galasso Glossy Greats	247
1978	TCMA 60'S I	112
1981	TCMA 60's II	477
1983	Franchise Brooks Robinson	16
1983	Yankee A-S Fifty Years	36
1983	Yankees 1961	2
1984-89	O'Connell and Son Ink	210
1987	Yankees 1961 TCMA	3
1988	Pacific Legends I	74
1989	Swell Baseball Greats	49
1990	HOF Sticker Book	61
1990	Pacific Legends	100
1990	Yankees 61 Ron Lewis	2
1991	Line Drive	4
1991	Swell Baseball Greats	75
1991	Upper Deck Sheets	16
1991	Yankees Rini Postcards 1961 1	11
1992	Action Packed ASG	31
1992	Yankees WIZ 60s	104
1992	Yankees WIZ All-Stars	63
1993	Upper Deck All-Time Heroes	107
1994	Ted Williams	63
1994	Ted Williams Memories	M28
1994	Upper Deck All-Time Heroes	131
1994	Upper Deck All-Time Heroes 125th	131
1994	Upper Deck Sheets	2
1997-98	Fleer Million Dollar Moments	27
1997-98	Fleer Million Dollar Moments Redemption	27
1998	Sports Illustrated World Series Fever	28
1998	Sports Illustrated World Series Fever Extra Edition	28
1998	Sports Illustrated World Series Fever First Edition	28

Phil Rizzuto

Year	Set Name	Card No.
1941	Double Play R330	61
1941	Double Play R330	63
1946-49	Sports Exchange W603	5-6
1947	Homogenized Bond	39
1947	Tip Top	57
1947	Yankees Team Issue	21
1947-65	PM10 Stadium Pins 2 1/8'	34
1947-66	Exhibits	187A

1951 Bowman #26

1991 Studio Previews #7

Year	Set Name	Card No.
1947-66	Exhibits	187B
1947-66	PM10 Stadium Pins 1 3/4'	175
1948	Bowman	8
1948	Yankees Team Issue	24
1949	Bowman	98A
1949	Bowman	98B
1949	Leaf	11
1949	Yankees Team Issue	19
1950	American Nut and Chocolate Co. Pennant	15
1950	Bowman	11
1950	Drake's	25
1950	Yankees Team Issue	19
1950-53	Royal Desserts	11
1951	Berk Ross	A3
1951	Bowman	26
1951	R423 Small Strip	90
1951	Topps Current All-Stars	9
1951	Topps Red Backs	5
1952	Berk Ross	54A
1952	Berk Ross	54B
1952	Bowman	52
1952	Royal Premiums	10
1952	Star Cal Large	70F
1952	Star Cal Small	84C
1952	Tip Top	32
1952	Tip Top	33
1952	Topps	11
1952	Wheaties	25A
1952	Wheaties	25B
1953	Bowman Color	9
1953	Bowman Color	93
1953	Exhibits Canadian	25
1953	Red Man	AL10
1953	Stahl Meyer	7
1953	Topps	114
1953-54	Briggs	39
1953-55	Dormand	101
1953-55	Dormand	101A
1954	Bowman	1
1954	Dan Dee	19
1954	New York Journal American	57
1954	Red Man	AL17
1954	Stahl Meyer	11
1954	Topps	17
1955	Bowman	10
1955	Stahl Meyer	11
1955	Topps	189
1956	Topps	113
1956	Topps Pins	29
1956	Yankees Team Issue	20
1960	Nu-Card Hi-Lites	45
1961	Nu-Card Scoops	445
1961	Topps	471
1967	Topps Venezuelan	186
1975	TCMA Guam	1
1975	Yankees All-Time Team TCMA	8
1977-84	Galasso Glossy Greats	37
1979	TCMA 50'S	144
1980	Yankees Greats TCMA	4
1980-83	Pacific Legends	82
1980-96	Perez-Steele Hall of Fame Postcards	219
1982	Diamond Classics	45
1982	GS Gallery All-Time Greats	10
1982	TCMA Stars of the 50's	3
1983	MLBPA Pins	15
1983	Topps Reprint 52	11
1983	Yankee A-S Fifty Years	37
1983	Yankee Yearbook Insert TCMA	3
1984	TCMA Playball 1946	7
1984-89	O'Connell and Son Ink	54
1986	Sportflics Decade Greats	22
1986	TCMA Superstars Simon	9
1986	TCMA Superstars Simon	19
1988	Pacific Legends I	10
1989	Swell Baseball Greats	111
1989	Yankee Citgo All-Time Greats	4
1990	Pacific Legends	101

Year	Set Name	Card No.
1990	Yankees Monument Park Rini Postcards	5
1990-97	Perez-Steele Great Moments	105
1991	Topps Archives 1953	114
1992	Bazooka Quadracard '53 Archives	2
1992	Upper Deck Sheets	16
1992	Yankees WIZ All-Stars	66
1993	Yoo-Hoo	15
1994	Topps Archives 1954	17
1994	Topps Archives 1954 Gold	17
1994	Yoo-Hoo	12
1995	Comic Images	6
1995	Comic Images Promo	1
1998	Donruss Signature Significant Signatures	13
1998	Sports Illustrated Then and Now	26
1998	Sports Illustrated Then and Now Extra Edition	26

Red Ruffing

Year	Set Name	Card No.
1925	Exhibits	69
1926	Exhibits	70
1929	Portraits and Action R316	77
1929-30	Exhibits Four-in-One	17
1932	U.S. Caramel R328	20
1933	Cracker Jack Pins	19
1933	George C. Miller R300	26
1933	Goudey R319	56
1934	Baby Ruth Gum	53
1934	Butterfinger Premiums R310	52
1934	Goudey Canadian V354	48
1934-36	Diamond Stars R327	60
1935	Goudey Puzzle R321	4D
1935	Goudey Puzzle R321	7D
1935	Goudey Puzzle R321	12D
1936	Exhibits Four-in-One W463-6	13
1936	National Chicle Fine Pen Premiums R313	92
1936	R311 Premiums	L11
1936	R312 Pastel Photos	20
1936	World Wide Gum V355	102
1937	O-Pee-Chee Batter Ups V300	136
1937	Wheaties BB6	2
1938	Our National Game Tabs	25
1939	Play Ball R334	3
1940	Play Ball R335	10
1940	Wheaties M4	1A
1940	Wheaties M4	1B
1941	Double Play R330	67
1941	Double Play R330	85
1941	Play Ball R336	20
1943	MP and Co. R302-1	22
1947-66	PM10 Stadium Pins 1 3/4'	191
1960	Fleer	63
1961	Fleer	74
1969-73	Equitable Sports Hall of Fame	BB19
1972	TCMA's the 30's	60
1972	TCMA's the 30's	61
1973	Seven-Eleven Trading Cups	64
1973	TCMA All-Time Greats	18
1975	Yankee Dynasty 1936-39 TCMA	39
1975	Yankees All-Time Team TCMA	10
1976	Great Plains Greats	35
1976	Rowe Exhibits	1
1976	Shakey's Pizza	105
1977-84	Galasso Glossy Greats	54
1980	Yankees Greats TCMA	9
1980-83	Pacific Legends	109
1980-87	SSPC HOF	106
1980-96	Perez-Steele Hall of Fame Postcards	106
1982	Mets Galasso '62	31
1982	Ohio Hall of Fame	11
1982	TCMA Greatest Pitchers	28
1983	Cardinals 1942-1946 TCMA	64
1983	Diamond Classics Series 2	107
1983	Donruss HOF Heroes	31
1986	Sportflics Decade Greats	14

Year	Set Name	Card No.
1989	HOF Sticker Book	83
1991	Conlon TSN	13
1991	Conlon TSN	227
1992	Yankees WIZ All-Stars	70
1992	Yankees WIZ HOF	28
1993	Conlon TSN	882
1994	Conlon TSN	1078
1994	Conlon TSN Burgundy	1078

Enos Slaughter

Year	Set Name	Card No.
1941	Cardinals W754	24
1941	Double Play R330	39
1946	Sears-East St. Louis PC783	50
1946-49	Sports Exchange W603	9-2
1947	Homogenized Bond	43
1947	Tip Top	163
1947-65	PM10 Stadium Pins 2 1/8'	38
1947-66	Exhibits	212
1947-66	PM10 Stadium Pins 1 3/4'	203
1948	Bowman	17
1948-49	Blue Tint R346	34
1949	Bowman	65
1949	Eureka Stamps	198
1949	Leaf	127
1950	American Nut and Chocolate Co. Pennant	17
1950	Bowman	35
1950	Drake's	36
1951	Bowman	58
1951	R423 Small Strip	96
1951	Topps Blue Backs	30
1952	Bowman	232
1952	Dixie Lids	22
1952	Dixie Premiums	22
1952	National Tea Labels	31
1952	Red Man	NL20
1952	Star Cal Large	81D
1952	Star Cal Small	93B
1952	Tip Top	39
1952	Topps	65
1953	Bowman Color	81
1953	Cardinals Hunter's Wieners	23
1953	Dixie Lids	21
1953	Dixie Premiums	21
1953	Northland Bread Labels	30
1953	Red Man	NL13
1953	Topps	41
1953-55	Dormand	133
1954	Bowman	62
1954	Cardinals Hunter's Wieners	26
1954	Dixie Lids	16
1954	Red Heart	28
1954	Red Man	NL19A
1954	Wilson	17
1955	A's Rodeo Meats	39
1955	A's Team Issue	24
1955	Bowman	60
1956	A's Rodeo Meats	10
1956	Topps	109
1957	Topps	215
1957	Yankees Jay Publishing	14
1958	Topps	142
1959	Topps	155
1959	Topps Venezuelan	155
1966	Cardinals Coins	11
1968	Laughlin World Series	43
1970	Fleer World Series	43
1971	Fleer World Series	44
1974	Laughlin All-Star Games	53
1975-76	Johnny Mize	16
1976	A's Rodeo Meat Commemorative	25
1976	Taylor/Schmierer Bowman 47	18
1977-84	Galasso Glossy Greats	40
1979	Diamond Greats	166
1979	TCMA 50'S	240

Year	Set Name	Card No.
1980-83	Pacific Legends	32
1980-87	SSPC HOF	194
1980-96	Perez-Steele Hall of Fame Postcards	191
1982	Diamond Classics	2
1983	Cardinals 1942-1946 TCMA	17
1983	Topps Reprint 52	65
1984-89	O'Connell and Son Ink	51
1985	Dallas National Collectors Convention	6
1985	TCMA Photo Classics	33
1985	TCMA Playball 1948	2
1985	Ultimate Baseball Card	15
1986	Sportflics Decade Greats	18
1988	Houston Show	16
1988	Pacific Legends I	84
1989	Pacific Legends II	137
1989	Perez-Steele Celebration Postcards	37
1989	Swell Baseball Greats	65
1990	Pacific Legends	50
1990	Swell Baseball Greats	54
1990-97	Perez-Steele Great Moments	29
1991	Conlon TSN	56
1991	Swell Baseball Greats	84
1991	Topps Archives 1953	41
1992	Action Packed ASG	15
1992	Action Packed ASG 24K	15G
1992	Bazooka Quadracard '53 Archives	13
1992	Cardinals McDonald's/Pacific	23
1992	Conlon TSN	642
1992	Upper Deck Sheets	11
1992	Yankees WIZ HOF	31
1993	Action Packed ASG Coke/Amoco	15
1993	Ted Williams	92
1993	Ted Williams Locklear Collection	7
1993	Upper Deck All-Time Heroes	115
1994	Conlon TSN Color Inserts	27
1994	Upper Deck All-Time Heroes	14
1994	Upper Deck All-Time Heroes	134
1994	Upper Deck All-Time Heroes 125th	14
1994	Upper Deck All-Time Heroes 125th	134
1997	Topps Stars Rookie Reprint Autographs	14
1997	Topps Stars Rookie Reprints	14
1998	Sports Illustrated Then and Now	31
1998	Sports Illustrated Then and Now Extra Edition	31
1998	Sports Illustrated World Series Fever	26
1998	Sports Illustrated World Series Fever Extra Edition	26
1998	Sports Illustrated World Series Fever First Edition	26

Bernie Williams

Year	Set Name	Card No.
1987	Ft. Lauderdale Yankees ProCards	21
1987	Oneonta Yankees ProCards	4
1988	Carolina League All-Stars Star	19
1988	Prince William Yankees Star	24
1988-89	Blanco Y Negro Puerto Rico Winter League Update	13
1989	Baseball America AA Prospects Best	AA5
1989	Columbus Clippers CMC	21
1989	Columbus Clippers Police	23
1989	Columbus Clippers ProCards	736
1989-90	Blanco Y Negro Puerto Rico Winter League	189
1990	Albany Yankees All Decade Best	33
1990	Albany Yankees Best	1
1990	Albany Yankees ProCards	1179
1990	Albany Yankees Star	22
1990	Best	26
1990	Bowman	439
1990	Bowman Tiffany	439
1990	Classic Blue	10
1990	CMC	789
1990	Donruss	689
1990	Eastern League All-Stars ProCards	EL45
1990	O-Pee-Chee	701

Year	Set Name	Card No.
1990	ProCards A and AA	31
1990	Score	619
1990	Star	54
1990	Topps	701
1990	Topps Tiffany	701
1990	Topps TV Yankees	66
1991	Albany Yankees Classic/Best Kraft	3
1991	Bowman	173
1991	Classic II	T61
1991	Classic III	T97
1991	Columbus Clippers Line Drive	123
1991	Columbus Clippers Police	23
1991	Columbus Clippers ProCards	612
1991	Fleer Update	49
1991	Line Drive AAA	123
1991	O-Pee-Chee Premier	128
1991	Red Foley Stickers	112
1991	Studio Previews	7
1991	Triple A All-Stars ProCards	AAA8
1991	Ultra Update	44
1991	Upper Deck	11
1992	Bowman	407
1992	Classic Game	102
1992	Columbus Clippers Fleer/ProCards	365
1992	Columbus Clippers Police	22
1992	Columbus Clippers SkyBox	123
1992	Donruss	344
1992	Fleer	247
1992	O-Pee-Chee	374
1992	O-Pee-Chee Premier	109
1992	Pinnacle	229
1992	Pinnacle Team 2000	24
1992	ProCards	106
1992	Score	401
1992	Score 100 Rising Stars	34
1992	Stadium Club	260
1992	Topps	374
1992	Topps Debut '91	185
1992	Topps Gold	374
1992	Topps Gold Winners	374
1992	Topps Micro	374
1992	Triple A All-Stars SkyBox	123
1992	Upper Deck	556
1992	Upper Deck Sheets	1
1992-97	Sports Illustrated For Kids II	475
1993	Bowman	623
1993	Donruss	577
1993	Finest	30
1993	Finest Refractors	30
1993	Flair	255
1993	Fleer	289
1993	Leaf	130
1993	O-Pee-Chee	363
1993	Pacific Spanish	215
1993	Pinnacle	7
1993	Pinnacle Team 2001	15
1993	Score	120
1993	Select	393
1993	SP	270
1993	Stadium Club	364
1993	Stadium Club First Day Issue	364
1993	Stadium Club Members Only Parallel	364
1993	Topps	222
1993	Topps Gold	222
1993	Topps Inagural Rockies	222
1993	Topps Inaugural Marlins	222
1993	Topps Micro	222
1993	Toys'R'Us	48
1993	Ultra	252
1993	Upper Deck	332
1993	Upper Deck	470
1993	Upper Deck Gold	332
1993	Upper Deck Gold	470
1993	Yankees Stadium Club	21
1994	Bowman	521
1994	Collector's Choice	298
1994	Collector's Choice Gold Signature	298

Trading Card Checklist

Year	Set Name	Card No.
1994	Collector's Choice Silver Signature	298
1994	Donruss	259
1994	Finest	279
1994	Finest Refractors	279
1994	Flair	326
1994	Fleer	251
1994	Fleer Extra Bases	142
1994	Leaf	4
1994	O-Pee-Chee	35
1994	Pacific	441
1994	Panini Stickers	106
1994	Pinnacle	139
1994	Pinnacle Artist's Proofs	139
1994	Pinnacle Museum Collection	139
1994	Score	339
1994	Score Gold Rush	339
1994	Select	140
1994	Sportflics	59
1994	Stadium Club	573
1994	Stadium Club First Day Issue	573
1994	Stadium Club Golden Rainbow	573
1994	Stadium Club Members Only Parallel	573
1994	Stadium Club Members Only Parallel	ST24
1994	Stadium Club Super Teams	ST24
1994	Stadium Club Team	198
1994	Stadium Club Team First Day Issue	198
1994	Topps	2
1994	Topps Gold	2
1994	Topps Spanish	2
1994	Triple Play	280
1994	Ultra	103
1994	Upper Deck	86
1994	Upper Deck Electric Diamond	86
1995	Collector's Choice	517
1995	Collector's Choice Gold Signature	517
1995	Collector's Choice Silver Signature	517
1995	Donruss	509
1995	Donruss Press Proofs	509
1995	Donruss Top of the Order	130
1995	Finest	209
1995	Finest Refractors	209
1995	Flair	290
1995	Fleer	85
1995	Leaf	105
1995	Leaf Limited	83
1995	Pacific	307
1995	Pacific Latinos Destacados	36
1995	Pinnacle	248
1995	Pinnacle Artist's Proofs	248
1995	Pinnacle Museum Collection	248
1995	Pinnacle Upstarts	US17
1995	Score	124
1995	Score Gold Rush	124
1995	Score Platinum Team Sets	124
1995	Select	28
1995	Select Artist's Proofs	28
1995	Sportflix	24
1995	Sportflix Artist's Proofs	24
1995	Stadium Club	290
1995	Stadium Club Members Only Parallel	290
1995	Stadium Club Super Team World Series	290
1995	Stadium Club Virtual Reality	150
1995	Stadium Club Virtual Reality Members Only	150
1995	Studio	79
1995	Summit	22
1995	Summit Nth Degree	22
1995	Topps	485
1995	Topps Cyberstats	277
1995	UC3	27
1995	UC3 Artist's Proofs	27
1995	Ultra	314
1995	Ultra Gold Medallion	314
1995	Upper Deck	209
1995	Upper Deck Electric Diamond	209
1995	Upper Deck Electric Diamond Gold	209
1996	Bazooka	7
1996	Bowman	109
1996	Bowman Foil	109
1996	Circa	70
1996	Circa Rave	70
1996	Collector's Choice	637
1996	Collector's Choice Gold Signature	637
1996	Collector's Choice Silver Signature	637
1996	Donruss	401
1996	Donruss Press Proofs	401
1996	Emotion-XL	99
1996	Finest	S2
1996	Finest Refractors	S2
1996	Flair	140
1996	Fleer	201
1996	Fleer Tiffany	201
1996	Leaf	16
1996	Leaf Limited	35
1996	Leaf Limited Gold	35
1996	Leaf Preferred	39
1996	Leaf Preferred Press Proofs	39
1996	Leaf Press Proofs Bronze	16
1996	Leaf Press Proofs Gold	16
1996	Leaf Press Proofs Silver	16
1996	Leaf Signature	17
1996	Leaf Signature Press Proofs Gold	17
1996	Leaf Signature Press Proofs Platinum	17
1996	Metal Universe	97
1996	Metal Universe Platinum	97
1996	MLB Pins	36
1996	Pacific	369
1996	Pacific Baerga Softball	3
1996	Pacific Estrellas Latinas	EL36
1996	Pacific Prisms	P123
1996	Pacific Prisms Gold	P123
1996	Panini Stickers	156
1996	Pinnacle	85
1996	Pinnacle Aficionado	71
1996	Pinnacle Aficionado Artist's Proofs	71
1996	Pinnacle Aficionado First Pitch Preview	71
1996	Pinnacle Starburst	47
1996	Pinnacle Starburst Artist's Proofs	47
1996	Pro Stamps	140
1996	Score	343
1996	Score Dugout Collection	B68
1996	Score Dugout Collection Artist's Proofs	B68
1996	Score Gold Stars	9
1996	Select	78
1996	Select Artist's Proofs	78
1996	Select Certified	25
1996	Select Certified Artist's Proofs	25
1996	Select Certified Certified Blue	25
1996	Select Certified Certified Red	25
1996	Select Certified Mirror Blue	25
1996	Select Certified Mirror Gold	25
1996	Select Certified Mirror Red	25
1996	Select Team Nucleus	6
1996	Sportflix	76
1996	Sportflix Artist's Proofs	76
1996	Stadium Club	210
1996	Stadium Club	289
1996	Stadium Club Extreme Players Bronze	289
1996	Stadium Club Extreme Players Gold	289
1996	Stadium Club Extreme Players Silver	289
1996	Stadium Club Members Only Parallel	210
1996	Stadium Club Members Only Parallel	289
1996	Studio	44
1996	Studio Press Proofs Bronze	44
1996	Studio Press Proofs Gold	44
1996	Studio Press Proofs Silver	44
1996	Summit	131
1996	Summit Above and Beyond	131
1996	Summit Artist's Proofs	131
1996	Summit Foil	131
1996	Team Out	88
1996	Topps	68
1996	Topps Chrome	24
1996	Topps Chrome Refractors	24
1996	Topps Gallery	31
1996	Topps Gallery Players Private Issue	31
1996	Topps Laser	16
1996	Ultra	109
1996	Ultra Gold Medallion	109
1996	Upper Deck	406
1996	Zenith	20
1996	Zenith Artist's Proofs	20
1996	Zenith Mozaics	22
1997	Bowman	227
1997	Bowman Chrome	56
1997	Bowman Chrome International	56
1997	Bowman Chrome International Refractors	56
1997	Bowman Chrome Refractors	56
1997	Bowman International	227
1997	Bowman International Best	BBI4
1997	Bowman International Best Atomic Refractor	BBI4
1997	Bowman International Best Refractor	BBI4
1997	Bowman's Best	43
1997	Bowman's Best Atomic Refractors	43
1997	Bowman's Best Refractor	43
1997	Circa	51
1997	Circa Boss	20
1997	Circa Rave	51
1997	Circa Super Boss	20
1997	Collector's Choice	175
1997	Collector's Choice	223
1997	Collector's Choice All-Star Connection	16
1997	Collector's Choice Teams	NY1
1997	Collector's Choice Toast of the Town	T21
1997	Cracker Jack	7
1997	Donruss	169
1997	Donruss	443
1997	Donruss Gold Press Proofs	169
1997	Donruss Gold Press Proofs	443
1997	Donruss Limited	93
1997	Donruss Limited	103
1997	Donruss Limited	173
1997	Donruss Limited Exposure	93
1997	Donruss Limited Exposure	103
1997	Donruss Limited Exposure	173
1997	Donruss Limited Exposure Non-Glossy	103
1997	Donruss Limited Fabric of the Game	42
1997	Donruss Preferred	111
1997	Donruss Preferred Cut to the Chase	111
1997	Donruss Preferred Precious Metals	22
1997	Donruss Signature	12
1997	Donruss Signature Autographs Century	135
1997	Donruss Signature Autographs Millenium	135
1997	Donruss Signature Platinum Press Proofs	12
1997	Donruss Silver Press Proofs	169
1997	Donruss Silver Press Proofs	443
1997	Donruss VxP 1.0	32
1997	E-X2000	36
1997	E-X2000 Credentials	36
1997	E-X2000 Essential Credentials	36
1997	Finest	45
1997	Finest	107
1997	Finest	331
1997	Finest Embossed	107
1997	Finest Embossed	331
1997	Finest Embossed Refractors	107
1997	Finest Embossed Refractors	331
1997	Finest Refractors	45
1997	Finest Refractors	107
1997	Finest Refractors	331
1997	Flair Showcase Diamond Cuts	19
1997	Flair Showcase Legacy Collection	51
1997	Flair Showcase Masterpieces	A51
1997	Flair Showcase Masterpieces	B51
1997	Flair Showcase Masterpieces	C51
1997	Flair Showcase Row 0	51
1997	Flair Showcase Row 1	51
1997	Flair Showcase Row 2	51
1997	Fleer	181
1997	Fleer	720
1997	Fleer Tiffany	181

Year	Set Name	Card No.
1997	Fleer Tiffany	720
1997	Leaf	111
1997	Leaf	386
1997	Leaf Fractal Matrix	111
1997	Leaf Fractal Matrix	386
1997	Leaf Fractal Matrix Die Cuts	111
1997	Leaf Fractal Matrix Die Cuts	386
1997	Leaf Warning Track	9
1997	Metal Universe	125
1997	Pacific	163
1997	Pacific Baerga Softball	2
1997	Pacific Fireworks Die Cuts	9
1997	Pacific Gold Crown Die Cuts	14
1997	Pacific Latinos of the Major Leagues	16
1997	Pacific Light Blue	163
1997	Pacific Prisms	55
1997	Pacific Prisms Gate Attractions	GA11
1997	Pacific Prisms Light Blue	55
1997	Pacific Prisms Platinum	55
1997	Pacific Prisms Sizzling Lumber	SL4B
1997	Pacific Silver	163
1997	Pinnacle	111
1997	Pinnacle Artist's Proofs	PP111
1997	Pinnacle Cardfrontations	20
1997	Pinnacle Certified	10
1997	Pinnacle Certified Mirror Black	10
1997	Pinnacle Certified Mirror Blue	10
1997	Pinnacle Certified Mirror Gold	10
1997	Pinnacle Certified Mirror Red	10
1997	Pinnacle Certified Red	10
1997	Pinnacle Inside Dueling Dugouts	12
1997	Pinnacle Museum Collection	111
1997	Pinnacle Press Plate Previews	111
1997	Pinnacle Totally Certified Platinum Blue	10
1997	Pinnacle Totally Certified Platinum Gold	10
1997	Pinnacle Totally Certified Platinum Red	10
1997	Pinnacle X-Press	46
1997	Pinnacle X-Press Men of Summer	46
1997	Score	5
1997	Score	503
1997	Score Artist's Proofs White Border	5
1997	Score Artist's Proofs White Border	503
1997	Score Heart of the Order	18
1997	Score Premium Stock	5
1997	Score Reserve Collection	503
1997	Score Showcase Series	5
1997	Score Showcase Series	503
1997	Score Showcase Series Artist's Proofs	5
1997	Score Showcase Series Artist's Proofs	503
1997	Score Stand and Deliver	11
1997	Select	174
1997	Select Company	174
1997	SP	122
1997	SP Special FX	28
1997	Sports Illustrated	127
1997	Sports Illustrated Extra Edition	127
1997	Stadium Club	57
1997	Stadium Club Instavision	I11
1997	Stadium Club Matrix	57
1997	Stadium Club Members Only Parallel	57
1997	Stadium Club Members Only Parallel	I11
1997	Strat-O-Matic All-Stars	61
1997	Studio	97
1997	Studio Hard Hats	19
1997	Studio Press Proof Gold	97
1997	Studio Press Proof Silver	97
1997	Topps	150
1997	Topps Chrome	57
1997	Topps Chrome Diamond Duos	DD2
1997	Topps Chrome Diamond Duos Refractors	DD2
1997	Topps Chrome Refractors	57
1997	Topps Gallery	103
1997	Topps Gallery Player's Private Issue	103
1997	Topps Inter-League Finest	ILM10
1997	Topps Inter-League Finest Refractors	ILM10
1997	Topps Stars	90
1997	Topps Stars Always Mint	90

Year	Set Name	Card No.
1997	Topps Team Timber	TT3
1997	UD3	26
1997	Ultra	107
1997	Ultra Gold Medallion	107
1997	Ultra Platinum Medallion	107
1997	Ultra Top 30	29
1997	Ultra Top 30 Gold Medallion	29
1997	Upper Deck	124
1997	Upper Deck	248
1997	Upper Deck	250
1997	Upper Deck Home Team Heroes	HT2
1997	Upper Deck Predictor	20
1997	Upper Deck Predictor Exchange	20
1997	Yankees McDonald's Pins	4
1997	Yankees Score	1
1997	Yankees Score Platinum	1
1997	Yankees Score Premier	1
1997	Zenith	24
1997-98	Fleer Million Dollar Moments	22
1997-98	Fleer Million Dollar Moments Redemption	22
1997-98	Topps Members Only 55	49
1998	Bowman	24
1998	Bowman Chrome	24
1998	Bowman Chrome Golden Anniversary	24
1998	Bowman Chrome Golden Anniversary Refractors	24
1998	Bowman Chrome International	24
1998	Bowman Chrome International Refractors	24
1998	Bowman Chrome Refractors	24
1998	Bowman Chrome Reprints	22
1998	Bowman Chrome Reprints Refractors	22
1998	Bowman Golden Anniversary	24
1998	Bowman International	24
1998	Bowman's Best	17
1998	Bowman's Best Atomic Refractors	17
1998	Bowman's Best Refractors	17
1998	Circa Thunder	51
1998	Circa Thunder Rave	51
1998	Circa Thunder Super Rave	51
1998	Collector's Choice	448
1998	Crown Royale	99
1998	Crown Royale Pillars of the Game	17
1998	Donruss	59
1998	Donruss	395
1998	Donruss Collections Donruss	59
1998	Donruss Collections Elite	427
1998	Donruss Collections Leaf	289
1998	Donruss Collections Preferred	588
1998	Donruss Collections Samples	59
1998	Donruss Crusade Green	31
1998	Donruss Crusade Purple	31
1998	Donruss Crusade Red	31
1998	Donruss Diamond Kings	13
1998	Donruss Diamond Kings Canvas	13
1998	Donruss Elite	27
1998	Donruss Elite Aspirations	27
1998	Donruss Elite Status	27
1998	Donruss Gold Press Proofs	59
1998	Donruss Gold Press Proofs	395
1998	Donruss MLB 99	18
1998	Donruss Preferred	38
1998	Donruss Preferred Great X-Pectations	26
1998	Donruss Preferred Great X-Pectations Die Cuts	26
1998	Donruss Preferred Great X-Pectations Samples	26
1998	Donruss Preferred Seating	38
1998	Donruss Preferred Title Waves	12
1998	Donruss Prized Collections Donruss	59
1998	Donruss Prized Collections Elite	427
1998	Donruss Prized Collections Leaf	289
1998	Donruss Prized Collections Preferred	588
1998	Donruss Production Line On-Base	17
1998	Donruss Production Line Power Index	14
1998	Donruss Signature	84
1998	Donruss Signature Proofs	84
1998	Donruss Silver Press Proofs	59

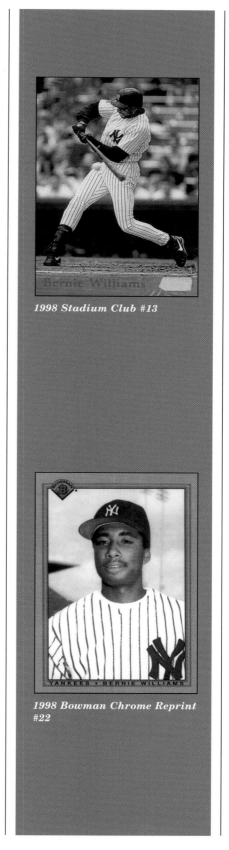

1998 Stadium Club #13

1998 Bowman Chrome Reprint #22

Trading Card Checklist

1997 Bowman Chrome #56

1990 Topps TV Yankees #34

Year	Set Name	Card No.
1998	Donruss Silver Press Proofs	395
1998	E-X2001	74
1998	E-X2001 Essential Credentials Future	74
1998	E-X2001 Essential Credentials Now	74
1998	Finest	177
1998	Finest Mystery Finest 2	M15
1998	Finest Mystery Finest 2	M17
1998	Finest Mystery Finest 2	M18
1998	Finest Mystery Finest 2	M35
1998	Finest Mystery Finest 2 Refractors	M15
1998	Finest Mystery Finest 2 Refractors	M17
1998	Finest Mystery Finest 2 Refractors	M18
1998	Finest Mystery Finest 2 Refractors	M35
1998	Finest Mystery Finest Oversize	2
1998	Finest Mystery Finest Oversize Refractors	2
1998	Finest No-Protectors	177
1998	Finest No-Protectors Refractors	177
1998	Finest Oversize	B2
1998	Finest Oversize Refractors	B2
1998	Finest Refractors	177
1998	Flair Showcase Legacy Collection	51
1998	Flair Showcase Legacy Collection Masterpieces	51
1998	Flair Showcase Row 0	51
1998	Flair Showcase Row 1	51
1998	Flair Showcase Row 2	51
1998	Flair Showcase Row 3	51
1998	Fleer	51
1998	Fleer	600
1998	Fleer Vintage '63	43
1998	Fleer Vintage '63 Classic	43
1998	Leaf	90
1998	Leaf Fractal Diamond Axis	90
1998	Leaf Fractal Foundations	90
1998	Leaf Fractal Materials	90
1998	Leaf Fractal Materials Die Cuts	90
1998	Leaf Fractal Materials Z2 Axis	90
1998	Leaf Fractal Matrix	90
1998	Leaf Fractal Matrix Die Cuts	90
1998	Leaf Rookies and Stars	11
1998	Leaf Rookies and Stars Longevity	11
1998	Leaf Rookies and Stars Longevity Holographic	11
1998	Leaf Rookies and Stars True Blue	11
1998	Leaf State Representatives	29
1998	Metal Universe	11
1998	Metal Universe Precious Metal Gems	11
1998	Pacific	161
1998	Pacific Aurora	64
1998	Pacific Aurora Pennant Fever	49
1998	Pacific Aurora Pennant Fever Copper	49
1998	Pacific Aurora Pennant Fever Platinum Blue	49
1998	Pacific Aurora Pennant Fever Red	49
1998	Pacific Aurora Pennant Fever Silver	49
1998	Pacific Gold Crown Die Cuts	24
1998	Pacific In The Cage	12
1998	Pacific Invincible	56
1998	Pacific Invincible Gems of the Diamond	81
1998	Pacific Invincible Moments in Time	12
1998	Pacific Invincible Platinum Blue	56
1998	Pacific Invincible Silver	56
1998	Pacific Invincible Team Checklists	19
1998	Pacific Latinos of the Major Leagues	28
1998	Pacific Omega	173
1998	Pacific Omega Online Inserts	11
1998	Pacific Omega Red	173
1998	Pacific Online	521
1998	Pacific Online	522
1998	Pacific Online Red	521
1998	Pacific Online Red	522
1998	Pacific Online Web Cards	521
1998	Pacific Online Web Cards	522
1998	Pacific Paramount	75
1998	Pacific Paramount Copper	75
1998	Pacific Paramount Gold	75
1998	Pacific Paramount Holographic Silver	75
1998	Pacific Paramount Inaugural	5

Year	Set Name	Card No.
1998	Pacific Paramount Platinum Blue	75
1998	Pacific Paramount Red	75
1998	Pacific Platinum Blue	161
1998	Pacific Red Threatt	161
1998	Pacific Silver	161
1998	Pinnacle Inside	51
1998	Pinnacle Inside Club Edition	51
1998	Pinnacle Inside Diamond Edition	51
1998	Pinnacle Inside Stand-Up Guys	19AB
1998	Pinnacle Inside Stand-Up Guys	19CD
1998	Pinnacle Inside Stand-Up Guys	20AB
1998	Pinnacle Inside Stand-Up Guys	20CD
1998	Pinnacle Inside Stand-Up Guys Samples	19AB
1998	Pinnacle Inside Stand-Up Guys Samples	19CD
1998	Pinnacle Inside Stand-Up Guys Samples	20AB
1998	Pinnacle Inside Stand-Up Guys Samples	20CD
1998	Pinnacle Performers	39
1998	Pinnacle Performers Launching Pad	18
1998	Pinnacle Performers Peak Performers	39
1998	Pinnacle Performers Swing for the Fences	25
1998	Pinnacle Plus	28
1998	Pinnacle Plus Artist's Proofs	PP15
1998	Pinnacle Plus Gold Artist's Proofs	PP15
1998	Pinnacle Plus Mirror Artist's Proofs	PP15
1998	Pinnacle Snapshots	NYY13
1998	Pinnacle Snapshots	NYY15
1998	Revolution	104
1998	Revolution Foul Pole	6
1998	Revolution Shadow Series	104
1998	Revolution Showstoppers	12
1998	Score	66
1998	Score Artist's Proofs	PP31
1998	Score Rookie Traded	12
1998	Score Rookie Traded Artist's Proofs	PP12
1998	Score Rookie Traded Artist's Proofs 1 of 1's	PP12
1998	Score Rookie Traded Showcase Series	PP12
1998	Score Rookie Traded Star Gazing	17
1998	Score Showcase Series	PP31
1998	SkyBox Dugout Axcess	74
1998	SkyBox Dugout Axcess Inside Axcess	74
1998	SP Authentic	143
1998	Sports Illustrated	125
1998	Sports Illustrated Extra Edition	125
1998	Sports Illustrated First Edition	125
1998	Sports Illustrated Opening Day Mini Posters	OD20
1998	Sports Illustrated Then and Now	47
1998	Sports Illustrated Then and Now	139
1998	Sports Illustrated Then and Now Extra Edition	47
1998	Sports Illustrated Then and Now Extra Edition	139
1998	Sports Illustrated World Series Fever	143
1998	Sports Illustrated World Series Fever Extra Edition	143
1998	Sports Illustrated World Series Fever First Edition	143
1998	SPx Finite	109
1998	SPx Finite Radiance	109
1998	SPx Finite Spectrum	109
1998	Stadium Club	13
1998	Stadium Club First Day Issue	13
1998	Stadium Club One Of A Kind	13
1998	Stadium Club Playing With Passion	P1
1998	Stadium Club Printing Plates	13
1998	Stadium Club Triumvirate Illuminator	T2B
1998	Stadium Club Triumvirate Illuminator	T16A
1998	Stadium Club Triumvirate Luminescent	T2B
1998	Stadium Club Triumvirate Luminescent	T16A
1998	Stadium Club Triumvirate Luminous	T2B
1998	Stadium Club Triumvirate Luminous	T16A
1998	Studio	32
1998	Studio Freeze Frame	21
1998	Studio Freeze Frame Die Cuts	21
1998	Studio Gold Press Proofs	32
1998	Studio MLB 99	18

Year	Set Name	Card No.
1998	Studio Silver Press Proofs	32
1998	Topps	293
1998	Topps Chrome	293
1998	Topps Chrome Refractors	293
1998	Topps Devil Rays	293
1998	Topps Diamondbacks	293
1998	Topps Gallery	85
1998	Topps Gallery Gallery Proofs	85
1998	Topps Gallery Original Printing Plates	85
1998	Topps Gallery Player's Private Issue	85
1998	Topps Gallery Player's Private Issue Auction	85
1998	Topps Gold Label Class 1	76
1998	Topps Gold Label Class 1 Black	76
1998	Topps Gold Label Class 1 One to One	76
1998	Topps Gold Label Class 1 Red	76
1998	Topps Gold Label Class 2	76
1998	Topps Gold Label Class 2 Black	76
1998	Topps Gold Label Class 2 One to One	76
1998	Topps Gold Label Class 2 Red	76
1998	Topps Gold Label Class 3	76
1998	Topps Gold Label Class 3 Black	76
1998	Topps Gold Label Class 3 One to One	76
1998	Topps Gold Label Class 3 Red	76
1998	Topps Minted in Cooperstown	293
1998	Topps Opening Day	120
1998	Topps Stars	10
1998	Topps Stars 'N Steel	44
1998	Topps Stars 'N Steel Gold	44
1998	Topps Stars 'N Steel Gold Holographic	44
1998	Topps Stars Bronze	10
1998	Topps Stars Gold	10
1998	Topps Stars Gold Rainbow	10
1998	Topps Stars Silver	10
1998	Topps SuperChrome	18
1998	Topps SuperChrome Refractors	18
1998	Topps Tek	7
1998	Topps Tek Diffractors	7
1998	UD3	89
1998	UD3	179
1998	UD3	269
1998	UD3 Die Cuts	89
1998	UD3 Die Cuts	179
1998	UD3 Die Cuts	269
1998	Ultra	51
1998	Ultra Double Trouble	15
1998	Ultra Gold Medallion	51
1998	Ultra Masterpieces	51
1998	Ultra Platinum Medallion	51
1998	Upper Deck	169
1998	Upper Deck National Pride	NP31
1998	Upper Deck Special F/X	91
1998	Yankees Score	6
1998	Yankees Score Platinum	6
1998	Zenith	72
1998	Zenith 5 x 7	12
1998	Zenith 5 x 7 Gold Impulse	12
1998	Zenith 5 x 7 Impulse	12
1998	Zenith Z-Gold	72
1998	Zenith Z-Silver	72
1999	Aurora	132
1999	Aurora On Deck Laser-Cuts	5
1999	Aurora Pennant Fever	13
1999	Aurora Pennant Fever Blue	5
1999	Aurora Pennant Fever Copper	5
1999	Aurora Pennant Fever Silver	5
1999	Aurora Styrotechs	13
1999	Finest Prominent Figures	PF27
1999	Fleer	22
1999	Fleer Diamond Magic	14
1999	Fleer Starting 9	22
1999	Fleer Vintage '61	22
1999	Fleer Warning Track	22
1999	Metal Universe	17
1999	Metal Universe Gem Masters	17
1999	Metal Universe Precious Metal Gems	17
1999	Pacific	305

Year	Set Name	Card No.
1999	Pacific	305A
1999	Pacific Crown Collection	198
1999	Pacific Crown Collection Latinos of the Major Leagues	15
1999	Pacific Crown Collection Platinum Blue	198
1999	Pacific Gold Crown Die Cuts	11
1999	Pacific Paramount	167
1999	Pacific Paramount Copper	167
1999	Pacific Paramount Fielder's Choice	13
1999	Pacific Paramount Holographic Silver	167
1999	Pacific Paramount Personal Bests	24
1999	Pacific Paramount Platinum Blue	167
1999	Pacific Platinum Blue	305
1999	Pacific Platinum Blue	305A
1999	Pacific Prism	102
1999	Pacific Prism Ahead of the Game	14
1999	Pacific Prism Diamond Glory	14
1999	Pacific Prism Holographic Blue	102
1999	Pacific Prism Holographic Gold	102
1999	Pacific Prism Holographic Mirror	102
1999	Pacific Prism Holographic Purple	102
1999	Pacific Private Stock	49
1999	Pacific Private Stock Platinum	49
1999	Pacific Private Stock PS-206	49
1999	Pacific Private Stock PS-206 Red	49
1999	Pacific Private Stock Vintage	49
1999	Pacific Red	305
1999	Pacific Red	305A
1999	Pacific Timelines	5
1999	Pinheads	29
1999	SkyBox Thunder	296
1999	SkyBox Thunder Rant	296
1999	SkyBox Thunder Rave	296
1999	SkyBox Thunder Super Rave	296
1999	SkyBox Thunder www.batterz.com	WB10
1999	SP Authentic	59
1999	Sports Illustrated	12
1999	Sports Illustrated	157
1999	Stadium Club Chrome	SCC19
1999	Stadium Club Chrome Refractors	SCC19
1999	Stadium Club Triumvirate Illuminator	T4C
1999	Stadium Club Triumvirate Luminescent	T4C
1999	Stadium Club Triumvirate Luminous	T4C
1999	Topps	222
1999	Topps	235
1999	Topps Chrome	222
1999	Topps Chrome	235
1999	Topps Chrome Refractors	222
1999	Topps Chrome Refractors	235
1999	Topps Opening Day	150
1999	Topps Stars 'N Steel	6
1999	Topps Stars 'N Steel Gold	6
1999	Topps Stars 'N Steel Gold Domed Holographic	6
1999	UD Choice	116
1999	UD Choice Prime Choice Reserve	116
1999	Ultra	141
1999	Ultra Gold Medallion	141
1999	Ultra Masterpieces	141
1999	Ultra Platinum Medallion	141
1999	Upper Deck Black Diamond	59
1999	Upper Deck Black Diamond A Piece of History	BW
1999	Upper Deck Black Diamond Double	59
1999	Upper Deck Black Diamond Quadruple	59
1999	Upper Deck Black Diamond Triple	59
1999	Upper Deck Ovation A Piece of History	BW

Dave Winfield

Year	Set Name	Card No.
1973	Padres Dean's	29
1974	O-Pee-Chee	456
1974	Padres Dean's	30
1974	Padres McDonald Discs	13
1974	Padres Team Issue	18
1974	Topps	456

Year	Set Name	Card No.
1974	Topps Stamps	100
1975	Hostess	37
1975	O-Pee-Chee	61
1975	Padres Dean's	30
1975	Topps	61
1975	Topps Mini	61
1976	Hostess	83
1976	O-Pee-Chee	160
1976	SSPC	133
1976	Topps	160
1977	Burger Chef Discs	130
1977	Hostess	44
1977	Kellogg's	28
1977	O-Pee-Chee	156
1977	Padres Schedule Cards	65A
1977	Padres Schedule Cards	65B
1977	Padres Schedule Cards	65C
1977	Padres Schedule Cards	65D
1977	Topps	390
1977	Topps Cloth Stickers	52
1977-79	Sportscaster	5702
1977-79	Sportscaster	8803
1978	Hostess	63
1978	Kellogg's	11
1978	O-Pee-Chee	78
1978	Padres Family Fun	38
1978	Topps	530
1979	Baseball Patches	97
1979	Hostess	125
1979	O-Pee-Chee	11
1979	Padres Family Fun	11
1979	Topps	30
1979	Topps Comics	31
1980	Burger King Pitch/Hit/Run	22
1980	Kellogg's	32
1980	O-Pee-Chee	122
1980	Topps	203
1980	Topps	230
1980	Topps Super	18
1981	All-Star Game Program Inserts	71
1981	Donruss	364
1981	Drake's	14
1981	Fleer	484
1981	Fleer Sticker Cards	25
1981	Kellogg's	21
1981	Perma-Graphic All-Stars	18
1981	Perma-Graphic Credit Cards	21
1981	Squirt	19
1981	Topps	370
1981	Topps Stickers	111
1981	Topps Super Home Team	72
1981	Topps Traded	855
1981	Yankees Photo Album	26
1982	Donruss	18
1982	Donruss	31
1982	Donruss	575
1982	Drake's	31
1982	FBI Discs	28
1982	Fleer	56
1982	Fleer	646
1982	Fleer	646B
1982	Fleer Stamps	110
1982	Fleer Stamps	113
1982	Kellogg's	12
1982	O-Pee-Chee	76
1982	O-Pee-Chee	352
1982	Perma-Graphic Credit Cards	14
1982	Perma-Graphic Credit Cards Gold	14
1982	Squirt	7
1982	Topps	553
1982	Topps	600
1982	Topps/O-Pee-Chee Stickers	137
1982	Topps/O-Pee-Chee Stickers	213
1982	Yankees Photo Album	26
1983	All-Star Game Program Inserts	72
1983	Donruss	409
1983	Donruss Action All-Stars	36

Trading Card Checklist

Year	Set Name	Card No.
1983	Drake's	31
1983	Fleer	398
1983	Fleer	633
1983	Fleer Stamps	219
1983	Fleer Stickers	39
1983	Kellogg's	15
1983	O-Pee-Chee	258
1983	Perma-Graphic All-Stars	8
1983	Perma-Graphic All-Stars Gold	7
1983	Perma-Graphic Credit Cards	34
1983	Perma-Graphic Credit Cards Gold	34
1983	Topps	770
1983	Topps Glossy Send-Ins	7
1983	Topps/O-Pee-Chee Stickers	99
1983	Yankees Roy Rogers Discs	12
1984	All-Star Game Program Inserts	161
1984	Donruss	51
1984	Drake's	32
1984	Fleer	143
1984	Fleer Stickers	5
1984	Fun Foods Pins	1
1984	Milton Bradley	29
1984	MLBPA Pencils	2
1984	Nestle 792	402
1984	Nestle 792	460
1984	Nestle Dream Team	6
1984	O-Pee-Chee	266
1984	O-Pee-Chee	378
1984	Ralston Purina	7
1984	Seven-Eleven Coins	E7
1984	Topps	402
1984	Topps	460
1984	Topps Cereal	7
1984	Topps Glossy All-Stars	8
1984	Topps Glossy Send-Ins	16
1984	Topps Rub Downs	29
1984	Topps Super	27
1984	Topps Tiffany	402
1984	Topps Tiffany	460
1984	Topps/O-Pee-Chee Stickers	190
1984	Topps/O-Pee-Chee Stickers	319
1984-89	O'Connell and Son Ink	63
1985	All-Star Game Program Inserts	72
1985	Donruss	51
1985	Donruss	651A
1985	Donruss	651B
1985	Donruss Action All-Stars	12
1985	Donruss Highlights	53
1985	Drake's	32
1985	Fleer	146
1985	Fleer	629
1985	Fleer Limited Edition	43
1985	Fleer Star Stickers	5
1985	General Mills Stickers	25
1985	KAS Discs	20
1985	Kitty Clover Discs	20
1985	Leaf/Donruss	127
1985	Leaf/Donruss	140
1985	O-Pee-Chee	180
1985	Police Mets/Yankees	Y4
1985	Seven-Eleven Coins	C3
1985	Seven-Eleven Coins	E5
1985	Seven-Eleven Coins	G3
1985	Seven-Eleven Coins	S5
1985	Seven-Eleven Coins	W5
1985	Subway Discs	23
1985	Thom McAn Discs	23
1985	Topps	180
1985	Topps	705
1985	Topps 3-D	18
1985	Topps Glossy All-Stars	17
1985	Topps Glossy Send-Ins	14
1985	Topps Rub Downs	30
1985	Topps Super	60
1985	Topps Tiffany	180
1985	Topps Tiffany	705
1985	Topps/O-Pee-Chee Stickers	186
1985	Topps/O-Pee-Chee Stickers	308
1985	Yankees TCMA Postcards	39
1985-86	Sportflics Prototypes	4
1985-86	Sportflics Prototypes	5
1986	Baseball Star Buttons	123
1986	Burger King All-Pro	2
1986	Donruss	248
1986	Donruss All-Stars	15
1986	Donruss Pop-Ups	15
1986	Dorman's Cheese	19
1986	Drake's	18
1986	Fleer	121
1986	Fleer Mini	26
1986	Fleer Sticker Cards	130
1986	Fleer Stickers Wax Box Cards	S4
1986	Leaf/Donruss	125
1986	Meadow Gold Blank Back	16
1986	Meadow Gold Stat Back	7
1986	MSA Jiffy Pop Discs	7
1986	O-Pee-Chee	70
1986	Quaker Granola	33
1986	Seven-Eleven Coins	E11
1986	Sportflics	49
1986	Sportflics Decade Greats	74
1986	Topps	70
1986	Topps	717
1986	Topps 3-D	29
1986	Topps Glossy All-Stars	8
1986	Topps Glossy Send-Ins	42
1986	Topps Mini Leaders	29
1986	Topps Super	60
1986	Topps Tiffany	70
1986	Topps Tiffany	717
1986	Topps/O-Pee-Chee Stickers	160
1986	Topps/O-Pee-Chee Stickers	298
1986	Topps/O-Pee-Chee Tattoos	1
1986	Woolworth's	33
1986	Yankees TCMA	36
1987	Boardwalk and Baseball	4
1987	Classic Game	11
1987	Donruss	20
1987	Donruss	105
1987	Donruss All-Stars	2
1987	Donruss Opening Day	243
1987	Donruss Pop-Ups	2
1987	Donruss Super DK's	20
1987	Drake's	5
1987	Fleer	120
1987	Fleer Glossy	120
1987	Fleer Limited Edition	42
1987	Fleer Mini	117
1987	Fleer Sticker Cards	126
1987	General Mills Booklets	2I
1987	Kay-Bee	33
1987	Key Food Discs	9
1987	Kraft Foods	33
1987	Leaf/Donruss	20
1987	Leaf/Donruss	70
1987	MSA Iced Tea Discs	9
1987	O-Pee-Chee	36
1987	O-Pee-Chee Box Bottoms	H
1987	Our Own Discs	9
1987	Ralston Purina	4
1987	Red Foley Sticker Book	28
1987	Seven-Eleven Coins	E15
1987	Sportflics	41
1987	Sportflics	153
1987	Sportflics Team Preview	7
1987	Stuart Panels	23
1987	Topps	770
1987	Topps Coins	26
1987	Topps Glossy All-Stars	17
1987	Topps Tiffany	770
1987	Topps Wax Box Cards	H
1987	Topps/O-Pee-Chee Stickers	152
1987	Topps/O-Pee-Chee Stickers	298
1987	Weis Market Discs	9
1988	Alaska Goldpanners All-Time AS '70s Team Issue	16
1988	Classic Red	170
1988	Donruss	298
1988	Donruss All-Stars	2
1988	Donruss Baseball's Best	244
1988	Donruss Pop-Ups	2
1988	Donruss Team Book Yankees	278
1988	Drake's	12
1988	Fleer	226
1988	Fleer Baseball All-Stars	44
1988	Fleer Baseball MVP's	43
1988	Fleer Glossy	226
1988	Fleer Mini	44
1988	Fleer Sluggers/Pitchers	43
1988	Fleer Sticker Cards	53
1988	Kay-Bee	33
1988	Leaf/Donruss	116
1988	MSA Jiffy Pop Discs	19
1988	Nestle	33
1988	O-Pee-Chee	89
1988	Panini Stickers	161
1988	Panini Stickers	231
1988	Score	55
1988	Score Box Cards	8
1988	Score Glossy	55
1988	Sportflics	7
1988	Sportflics Gamewinners	7
1988	Star Stickers Winfield	1
1988	Star Stickers Winfield	2
1988	Star Stickers Winfield	3
1988	Star Stickers Winfield	4
1988	Star Stickers Winfield	5
1988	Star Stickers Winfield	6
1988	Star Stickers Winfield	7
1988	Star Stickers Winfield	8
1988	Star Stickers Winfield	9
1988	Star Stickers Winfield	10
1988	Star Winfield	1
1988	Star Winfield	2
1988	Star Winfield	3
1988	Star Winfield	4
1988	Star Winfield	5
1988	Star Winfield	6
1988	Star Winfield	7
1988	Star Winfield	8
1988	Star Winfield	9
1988	Star Winfield	10
1988	Star Winfield	11
1988	Star Winfield	12
1988	Starting Lineup All-Stars	36
1988	Starting Lineup Yankees	20
1988	Tara Plaques	48
1988	Topps	392
1988	Topps	459
1988	Topps	510
1988	Topps Big	24
1988	Topps Cloth	119
1988	Topps Glossy All-Stars	8
1988	Topps Glossy Send-Ins	46
1988	Topps Tiffany	392
1988	Topps Tiffany	459
1988	Topps Tiffany	510
1988	Topps UK Minis	85
1988	Topps UK Minis Tiffany	85
1988	Topps/O-Pee-Chee Sticker Backs	54
1988	Topps/O-Pee-Chee Stickers	159
1988	Topps/O-Pee-Chee Stickers	302
1989	Bowman	179
1989	Bowman Tiffany	179
1989	Cadaco Ellis Discs	61
1989	Classic Light Blue	32
1989	Donruss	159
1989	Donruss All-Stars	6
1989	Donruss Bonus MVP's	BC11
1989	Donruss Grand Slammers	6
1989	Donruss Pop-Ups	6

Year	Set Name	Card No.
1989	Fleer	274
1989	Fleer Baseball All-Stars	44
1989	Fleer Baseball MVP's	43
1989	Fleer Exciting Stars	43
1989	Fleer Glossy	274
1989	Fleer Heroes of Baseball	43
1989	Fleer League Leaders	43
1989	Fleer Superstars	43
1989	Kay-Bee	32
1989	Key Food Discs	13
1989	King-B Discs	16
1989	MSA Iced Tea Discs	13
1989	O-Pee-Chee	260
1989	O-Pee-Chee Box Bottoms	P
1989	Our Own Tea Discs	13
1989	Panini Stickers	240
1989	Panini Stickers	409
1989	Red Foley Sticker Book	128
1989	Score	50
1989	Score Hottest 100 Stars	3
1989	Score Scoremasters	41
1989	Sportflics	24
1989	Tetley Tea Discs	13
1989	Topps	260
1989	Topps	407
1989	Topps Ames 20/20 Club	32
1989	Topps Baseball Talk/LJN	42
1989	Topps Big	314
1989	Topps Coins	58
1989	Topps Doubleheaders Mets/Yankees Test	15
1989	Topps Glossy All-Stars	8
1989	Topps Glossy Send-Ins	21
1989	Topps Hills Team MVP's	32
1989	Topps Mini Leaders	67
1989	Topps Tiffany	260
1989	Topps Tiffany	407
1989	Topps UK Minis	84
1989	Topps Wax Box Cards	P
1989	Topps/O-Pee-Chee Sticker Backs	20
1989	Topps/O-Pee-Chee Stickers	149
1989	Topps/O-Pee-Chee Stickers	315
1989	TV Sports Mailbags	81
1989	Upper Deck	349
1989	Weis Market Discs	13
1989	Yankees Score Nat West	7
1989-91	Sports Illustrated For Kids I	282
1990	All-American Baseball Team	23
1990	Bowman	432
1990	Bowman Tiffany	432
1990	Donruss	551
1990	Donruss Best AL	87
1990	Fleer	458
1990	Fleer Canadian	458
1990	Fleer Update	81
1990	Kay-Bee	32
1990	Leaf	426
1990	M.V.P. Pins	71
1990	MLBPA Baseball Buttons (Pins)	64
1990	O-Pee-Chee	380
1990	Pubs.Int'l. Stickers	298
1990	Pubs.Int'l. Stickers	550
1990	Score	307
1990	Score Rookie/Traded	1T
1990	Sportflics	87
1990	Topps	380
1990	Topps Ames All-Stars	1
1990	Topps Big	20
1990	Topps Hills Hit Men	17
1990	Topps Tiffany	380
1990	Topps Traded	130T
1990	Topps Traded Tiffany	130T
1990	Topps TV Yankees	34
1990	Upper Deck	337
1990	Upper Deck	745
1990-93	Topps Magazine	50
1991	Angels Smokey	3
1991	Bowman	210

Year	Set Name	Card No.
1991	Donruss	468
1991	Fleer	329
1991	Foul Ball	27
1991	Jimmy Dean	22
1991	Leaf	499
1991	O-Pee-Chee	630
1991	O-Pee-Chee Premier	130
1991	Panini French Stickers	184
1991	Panini Stickers	132
1991	Petro-Canada Standups	5
1991	Post Canadian	28
1991	Red Foley Stickers	102
1991	Score	83
1991	Score 100 Superstars	66
1991	Stadium Club	263
1991	Stadium Club Members Only	9
1991	Starshots Pinback Badges	54
1991	Studio	30
1991	Topps	630
1991	Topps Desert Shield	630
1991	Topps Micro	630
1991	Topps Tiffany	630
1991	Topps Triple Headers	A3
1991	Ultra	54
1991	Upper Deck	337
1992	Blue Jays Fire Safety	34
1992	Blue Jays Pins	13
1992	Bowman	315
1992	Classic Game	194
1992	Donruss	133
1992	Donruss Update	U18
1992	Fleer	72
1992	Fleer	686
1992	Fleer Update	67
1992	High 5	15
1992	L and K Decals	30
1992	Leaf	171
1992	Leaf Black Gold	171
1992	O-Pee-Chee	5
1992	O-Pee-Chee	792
1992	O-Pee-Chee Premier	150
1992	Pepsi Diet MSA	30
1992	Pinnacle	375
1992	Pinnacle Rookie Idols	18
1992	Red Foley Stickers	100
1992	Score	32
1992	Score 100 Superstars	9
1992	Score Factory Inserts	B10
1992	Score Rookie/Traded	7T
1992	Score/Pinnacle Promo Panels	7
1992	Stadium Club	745
1992	Studio	260
1992	Topps	5
1992	Topps	792
1992	Topps Gold	5
1992	Topps Gold	792
1992	Topps Gold Winners	5
1992	Topps Gold Winners	792
1992	Topps Kids	96
1992	Topps Micro	5
1992	Topps Micro	792
1992	Topps Traded	130T
1992	Topps Traded Gold	130T
1992	Ultra	454
1992	Upper Deck	28
1992	Upper Deck	222
1992	Upper Deck	734
1992	Upper Deck Home Run Heroes	HR17
1992	Yankees WIZ 80s	204
1992	Yankees WIZ All-Stars	86
1992-94	Highland Mint Mint-Cards Topps	50
1992-94	Highland Mint Mint-Cards Topps	51
1992-97	Sports Illustrated For Kids II	170
1993	Blue Jays Donruss 45	14
1993	Blue Jays Donruss World Series	7
1993	Bowman	565
1993	Classic Game	98

1989 Donruss Grand Slammers #6

1988 Topps #392

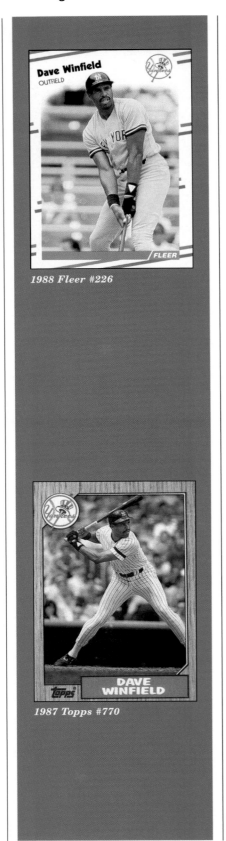

1988 Fleer #226

1987 Topps #770

Year	Set Name	Card No.
1993	Diamond Marks	118
1993	Donruss	643
1993	Donruss Elite	35
1993	Donruss Elite Supers	17
1993	Donruss Spirit of the Game	SG1
1993	Duracell Power Players I	24
1993	Finest	162
1993	Finest Refractors	162
1993	Flair	243
1993	Fleer	343
1993	Fleer Final Edition	241
1993	Fleer Final Edition Diamond Tribute	9
1993	Fleer Golden Moments	A3
1993	Fun Pack	196
1993	Humpty Dumpty Canadian	12
1993	Leaf	423
1993	Leaf	DW
1993	Metz Baking	40
1993	O-Pee-Chee	371
1993	O-Pee-Chee Premier	28
1993	O-Pee-Chee World Champions	17
1993	O-Pee-Chee World Series Heroes	4
1993	Pacific Jugadores Calientes	18
1993	Pacific Spanish	528
1993	Pinnacle	295
1993	Pinnacle	438
1993	Pinnacle	483
1993	Pinnacle	486
1993	Pinnacle Cooperstown	10
1993	Pinnacle Cooperstown Dufex	10
1993	Pinnacle Home Run Club	32
1993	Rainbow Foods Winfield	1
1993	Rainbow Foods Winfield	2
1993	Rainbow Foods Winfield	3
1993	Rainbow Foods Winfield	4
1993	Rainbow Foods Winfield	5
1993	Rainbow Foods Winfield	6
1993	Rainbow Foods Winfield	7
1993	Rainbow Foods Winfield	8
1993	Rainbow Foods Winfield	9
1993	Rainbow Foods Winfield	10
1993	Score	521
1993	Score	620
1993	Select	32
1993	Select Rookie/Traded	9T
1993	SP	252
1993	Stadium Club	206
1993	Stadium Club	609
1993	Stadium Club First Day Issue	206
1993	Stadium Club First Day Issue	609
1993	Stadium Club Members Only	28
1993	Stadium Club Members Only Parallel	206
1993	Stadium Club Members Only Parallel	609
1993	Stadium Club Murphy	1
1993	Studio	77
1993	Topps	131
1993	Topps Black Gold	44
1993	Topps Gold	131
1993	Topps Inagural Rockies	131
1993	Topps Inaugural Marlins	131
1993	Topps Magazine Jumbo Rookie Cards	2
1993	Topps Micro	131
1993	Topps Traded	83T
1993	Triple Play Gallery	GS5
1993	Ultra	589
1993	Upper Deck	40
1993	Upper Deck	786
1993	Upper Deck Gold	40
1993	Upper Deck Gold	786
1993	Upper Deck Season Highlights	HI19
1993	Upper Deck Then And Now	TN9
1994	Bowman	300
1994	Bowman's Best	R6
1994	Bowman's Best Refractors	R6
1994	Collector's Choice	302
1994	Collector's Choice Gold Signature	302
1994	Collector's Choice Silver Signature	302

Year	Set Name	Card No.
1994	Donruss	336
1994	Donruss	550
1994	Donruss Diamond Kings	DK29
1994	Donruss Diamond Kings Jumbo	DK29
1994	Donruss Special Edition	336
1994	Finest	215
1994	Finest Jumbos	215
1994	Finest Refractors	215
1994	Flair	79
1994	Flair Outfield Power	10
1994	Fleer	223
1994	Fleer Extra Bases	126
1994	Fleer Extra Bases Game Breakers	30
1994	Fleer Golden Moments	3
1994	Fleer Golden Moments Jumbo	3
1994	Fun Pack	32
1994	Fun Pack	202
1994	Kraft	15
1994	Leaf	137
1994	Leaf Limited	52
1994	Leaf Statistical Standouts	8
1994	O-Pee-Chee	53
1994	Pacific	371
1994	Panini Stickers	97
1994	Pinnacle	332
1994	Pinnacle Artist's Proofs	332
1994	Pinnacle Museum Collection	332
1994	Pinnacle Tribute	TR3
1994	Score	407
1994	Score	629
1994	Score Gold Rush	407
1994	Score Gold Rush	629
1994	Select	84
1994	Select	SS2
1994	SP	187
1994	SP Die Cuts	187
1994	Sportflics	63
1994	Stadium Club	288
1994	Stadium Club Dugout Dirt	DD2
1994	Stadium Club First Day Issue	288
1994	Stadium Club Golden Rainbow	288
1994	Stadium Club Members Only Parallel	288
1994	Stadium Club Members Only Parallel	DD2
1994	Studio	202
1994	Topps	430
1994	Topps Gold	430
1994	Topps Spanish	430
1994	Triple Play	260
1994	Triple Play Medalists	15
1994	Ultra	92
1994	Ultra Career Achievement	5
1994	Upper Deck	81
1994	Upper Deck Electric Diamond	81
1994-95	Pro Mags	79
1995	Blue Jays U.S. Playing Cards	6D
1995	Blue Jays U.S. Playing Cards	13C
1995	Bowman	434
1995	Collector's Choice	54
1995	Collector's Choice	280
1995	Collector's Choice Gold Signature	54
1995	Collector's Choice Gold Signature	280
1995	Collector's Choice SE	115
1995	Collector's Choice SE Gold Signature	115
1995	Collector's Choice SE Silver Signature	115
1995	Collector's Choice Silver Signature	54
1995	Collector's Choice Silver Signature	280
1995	Emotion	40
1995	Finest	249
1995	Finest Refractors	249
1995	Flair	254
1995	Fleer	151
1995	Fleer Update	43
1995	Leaf	372
1995	Pacific	259
1995	Pacific Gold Prisms	7
1995	Pacific Prisms	83
1995	Pinnacle	367

Year	Set Name	Card No.
1995	Pinnacle Artist's Proofs	367
1995	Pinnacle Museum Collection	367
1995	Score	80
1995	Score Gold Rush	80
1995	Score Platinum Team Sets	80
1995	Select	226
1995	Select Artist's Proofs	226
1995	SP	26
1995	SP	149
1995	SP Championship	148
1995	SP Championship Die Cuts	148
1995	SP Silver	26
1995	SP Silver	149
1995	Stadium Club	533
1995	Stadium Club Members Only Parallel	533
1995	Stadium Club Members Only Parallel	RL36
1995	Stadium Club Ring Leaders	RL36
1995	Stadium Club Super Team World Series	533
1995	Summit	75
1995	Summit Nth Degree	75
1995	Topps	158
1995	Topps Cyberstats	38
1995	UC3	50
1995	UC3 Artist's Proofs	50
1995	Ultra	283

Year	Set Name	Card No.
1995	Ultra Gold Medallion	283
1995	Upper Deck	95
1995	Upper Deck Electric Diamond	95
1995	Upper Deck Electric Diamond Gold	95
1995	Upper Deck Special Edition	160
1995	Upper Deck Special Edition Gold	160
1995	Zenith	23
1996	Collector's Choice	123
1996	Collector's Choice Gold Signature	123
1996	Collector's Choice Silver Signature	123
1996	Donruss	275
1996	Donruss Press Proofs	275
1996	Fleer	104
1996	Fleer Tiffany	104
1996	Pinnacle	87
1996	Pinnacle Starburst	49
1996	Pinnacle Starburst Artist's Proofs	49
1996	Score	83
1996	Score Dugout Collection	A66
1996	Score Dugout Collection Artist's Proofs	A66
1996	Ultra	56
1996	Ultra Gold Medallion	56
1996	Upper Deck	100
1997	Blue Jays Sizzler	43

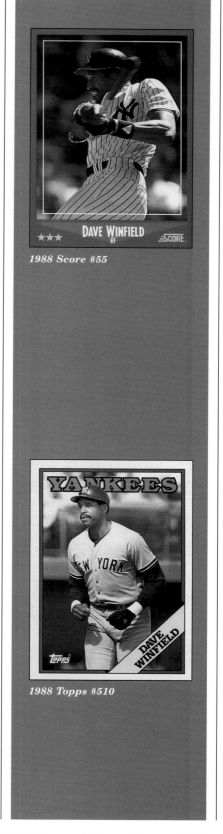

1988 Score #55

1988 Topps #510

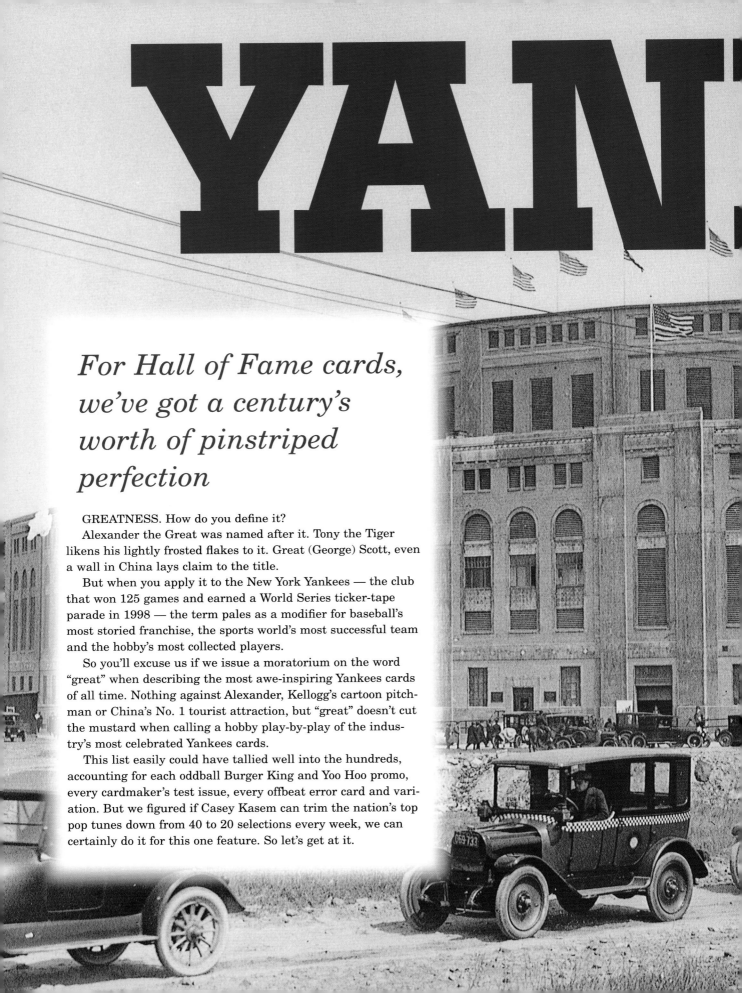

YAN

For Hall of Fame cards, we've got a century's worth of pinstriped perfection

GREATNESS. How do you define it?

Alexander the Great was named after it. Tony the Tiger likens his lightly frosted flakes to it. Great (George) Scott, even a wall in China lays claim to the title.

But when you apply it to the New York Yankees — the club that won 125 games and earned a World Series ticker-tape parade in 1998 — the term pales as a modifier for baseball's most storied franchise, the sports world's most successful team and the hobby's most collected players.

So you'll excuse us if we issue a moratorium on the word "great" when describing the most awe-inspiring Yankees cards of all time. Nothing against Alexander, Kellogg's cartoon pitchman or China's No. 1 tourist attraction, but "great" doesn't cut the mustard when calling a hobby play-by-play of the industry's most celebrated Yankees cards.

This list easily could have tallied well into the hundreds, accounting for each oddball Burger King and Yoo Hoo promo, every cardmaker's test issue, every offbeat error card and variation. But we figured if Casey Kasem can trim the nation's top pop tunes down from 40 to 20 selections every week, we can certainly do it for this one feature. So let's get at it.

KHeaven

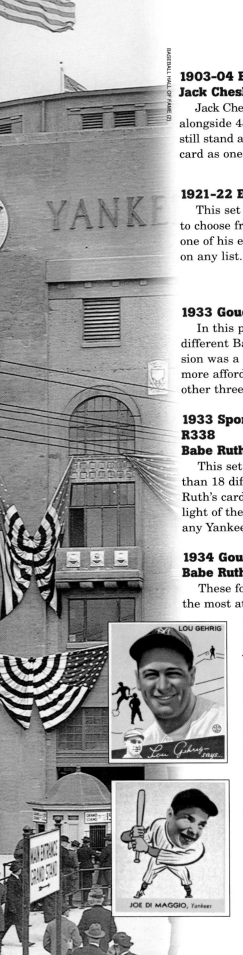

1910

1903-04 Breisch Williams E107 Jack Chesbro #19

Jack Chesbro recorded an amazing 41 wins alongside 48 complete games in 1904. Both still stand as post-1900 records, as does this card as one of the earliest Yankees issues.

1920

1921-22 E121 Babe Ruth #86B

This set offers several Babe Ruth issues to choose from, but this three-photo issue is one of his earliest cards and ranks as a classic on any list.

1930

1933 Goudey R319 Babe Ruth #144

In this popular vintage set you'll find four different Babe Ruth cards. The batting version was a double print, therefore it's slightly more affordable than his other three.

1933 Sport Kings R338 Babe Ruth #2

This set covered more than 18 different sports. Ruth's card is the highlight of the set as well as any Yankees collection.

1934 Goudey Premiums R309-1 Babe Ruth #4

These four oversized Goudeys were some of the most attractive premiums ever issued measuring approximately 5-1/2-by-9 inches. Babe's card is the crown jewel of this set.

1934 Goudey R320 Lou Gehrig #37

Even the cards that don't feature Lou Gehrig still carry his name and likeness, but the Iron Horse's full-color issue is beyond compare.

1938 Goudey Heads Up R323 Joe DiMaggio #250

Who says Upper Deck invented goofy protruding-head cards? Goudey was printing 'em back in the '30s and Joe D's issue is one its most famous large-noggin issues.

1939 Play Ball R334 Joe DiMaggio #26

Thanks to Gum Incorporated's innovations — actual player photos and a larger card size — DiMaggio's Play Ball was an original groundbreaker. Those overprinted with "sample card" are in shorter supply and command a substantial premium.

1940

1948 Bowman Yogi Berra #6

This set was the first major trading card issue of the post-war era and therefore contains several key Rookie Cards. You might not think it's much to look at, but Yogi Berra's card is second only to Stan Musial's Rookie Card in terms of value, but it's the only '40s-era Yankees card to make our list.

1950

1950 Bowman Casey Stengel #217

When it comes to manager cards, Casey Stengel's issue from the '50 Bowman set is an artful rendition of one of baseball's most prominent managers. This portait of Stengel truly captures the feel of the Yankees' most famous skipper.

1951 Bowman Mickey Mantle #253

Even though Mantle's '52 Topps gets all the pub (and has for decades), this is No. 7's true Rookie Card and

should make the top five of any serious Yankees collector's want list.

Heck, this issue carries so much weight
that one Gem-Mint copy graded PSA-10
reportedly sold for as much as $100,000. And
when you talk about hobby respect, 100,000
clams is a pretty good indicator that this card
receives more than just about any Yankees
card.

1951 Bowman
Whitey Ford #1

What would a
Yankees collection be
without one of its
finest pitchers? But
as card No. 1 in the
set, Whitey Ford's
condition-sensitive
issue makes the
chase twice as chal-
lenging for those in
search of Near-Mint
specimens.

1951 Topps Current All-Stars
Yogi Berra #1

Topps was always experimenting with new
types of sets and concepts. Therefore this die-
cut card features the three-time MVP just
before landing the first of his awards.

1952 Topps Mickey Mantle #311

What can we say about this card that has-
n't already been said.
The Series II release
of '52 Topps, which
contained Mantle's
card, was largely
ignored by collectors
who had already
turned their attention
to football. This
unsold product was
stored in a warehouse
until the 1960s when
it was finally dumped off a garbage scow into
the Atlantic Ocean, giving rise to this card's
legendary scarcity.

1953 Bowman Color
Phil Rizzuto/ Billy Martin #93

No card pictures the heart and soul of the
Yankees better than this multi-player issue.
Lifelong friends Rizzuto and Martin were
among the first to be featured on the modern
multi-player cards.

1953 Topps Mickey Mantle #82

For pure aesthetics, the '53 Topps Mantle
is unmatched. Although line drawings ren-
dered in full color were the standard of the
day, this issue stands apart as one of the best.

1954 Topps Sports Illustrated
Mickey Mantle

This card was never issued in packs,
although readers of the second issue
of Sports Illustrated saw this design
as part of a special baseball card lay-
out. Although printed on magazine
paper stock, this mock-up is an accurate representation of Mick's early
days on a card that never was.

1955 Red Man
Whitey Ford #AL3

The 1950s were a prime time for
both regional and national oddball
sets and the Red Man issues portrayed many of the day's leading
players. Today, cards with the
coupon still attached carry a premium, but Ford's is a keeper with
or without it.

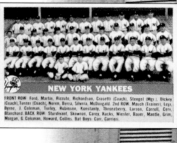

1956 Topps
Yankees Team Card #251

This was the first card of the
Yankees team issued during the
Stengel era and features Hall of Famers such
as Mantle, Berra, Ford and Stengel during
the peak of the Yankees' glory years.

1957 Topps Mickey Mantle #95

Take a gander at Mickey coming off his
Triple Crown year in the full bloom of youth.
This issue is considered by many to be from

the most attractive
set Topps ever made.
Clear photos and
uncluttered fronts
truly make the differ-
ence with this card.

1957 Topps
Mickey Mantle/
Yogi Berra #407

Also from the '57
set, this one's tough
to find in really sharp condition because it
ended the bricks in many shoe boxes. Mantle
and Berra combined for five MVPs during a
seven-year period from 1951 through 1957,
and were the lifeblood of the Yankees. This

card is a perfect reminder of that fact.

1960

1961 Topps Don Larsen #402

When you combine the Hope Diamond of World Series records with a special Topps highlight card, you get a Don Larsen perfect game tribute that's worth more than its $30 asking price.

1962 Topps Roger Maris #313

From the same price range as the Larsen issue comes this Maris masterpiece that captures his historic 61st blast. This card is overflowing with Yankees history.

1962 Topps Babe Ruth/ Lou Gehrig #140

It's a cardboard pairing that shows why it's great to be a Yankees fan — the most feared hitting duo in history wore pinstripes.

1962 Topps HR Leader Mickey Mantle/ Roger Maris #53

It's the M&M boys on a league leader card touting the only statistic anyone cared about in 1961 — home runs.

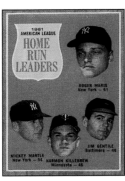

1965 Topps Mickey Mantle #134

You want drama? Mantle's Game 3 World Series homer in the bottom of the ninth sure qualifies. The Yanks still lost to St. Louis in seven, but this card's a testament to one of the game's most clutch hitters.

1969 Topps Mickey Mantle #500A

Heck, it's expensive enough assembling a collection of Mantle cards, but if you've got the cash, there's always the variation to chase. The white lettered version (Mantle is spelled

with white letters) of his '69 Topps is a short-printed prize that will run you about 3 times the regular version. But for most, this more common yellow-lettered version will do just fine.

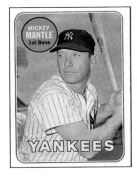

1970

1971 Topps Thurman Munson #5

When you list the player names that are synonymous with Yankees baseball, the great backstop Thurman Munson comes to mind. The black-bordered '71 Topps set is a stunning issue in its own right, but Munson's card is a fitting tribute to the all-time Yankees favorite.

1978 Topps Reggie Jackson #7 World Series Record Breaker

Sometimes the greatest cards are greatly overlooked. Such is this case with this $3 issue that marks Reggie's record-breaking five-homer performance in the 1977 World Series.

1980

1984 Donruss Don Mattingly #248

Few cards drove the hobby the way Donnie Baseball's Rookie Card did back in the '80s. It still packs hobby heat even today. This '84 Donruss set also carries the RC of Darryl Strawberry, but the Yankees card of choice from this set has been, and will likely always be, the team's most popular first baseman since Lou Gehrig.

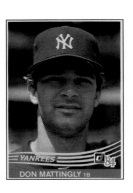

1990

1990 Upper Deck Heroes Reggie Jackson #AU1

This card qualifies as the hobby's first serial-numbered insert and features the autograph of Mr. October. Pricey, yes. Worth it? Most definitely.

1991 Score Mantle Autograph

It wasn't long after Upper Deck's entree into autographs that Mickey's 'graph popped up in '91 Score. The cardmaker couldn't have made a better selection.

1992 Score Joe DiMaggio Autograph

How do you top a Mickey Mantle auto-graph from '91? Well, you go out and sign Joe D — only one of the toughest autographs in the trading card business.

1993 SP Derek Jeter RC #279

Few Yankees cards are hotter than Jeter's. Derek's the Bronx Bomber that draws the most hobby attention and his con-dition-sensitive, foil-drenched SP Rookie Card is the debut of choice. Plus that foil-framed fielding pose is distinct issue worthy of special attention.

1994 Upper Deck All-Time Heroes Autographs Mickey Mantle #3

Mickey signed 1,000 cards for this promo-tion, which also included George Brett, Reggie Jackson and Tom Seaver. Each card came with a certificate that could be registered with Upper Deck. Let's be honest, who wouldn't want to own one of these?

1996 Leaf Signature Autographs Derek Jeter #118

Even though Donruss' first attempt at the all-autograph issue boasted a less-than-stellar lineup, the good news is that a young Yankees shortstop named Jeter made the cut and now stands as one of the key issues in the set.

1996 Topps Mickey Mantle #7

For four bucks you can own Topps' cur-tain call for card #7. The 1996 set featured Mantle as card #7 and has since retired it for future Topps issues in honor of Mickey. Topps struck upon the perfect promotion by honoring Mantle in a manner befitting this trading card legend.

1997 Donruss Signature Series Signifi-cant Signatures Don Mattingly #14

This is Mattingly's only autographed base-ball insert (he can also be found on an auto-graphed 1992 Pro Line football issue) and a must have for any modern Yankees collector. It's the most popular (and valuable) card in the 22-card set.

1997 Donruss Signature Series Significant Signatures Yogi Berra #3

A modern-day tribute to this Yan-kees legend reminds younger collectors that there were New York backstops before Jorge Posada.

1998 Topps Stars Rookie Reprint Autograph Whitey Ford

The combination of Whitey's Rookie Card reprint and his certified autograph is a win-win for collectors at around $60.

1999 Upper Deck Babe Ruth A Piece of History

Last but not least, Upper Deck's boldest insert innovation yet mounts an actual Babe Ruth game-used bat chip and a cut signature to a limited insert set for its 10th anniversary product. Love it or hate it. It's original. It's definitely authentic. And it's the Babe.

Autographs
By Theo Chen

Babe Ruth/Lou Gehrig autographed photo

The Texas Rangers' spring training facility in Port Charlotte, Fla., is in the loneliest corner of the Grapefruit League, halfway between Fort Myers and Sarasota on Florida's Gulf Coast. I made the trek to Port Charlotte in 1997 as part of my annual spring training trip, in an attempt to score some autographs of the visiting Yankees, who were coming off their first World Series title in two decades.

I was hoping that maybe, just maybe, the long drive from Tampa/St. Pete would deter Yankees fans and fellow autograph seekers from joining me. Alas, it was not to be. The usually tranquil Port Charlotte County Stadium became a raucous madhouse. And that was before the Yankees team buses arrived.

I spent the rest of the afternoon sweating profusely and getting jostled by pinstripe-clad fans. I left the stadium virtually empty-handed that day. I did gain new respect for the incredible, rock star-like popularity that follows this hallowed franchise.

If anything, the throngs have grown since then, with the Yankees capturing their second World Series in three years, and again with the addition of future Hall of Fame hurler Roger Clemens. The insatiable demand for autographs of today's Yankee superstars, of course, is inexorably linked to the team's storied past, which boasts a roster of legends unmatched in the history of American team sports.

The allure of the Yankee pinstripes means that signatures of

standouts past and present will always carry value above and beyond what their statistics would suggest. For example, the most renowned Yankee of the 1980s, Don Mattingly, can easily bring $50 per signature at a card show, even though his Hall of Fame chances are questionable. Other borderline Hall of Famers such as Joe Carter, Andre Dawson, Dave Parker or Jim Rice would be lucky to bring half as much per signature. Now that you have an idea of the phenomenon you're dealing with, here are some specific anecdotes, insights and tips for collecting autographs of Yankees past and present:

RETIRED PLAYERS
Yogi Berra

With the passing of Joe DiMaggio and Mickey Mantle before that, Berra probably now should be considered the "Greatest Living Yankee." Berra normally makes a few card show appearances a year and charges $40-$50 for flats. His signature is neat, but he normally signs very small. Now that Yogi and George Steinbrenner have reconciled, you might see him attend more official team events. If you run into him at such a venue, Yogi will usually sign for free, but only one per person.

Joe DiMaggio

The Yankee Clipper's recent passing has driven up his autograph values — even a cut signature will set you back at least $100, and a signed photo will cost twice that. Joe signed at card shows beginning in the 1980s, but the

supply never kept up with demand. The last few years of his life, Joe charged $150 to sign baseballs and $175 for small flats. Joe always was very picky about what he signed, and at every appearance he could be counted on to refuse to sign a particular item for no apparent reason. He steadfastly refused to sign any pictures of himself with Marilyn Monroe.

DiMaggio's signature was among the most-forged in baseball before his death, and you can expect the problem to get worse now that demand is peaking. This is complicated by the fact that Joe had some very good ghost-signers handling his fan mail for a while. In addition to his show appearances, Joe did many private signings with B&J Collectibles. A semi-recluse during the 1990s, even when in public he rarely signed for free.

Whitey Ford

The dominant Yankee pitcher of the 1950s, Whitey's World Series success ensured his Hall of Fame induction. Ford makes several card show appearances annually, and his fee of $20-$30 must be considered a pretty good deal these days.

Lou Gehrig

The early death of baseball's original Iron Man is one major reason his signature is among the most sought after in American

Lou Gehrig autographed ball

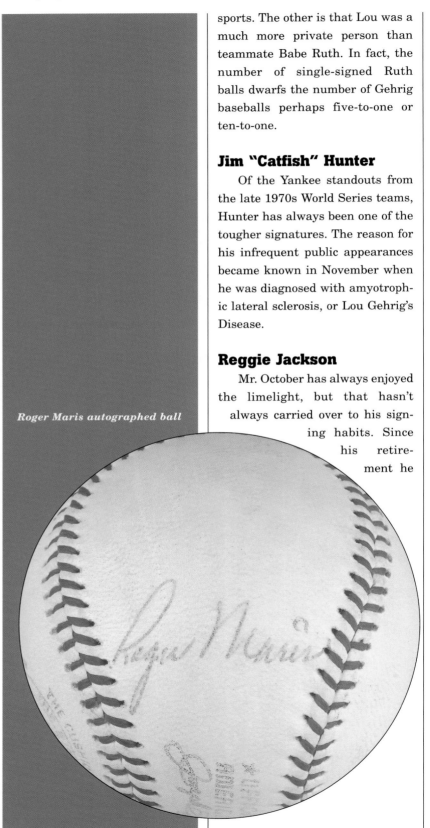

Roger Maris autographed ball

sports. The other is that Lou was a much more private person than teammate Babe Ruth. In fact, the number of single-signed Ruth balls dwarfs the number of Gehrig baseballs perhaps five-to-one or ten-to-one.

Jim "Catfish" Hunter

Of the Yankee standouts from the late 1970s World Series teams, Hunter has always been one of the tougher signatures. The reason for his infrequent public appearances became known in November when he was diagnosed with amyotrophic lateral sclerosis, or Lou Gehrig's Disease.

Reggie Jackson

Mr. October has always enjoyed the limelight, but that hasn't always carried over to his signing habits. Since his retirement he became a Yankees special advisor, which included occasionally working out and traveling with the team. He also was involved with the early years of Upper Deck and Upper Deck Authenticated. In both roles, Reggie often signed for free, but every once in a while would give a curt refusal. The easiest way to get Reggie today is via his Mr. October Foundation for Kids — the turnaround is very quick, and the money goes to a good cause.

Don Larsen

The only pitcher to throw a World Series perfect game had an otherwise average career, but that game will always set him apart. He is a very gracious signer at banquets and other events, his card show fee usually is about $15, and he also has an official website that offers signed memorabilia at http://www.nidlink.com/~bhbi/yan kee/main.html.

Mickey Mantle

Mantle once joked that when he arrived at the Pearly Gates, St. Peter would let him in — but only if Mantle would sign a baseball for him.

The Mick was among the very first players to cash in on the memorabilia craze, charging a few bucks per signature at early '80s card shows. Don't you wish you had a time machine? Mantle was a pretty consistent in-person signer throughout his retirement, although in his later years he was able to easily charge triple digits at shows, and he also signed memorabilia for Upper Deck Authenticated.

After Mantle's passing, the quantity of signatures on the market seemed to increase. In truth, the percentage of fakes probably is less than some autograph dealers would have you believe, although the bogus ones out there are pretty good.

Roger Maris

The McGwire mania of 1998 brought sudden attention to Maris, resulting in an increase in autograph values, and the number of fakes. Roger died in 1985, just as the card market was about to explode. Maris did sign at a couple shows late in life, but there seem to be a suspicious number offered for sale all of a sudden.

Don Mattingly

No doubt about it, Mattingly was a true class act and the best player in baseball for at least three seasons. He was a willing in-person signer and remains an icon among Yankees fans. His current signature value, however, probably is overvalued unless he makes it to Cooperstown.

Thurman Munson

Munson's airplane crash in 1979 ended a very promising catching career. It also created something of a cult hero status for Baby Boomer Yankee fans. This demand, combined with an obviously limited supply of signatures, has made Munson autographs very valuable.

Phil Rizzuto

The Scooter had to wait a long, long time, but his eventual Hall of Fame induction seemed predes-

tined. Even so, his autograph values almost doubled, even though his Yankee broadcasting career made him very accessible.

Babe Ruth

There probably are only two other men in American sports history who compare to Ruth in terms of charisma, fame, historical importance and stature: Muhammad Ali and Michael Jordan. Therefore, even though the number of Ruth autographs on the market is plentiful for his era — he died in 1948 and rarely refused a request — the values are demand-driven.

Dave Winfield

Despite Steinbrenner's unfair "Mr. May" criticism, Winfield probably will be best remembered for his Yankee exploits when he makes it to Cooperstown. For some reason, Dave has done very few card shows since his retirement, but he's been reasonably cooperative at other events I've seen him at.

ACTIVE PLAYERS
Roger Clemens

The Rocket was never an easy autograph in previous stints with the Red Sox or Blue Jays — "moody and inconsistent" would be the most accurate descriptive words. Sometimes he seemed to dislike being asked, other times he almost seemed to enjoy interacting with fans. Joining the Yankees increases the pressure on him, but also will allow him to enjoy winning again.

At a February 1998 awards banquet in Dallas, Clemens only

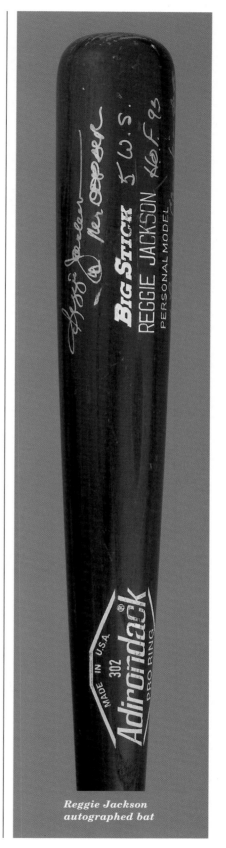

Reggie Jackson autographed bat

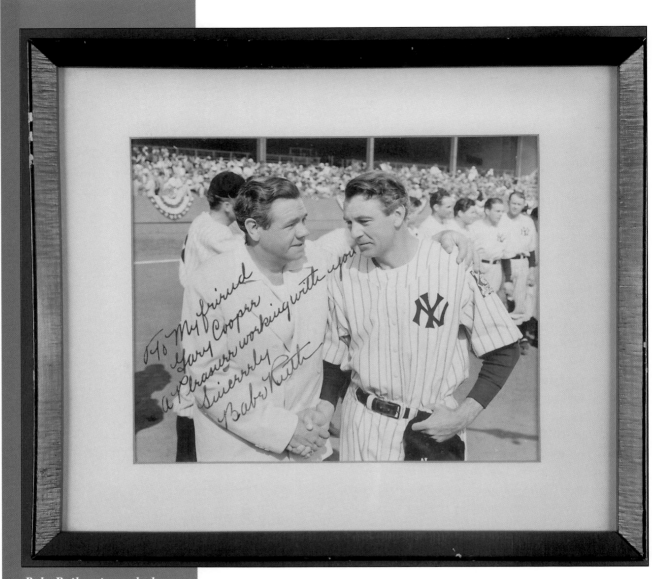

**Babe Ruth autographed
photo for Gary Cooper**

signed for a couple people. Lucky me, he was on my flight to the Super Show in Atlanta the next morning, and my seat was right behind his. I followed him off the plane and got him in the terminal — good thing I had my 1997 All-Star Game cap in my carry-on luggage.

David Cone

His card show fee usually starts at $30, but if you catch him at the team hotel or at the park, he almost always signs for free.

Derek Jeter

The standout shortstop's matinee idol looks and popularity creates crowd control problems wherever he goes. But he seems to genuinely care about fans and signs quite a bit at the park.

Chuck Knoblauch

In his last few years with the Twins, Chuck was very tough to get at times. An agent who represented other Twins players told me he was taken aback by how rarely Chuck deigned to sign at the team hotel. Joining the Yankees hasn't changed him much. I was lucky enough to get him in downtown Minneapolis during Chuck's last Twinsfest appearance in 1997.

Bernie Williams

Only Jeter is more popular among current Yankees. But unlike Derek, Bernie seems a bit unsure how to handle the attention he draws, thus he doesn't sign as much. At the few card shows he does, fees usually start at $40, which seems a bit much for a guy who didn't contribute much during the 1998 postseason.

Babe Ruth autographed photo

Autographs Price Guide

Retired Players

Baker, Frank - (1955) d. 1963
3 X 5	200.00
8 X 10 Photo	600.00
B&W HOF Signed Postcard	1200.00
Single Signed Ball	3500.00

Berra, Yogi - (1972)
3 X 5	8.00
8 X 10 Photo	20.00
Gold HOF Signed Postcard	20.00

Lou Gehrig autographed photo

Perez-Steele Signed Postcard	25.00
Signed Bat	150.00
Single Signed Ball	40.00

Chance, Frank - (1946) d. 1924
3 X 5	600.00
Signed Document	2000.00
Single Signed Ball	7500.00

Chesbro, Jack - (1946) d. 1931
3 X 5	1000.00
Signed Document	3000.00

Combs, Earle - (1970) d. 1976
3 X 5	20.00
8 X 10 Photo	125.00
Canceled Check	100.00
Gold HOF Signed Postcard	40.00
Single Signed Ball	2000.00

Coveleski, Stan - (1969) d. 1984
3 X 5	15.00
8 X 10 Photo	50.00
Gold HOF Signed Postcard	25.00
Single Signed Ball	500.00

Dickey, Bill - (1954) d. 1993
3 X 5	15.00
8 X 10 Photo	50.00
B&W HOF Signed Postcard	50.00
Canceled Check	250.00
Gold HOF Signed Postcard	35.00
Perez-Steele Signed Postcard	75.00
Single Signed Ball	300.00

DiMaggio, Joe - (1955)
3 X 5	75.00
8 X 10 Photo	125.00
B&W HOF Signed Postcard	175.00
Gold HOF Signed Postcard	150.00
Perez-Steele Signed Postcard	250.00
Signed Bat	1800.00
Single Signed Ball	250.00

Durocher, Leo - (1994) d. 1991
3 X 5	25.00
8 X 10 Photo	40.00
Single Signed Ball	175.00

Ford, Whitey - (1974)
3 X 5	8.00
8 X 10 Photo	20.00
Canceled Check	35.00
Gold HOF Signed Postcard	20.00
Perez-Steele Signed Postcard	25.00

Signed Bat	100.00
Single Signed Ball	35.00

Gehrig, Lou - (1939) d. 1941
3 X 5	1000.00
8 X 10 Photo	4500.00
Single Signed Ball	8000.00

Gomez, Lefty - (1972) d. 1988
3 X 5	15.00
8 X 10 Photo	50.00
Canceled Check	125.00
Gold HOF Signed Postcard	20.00
Perez-Steele Signed Postcard	75.00
Single Signed Ball	350.00

Griffith, Clark - (1946) d. 1955
3 X 5	200.00
8 X 10 Photo	600.00
B&W HOF Signed Postcard	750.00
Single Signed Ball	3500.00

Grimes, Burleigh - (1964) d. 1985
3 X 5	15.00
8 X 10 Photo	75.00
Canceled Check	60.00
Gold HOF Signed Postcard	25.00
Perez-Steele Signed Postcard	200.00
Single Signed Ball	300.00

Howard, Elston d. 1980
3 X 5	100.00
8 X 10 Photo	350.00
Single Signed Ball	1000.00

Hoyt, Waite - (1969) d. 1984
3 X 5	20.00
8 X 10 Photo	75.00
Canceled Check	125.00
Gold HOF Signed Postcard	50.00
Single Signed Ball	450.00

Hunter, Catfish - (1987)
3 X 5	5.00
8 X 10 Photo	15.00

Gold HOF Signed Postcard	7.00
Perez-Steele Signed Postcard	10.00
Signed Bat	50.00
Single Signed Ball	30.00

Jackson, Reggie - (1993)
3 X 5	10.00
8 X 10 Photo	25.00
Gold HOF Signed Postcard	50.00
Perez-Steele Signed Postcard	50.00
Signed Bat	250.00
Single Signed Ball	60.00

Jensen, Jackie d. 1982
3 X 5	25.00
8 X 10 Photo	50.00
Canceled Check	100.00
Single Signed Ball	175.00

Keeler, Willie - (1939) d. 1923
3 X 5	1000.00
Signed Document	2500.00
Single Signed Ball	10000.00

Lazzeri, Tony - (1991) d. 1946
3 X 5	350.00
8 X 10 Photo	850.00
Single Signed Ball	3500.00

Maglie, Sal d. 1992
3 X 5	25.00
8 X 10 Photo	50.00
Canceled Check	60.00
Single Signed Ball	250.00

Mantle, Mickey - (1974) d. 1995
3 X 5	50.00
8 X 10 Photo	125.00
Gold HOF Signed Postcard	150.00
Perez-Steele Signed Postcard	250.00
Signed Bat	2000.00
Single Signed Ball	225.00

Maris, Roger d. 1985
3 X 5	175.00
8 X 10 Photo	500.00
Single Signed Ball	1200.00

Martin, Billy d. 1989
3 X 5	15.00
8 X 10 Photo	50.00
Single Signed Ball	200.00

Mattingly, Don
3 X 5	12.00
8 X 10 Photo	30.00
Signed Bat	175.00
Single Signed Ball	50.00

McCarthy, Joe - (1957) d. 1978
3 X 5	40.00
8 X 10 Photo	150.00
B&W HOF Signed Postcard	100.00
Gold HOF Signed Postcard	75.00
Single Signed Ball	1200.00

Mize, Johnny - (1981) d. 1993
3 X 5	10.00
8 X 10 Photo	25.00
Gold HOF Signed Postcard	15.00
Perez-Steele Signed Postcard	25.00

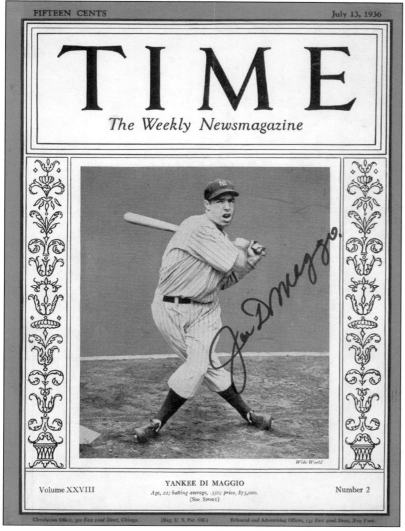

Joe DiMaggio autographed 1936 Time magazine

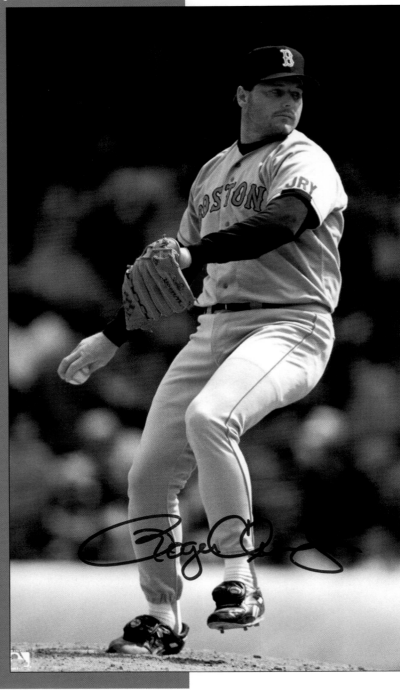

Roger Clemens autographed photo

Signed Bat	150.00
Single Signed Ball	75.00
Munson, Thurman d. 1979	
3 X 5	175.00
8 X 10 Photo	400.00
Canceled Check	600.00
Single Signed Ball	1500.00
O'Doul, Lefty d. 1969	
3 X 5	75.00

8 X 10 Photo	200.00
Single Signed Ball	1500.00
Pennock, Herb - (1948) d. 1948	
3 X 5	200.00
8 X 10 Photo	600.00
Canceled Check	1200.00
Single Signed Ball	3000.00
Perry, Gaylord - (1991)	
3 X 5	5.00
8 X 10 Photo	15.00
Canceled Check	25.00
Gold HOF Signed Postcard	7.00
Perez-Steele Signed Postcard	15.00
Signed Bat	50.00
Single Signed Ball	25.00
Rickey, Branch - (1967) d. 1965	
3 X 5	150.00
8 X 10 Photo	400.00
Canceled Check	800.00
Single Signed Ball	2000.00
Rizzuto, Phil - (1994)	
3 X 5	8.00
8 X 10 Photo	15.00
Gold HOF Signed Postcard	20.00
Perez-Steele Signed Postcard	25.00
Signed Bat	125.00
Single Signed Ball	30.00
Ruffing, Red - (1967) d. 1986	
3 X 5	25.00
8 X 10 Photo	100.00
Gold HOF Signed Postcard	75.00
Single Signed Ball	500.00
Ruth, Babe - (1936) d. 1948	
3 X 5	750.00
8 X 10 Photo	2500.00
Canceled Check	1600.00
Single Signed Ball	5500.00
Schalk, Ray - (1955) d. 1970	
3 X 5	50.00
8 X 10 Photo	150.00
B&W HOF Signed Postcard	275.00
Gold HOF Signed Postcard	450.00
Single Signed Ball	1200.00
Sewell, Joe - (1977) d. 1990	
3 X 5	15.00
8 X 10 Photo	40.00
Canceled Check	25.00
Gold HOF Signed Postcard	20.00
Perez-Steele Signed Postcard	50.00
Single Signed Ball	125.00
Slaughter Enos - (1985)	
3 X 5	5.00
8 X 10 Photo	15.00
Canceled Check	35.00
Gold HOF Signed Postcard	7.00
Perez-Steele Signed Postcard	15.00
Signed Bat	75.00
Single Signed Ball	25.00
Vance, Dazzy - (1955) d. 1961	
3 X 5	200.00
8 X 10 Photo	500.00
Single Signed Ball	2000.00

Waner, Paul - (1952) d. 1965

3 X 5	150.00
8 X 10 Photo	300.00
B&W HOF Signed Postcard	350.00
Single Signed Ball	2000.00

Winfield, Dave

3 X 5	8.00
8 X 10 Photo	20.00
Signed Bat	100.00
Single Signed Ball	50.00

Active Players

Boggs, Wade

8 X 10 Photo	20.00
Authentic Jersey	200.00
Signed Card	10.00
Signed Bat	75.00
Signed Cap	50.00
Signed Helmet	90.00
Single Signed Ball	35.00

Clemens, Roger

8 X 10 Photo	30.00
Authentic Jersey	300.00
Signed Card	20.00
Signed Bat	130.00
Signed Cap	80.00
Signed Helmet	150.00
Single Signed Ball	50.00

Cone, David

8 X 10 Photo	20.00
Authentic Jersey	200.00
Signed Card	10.00
Signed Bat	70.00
Signed Cap	50.00
Signed Helmet	75.00
Single Signed Ball	30.00

Jeter, Derek

8 X 10 Photo	30.00
Authentic Jersey	300.00
Signed Card	20.00
Signed Bat	130.00
Signed Cap	80.00
Signed Helmet	150.00
Single Signed Ball	50.00

Knoblauch, Chuck

8 X 10 Photo	20.00
Authentic Jersey	200.00
Signed Card	10.00
Signed Bat	75.00
Signed Cap	50.00
Signed Helmet	75.00
Single Signed Ball	30.00

Martinez, Tino

8 X 10 Photo	20.00
Authentic Jersey	220.00
Signed Card	12.00
Signed Bat	90.00
Signed Cap	60.00
Signed Helmet	100.00
Single Signed Ball	40.00

Pettitte, Andy

8 X 10 Photo	20.00
Authentic Jersey	220.00

Signed Card	12.00
Signed Bat	90.00
Signed Cap	60.00
Signed Helmet	100.00
Single Signed Ball	40.00

Williams, Bernie

8 X 10 Photo	25.00
Authentic Jersey	250.00
Signed Card	12.00
Signed Bat	100.00
Signed Cap	75.00
Signed Helmet	125.00
Single Signed Ball	40.00

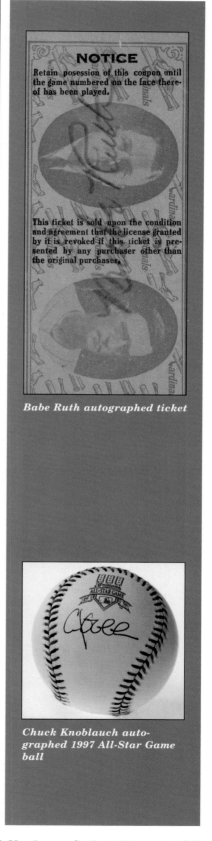

Babe Ruth autographed ticket

*Chuck Knoblauch auto-
graphed 1997 All-Star Game
ball*

World Series Collectibles
By Dan Schlossberg

Yankee fans always want a piece of the action — especially a piece that played a part in one of the team's 35 World Series appearances.

There's plenty to go around, since the Yankees won more pennants (24) and reached the Fall Classic more often than any other major league team. They are also the only franchise to forge five straight World Championships — a feat they executed twice (1936-41 and 1949-53).

Big moments of World Series history often involved players in pinstripes: Babe Ruth's called-shot homer in 1932, Don Larsen's perfect game in 1956, and Reggie Jackson's three-homer game in 1977 come to mind immediately.

"Yankees World Series stuff is in tremendous demand," said long-time memorabilia dealer Bill

1922 World Series at New York Polo Grounds

Jacobowitz of Livingston, N.J. "Any uniforms or any kind of equipment actually used in a World Series game is especially valuable. In the most recent World Series, the special emblems and patches worn on the uniforms and hats would have significant value."

According to Jacobowitz, who opened his first card store and ran the first memorabilia show in New Jersey 24 years ago, game-used bats have more value than game-used balls.

"If you can get a game-used Mickey Mantle World Series bat, accompanied by a letter of authenticity from him or a member of his family, that bat could be worth $50-$100,000," he says. "It's that nuts out there.

"If you could actually get one of his 18 home run balls — especially if Mantle signed it and you have a letter of authenticity from a family member — who knows what it might bring? Some of the Mark McGwire and Sammy Sosa home run balls in that auction last year went for more than a million dollars. All you need in any auction is two guys who want the item."

Although Mantle passed away in 1995, Larsen can still authenticate artifacts from his perfect game.

"If he had a ball or any part of his uniform from the perfect game, it's amazing what kind of money they would bring," Jacobowitz says. "Any kind of equipment, especially with a letter from the player, would be great. The people buying these things are not kids, but businessmen and corporations who want to display them. The letter of authenticity also becomes a collectible."

A Yankees World Series appearance is invariably a financial bonanza for card store owners in the New York metropolitan area.

"It's a real shot in the arm when the Yankees win," says Jacobowitz, who sells cards, autographs and memorabilia from a second-floor store called Skybox Baseball Cards.

"Last year, there was a tremendous rush to buy this stuff. I got in Yankees posters, yearbooks, even newspapers showing the Yankees winning and blew them out. Same thing with the championship publication the team produced afterthe season. I had zero left in my store because of the tremendous publicity.

"If you want World Series collectibles, and especially Yankees World Series collectibles, you'll have enough to collect for the rest of your life."

The list of collectibles is lengthy.

Ticket stubs from Ruth's called-shot game have sold for more than $600 each, while stubs from Larsen's perfect game bring $400. A mint-condition ticket from 1921, the first Yankee World Series, is valued at $1,200. Even the ticket from the relatively-recent Reggie Jackson three-homer game of Oct. 18, 1977, has a significant value attached ($90).

Programs from the Larsen game have sold for $500, while 1977 World Series programs are priced at $15.

Team-signed World Series baseballs cost considerably more: $18,000 for the 1927 Yankees; $10,000 for the '28 team; $4,000 for the 1951 edition; $3,000 for the first Yankees World Champions, in 1923; $2,000 for the 1961 juggernaut led

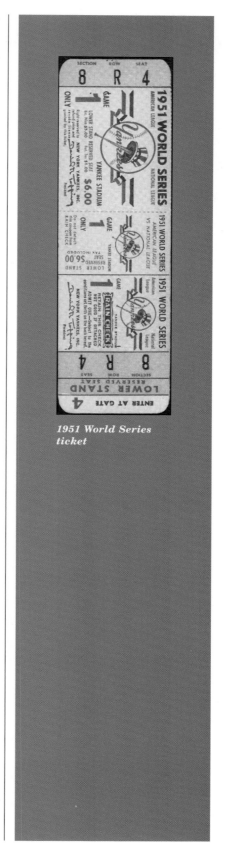

1951 World Series ticket

by Mantle and Roger Maris; $1,000 for the 1958 Yankees; and $600 for the 1996 team that upset the favored Atlanta Braves.

Single-signed balls of more recent vintage cost much less: official 1998 World Series balls signed by Orlando (El Duque) Hernandez and Mariano Rivera, respectively, were advertised at $60 and $65, respectively, earlier this year.

The Adirondack bat Mantle used to hit his 18th and last World Series home run in 1964 Game 7 was listed at $26,000 in a 1993 paperback that carried Mickey Mantle Memorabilia. Its value keeps escalating.

Press pins — initially issued to credentialed media covering the World Series have also found a niche as a baseball collectible. Issued since 1911 (with the exception of the war-shortened 1918 season), there are 67 variations featuring Yankees teams: home and away versions for every year but 1921-23, when single pins represented both New York clubs (the Yankees and Giants).

The 1921 and 1922 pins are priced at $3,000, with the 1923 pin

Joe DiMaggio

at $3,200. One of the most valuable Yankee-related press pins is the home-club version from 1927, when the team's top performers were Babe Ruth and Lou Gehrig. Its value is $2,800 and climbing.

The Yankees also produced a pair of phantom pins — jewelry rushed to mint before the pennant race was decided. The Yankees phantom of 1948, when Cleveland won the pennant, is worth $1,500, while the 1987 Yankee phantom is valued at $200.

Earlier this year, the California-based SportsCards Plus was selling three different editions (1953, 1956, and 1960) of the original Balfour Company press pins, neatly packaged with the original art in a Balfour folder display. The asking price was $995.

World Series rings are less common — mainly because they weren't routinely presented to players on winning teams, as they are today.

According to Yogi Berra, who played in a record 14 different World Series, "We didn't get rings all the time. Mr. Weiss (Yankees general manager George Weiss) gave us a choice. I kept two rings, from my first World Series in 1947 and from 1953, after we won five in a row. Other years I got a Rolex watch, a sterling silver cigarette box, and a sterling silver tray."

During a 19-year career in the majors, Berra made the All-Star team 15 times and won three American League MVP awards. But he has one regret from his rookie season: forgetting to keep the bat he used to hit the first pinch-homer in World Series history.

"I wish I had kept it," he said earlier this year from his new museum in Montclair, N.J. "But at that time you didn't think about what's happening now."

Berra's 1947 Series ring, plus some of the rings he later won as a coach with the 1977-78 Yankees, are on display at his museum, located in a corner of the Montclair State University campus.

According to museum director Dave Kaplan, "Our most prized possession is Yogi's catcher's mitt from Don Larsen's perfect game. It was immediately bronzed by (equipment man) Pete Sheehy and Yogi kept it all these years. It's almost the centerpiece of the museum."

It gained a competitor in April, however, when a new item arrived on temporary loan from the current Yankee team: the 1998 World Championship trophy.

At the Babe Ruth Museum, located near his Baltimore birthplace, there's a rotating collection of all the press pins from World Series that involved Ruth. But curator Greg Schwalenberg prefers another item.

"My personal favorite," he says, "is the watch given to Babe after the 1932 World Series. I'm not sure every player got the watch or just the Babe. It was donated to us by his family. We do have different World Series programs but the called-shot watch sticks out in my mind."

At the National Baseball Hall of Fame & Museum, in the Central New York hamlet of Cooperstown, a highlight of the World Series room is a collection of rings dating back to 1922. The "called shot" bat used by

Yankee Pennant Winners

With 35 World Series appearances and 24 World Championships, the Yankees have produced more Fall Classic memorabilia than any other team. They had pennant-winning clubs in the following seasons:

1921	*1952
1922	*1953
*1923	1955
1926	*1956
*1927	1957
*1928	*1958
*1932	1960
*1936	*1961
*1937	*1962
*1938	1963
*1939	1964
*1941	1976
1942	*1977
*1943	*1978
*1947	1981
*1949	*1996
*1950	*1998
*1951	

(*) World Champions

Yogi Berra/Don Larsen – 1956 World Series

Ruth against the Cubs in 1932 is on display, along with the bat swung by Pittsburgh's Bill Mazeroski against the Yankees in 1960 when he delivered the first home run to end a World Series.

The Hall also has jerseys of every Yankee manager to win a World Championship (Miller Huggins, Joe McCarthy, Bucky Harris, Casey Stengel, Ralph Houk, Billy Martin, Bob Lemon, and Joe Torre).

In addition, a new annual exhibit called "Hail to the Champs" features the defending world champions.

"Historically speaking, the Yankees have dominated baseball unlike any other franchise," says Hall of Fame curator Ted Spencer. "There are many significant artifacts from members of the 1998 champion Yankees on display in 'Hail to the Champs.'"

Specific World Series items in the exhibit include game-used bats from each of the starting position players in the decisive Game 4, the bat used by Scott Brosius to earn World Series MVP honors, plus a 1998 World Series press pin and program.

Cooperstown's World Series collection will be enhanced this fall with the addition of hand-picked memorabilia from world-famous collector Barry Halper of Livingston, N.J. Paul Beeston, president and chief operating officer of Major League Baseball, and National League president Len Coleman were among the baseball officials who personally selected items for baseball to purchase for the purpose of donation to the Hall of Fame.

Baseball acquired about 20 per cent of the Halper collection, with most of the rest sent to Sotheby's New York for a live one-week auction in September, followed by six months on the Internet.

All of Halper's World Series rings and pins (including many phantoms) went to the auction house, but other Fall Classic pieces were divided.

"I had a ticket from every World

Series — both American and National League teams — dating back to 1903," says Halper, a retired paper products executive who started collecting in 1948. "From 1919-21, the World Series was a best-of-nine. I had eight different Polo Grounds tickets from one year because the Series went eight games."

Halper, one of George Steinbrenner's limited partners in the current Yankee ownership group, acquired the tickets primarily from flea markets and shows.

He also made it a point to acquire as many items as possible relating to Babe Ruth, to whom he bears some resemblance.

"I had more Babe Ruth things than anybody else," says Halper, long considered the Babe Ruth of collecting. "I kept one picture of Babe standing in front of a Rolls Royce in the late 1920s or early 1930s. He's wearing light pants with a dark blue blazer, with his hands on the driver's side of the car. Hundreds of people are standing across the street in the background. The caption says it all, 'The Babe With the Rolls.'"

An ardent fan of the Yankees in general and Ruth in particular, Halper's collection included Ruth's camel-hair coat (since sent to the Hall of Fame) and even a lock of his hair (sent to Sotheby's). Another personal item that belonged to Ruth might have helped the 1996 Yankees win a World Championship, according to Halper.

"I had a display I called 'From the Babe's boudoir,'" he says. "I had a nail file, mirror, brush, comb, a shoe horn, and a toothbrush holder

that was a clear glass cylinder with a silver top. Everything said GHR for George Herman Ruth.

"I've used a few of them. You could take the file out and hold it in the palm of your hand. I've used it at certain Yankee games, rubbing the GHR for good luck. It worked in Atlanta, when the Yankees were down two games to none in the 1996 World Series, so I kept doing it."

When Barry Halper thinks about Babe Ruth, there's an automatic link to the World Series.

"To me, the first thing that comes to mind is 1932, Game 3, The Babe points. Whether it's true or not doesn't make a difference; that's academic. The Babe made a statement and created all this controversy.

"In my years of collecting, I enjoyed writing to the players associated with that game. Of the 10 letters I received back, six said he did not call the shot and four said he did. Those who said he did not included Gabby Hartnett, the catcher, and Billy Herman, who said he would have gotten the next pitch in his ear.

"One of the last times I talked to Frank Crosetti, who played shortstop in that game, I told him I had a 1932 souvenir bat from the World Series and wanted him to sign it.

I also asked him if the Babe pointed. He said no: Why should the Babe point to center field if all his home runs went to right field? But he hit the next pitch over the center field wall — and I bet he didn't hit one to center field all year long.

1998 Yankees team autographed ball

Derek Jeter

"Everybody agrees on one thing: The Babe pointed. Where he pointed and what he said to the pitcher, we don't know. So the controversy lives."

Perhaps a Paul Gallico press pass, part of the Halper collection, provides the answer. "In his writing, it says at the top, 'Babe knocked home run.' On the bottom, it says, 'Babe pointed.'"

In another Yankee World Series 15 years later, Berra hit the first pinch-homer in the World Series while wearing his rookie number — 35 — and Bill Bevens pitched 8 2/3 hitless innings against Brooklyn before surrendering a Cookie

Lavagetto hit that ended the no-hitter and the game (two base-runners who reached on walks scored the tying and winning runs). The Berra and Bevens uniforms belonged to Halper before going to the Hall of Fame and Sotheby's, respectively.

One of the prizes of Sotheby's Halper auction may be Joe DiMaggio's last World Series ring, from 1951. Preliminary estimates of its value range up to $75,000.

Although Sotheby's prices may make Halper into the Aristotle Onassis of baseball memorabilia collectors, fans can still find affordable pieces of Yankee World Series history.

While the 1999 Yankees were shaking out the winter cobwebs at Legends Field in Tampa, a Las Vegas company called American Memorabilia was selling a single-signed Derek Jeter 1998 World Series baseball for $59.99, a Jeter-signed 1998 Series hat for $79.99, and a 1998 Yankee World Series ball containing 25 signatures for $900.

At the same time, the Danbury Mint of Norwalk, CT produced a set of 22kt gold trading cards honoring the 1998 Yankees.

Across the top of each front was a line that read "1998 World Champions." A team logo marked the lower left, across from the player's name and position on the lower right. The focus of the front was the player's likeness, while regular-season and postseason stats comprised the flip side. Few could argue with the per-card cost: $9.95 plus 95 cents shipping.

If cost is the major consideration, viewing World Series memorabilia is invariably less expensive than owning it. Authenticated game-used items, especially if signed by any of the 15 Yankees with retired numbers, often command top dollar in the collectibles market. Material from the Big Four of Ruth, Gehrig, DiMaggio, and Mantle could prove astronomical.

But long-time Yankees fans — especially successful executives with office display room — relish the chance to show their support by showcasing celebrated items from the team's storied history. They will certainly pay for the privilege.

1998 World Series black bat

World Series Collectibles Price Guide

World Series Programs

World Series programs are the most popular item in the publication field. Programs prior to 1920 are difficult to find and command a premium in top condition. Programs prior to 1910 are quite scarce; only a few copies from 1903 are known to exist. Programs thru 1935 are graded in Ex-Ex-Mt condition. Programs after 1935 are graded in Ex-Mt-Nr-Mt condition.

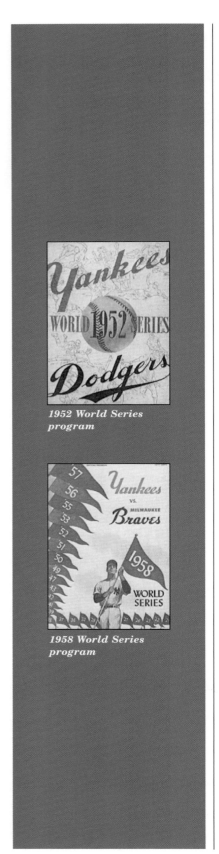

1952 World Series program

1958 World Series program

	Nr-Mt	Ex-Mt
1921 New York Yankees	2000.00	1200.00
1922 New York Yankees	2000.00	1200.00
1923 New York Yankees	2000.00	1200.00
1926 New York Yankees	1500.00	900.00
1927 New York Yankees	3500.00	2000.00
1928 New York Yankees	1500.00	900.00
1932 New York Yankees	1000.00	700.00
1936 New York Yankees	500.00	250.00
1937 New York Yankees	500.00	250.00
1938 New York Yankees	400.00	200.00
1939 New York Yankees	400.00	200.00
1941 New York Yankees	350.00	175.00
1942 New York Yankees	300.00	150.00
1943 New York Yankees	250.00	125.00
1947 New York Yankees	300.00	150.00
1949 New York Yankees	250.00	125.00
1950 New York Yankees	150.00	90.00
1951 New York Yankees	150.00	90.00
1952 New York Yankees	125.00	75.00
1953 New York Yankees	125.00	75.00
1955 New York Yankees	150.00	90.00
1956 New York Yankees	175.00	100.00
1957 New York Yankees	125.00	75.00
1958 New York Yankees	125.00	75.00
1960 New York Yankees	75.00	50.00
1961 New York Yankees	150.00	75.00
1962 New York Yankees	100.00	60.00
1963 New York Yankees	60.00	40.00
1964 New York Yankees	75.00	50.00
1976 New York Yankees	20.00	12.00
1977 New York Yankees	15.00	8.00
1978 New York Yankees	15.00	8.00
1981 New York Yankees	15.00	8.00
1996 New York Yankees	10.00	6.00

World Series Ticket Stubs

The value for complete World Series tickets is generally double that of a stub. Complete World Series tickets prior to 1920 are valued even higher. Ticket stubs for historic World Series contests, such as Don Larsen's 1956 perfect World Series game, or Babe Ruth's famous called shot game, can command anywhere from 3 to 6 times that of a regular stub. Stubs prior to 1935 are graded in Ex-Ex-Mt condition. Stubs after 1935 are graded in Ex-Mt-Nr-Mt condition.

	Nr-Mt	Ex-Mt
1921 New York Yankees	600.00	350.00
1922 New York Yankees	600.00	350.00
1923 New York Yankees	600.00	350.00

	Nr-Mt	Ex-Mt
1926 New York Yankees	400.00	250.00
1927 New York Yankees	500.00	300.00
1928 New York Yankees	350.00	200.00
1932 New York Yankees	200.00	125.00
1936 New York Yankees	150.00	90.00
1937 New York Yankees	150.00	90.00
1938 New York Yankees	150.00	90.00
1939 New York Yankees	150.00	90.00
1941 New York Yankees	125.00	75.00
1942 New York Yankees	150.00	90.00
1943 New York Yankees	150.00	90.00
1947 New York Yankees	150.00	90.00
1949 New York Yankees	125.00	75.00
1950 New York Yankees	125.00	75.00
1951 New York Yankees	125.00	75.00
1952 New York Yankees	125.00	75.00
1953 New York Yankees	125.00	75.00
1955 New York Yankees	75.00	50.00
1956 New York Yankees	75.00	50.00
1957 New York Yankees	75.00	50.00
1958 New York Yankees	75.00	50.00
1960 New York Yankees	70.00	45.00
1961 New York Yankees	90.00	60.00
1962 New York Yankees	75.00	50.00
1963 New York Yankees	60.00	40.00
1964 New York Yankees	70.00	45.00
1976 New York Yankees	45.00	30.00
1977 New York Yankees	45.00	30.00
1978 New York Yankees	45.00	30.00
1981 New York Yankees	40.00	25.00
1996 New York Yankees	35.00	20.00

World Series Press Pins

World Series press pins were first introduced by the Philadelphia Athletics during the 1911 Fall Classic. The press pin was intended to keep non-press personnel out of the press box. Today, World Seres press pins are given to members of the media more as a symbolic gesture.

	Nr-Mt	Ex-Mt
1921 New York Yankees	3000.00	1500.00
1922 New York Yankees	3000.00	1500.00
1923 New York Yankees	3200.00	1600.00
1926 New York Yankees	1250.00	650.00
1927 New York Yankees	2800.00	1800.00
1928 New York Yankees	1800.00	1000.00
1932 New York Yankees	1000.00	500.00
1936 New York Yankees	700.00	350.00
1937 New York Yankees	800.00	400.00
1938 New York Yankees	700.00	350.00
1939 New York Yankees	700.00	350.00
1941 New York Yankees	700.00	350.00
1942 New York Yankees	600.00	300.00
1943 New York Yankees	600.00	300.00
1947 New York Yankees	700.00	350.00
1949 New York Yankees	600.00	300.00
1950 New York Yankees	350.00	175.00
1951 New York Yankees	300.00	150.00
1952 New York Yankees	300.00	150.00
1953 New York Yankees	300.00	150.00

1955 New York Yankees	300.00	150.00
1956 New York Yankees	300.00	150.00
1957 New York Yankees	200.00	100.00
1958 New York Yankees	200.00	100.00
1960 New York Yankees	175.00	100.00
1961 New York Yankees	250.00	150.00
1962 New York Yankees	175.00	100.00
1963 New York Yankees	175.00	100.00
1964 New York Yankees	175.00	100.00
1976 New York Yankees	150.00	75.00
1977 New York Yankees	150.00	75.00
1978 New York Yankees	100.00	50.00
1981 New York Yankees	100.00	50.00
1996 New York Yankees	150.00	75.00

World Series Phantom Press Pins

Major League baseball allows teams it considers World Series contenders to produce post season materials prior to the end of the season. These materials include tickets, press pins, etc.. Phantom World Series Press Pins were produced but never formerly released by non-title ball-clubs

	Nr-Mt	Ex-Mt
1948 New York Yankees	1500.00	900.00
1987 New York Yankees	200.00	125.00

World Series Black Bats

World Series Commemorative Black Bats are produced in limited numbers by Hillerich & Bradsby. The only bat not produced by H&B was the 1934 Tigers model. Black bats are given to various VIP's, league and team officials each December. Post 1937 Black Bats contain facimile player signatures, usually in either green or gold ink. Pre-1938 bats are brown in color, rather than the traditional black. Beginning in 1991, the number of Black Bats issued fell sharply from previous years and command premium prices.

	Nr-Mt	Ex-Mt
1936 New York Yankees	2500.00	1500.00
1937 New York Yankees	2500.00	1500.00
1938 New York Yankees	1200.00	700.00
1939 New York Yankees	1200.00	700.00
1941 New York Yankees	1500.00	900.00
1942 New York Yankees	600.00	400.00
1943 New York Yankees	600.00	400.00
1947 New York Yankees	750.00	500.00
1949 New York Yankees	600.00	400.00
1950 New York Yankees	500.00	300.00
1951 New York Yankees	1500.00	900.00
1953 New York Yankees	500.00	300.00
1955 New York Yankees	1000.00	600.00
1956 New York Yankees	600.00	400.00
1957 New York Yankees	500.00	300.00
1958 New York Yankees	500.00	300.00
1960 New York Yankees	500.00	300.00
1961 New York Yankees	800.00	500.00
1962 New York Yankees	500.00	300.00
1963 New York Yankees	400.00	250.00
1964 New York Yankees	400.00	250.00
1976 New York Yankees	300.00	175.00
1977 New York Yankees	400.00	300.00
1978 New York Yankees	500.00	300.00
1981 New York Yankees	300.00	175.00
1996 New York. Yankees	750.00	500.00

1937 World Series press pin

1936 World Series press pin

1956 World Series black bat

Game-Used Memorabilia

By Dan Schlossberg

Don't let anyone suggest otherwise: There's a huge market for game-used equipment and uniforms. And most of the prized possessions once belonged to Yankee greats.

As long ago as the mid-1970s, when collecting was in its infancy, the Yankees realized a handsome profit by selling items from the old Yankee Stadium, prior to its renovation.

Three retired numbers — Babe Ruth's No. 3, Lou Gehrig's No. 4, and Joe DiMaggio's No. 5 — that had hung in the old stadium were sold for $30,000 each while original seats went for $1,000 apiece.

And uniforms of the stars invariably command big bucks.

"A Joe DiMaggio uniform in nice condition would be worth at least $100,000," said Bill Jacobowitz, owner of Skybox Baseball Cards in Livingston, N.J. "And another interesting item is a nice, signed No. 6 Mickey Mantle (worn during his 1951 rookie year).

"Of all the old-timers, Mantle is by far the best seller. In my 24 years of business, the week after

Game-used 1978 World Series ball

Mantle passed away was the best I've ever had. I literally ran out of Mantle merchandise and had to send a driver 120 miles roundtrip to one of my wholesalers. I had nothing left and had run a big ad.

"Many of the people who saw DiMaggio play have passed away or are elderly and not into collecting. But Mantle is for people 40-55 years old who have the money to buy stuff and display it. They'll pay high prices for Mantle items."

Mantle's No. 7 road uniform from 1952, his first full season, and an unsigned DiMaggio road uniform from 1939, his first MVP campaign, were some of the most highly coveted items at Leland's June 1999 auction, one of three the New York auction house held that year. Game-used jerseys and bats were also available.

On Sept. 13, the ninth annual Phil Rizzuto Celebrity Golf Tournament, at Brooklake Country Club of Florham Park, N.J., will use Yankee memorabilia to raise funds by auction for St. Joseph's School for the Blind of Jersey City, N.J. According to organizer Ed Lucas, bats and uniforms contributed by past and present Yankee stars — including Don Mattingly, Wade Boggs and Dave Righetti — fuel the bidding.

Also in September, the bulk of the famed Barry Halper collection will be auctioned by Sotheby's New York.

Halper had 1,053 uniforms, most of them signed, hanging on a dry cleaner's rack rigged to respond to the dialing of the matching jersey number. In the collection were numbers nobody remembers: rookie tops worn by Joe DiMaggio (No. 9 in 1936), Yogi Berra (No. 35 in 1947), Whitey Ford (No. 19 in 1950), and Mickey Mantle (No. 6 in 1951), among others.

The world-famous Livingston, N.J. collector, who still owns a small piece of the Yankees, also had bats, balls, hats, gloves and other gear acquired over a half-century of baseball treasure hunting.

If it existed, chances are Halper had it. He owned Mickey Mantle's only Triple Crown as well as Babe Ruth's last bat.

"That bat was used on June 13, 1948, the day the Yankees retired Ruth's number," Halper explained. "Eddie Robinson (the Cleveland

first baseman) asked the batboy to bring the bat up to the Babe because it looked like he needed help. The picture of Ruth leaning on the bat won a Pulitzer Prize.

"When Babe came back to the dugout, Robinson walked him into the clubhouse and asked him to sign the bat. I eventually got it from Eddie in the 1970s."

Ironically, the bat the batboy grabbed belonged to Bob Feller, star pitcher of the visiting

Series Bats Score Big

For many years, the Hillerich & Bradsby Company, makers of Louisville Slugger bats, has created commemorative bats for players of all teams that reach the World Series.

Players already using Louisville Sluggers got bats similar to their regular models, with the words "1998 World Series" stamped on the barrel in the space usually reserved for the team name.

The bats were never used in games because players are a superstitious lot who prefer to stick with bats already in their regular rotation. They weren't about to change equipment just because it had the words "World Series" on it.

The Louisville Slugger company also created post-World Series bats branded with the names of participating players from each team. Those under contract to Louisville Slugger got bats emblazoned with their already-on-file signatures, while others got bats with their names in block letters. Names of all players and coaches appeared on each bat, along with the name of the team and an added line that says

"World Champions" on bats created for the winners.

Although such bats are sent to individual teams for their use only, a few have found their way into the memorabilia marketplace, where they have commanded high prices.

According to Dan Burgess, spokesman for the Louisville Slugger Museum, collectors can buy a $69 replica of the World Series bat, complete with World Series and team logos, and have their names stamped on the barrel. Miniature versions bats bearing player names (including Ruth, Gehrig, DiMaggio and Mantle) are on sale at the museum's gift shop for $3.75.

For further information, check out the Louisville Slugger website (www.slugger.com) or call its toll-free number (800-282-BATS).

— Dan Schlossberg

Reggie Jackson game-used bat

Cleveland Indians. Years later, when Feller saw it in Halper's museum, he asked to sign it. Feller wrote, "This was my bat. Now it's yours. The Babe's last bat." Feller also gave Halper a supporting affidavit bearing the signatures of Dale Mitchell, Eddie Robinson and Bob Lemon.

Halper later loaned the bat to Feller for a one-year temporary display at the pitcher's museum in his hometown of Van Meter, Iowa.

The best place to see famous Yankee bats remains the Baseball Hall of Fame.

Its collection includes the bats used for Babe Ruth's 60th home run in 1927, his called-shot homer in the 1932 World Series, and Roger Maris' 61st home run in 1961.

The Hall also has a Joe DiMaggio bat from 1939, when the Yankee Clipper won the first of his three MVP awards; the bat Mantle used to slam a 565-foot Yankee Stadium homer against a stunned Chuck Stobbs of the Washington Senators; and the bat Bernie Williams used when he became the first man to homer from both sides of the plate in a playoff game.

Visitors can view gloves used by smooth-fielding third basemen Graig Nettles and Clete Boyer, Tony Kubek's Rookie of the Year trophy, and Phil Rizzuto's Hickock Award, given annually to the athlete of the year. There are even Yankee jerseys from each of the eight managers to win a World Championship.

Last year's World Championship team has its own exhibit, "Hail to the Champs," that includes Derek Jeter's spikes, bats used by September phenoms Shane Spencer and Ricky Ledee, and one of the two home jerseys worn by Yankee manager Joe Torre during the season.

"We also have the bat Scott Brosius broke while hitting a single in the last game of the World Series," said Jeff Idelson, a former Yankees publicist who is now communications director for the Hall of Fame. "How can I forget that? I was there and got it from him."

Cooperstown's collection goes far beyond bats and balls. Babe Ruth's larger-than-life legacy lives on in the 60-year-old museum

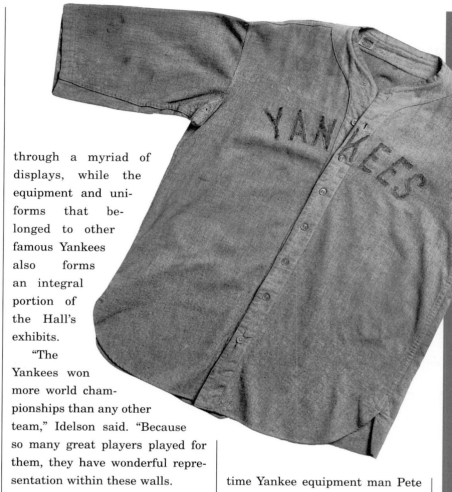

through a myriad of displays, while the equipment and uniforms that belonged to other famous Yankees also forms an integral portion of the Hall's exhibits.

"The Yankees won more world championships than any other team," Idelson said. "Because so many great players played for them, they have wonderful representation within these walls.

"We have a ton of stuff from Lou Gehrig — including his locker. We also have his wife Eleanor's scrapbook that was depicted in Pride of the Yankees, plus the movie version. And we have a number of pieces of Gehrig equipment from throughout his career. When Eleanor passed away, the Gehrig estate bequeathed everything that was Yankee-related to us."

Joe DiMaggio's old Yankee Stadium locker also resides in the Hall of Fame, along with a home uniform worn during his final season in 1951 and bats, gloves, and spikes DiMaggio used during his brilliant 13-year career.

Thanks to the foresight of long-time Yankee equipment man Pete Sheehy, Mickey Mantle also used DiMaggio's locker. When DiMaggio retired after the 1951 campaign, Sheehy simply assigned his locker to the team's next superstar-in-waiting.

It was also Sheehy who helped Barry Halper acquire many of his most famous uniforms. He put Halper in touch with the relatives of former clubhouse men who had inherited the items. Relatives of the old Columbia University clubhouse man had Lou Gehrig's old college togs, as well as his first pro uniform: from the 1921 Hartford club, where he used the name Lewis to protect his amateur status.

Retired Yankee Numbers

Memorabilia from a player whose number was retired is often more valuable. The Yankees have retired 15 numbers, more than any other club. They are:

1	Billy Martin
3	Babe Ruth
4	Lou Gehri
5	Joe DiMaggio
7	Mickey Mantle
8	Yogi Berra
8	Bill Dickey
9	Roger Maris
10	Phil Rizzuto
15	Thurman Munson
16	Whitey Ford
23	Don Mattingly
32	Elston Howard
37	Casey Stengel
44	Reggie Jackson

Gehrig's 1927 uniform, along with those of Ruth and other studs from that Murderer's Row club, were unearthed in the attic of a man living in upstate Coxsackie, N.Y.

Depending upon their condition, typical player uniforms sell for up to $600, while uniforms of stars command up to $1,500 and superstars may draw twice as much. Jerseys worn by the Yankees' Big Four — Ruth, Gehrig, DiMaggio and Mantle — zoom off the price chart. Signed suits are worth more.

Because counterfeiting is a problem, it's always advisable to have a letter of authenticity from a reliable source, such as the player or his family.

Any pre-1929 uniform with a number on the back is not genuine; the 1929 Yankees became the first team to assign player numbers, matching each man with his position in the batting order (3 for Ruth, 4 for Gehrig, etc.). Prior to numbering, jerseys had players' names sewn inside.

Ruth wore no number on his back when he swung the 40-ounce, 35-inch bat acquired for $23,000 by Upper Deck Trading Card Company of Carlsbad, Calif., at a June 1997 auction. Two months later — to the dismay of many baseball historians — the cracked bat was carved into 200 slivers for Piece of History cards randomly inserted into Series 1 card packs.

The Yogi Berra Museum, opened on the campus of Montclair (N.J.) State University late last year, has a bat from Babe Ruth's last season (with the Boston Braves), a glove Berra used while playing sandlot ball at age 14, and uniforms from Joe DiMaggio (1939), Mickey Mantle (1952) and Berra (1961 and 1963).

The 25-year-old Babe Ruth Museum, which doubles as the official museum of the Baltimore Orioles, has various bats Ruth used during his career plus a pair of pinstriped pants from the 1930s

with the Ruth name stitched inside. But a Ruth jersey tops its want list.

According to curator Greg Schwalenberg, "If there's one thing we'd really like to have that we don't, it's a Ruth jersey. We've borrowed some from collectors for special displays but we don't have a game-used jersey. And that's what people want to see."

The centerpiece of the Louisville Slugger Museum, opened three years ago, is a 1927 Babe Ruth bat protected behind a glass case. What makes the 46-ounce, 42-inch bat unusual is the series of 21 notches — one for every homer he hit before the bat cracked — around the trademark oval.

"There's a lot of Yankee presence in our museum," said spokesman Dan Burgess. "We try to keep

things as interactive and changeable as possible. After Joe DiMaggio's passing, we put together a temporary DiMaggio display that included some models of his bats. We also have some Lou Gehrig bats in our collection."

Ogling a prized Yankee collectible is one thing; purchasing it is something else.

In 1998, several Joe DiMaggio items were included in an auction held by Ron Oser Enterprises. A signed 1947 game-used home jersey went for $82,027, a 1941 pair of spikes worn during the 56-game hitting streak went for $36,094, and a game-used 1942 cap went for $22,188.

The 1958 All-Star Game bat Mickey Mantle used in Baltimore that summer carries a $16,000 price tag. It's a Louisville 125

Roger Maris game-worn jersey

Opposite: Babe Ruth

model with the All-Star stamp and Mantle's name burned into the barrel.

Another game-used Mantle bat, a 35-inch Louisville Slugger MM 125 with a minor crack on the handle and P104 on the knob, was among the last he used. Its estimated value is $8,000.

More contemporary uniforms and equipment are available from the Sports Warehouse of Wilsonville, Ore. Owner Robb Wochnick recently acquired several hundred 1996-97 batting practice jerseys, 350-400 game-used bats, 150 caps, and dozens of other items, including team equipment bags.

Frequent memorabilia auctions — both live and via the Internet — also include items of interest to Yankee collectors.

A highly coveted blend of old and new appeared on the market late last year, when the Yankees honored Joe DiMaggio with a limited edition commemorative ball.

The same official Rawlings American League ball used for games at Yankee Stadium, it was given to fans that attended the game on Sept. 27, 1998. The ball contained a Yankee logo with a cartoon DiMaggio superimposed. Unsigned versions of the ball now sell for $25, though anything containing Joe D's signature — especially if it also had No. 5 or HOF 1955 (the year of his Hall of Fame induction) — would cost much more.

Another Rawlings item, a game-used No. 24 Rawlings sweatshirt worn under his Oakland uniform by Rickey Henderson in 1980, carries a price tag of $225. It's of interest to Yankee fans because Henderson played for the team from 1985-89 and this year became one of the few superstars to play for both the Yankees and Mets. Since he's the single-season and career leader in stolen bases, the best leadoff man in baseball history, and a sure-fire Hall of Famer five years after retirement, Henderson's game-worn equipment can only increase in value.

The same rule of thumb applies to anyone good enough to reach Cooperstown. Among the Yankee greats who did are Babe Ruth, Lou Gehrig, Joe DiMaggio, Mickey Mantle, Phil Rizzuto, Whitey Ford and Bill Dickey — all of whom spent their entire careers in the Bronx. Catfish Hunter and Reggie Jackson, who arrived in mid-career, also chose Yankee hats for their Cooperstown plaques.

Also representing the Yankees in the Hall of Fame are Ed Barrow, Jack Chesbro, Earle Combs, Lefty Gomez, Waite Hoyt, Miller Huggins, Tony Lazzeri, Joe McCarthy, Herb Pennock, Red Ruffing, Casey Stengel and George Weiss.

Landing any item used by any of them — signed or unsigned — would be a major coup for any collector who identifies with baseball's most successful franchise.

Pennants

1940s Joe DiMaggio	1500.00
1950s New York Yankees "American League Champions"	250.00
1950s New York Yankees "Uncle Sam"	175.00
1961 New York Yankees "Team Photo"	600.00
1955 World Series Yankees vs Dodgers	3200.00
1956 World Series Yankees vs Dodgers	1000.00

* Values for the following pennants were determined from actual sales information and auction results.

* Certain pennant photos are courtesy of Mastro and Steinbach, Lelands, Hunt Auctions, Inc.

Yearbooks

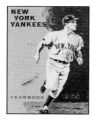

Jay Publishing issued unofficial Yankee's Yearbooks between 1952 and 1965. The Jay Yearbooks were available through various mail order sources and souvenir outlets outside Yankee Stadium.

	Nr-Mt	Ex-Mt
1950 (First Year)	325.00	250.00
1951	200.00	125.00
1952	150.00	100.00
1952 (Jay)	100.00	60.00
1953	150.00	100.00
1953 (Jay)	100.00	60.00
1954	150.00	100.00
1954 (Jay)	100.00	60.00
1955	275.00	200.00
1955 (Revised)	250.00	175.00
1955 (Jay)	100.00	60.00
1956	125.00	75.00
1956 (Revised)	125.00	75.00
1956 (Jay)	75.00	50.00
1957	225.00	150.00
1957 (Revised)	225.00	150.00
1957 (Jay)	75.00	50.00
1958	150.00	100.00
1958 (Revised)	150.00	100.00

1958 (Jay)	75.00	50.00
1959	150.00	100.00
1959 (Revised)	150.00	100.00
1959 (Jay)	75.00	50.00
1960	150.00	100.00
1960 (Revised)	150.00	100.00
1960 (Jay)	75.00	50.00
1961	150.00	100.00
1961 (Revised)	175.00	100.00
1961 (Jay)	75.00	50.00
1962	100.00	60.00
1962 (Revised)	100.00	60.00
1962 (Revised #2)	100.00	60.00
1962 (Revised #3)	100.00	60.00
1962 (Jay)	60.00	40.00
1963	75.00	50.00

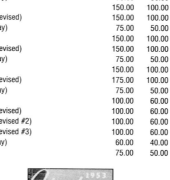

1963 (Revised)	75.00	50.00
1963 (Jay)	40.00	25.00
1964	75.00	50.00
1964 (Revised)	75.00	50.00
1964 (Revised #2)	75.00	50.00
1964 (Revised #3)	75.00	50.00

1964 (Jay)	35.00	20.00
1965	60.00	40.00
1965 (Revised)	60.00	40.00
1965 (Jay)	35.00	20.00
1966	50.00	30.00
1966 (Revised)	50.00	30.00
1966 (Revised #2)	50.00	30.00
1966 (Revised #3)	50.00	30.00
1967	50.00	30.00
1967 (Revised)	50.00	30.00
1968	25.00	15.00
1969	40.00	25.00
1970	60.00	40.00
1971	7.00	4.00
1972	15.00	9.00
1973	15.00	9.00
1974	15.00	9.00
1975	15.00	9.00
1976	20.00	12.00
1977	10.00	6.00
1978	10.00	6.00
1979	10.00	6.00
1980	10.00	6.00
1981	15.00	9.00
1982	7.00	4.00
1983	7.00	4.00
1984	10.00	6.00
1985	7.00	4.00
1986	7.00	4.00
1987	7.00	4.00
1988	10.00	6.00
1989	10.00	6.00
1990	10.00	6.00
1991	10.00	6.00
1992-PRESENT	10.00	6.00

Vintage Comic Price Guide

1940-41 Sport Comics

This real-life drama series depicted modern-day athletes. The title was changed to True Sport Picture Stories after the fourth issue. Published by Street & Smith Publications.

	Ex-Mt	Ex
Lou Gehrig Story (#1, Oct.,1940)	200.00	125.00
Gene Tunney Story (#2, Oct.,1940)	100.00	60.00
Phil Rizzuto Story (#3, Oct.,1940)	75.00	50.00
Frank Leahy Story (#4, Nov.,1941)	75.00	50.00

1941-46 Real Heroes Comics

Published by Parents' Institute.

	Ex-Mt	Ex
Lou Gehrig Story (#6)	100.00	60.00
Pete Gray Story (#14)	25.00	15.00

1941-50 True Comics

The True Comics series was based on real-life stories. The series lasted nine years. Published by True Comics/Parents' Magazine Press.

	Ex-Mt	Ex
Marathon Run Story (#1, April,1941)	100.00	60.00
Baseball Hall of Fame Story (#3, Aug.,1941)	60.00	40.00
Joe Louis Story (#5, Oct.,1941)	40.00	25.00
World Series Story (#6, Nov.,1941)	50.00	30.00
Football Stars (#7, Dec.,1941)	30.00	20.00
Basketball's Origin (#11, April,1942)	30.00	20.00
Bob Feller Story (#15, Aug.,1942)	30.00	20.00
Brooklyn Dodgers Story (#17, Oct.,1942)	30.00	20.00
Barney Ross Story (#24, May,1943)	20.00	12.00
Walt & Walker Cooper (#30, Dec.,1943)	20.00	12.00
Red Grange Story (#31, Dec.,1943)	20.00	12.00

Rube Waddell Story (#37, July,1944)	20.00	12.00
Rube Marquard Story (#49, May,1946)	20.00	12.00
Dixie Walker Story (#50, July,1946)	20.00	12.00
Jim Jeffries Story (#58, Mar.,1947)	20.00	12.00
Indianapolis Speedway (#60, May,1947)	20.00	12.00
Bob Feller Story (#61, June,1947)	20.00	12.00
Wally Butts Story (#65, Oct.,1947)	20.00	12.00
Guide to Football Formations (#66, Nov.,1947)	20.00	12.00
Univ. of Michigan Basketball (#70, Mar.,1948)	20.00	12.00
Joe DiMaggio Cover (#71, May,1948)	125.00	75.00
Jackie Robinson Story (#72, July,1948)	40.00	25.00
Story of the Marathon (#73, Sept.,1948)	15.00	9.00
Special Football Tips (#74, Nov.,1948)	15.00	9.00
Stan Musial Cover (#78, Aug.,1949)	100.00	60.00
Red Grange Story (#81, Feb.,1950)	75.00	50.00

1942-49 True Sport Picture Stories

This real-life drama series depicted modern-day athletes. The title was changed from Sport Comics after that series' fourth issue. Published by Street & Smith Publications.

	Ex-Mt	Ex
Joe DiMaggio Cover (#5, Feb.,1942)	200.00	125.00
Billy Conn Cover (#6, Apr.,1942)	60.00	40.00
Mel Ott Cover (#7, June,1942)	60.00	40.00
Lou Ambers Cover (#8, Aug.,1942)	50.00	30.00
Pete Reiser Cover (#9, Oct.,1942)	60.00	40.00
Frankie Sinkwich Cover (#10, Dec.,1942)	50.00	30.00
Red Grange Cover (#11, Feb.,1943)	60.00	40.00
Jack Dempsey Cover (#12, Apr.,1943)	60.00	40.00
Willie Pep Cover (Vol.2 #1, June,1943)	50.00	30.00
Mort Cooper Cover (Vol.2 #2,Aug.,1943)	40.00	25.00
Carl Hubbell Cover (Vol.2 #3, Oct.,1943)	40.00	25.00
Baseball of Tomorrow (Vol.2 #4, Dec.,1943)	40.00	25.00
Don Hutson Cover (Vol.2 #5, Feb.,1944)	40.00	25.00
Dixie Walker Cover (Vol.2 #6, Apr.,1944)	40.00	25.00
Stan Musial Cover (Vol.2 #7, June,1944)	60.00	40.00
Famous Boxers Cover (Vol.2 #8, Aug.1944)	50.00	30.00
Negro Leagues Stars Cover (Vol.2 #9 ,Oct.,1944)	100.00	60.00
Connie Mack Cover (Vol.2 #10, Dec.,1944)	60.00	40.00
Winning Basketball Plays (Vol.2 #11, Feb.,1945)	40.00	25.00
Eddie Gottlieb Cover (Vol.2 #12, Apr.,1945)	40.00	25.00
Bill Conn Cover (Vol.3 #1, June,1945)	40.00	25.00
Philadelphia A's Cover (Vol.3 #2, Aug.,1945)	50.00	30.00
Leo Durocher Cover		

(Vol.3 #3, Oct.,1945)	50.00	30.00
Football Plays (Vol.3 #4, Nov.,1945)	40.00	25.00
Curley Lambeau Cover (Vol.3 #5, Jan.,1946)	40.00	25.00
Bowling with Ned Day (Vol.3 #6, Mar.,1946)	40.00	25.00
Home From War/DiMaggio (Vol.3 #7, May,1946)	75.00	50.00
Billy Conn vs. Joe Lous (Vol.3 #8, July,1946)	75.00	50.00
Mexican Baseball (Vol.3 #9, Sept.1946)	50.00	30.00
Don "Dopey" Dillock (Vol.3 #10, Nov.,1946)	40.00	25.00
Death Scores a Touchdown (Vol.3 #11, Jan.,1947)	40.00	25.00
Red Sox vs. Senators (Vol.3 #12, March,1947)	50.00	30.00
Spring Training (Vol4 #1, May,1947)	40.00	25.00
How To Pitch (Vol.4 #2, July,1947)	40.00	25.00
Joe Fulks Cover (Vol.4 #3, Sept.,1947)	40.00	25.00
Get Ready for Olympics (Vol.4 #4, Nov.,1947)	40.00	25.00
Hugh Casey Cover (Vol.4 #5, Jan.,1948)	40.00	25.00
Jackie Robinson Cover (Vol.4 #6, Mar.,1948)	75.00	50.00
How to Bowl Better (Vol.4 #7, May,1948)	30.00	20.00
Joe Wolcott & Joe Louis (Vol.4 #8, July,1948)	50.00	30.00
Bill McCahan Cover (Vol.4 #9, Sept.,1948)	30.00	20.00
Great Football Plays (Vol.4 #10, Nov.,1948)	30.00	20.00
Steve Van Buren Cover (Vol.4 #11, Jan.,1949)	40.00	25.00
Basketball Cover (Vol.4 #12, Mar.,1949)	30.00	20.00
Satchel Paige Cover (Vol.5 #1, May,1949)	75.00	50.00
History of Boxing (Vol.5 #2, July,1949)	30.00	20.00

1944-47 It Really Happened

Published by William H. Wise/Visual Editions.

	Ex-Mt	Ex
Lou Gehrig Story (#5)	60.00	40.00
Man O'War Story (#8)	75.00	50.00
Honus Wagner Story (#10)	30.00	20.00

1946-47 Picture News in Color and Action

Published by 299 Lafayette Street Corporation.

	Ex-Mt	Ex
America's 1st Girl Boxer (#2, Feb., 1946)	50.00	30.00
Jackie Robinson Story (#4, Apr., 1946)	60.00	40.00
Hank Greenberg Story (#5, May, 1946)	40.00	25.00
Joe Louis Cover (#6, June, 1946)	50.00	30.00
Joe DiMaggio Story (#9, Nov.- Dec., 1946)	75.00	50.00

1946-49 Real Fact Comics

Published by National Periodical Publications.

	Ex-Mt	Ex
Jackie Robinson Story (#2, 1946)	150.00	90.00
Joe DiMaggio Story (#4, 1946	150.00	90.00

1946-48 Sports Stars

Published by Sports Stars Inc./Parents' Institute.

	Ex-Mt	Ex
Johnny Weissmuller Cover (#1, Feb., 1946)	125.00	75.00
Mel Ott Story (#2, April, 1946)	75.00	50.00
Joe DiMaggio Cover (#3, June, 1946)	125.00	75.00
Pepper Martin Story (#4, August, 1946)	75.00	50.00

1949-51 Babe Ruth Sports Comics

The popular series was launched shortly after Babe Ruth's death in 1948 and lasted 11 issues. Published by Harvey Publications

	Ex-Mt	Ex
Basketball Cover (April,1949)	75.00	50.00
Baseball Cover (June,1949)	75.00	50.00
Joe DiMaggio Cover (Aug.,1949)	100.00	60.00
Bob Feller Cover (Oct.,1949)	75.00	50.00
Football Cover (Dec.,1949)	50.00	30.00
George Mikan Cover (Feb.,1950)	40.00	25.00
Sugar Ray Robinson (May,1950)	30.00	20.00
Yogi Berra (Aug.,1950)	60.00	40.00
Stan Musial Cover (Oct.,1950)	60.00	40.00
Kyle Rote (Dec.,1950)	30.00	20.00
Basketball Cover (Feb.,1951)	30.00	20.00

1949 The Pride of the Yankees

The Lou Gehrig Story. Published by Magazine Enterprises.

	Ex-Mt	Ex
Lou Gehrig Cover (1949)	250.00	150.00

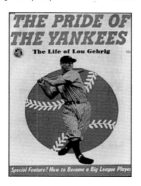

1950-51 Sport Thrills

Published by Curtis Publications/Star Publications.

	Ex-Mt	Ex
T. Williams/T. Cobb Stories (#11, Nov.,1950)	100.00	60.00
J. DiMaggio/P. Rizzuto Stories (#12, Nov.,1950)	75.00	50.00
J. Robinson/P. Reese Cover (#13, May,1951)	100.00	60.00
J. Weismuller Story (#14, May,1951)	50.00	30.00
Yankees Cover (#15, Nov.,1951)	75.00	50.00

1951-52 Baseball Thrills

Published by Ziff-Davis Publishing Co.

	Ex-Mt	Ex
Bob Feller Predicts Pennant (#1, Summer,1951)	150.00	90.00
Yogi Berra Story (#2, Summer,1951)	100.00	60.00
Joe DiMaggio Story (#3, Summer,1952)	100.00	60.00

1951 Phil Ruzzuto Baseball Hero

Published by Fawcett Publications

	Ex-Mt	Ex
Phil Ruzzuto Cover (1951)	150.00	90.00

1951 Yogi Berra Baseball Hero

Published by Fawcett Publications

	Ex-Mt	Ex
Yogi Berra Cover (1951)	175.00	100.00

1952 Baseball Heroes

Published by Fawcett Publications

	Ex-Mt	Ex
Ruth, others on Cover (1952)	200.00	125.00

1952 Thrilling True Story of Baseball

Published by Fawcett Publications

	Ex-Mt	Ex
Giants Players on Cover (1952)	250.00	150.00
Yankees Players on Cover (1952)	275.00	175.00

Starting Lineup® Figurines

1988 Baseball

Jack Clark	9.00	18.00
Rickey Henderson	12.00	24.00
Don Mattingly	15.00	25.00
Willie Randolph	8.00	16.00
Dave Righetti	8.00	16.00
Dave Winfield	20.00	40.00

1990 Baseball

Jesse Barfield	5.00	10.00
Roberto Kelly	8.00	16.00
Don Mattingly Batting	7.00	14.00
Don Mattingly Power	10.00	20.00
Dave Righetti	5.00	10.00
Steve Sax	5.00	10.00
Dave Winfield	18.00	30.00

1991 Baseball

Roberto Kelly	5.00	10.00
Kevin Maas	5.00	10.00
Don Mattingly	8.00	16.00
Steve Sax	5.00	10.00

1991 Baseball Headline Collection

Don Mattingly	25.00	40.00

1992 Baseball

Kevin Maas	5.00	10.00
Danny Tartabull EXT	5.00	10.00

1993 Baseball

Roberto Kelly	5.00	10.00

1994 Baseball

Wade Boggs	5.00	10.00
Jimmy Key	7.00	14.00
Don Mattingly	8.00	14.00

1994 Cooperstown Collection

Lou Gehrig	8.00	15.00
Reggie Jackson	18.00	30.00

1995 Baseball

Jim Abbott	6.00	10.00
Paul O'Neill	6.00	10.00

Above: 1989 Mantle and DiMaggio. Right: 1989 Mantle

1989 Baseball

Ricky Henderson	9.00	18.00
Al Leiter	7.00	14.00
Don Mattingly	15.00	25.00
Mike Pagilarulo	5.00	10.00
Dave Righetti	9.00	18.00
Don Slaught	6.00	12.00
Dave Winfield	15.00	25.00

1989 Baseball Greats

Mickey Mantle/Joe DiMaggio	50.00	90.00
Babe Ruth/Lou Gehrig G/W	25.00	40.00
Babe Ruth/Lou Gehrig W/G	25.00	50.00
Babe Ruth/Lou Gehrig W/W	30.00	60.00

1995 Cooperstown Collection Babe Ruth

1988 Don Mattingly

1989 Joe DiMaggio

1996 Derek Jeter

*1997 Cooperstown
Collection Babe Ruth*

1995 Cooperstown Collection

Whitey Ford	7.00	12.00
Babe Ruth	10.00	20.00

1996 Baseball

David Cone	6.00	10.00
Derek Jeter	40.00	65.00
Don Mattingly EXT	10.00	20.00
Paul O'Neill	6.00	10.00

1996 Cooperstown Collection 12" Figures

Lou Gehrig	15.00	30.00
Babe Ruth	15.00	30.00

1997 Baseball

Derek Jeter EXT	15.00	25.00
Tino Martinez	18.00	30.00
Andy Pettitte EXT	15.00	25.00
Bernie Williams	15.00	25.00

1997 Cooperstown Collection

Mickey Mantle	12.00	20.00

1997 Cooperstown Stadium Stars

Mickey Mantle	20.00	35.00
Babe Ruth	18.00	30.00

1998 Baseball

Hideki Irabu EXT	10.00	20.00
Derek Jeter	10.00	18.00
Mariano Rivera	10.00	20.00
Bernie Williams	6.00	12.00

1998 Baseball 12" Figures

Derek Jeter	18.00	30.00

1998 Baseball Classic Doubles

Yogi Berra/Thurman Munson	15.00	25.00
Derek Jeter/Rey Ordonez	18.00	30.00
Babe Ruth/Roger Maris	15.00	25.00

1998 Baseball Freeze Frames

Derek Jeter	20.00	35.00

1998 Stadium Stars

Bernie Williams	15.00	25.00

1998 Cooperstown Collection

Yogi Berra	6.00	10.00

1999 Baseball

David Cone	6.00	12.00
Derek Jeter	7.50	15.00
Tino Martinez	*	*

"Yankee Stadium Classic" by William Feldman, 1991

Contributors

Book design by Sara Maneval.

Editorial Credits

Marty Appel, who contributed the introduction and Mickey Mantle feature to this book, directed public relations for The Topps Company and worked in the Yankees' organization in a number of capacities from 1968–1992. He now acts as a spokesman for the Topps Company and owns Marty Appel Public Relations.

Theo Chen, who contributed the autograph chapter introduction to this book, is a freelance writer based in Oceanside, Calif., and writes regular autograph columns for several Beckett magazines.

Mike Pagel, who contributed the Joe DiMaggio story to this book, is an associate editor at Beckett Publications. Dick Dobbins, a Bay Area baseball historian also contributed to the story.

Dan Schlossberg, who contributed the trading card, World Series memorabilia and game-used chapter introductions to this book, is a freelance writer based in Fair Lawn, N.J. He is baseball editor of *Legends Sports Memorabili*a and the *Encyclopedia Americana Annual* and contributor to many baseball publications. He is also the author of *The New Baseball Catalog* and 19 other books about the game.

Photo Credits

Mastro Fine Sports Auctions contributed many photos of New York Yankees collectibles and autographed memorabilia to this book.